LEISURE AND RECREATION IN CANADIAN SOCIETY

An Introduction

Dedication:

To my wife Pinelopi, with all my love.

LEISURE AND RECREATION IN CANADIAN SOCIETY

An Introduction

GEORGE KARLIS

University of Ottawa

THOMPSON EDUCATIONAL PUBLISHING, INC.
Toronto

Information on how to obtain copies of this book may be obtained from:

Website: www.thompsonbooks.com
E-mail: publisher@thompsonbooks.com
Telephone: (416) 766-2763
Fax: (416) 766-0398

National Library of Canada Cataloguing in Publication

Karlis, George, 1960-

Leisure and recreation in Canadian Society : an introduction / George Karlis.

Includes bibliographical references and index.
ISBN 1-55077-138-8

1. Leisure—Canada—Textbooks. 2. Recreation—Canada—Textbooks. I. Title.

GV55.K37 2004   790'.0971   C2004-902455-8

Copy Editing: Elizabeth Phinney
Cover Design: Elan Designs
Photo Research: Jane Affleck
Cover photomontage: photos reproduced by permission of Canapress: Betty Sullivan does biceps curl/Minuo Senior Centre 2002 (Chuck Stoody); Grade 9 student during outdoor session for physical education class/Kingston 2004 (Michael Lea); Lion Dancers peform during Chinese New Year festivities, 2003 (Frank Franklin II); Young boy dances in international peace powwow/ Lethbridge 2002 (Ian Martens);

Every reasonable effort has been made to acquire permission for copyrighted materials used in this book and to acknowledge such permissions accurately. Any errors or omissions called to the publisher's attention will be corrected in future printings.

We acknowledge the support of the Government of Canada through the Book Publishing Industry Development Program for our publishing activities. We acknowledge the support of the Government of Ontario through the Ontario Media Development Corporation Book Initiative.

Printed in Canada.
1 2 3 4 5   08 07 06 05 04

Contents

PREFACE

Although the history of leisure and recreation in Canada can be traced to the events and activities prior to Confederation, the study of leisure and recreation in Canadian society is relatively young. It was not until the 1960s that the study of leisure and recreation became an academic discipline in Canadian universities and colleges. It was also during this decade that the active dissemination of Canadian-based research on leisure and recreation started to blossom. Yet, it was not until the 1970s that the first Canadian-based journals of leisure studies were introduced.

Leisure and recreation is an important part of the service industry of society. We all need leisure and recreation, we all want to experience it, and we all desire to have our leisure and recreation needs served by the service sector of society. Moreover, leisure and recreation is big business, meaning that how and by which means our leisure and recreation needs are served usually depends on the distribution of monies, discretionary income, and the state of the economy in general.

In Canada, there are three leisure and recreation service sectors: the public, commercial and voluntary sectors. Although each of these has a unique mandate with differing objectives, all have the same main goal; that is, the provision of leisure and recreation services. These three broad leisure and recreation service sectors provide the over 31 million Canadians living in Canada with an abundance of leisure and recreation options to meet the needs that have evolved out of who we are, where we have come from, and our personal, cultural and national identity.

This text seeks to provide an overview of past and present leisure and recreation in Canadian society, while also attempting to discern what might unfold in the future. The opening chapters lay the groundwork for the study of leisure and recreation in Canada, followed by chapters that contain an overview of the history, current state of condition, and possible future happenings and scenarios in leisure and recreation.

Chapter 1 examines the reasons for studying leisure and recreation in Canada, followed by an introduction to the leisure and recreation service industry in Canada and concludes with a brief description of the relationship between leisure, recreation and what it means to be Canadian. Chapter 2 introduces the concepts of leisure and recreation and every effort has been made to include Canadian-based research. Chapter 3 provides a historical overview of leisure and recreation in Canada, and in Chapter 4, the public sector of leisure is explored. Chapter 5 examines the commercial recreation sector, and Chapter 6 focuses on what is often referred to as the largest sector of the leisure and recreation field, the voluntary sector, while Chapter 7 focuses on the relationship between leisure, recreation and community development. In Chapter 8, Canadian culture, multiculturalism and ethnicity are explored.

Chapter 9 examines Canada's Aboriginal Peoples and their unique cultural-specific leisure and recreation needs. Chapter 10 focuses on the leisure and recreation pursuits and experiences of Canadians and discusses what Canadians do for leisure and recreation while also reviewing research in leisure studies that explores the leisure and recreation patterns for selected groups of Canadians. Chapter 11 is devoted to tourism in Canada. Chapter 12 examines education, research journals and conferences in leisure studies in Canada and provides an overview of university and community college leisure studies programs. Chapter 13 highlights some of the major social trends that currently face Canadian society and that may, in time, shape the future of leisure and recreation in Canada.

It should be noted that my original goal in preparing this textbook was to restrict the content used to Canadian or Canadian-based research. Although this has been a difficult task, I am pleased to say that most chapters in this text are put together solely through the use of Canadian-based research. I would like further to state that I have attempted to present research from as many Canadian or Canadian-based leisure studies researchers as possible. This, however, has also been a difficult task, as few of us exist in this young discipline.

This text has been prepared for use in post-secondary leisure studies or related programs. However, its detailed overview of leisure and recreation in Canada may be of interest to a general readership outside of post-secondary leisure studies or related programs. The nature of the content provides useful information to all levels of college, undergraduate and graduate studies. Each chapter commences with five learning objectives to guide students to focus on pertinent material and ends with study questions, selected websites and key concepts.

To assist university and college course instructors and their students, I have created a supplementary instructor's manual. The instructor's manual has been designed to follow the layout of each chapter of the text. For each chapter, the instructor's manual provides learning objectives, a summary of key points and a series of questions to help instructors and students prepare for examinations.

George Karlis, Ph.D.
April 2004

ACKNOWLEDGMENTS

During the early years of my academic career, I was blessed to have the help and encouragement of a dedicated mentor – the late Alex Wright (Acadia University). The passion for leisure and recreation research that Alex possessed aided in motivating me to complete this manuscript. Although Alex passed away several years ago, I think of him often and am grateful for the direction and guidance he provided me.

I would also like to thank the over five thousand students that I have taught throughout the past thirteen years. Not only have I taught you, I have also learned from you.

The writing of this text would not have been possible without the valuable insight, assistance, patience and encouragement provided to me by my wife, Pinelopi. I wish to thank her for her unconditional love, for her humour and for being by my side throughout the entire process. I thank her for continuing to support me in all my endeavours.

I would especially like to thank my parents, Nicholas and Ioanna, for their continued love, patience and support throughout the entire writing process. I am grateful to them both for their faith in me and my abilities. I am blessed to have them in my life.

I would also like to thank my brother Jim, my sister-in-law Georgina and my niece Ioanna for all their love and support; my father-in-law and mother-in-law, John and Ekaterina Makrodimitris, for their love and assistance; and my brother-in-law Agisi, sister-in-law Monica and nephew Jonathan for their support and encouragement.

Also, I thank all of my friends at the law firm of Gorman & Williams in Baltimore, Maryland, both for their enthusiasm and encouragement and for allowing me to use their office space and facilities during the writing of this text.

The completion of this text would not have been possible without the editorial work and support of the staff of Thompson Educational Publishing. In particular, I wish to thank Keith Thompson for his dedication and commitment. I would also like to acknowledge the contributions of Paul Challen and Elizabeth Phinney.

1
INTRODUCING LEISURE AND RECREATION

LEARNING OBJECTIVES

- To examine why we should study leisure and recreation in Canadian society.
- To describe the benefits of leisure and recreation.
- To explore the perceptions of Canadians towards leisure and recreation.
- To introduce leisure and recreation research in Canada.
- To review the relationship between leisure, recreation and Canadian identity.

Canada is an industrialized society in which most of us distinguish our work from non-work time and our leisure from our non-leisure time. For some of us, leisure and recreation can be experienced during any part of our daily lives, at work or during non-work time. For others, leisure may be time-specific and occur only during a specific time frame. Nonetheless, one thing is certain: leisure and recreation is an interesting phenomenon that merits study. This chapter begins by discussing why we should study leisure and recreation in Canada. The second part introduces the leisure and recreation service industry. The third part presents directions of leisure and recreation research in Canada. The fourth part introduces leisure and recreation in Canadian society. Finally, the fifth part discusses the relationship between leisure, recreation and being Canadian.

"Leisure is the mother of Philosophy."

— Thomas Hobbes (1588-1679), British philosopher. *Leviathan*, pt. 4, ch. 46 (1651).

WHY STUDY LEISURE AND RECREATION?

In 1992, *Recreation Canada* published an article compiled by Susan Markham, which consisted of contributions from five retired recreation professionals: Roy Ellis, Lloyd Minshall, Bob Secord, Cor Westland and Ray Wittenburg. Each of these contributors agreed that leisure and recreation is an industry that: (1) considers community development, (2) consists of volunteers, (3) takes into consideration the needs and capacities of the entire human organism, and (4) has unlimited potential.

By examining the points expressed by these retired recreation professionals it is easy to understand why it is important to study leisure and recreation. Leisure and recreation plays an important role in the development of the lives of individuals, the development of communities and the sustainability of healthy communities. Leisure and recreation is important for the individual, for groups of individuals and for society as a whole.

Although it would be impossible to compile a comprehensive list as to why one should study leisure and recreation in Canada, here are a few reasons: (1) to better understand ourselves, (2) to best address the leisure and recreation needs of ourselves and others, (3) to improve our quality of life and the quality of life of our community, (4) for social reasons, (5) to help us adjust to life stages and the life cycle, (6) to better understand the society we live in, and (7) to make a valuable contribution to the leisure and recreation service industry and to society as a whole.

Most people who study leisure and recreation do it as preparation for work, are researchers, or are academics. Most of us go through life without even thinking about the study of leisure and recreation, or at the very least, knowing that the study of leisure and recreation exists. For many, the mere idea of studying leisure and recreation tends be viewed as a joke. However, the study of leisure and recreation is serious business. If leisure and recreation pursuits take up a minimum of one-third of our time, then these pursuits must be important to us.

The more rushed and complex out lives become, the more we value time as a limited commodity. To ascertain the best use of our time, we must make leisure and recreation decisions and choices. We must be selective of and informed about our leisure and recreation options. Leisure and recreation, like public health and health-care services, is a public good. It is a service that leads to the enhancement of quality of life and the betterment of the individual and the community. It provides a much needed service to the individual, to the community and to society as a whole. The following nine connections between leisure, recreation and health were put forth by Wharf Higgins (1995):

- Leisure and recreation practitioners, such as subsidized public recreation and non-discriminatory pricing and registration policies, contribute towards reducing inequities.

- Increasing the prevention of disease will be realized through public leisure and recreation services that offer all citizens opportunities for promoting their own physical and mental health.

- Leisure education and counseling and therapeutic recreation services are integral to enhancing the coping ability of people.

- Community recreation and leisure programs contribute towards promoting individual self-care and self-help practices.

- Public recreation encourages and facilitates the development of mutual aid and social support in the community.

- Leisure and recreation agencies take a leadership role in the creation of healthy environments.

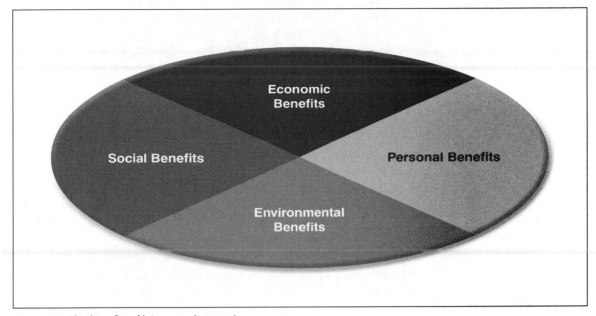

Figure 1.1: The benefits of leisure and recreation.

- Leisure and recreation practitioners are important catalysts in fostering public participation in community life.

- As a local, decentralized and intersectoral service, recreation and leisure programs strengthen community health services.

- Through the collaborative working relationships with other health and social services, leisure and recreation leaders are active participants in coordinating healthy public policy (pp. 24-28).

The benefits that may be gained from leisure and recreation are diverse and varied. In an attempt to conceptualize the magnitude of benefits, the Parks and Recreation Federation of Ontario, in conjunction with the Ontario Ministry of Tourism and Recreation, published *The Benefits of Parks and Recreation: A Catalogue* in 1992. This catalogue depicts four types of benefits that may be gained through leisure and recreation experiences: personal benefits, social benefits, economic benefits and environmental benefits (See Figure 1.1).

The **personal benefits of leisure and recreation** are: (1) a contribution to a full and meaningful life, (2) health insurance, (3) essential to stress management, (4) a source of self-esteem and positive self-image, (5) the leading of balanced lives, (6) the achievement of our full potential and the gain of life satisfaction, (7) children's play as essential to the human development process, (8) the provision of positive lifestyle choices and alternatives, and (9) giving people satisfaction and improving their quality of life.

The **social benefits of leisure and recreation** include: (1) the building of strong communities, (2) the reduction in alienation, loneliness and anti-social behaviours, (3) the promotion of ethnic and cultural harmony, (4) the building of strong families, (5) the provision of opportunities for community involvement, shared management and ownership of resources, (6) integrated and accessible leisure services, (7) the foundations of community pride, and (8) the enhancement of protective services for latchkey children through after-school programs.

The **economic benefits of leisure and recreation** were presented as follows: (1) preventative health service, (2) contribution to a productive work force, (3) the yielding of big economic returns, (4) the motivation of business relocation and expansion in communities, (5) the reduction of the high cost of vandalism and criminal activity, (6) a catalyst for tourism, and (7) investments in environmental protection that pay for themselves.

Finally, the **environmental benefits of leisure and recreation** are: (1) the environmental health of the community, (2) environmental protection and rehabilitation, (3) investing in the environment leading to an increase in neighbourhood property value, and (4) insurance for a new and improved environmental future.

THE LEISURE AND RECREATION SERVICE INDUSTRY

In 1978, a retreat of recreation professionals, sponsored by the Ontario Ministry of Culture and Recreation, resulted in a document entitled *The Elora Prescription*. The intent of the *The Elora Prescription* was to examine past and present social trends while trying to predict the future of recreation. It posited that the individual is her or his own best recreation resource – that is, our leisure and recreation lifestyle depends on personal choice. *The Elora Prescription* argued that it is up to the individual to find happiness in leisure and recreation through personal lifestyles and personal choices. To what extent is this true today? Does our satisfaction with our leisure and recreation rest fully with ourselves? Does the leisure and recreation service sector not have an impact on the type of leisure and recreation activities we may engage in and, ultimately, the degree of satisfaction that we may derive?

In Canada, the leisure and recreation service sector consists of public, commercial and volunteer organizations. Each of these sectors offers leisure and recreation services, yet the reasons and the means used differ. Traditionally in Canada, the public sector was most relied upon to fulfill the basic leisure and recreation needs. Today, however, government services have become subject to downsizing and reduced resources. The public service sector of leisure and recreation has changed from one that was concerned to providing the plethora of required basic leisure and recreation services to one that provides only a basic amount. As a result, Canada has witnessed an expansion of services in the commercial and voluntary service sectors of leisure and recreation.

Photo: Health Canada.

Building strong families is one of the benefits of recreation programs.

Without doubt, economics and the distribution of monies are paramount in shaping the leisure and recreation service sector. As far as the public sector is concerned, lack of public subsidies often translates into the reduction or even the elimination of leisure and recreation services. Economic trends in society also shape what and how we participate in leisure and recreation. The availability of discretionary or disposable income means a greater expenditure in leisure and recreation activities and services. Thus, the better the economy, the more money we have, and the more we spend on leisure and recreation.

Despite changes in the leisure and recreation service sector, the value of leisure, and in particular, the value placed by society on public leisure and recreation services, continues. The results of a Canadian national survey conducted by the Angus Reid Group of Winnipeg reports that Canadians tend to have a strong perception towards leisure and recreation and, in particular, the importance of public sector leisure and recreation services. More specifically, the results of this study as presented by Harper, Neider and Godbey (1997) reveal that: (1) 57 percent of Canadians have the same or more free time as compared to the past, (2) 83 percent of Canadians use local government parks and recreation services, and (3) 86 percent feel that their local parks provide them with benefits. Furthermore, it was also reported that 86 percent of respondents believe that the absence of parks and recreation services would have an impact on them personally and on their community.

The promotion of all aspects of wellness is a major goal of the leisure and recreation service industry. Physical fitness is a major objective of leisure and recreation programs, while stress reduction and overall mental health are benefits also pursued through leisure and recreation services and experiences (Karlis and Dawson, 1994). Such services are thus important services for individual and community development in Canada. But does "equality for all" truly exist in Canada when it comes to the provision of leisure and services?

For a society to be **"recreationally complete,"** opportunity, accessibility and recognition by the leisure and recreation service sector is necessary (Karlis, 1998a). But which part of the service sector should be responsible for ensuring that Canadian society is "recreationally compete?" Within the various levels of government, it appears evident on the part of the public sector that it shall not be the major provider of leisure and recreation but rather will enable and assist the commercial and voluntary sectors to provide necessary leisure and recreation services. Yet, the commercial and voluntary sectors tend to have restrictive parameters in the provision of leisure and recreation services – the commercial sector through high user fees, and the voluntary sector through limited mandates and resources. Perhaps education is the key to enhancing "recreational completeness" in Canadian society. Through education, leisure and recreation practitioners, administrators, professionals, academics and students may become more aware of how effectively to address the issues of opportunity, accessibility and recognition.

THE ELORA PRESCRIPTION

In 1978, *The Elora Prescription* argued that the individual is her or his own best resource. In the past twenty-five years, this continues to be true. However, it can be said that the pursuit of recreation experiences depends not only on the individual but also on the capacity of the recreation industry to assist in addressing the recreation needs of individuals. For the service industry to aid in the fulfillment of the recreation needs of society, it must

- be accessible,
- provide opportunities,
- entail equal service provision,
- offer a barrier free environment, and
- consist of effective communication channels.

DIRECTIONS OF LEISURE AND RECREATION RESEARCH

In one of the first major leisure and recreation conferences held in Canada, the *Conference on Leisure* in Montmorency, Quebec, in 1969, Norman Pearson commented on the lack of leisure and recreation research in Canada. He argued that "it is not enough to simply assume that the patterns found in the U.S.A. apply to Canada" (1969: 81). Pearson went on to state that "we urgently need, for Canada viewed as a whole, an inventory of the available and potential resources for leisure and recreation; studies of the supplies of recreation resources, the demand for recreation, the economics of recreation, and of the problems relating all three to assure present and future generations the basic resources for whatever patterns of leisure use they may choose" (ibid.).

A little more than a decade later, leisure and recreation studies had emerged into a growing field in Canada. However, at that time, it was not yet known how research in the field would shape or develop. In 1981, Stephen Smith posited that the muse of leisure studies may create either a desert, a jungle or a garden. The desert scenario would be a dry one with minimal research produced. The jungle would consist of research that is widespread yet lost and ignored, whereas the garden would consist of research that is plentiful, including the creation of new ways and new ideas.

Today it appears that leisure and recreation research in Canada has indeed evolved into a "garden." In the past three decades, leisure and recreation research has experienced exponential growth (Jackson, 2000/2001). Leisure research has also shifted away from the parent disciplines (i.e., sociology, psychology, physical education) and has been carried out largely within the leisure studies field (ibid.). Yet, one of the major criticisms of leisure and recreation research in Canada is that it has failed to adequately address the concerns of the practice. A gap exists between the researcher and the practitioner as current levels of interaction between the two groups is minimal (Nogradi, 1992; Beaman, 1978). For one reason or another, those academics and scientists doing research in the field often find that their work remains on the shelf, collecting dust. Since leisure studies is a discipline concerned with people, and since a large portion of research in the field, whether applied or not, can have a significant impact on how the leisure and recreation needs of society are addressed, the gap between the practitioner and researcher needs to be eliminated or, at the very least, reduced.

One means of reducing this gap is by understanding and applying **technology transfer**. Technology transfer is concerned with enhancing the recreation practitioner's awareness of research (Karlis, 1991a). More specifically, technology transfer focuses on eliminating the gap between the researcher and the practitioner through the passing on of knowledge from one channel to the other. For technology transfer to exist, practitioners must be made aware of current research, its location and how to access it. For technology transfer to exist, research in leisure and recreation must address the practical and social needs of society and focus on

Photo: Parks Canada.

Research in leisure studies contributes to a healthy future for Canadians.

WHAT IS LEISURE STUDIES?

It's All about People

Leisure studies is an academic discipline that focuses on people. This academic program has evolved out of the need to understand why we behave in certain ways during periods of intrinsic and extrinsic freedom. This discipline examines the behaviour of individuals, groups, communities and society.

The purpose of leisure studies is to better the state of society by enhancing the quality of life of its citizens. The intent of leisure studies is to explore and better understand the behaviour patterns of people through an analysis of their leisure and recreation needs, wants, preferences, attitudes and participation patterns.

Leisure Studies Degrees and Diplomas

In Canada, both universities and community colleges offer programs in leisure studies. University degree programs tend to be four years in length; some universities, such as the University of Ottawa, also offer three-year degree programs. Community college programs tend to be two years in length, but related programs are offered that take only one year to complete.

To successfully complete university or community college leisure studies programs, students must complete a series of courses that explore the foundation and nature of leisure behaviour. Courses that students must complete in order to be granted a degree or diploma in Leisure Studies include: Leisure in Canadian Society, Introduction to Leisure, Recreation and Political Processes, Recreation and Selected Populations, Theories of Play, The Philosophy of Leisure, The Sociology of Leisure, The Anthropology of Leisure, The Economics of Leisure, Leisure and the Law, Leisure and Community Development, Women and Leisure, Recreation Resource Management, The Administration of Leisure and Recreation Services, The Voluntary Sector of Leisure and Recreation, Commercial Recreation Services, Site Design, Leisure and the Environment, Therapeutic Recreation, Recreation and Special Populations, Leisure and the Aged, The Future of Leisure and Recreation, Technology and Recreation, Marketing Leisure Services, and Leisure in Global Societies.

The Multidisciplines of Leisure

Leisure studies is a multidisciplinary field, which relies very much on theories and knowledge from other academic fields. For example, courses on the sociology of leisure often reflect on the work of Abraham Maslow, while courses on the future of leisure utilize the research of David Foot.

Although a case may be made that almost all academic disciplines relate, in some shape or form, to leisure studies, some disciplines have a closer relationship than others. These include: Psychology, Sociology, Physical Education, Anthropology, Economics, Environmental Studies, Forestry, Canadian Studies, Human Kinetics, and Health Sciences.

The Profession

Most students of leisure studies intend to pursue a career in the profession. As the field is multidisciplinary, there are many employment possibilities for graduates. These include: Municipal Recreation Director, Program Planner, Recreation Resource Coordinator, Recreation Service Administrator, Social Service Director, Physical Education Teachers, Tour Guides, Forest Rangers, Community Activity Planners, Sport Team Coaches and Training Staff, Tourism Researchers, Leisure Counsellors, Leisure Educators, Park Supervisors, Travel Agents and Managers of Sport Teams.

Leisure studies graduates of four-year university degree programs may choose to enter post-graduate or professional education programs, which lead to a professional career. Post-graduate or professional career alternatives for students include: MBA studies, law school, teachers education programs, social work studies, landscape design programs, and doctoral studies.

THE BENEFITS OF RESEARCHING LEISURE AND RECREATION

Leisure studies research benefits the individual, the community, and society as a whole as it

• helps us better understand ourselves, our community and society;
• aids in recognizing the needs, wants and desires of individuals, community and society;
• assists in recognizing participation patterns and trends;
• aids in policy making;
• enhances awareness of the importance of leisure and recreation; and
• provides program, facility and service suggestions for leisure and recreation organizations.

applied research that can be of benefit to the industry. For technology transfer to take place, both the researcher and the practitioner must make a constant effort to mutually exchange and share information; that is, both must make changes from what has traditionally occurred (Nogradi, 1992).

In her keynote address to the delegates of the 7th Canadian Congress on Leisure Research on May 13, 1993, Karla Henderson articulated that in the 1990s and beyond leisure and recreation research needs to focus on "the changer and the changed." During her presentation, Henderson argued that leisure and recreation researchers need to understand new ways of change to incorporate new ways of thinking. Problems with some leisure and recreation research are deficient theoretical assumptions, inadequate methodologies, a failure to discern meanings and a failure to provide a framework for social action leading to change.

The main point raised by Henderson is that leisure and recreation researchers, in Canada and elsewhere, need to make a difference. To this end, Henderson presented ten guidelines directing the leisure and recreation researcher to accomplish this change. These are to: (1) develop a mindset that makes social and personal change an aspect to be considered in leisure research, (2) ground research in theory, (3) consider the multiple research methods available, (3) consider the *Verstehn* of research, (5) address the importance of "meaning-making," (6) make research a long-term commitment, (7) acknowledge that research in not value free, (8) reduce the researcher-practitioner gap, (9) believe that researchers are always educators, and (10) define research as a process as well as a product (Henderson, 1993: 3-4).

More recently, Pedlar and Hutchison (1999) proposed that enhancing the participatory process in leisure and recreation research would move the social agenda of leisure and recreation forward. For Pedlar and Hutchison, the direction of leisure research in Canada needs to capture the perspective of citizens. Leisure and recreation research should not be focused simply on the collection of empirical data but should focus on research means that engage citizens in the "process of self-determined leisure and recreation as meaningful aspects of daily life" (p. 22).

Leisure and recreation is a people-oriented industry, one that is concerned with changing the community for the better. This process of community change is an ongoing one as the leisure and recreation needs of society are constantly evolving. To better understand leisure and recreation in Canada, the direction of leisure research needs to address issues such as power, social structures, group formation and politics. Moreover, the direction of research in leisure studies needs to include the participants, the people who are directly affected by the research at hand.

Participatory action research (PAR), an approach to data collection that brings together leisure studies researchers and citizens, was extensively used in the 1990s by Canadian-based leisure studies researchers (see Haasen, Hornibrook and Pedlar, 1998; Arai, 1996; Pedlar, Gilbert and Gove, 1993). It may thus be that participatory action research is a growing trend in leisure studies research. For this trend to grow, Pedlar and Hutchison (1999) posit that the agenda for leisure research has to focus on truly understanding the viewpoints of citizens. That is, "the nature of involvement needs to be such that genuine participatory research processes allow for learning-as-you-go, empowerment, and supportive relationships which serve to diminish power imbalances between the leisure research community and citizens who may thus play a more active part in shaping the social agenda" (p. 22).

"As members of Parliament, our health is at risk, considering the long hours we work, the stressful nature of our employment, the dietary regimes that we keep and our overall lack of opportunity for physical activity."

— The Hon. Eleni Bakopanos, Parliamentary Secretary to the Minister of Human Resources and Skills Development, *The Hill Times*, 22-28 March 2004.

LEISURE AND RECREATION IN CANADIAN SOCIETY

Leisure and recreation has been a part of Canadian society since before Confederation. In fact, leisure and recreation has been a part of Canadian society for over 4,000 years as people have lived, hunted and raised families in this great nation. Canada's rich culture, history, environment, outdoor opportunities, climate and geographical location all help in being determining factors for leisure and recreation in Canadian society. Leisure and recreation opportunities in Canada are endless. Among and included in these opportunities are the following: national and provincial parks, wildlife sanctuaries, a vast marine ecosystem, canoe trips in the arctic wilderness, hiking and nature trails, multicultural centres and ethnic community organizations, and public and private gardens.

Recent statistics released by Statistics Canada (1998a) reveal that, on average, Canadians experience 5.6 hours of free time per day. These same statistics indicate that Canadians engage in 7.8 hours of paid work and related activities per day, whereas 10.6 hours per day is for sleep, meals and other personal activities. To complete the daily hourly breakdown, Statistics Canada identifies 4.4 hours per day of unpaid work and .6 hours per day of education and related activities.

From the aforementioned statistics, it is evident that the free time category occupies a significant portion of our time. Although not as much as the sleep, meals and other personal activities category, and the paid work and activity category, the free time category, the period in which we engage in leisure and recreation, makes up a huge part of each day that we live. This is the time period in which we tend to pursue leisure and recreation activities and experiences that we enjoy.

Time budget studies show that Canadians do have free time. How is this free time occupied by leisure and recreation? What active and/or passive leisure and recreation pursuits do Canadians experience? These questions will be addressed throughout this text as we explore leisure and recreation in the past, present and future in Canada. One thing that is certain is that free time is a limited commodity. For this reason, we see people rushing through shopping malls on Friday evenings, or experience Saturday morning traffic jams as we drive our children to ballet or piano lessons. We continue to place high value on this free time period and thus rush to do as much as we can, often resulting in stress.

LEISURE AND RECREATION ... ON BEING CANADIAN

Scott claims that leisure and recreation "reflects on culture, identity, and nationalism, and it can be the sources of much focus and pride" (1998: 5). Leisure and recreation are indeed key factors in determining not only who we are, but also in building national pride and social cohesiveness. The gold medal ice hockey accomplishment of the Canadian men's and women's teams during the 2002 Winter Olympics are excellent examples as to how leisure and recreation can build on culture and identity through our national sport of hockey. From coast to coast, the ice hockey matches of the 2002 Winter Olympics were followed religiously by Canadians, bringing our country together and helping to enhance nationalism and national pride.

The leisure and recreation industry is an important part of culture. It helps shape, determine and identify the culture of a society, and Canada is no exception. In Canada, Canadian broadcasting, cable TV, film making, recording, and the performing arts all help define Canadian culture (Watson, 1988). Activities such as the Grey Cup, the 6/49 lottery, and the Calgary Stampede all help determine the Canadian way of life and our cultural identity.

Not long ago, the administrative bodies of the Canadian Football League decided to expand to the U.S. market, and a number of U.S.-based teams were added to the league. Many Canadians were critical of this so-called business move to save the league as the Canadian Football League is the oldest professional league that is 100 percent based in Canada. In fact, the event of the Grey Cup, the championship game with weeklong cultural activities bringing together western and eastern Canada was seen to be jeopardized as U.S. teams began to compete and even win this trophy, as did the football team from Baltimore, Maryland. No doubt, a part of our culture had been taken over by the inclusion of U.S.-based teams into an all-Canadian home-based league, and more so by the winning of the Grey Cup by a U.S.-based team.

The Canadian Football League did not last in the U.S. Today, it is back to its original form with nine teams, all Canadian based. The Grey Cup remains a national event that brings together the country through an exposure of the western and the eastern cultural heritages of this vast land. The Grey Cup is once again a purely Canadian cultural event. As Watson (1988: 81) states, "if any Canadian cultural event satisfies the definition of a public good – and few do – it is the Grey Cup."

In addition to sports, there are many other leisure and recreation activities that help define us as Canadians. Indeed, the leisure and recreation activities we choose to engage in, and the activities we prefer and have access to, are largely determined by the society we live in and the democratic principles we uphold. Throughout this text, the reader will be introduced to how various government acts and policies of leisure and recreation in Canada have helped shaped our Canadian identity and culture. We will explore the role the public sector plays, the fundamental principles of Canadian society, such as democracy, and the

THE LEISURE INFORMATION NETWORK (LIN)

Spreading the Word Electronically about Leisure and Recreation

In Canada and North America, leisure and recreation students, practitioners, researchers and academics have been brought closer together through the existence of a Canadian-based Internet site – The Leisure Information Network (LIN).

Initiated by the Ontario Ministry of Citizenship, Culture and Recreation and the Fitness Program of Health Canada, the intent of LIN is to aid individuals and organizations interested in recreation, culture and sport through knowledge acquisition and information dissemination. The purpose of LIN is to provide "knowledge management services" to the leisure sector while also "fostering on-line knowledge exchange." (The leisure sector, according to LIN, consists of a community or individual, and organizations and agencies. Each of these must have an interest in the development of healthy individuals, and the development of healthy communities.) To fulfill this purpose LIN collects, archives and spreads pertinent information related to leisure and recreation.

The LIN Website

The LIN website offers a "Bulletin Board" for the posting of specific announcements or areas of interest in the leisure and recreation industry and a "Career Centre" that allows for the submission of resumes; a resume job bank; a means to submit job openings; and a place to search for job openings. The job listings that appear in the LIN website are categorized under the following headings: Active Living, Recreation, Health, Education and Sport.

For students this Canadian established and operated website offers information on the National Recreation Database; careers in parks and recreation; program standards; colleges and universities; and organizations in the field of leisure and recreation.

The "What's New" section informs site visitors of recent happenings and developments in the leisure sector. It contains "Custom Information Service," "Join LIN News," "Latest News" and "Events Listing."

The "Resource Center" provides a wide array of useful information to everyone from students doing research to practitioners looking to understand growing trends in the leisure sector. Users can choose from: "Recreational Database," "Further Research," "Government Contacts," "E-mail Directory," "Journal of Leisurability," "Related Links," "Mailing Lists," "Journals," "LIN News Archive," "Conference Papers," "Custom Information Service," "Current Awareness Service," "Youth At Risk Database," "Leisurability Publications," "Skills Program" and "Benefits Online."

For more information on Leisure Information Network, visit the LIN website at www.lin.ca.

Source: <http://www.lin.ca>.

Photo: Health Canada.

impact that our Charter of Rights and Freedoms has had on our leisure and recreation choices. We will also look at how demographics and social factors in Canada determine not only who were are and what we participate in but also how our leisure and recreation pursuits shape our personal and cultural identities.

CONCLUSION

It is important to study leisure and recreation, not only for the sake of understanding and exploration, but also to learn how better to address our individual and social needs and to be in a position to better serve society. To be able to study and learn about leisure, leisure studies has been developed in Canada as a discipline and area of inquiry.

Leisure studies is a young discipline in Canada with the dissemination of Canadian research commencing in the 1960s. Trends in leisure and recreation research indicate that more is needed to better understand means and ways to serve the community. As the benefits of leisure and recreation are plentiful and have come to the forefront of Canadian society, and as Canadians realize that leisure and recreation is an important part of our daily lives, our lifestyle, and our cultural identity, it has become more important than ever to have a solid understanding of leisure and recreation in Canada.

CHAPTER 1: INTRODUCING LEISURE AND RECREATION

Study Questions

1. List six reasons why we should study leisure and recreation in Canada.

2. What are Dwarf Higgins' nine propositions of leisure, recreation and health?

3. Compare and contrast the four benefits of leisure and recreation.

4. What is posited in *The Elora Prescription*?

5. Which leisure and recreation service sector(s) has expanded? Why?

Selected Websites

- **Canadian Parks and Recreation Association**
  http://www.cpra.ca

- **National Recreation and Parks Association**
  http://www.nrpa.org

- **Ontario Ministry of Tourism and Recreation**
  http://www.tourism.gov.on.ca

Key Concepts

- **Personal benefits of leisure and recreation**

- **Social benefits of leisure and recreation**

- **Economic benefits of leisure and recreation**

- **Environmental benefits of leisure and recreation**

- **"Recreationally complete"**

- **Technology transfer**

- **Participatory action research**

2
CONCEPTS OF LEISURE AND RECREATION

LEARNING OBJECTIVES

- To explore the conceptual makeup of leisure and recreation.
- To examine the concepts of leisure and recreation from Canadian-based research.
- To depict the purposes of leisure and recreation in Canadian society.
- To conceptualize leisure and recreation in Canada.
- To examine the relationship between leisure, recreation and play.

To examine leisure and recreation in Canadian society it is necessary to first understand the concepts of leisure and recreation. Throughout this text, the concepts of leisure and recreation often appear together. On the surface it may seem that leisure and recreation mean the same thing, yet differences exist. This chapter examines the concepts of leisure and recreation mostly, yet not exclusively, from a Canadian perspective, as most contemporary research on the concepts of leisure and recreation evolves out of the United States. The concept of play is also introduced as its meaning is closely linked to that of leisure and recreation.

This chapter commences with a brief overview of the foundation of the concepts of leisure and recreation in Canada. The concept of leisure is explored, followed by the depiction of Canadian-based research on the concept of leisure. A conceptualization of leisure in Canada is put forth, and the purpose of leisure in Canada is presented. The concept of recreation is examined, followed by the introduction of Canadian-based research. A conceptualization of recreation in Canada is offered, and the purpose of recreation in Canada is explored. The chapter ends with a brief analysis of a concept related to leisure and recreation, that of play.

"Play for young children is not recreation activity.... It is not leisure-time activity nor escape activity.... Play is thinking time for young children. It is language time. Problem-solving time. It is memory time, planning time, investigating time. It is organization-of-ideas time, when the young child uses his mind and body and his social skills and all his powers in response to the stimuli he has met."

— James L. Hymes, Jr., U.S. child development specialist, author. *Teaching the Child Under Six*, ch. 4 (1968).

THE FOUNDATION OF THE CONCEPTS OF LEISURE AND RECREATION

Most Canadian leisure studies researchers, those Canadian-born, have obtained their higher degrees, in particular their Ph.D., from American universities. Until the 1990s, no Ph.D. program in leisure

WHAT'S IN A NAME?

Agreeing on a global definition of leisure is difficulty because:

- The notion of leisure is cultural specific.
- Leisure means different things to different people.
- The meaning of leisure for each individual is case specific.
- The word "leisure" does not exist in all languages.
- Leisure can be anything for anybody at any time, meaning that the way we define leisure may be different in the future than it is today or was yesterday.

studies had been successfully implemented in Canada. Prior to the 1990s, Canadians interested in doing leisure studies research, for one reason or another, were reluctant to go to the United States or elsewhere to pursue a Ph.D. in leisure studies. Many of those interested in leisure studies research ended up exploring this area in related disciplines such as psychology, sociology, education and physical fitness. As a result, many Canadian leisure studies researchers have not obtained a higher degree in leisure studies, while most have been trained in disciplines related to leisure and recreation. Thus, most of the conceptualizations of leisure and recreation that we currently use have come from researchers trained in other disciplines (Karlis, 2000; Bregha, 1978).

Leisure studies as a discipline of higher education has existed in the United States since the 1930s. In Canada, it came into being in the 1960s. This discipline had its "head start" in the neighbouring United States and thus much of the research used in Canada has been adopted from there. The similar nature of these two societies, their geographic proximity, and cross-border media communication channels have made it easy for research conducted in the United States to have a direct impact on leisure studies in Canada.

Early American researchers in leisure studies put forth the conceptual framework used in this field. Foundations for key concepts of leisure studies – leisure, recreation and play – were identified and defined by researchers such as Brightbill (1960), Larabee and Meyersohn (1958), Nash (1953) and Neumeyer and Neumeyer (1949). Thus, when the discipline of leisure studies was established in Canada in the 1960s, the foundational concepts had already been defined. Canadian researchers of leisure studies adopted the foundational concepts from United States-based researchers, a task that was easy, as many of the first leisure studies researchers in Canada were either American or had been trained in the United States.

Today, Canadian leisure studies researchers continue to rely extensively on foundational conceptual research coming from the United States and other countries. Few Canadian researchers have attempted to re-conceptualize leisure, recreation and play, choosing rather to rely upon the traditional established notions. In addition, Canadian leisure studies researchers tend to not agree on the meaning of "leisure," while using the word "leisure" in many different ways. Swedburg (2002), in a study of the grammatical uses of leisure conducted at the 9th Canadian Congress on Leisure Research, found that the word "leisure" tends be used more often as an adjective or a noun. In no cases was "leisure" used as an adverb or verb.

Every possible effort has been made in this book to incorporate Canadian-based research. However, in this chapter, a review of North American literature is used to describe the concepts of leisure and recreation. Then, Canadian-based research on leisure and recreation concepts are presented and discussed. Finally, a definition for leisure and recreation based on Canadian society is introduced.

THE CONCEPT OF LEISURE

From a review of existing literature on the concept of leisure, three viewpoints have been identified: (1) leisure as discretionary time, (2) leisure as free-time activity, and (3) leisure as personal experience and state of being (see Table 2.1).

• Leisure as Discretionary Time

Kraus (1994) states that the most common meaning associated with the concept of leisure in Western nations such as Canada and the United States is **leisure as discretionary time**.

According to this perspective, leisure is time free from work, work-related responsibilities and household obligations, and other social and personal obligations. Study, travel, self-maintenance and housekeeping obligations are non-leisure experiences, meaning that leisure is a time period in which free or self-driven experiences are undertaken away from work and other obligations. Leisure is thus time that is "left over" after work and other obligations necessary for survival have been fulfilled. Leisure is the opposite of work and other obligations. It is a set time period apart from all other time periods in our daily time including that required for sleep. If, for example, we devote eight hours of our day to work and other obligations, and sleep for another eight hours, then leisure as discretionary time refers to the remaining eight hours that complete the twenty-four-hour time clock. Leisure as discretionary time is that time-period apart from the obligations of work, family, and society.

When leisure is defined as discretionary time, it can be objectively measured (Neulinger, 1974). Simply put, there is leisure time and there is non-leisure time. Everything we do during leisure time determines our leisure, and everything we do during our non-leisure time determines our experiences outside of leisure. It is thus possible to measure not only

Table 2.1: Three Viewpoints of the Concept Leisure

Viewpoint	Necessary Condition
Discretionary Time	Time free from work, work-related responsibilities, household obligations and other social and personal obligations.
Free Time Activity	"Activities" and the nature of these activities that are experienced outside of work and obligations.
Personal Experience and State of Being	Any experience, at any time, that is self-satisfying. A personally chosen, self-fulfilling experience or activity that may be planned or experienced spontaneously.

PROHIBITED ACTIVITIES?

Most Canadian-based definitions of leisure tend to define leisure according to what it "is" rather than what it "is not." In Canada, there are certain activities that some may call leisure that our legal system prohibits, such as smoking marijuana or prostitution.

Although these activities have social, moral, legal and economic ramifications, some argue that these activities are indeed leisure.

the time we have for leisure, but also the leisure pursuits that we experience during this leisure time. As leisure is time-specific, it is easy to determine what is and what is not leisure.

• **Leisure as Free Time Activity**

The understanding of **leisure as free time activity** generally assumes that leisure consists of more than just discretionary time. Leisure is the activities that we experience voluntarily during discretionary time. Leisure is free time activity when it is experienced outside of work (Scott, 1998; LeClair, 1992). It is the "activities" and the nature of these activities that determine whether or not certain non-work time pursuits are leisure.

Leisure activities tend to be defined by society. In Canada, municipal recreation services (e.g., the City of Ottawa) put together leisure activity program calendars delivered during the fall, winter, spring and summer periods, identifying leisure activities according to the programs offered. Within these calendars, we find cooking classes, hockey camps, weightlifting for seniors, and aerobics under the heading "leisure activities." Leisure as free time activity is thus a reflection of the type of activities that have been determined by society to be leisure activities.

It is important to note that, according to this conceptualization of leisure, the operant word is "voluntarily" experienced, meaning that leisure as free time activity can be self-chosen, personally defined leisure pursuits such as voluntary activity and community service. Thus, leisure as free time activity is a viewpoint based on the perception one has towards certain activities during free time. Unlike the discretionary time viewpoint, leisure as free time activity refers to the fact that only some and not all activities engaged in during discretionary time are leisure.

As is the case with leisure as discretionary time, leisure as free time activity is also objectively determined (Neulinger, 1974). It is easy to measure the type of activities identified as leisure and engaged in during free time. The mere fact that the leisure experience is restricted to "free time" makes it possible to objectively analyze what is and what is not leisure. Leisure is objectively determined by the nature and type of activities experienced during free time.

• **Leisure as Personal Experience and State of Being**

The subjective nature of **leisure as personal experience and state of being** is complex, as this perspective extends beyond leisure as discretionary time and leisure as free time activity to leisure as experience, any experience, at any time, that is self-satisfying (Hollands, 1998). Kraus (1994: 10) posits that social psychologists describe this orientation of leisure according to two basic characteristics: (1) it must involve perceived freedom in selecting activities without compulsion or the hope for extrinsic rewards, and (2) it has the potential to involve all aspects of the individual's personality and, in its highest form, to reach a state of what has been called " self-actualization" – achieving one's fullest potential as a human being. Leisure is thus a personally chosen, self-ful-filling experience or activity that may be planned or experienced spontaneously.

Leisure as personal experience or state of being is an all-inclusive con-ceptualization consisting of all the above. Leisure is anything for anyone at any given point in time and any place. According to this perspective of leisure, leisure is discretionary time, free time activity, personal experi-ence, a state of being and a distinct part of each human life. Since we are all individuals, with differing internal thoughts, emotions, values and feelings, leisure is case-specific. Leisure is something, anything, and can be different for everyone. Leisure is something that can be experienced by anyone at any time, including during work and other social and per-sonal obligations. Leisure is a personal experience that is free from con-straints (Westland, 1991). Leisure is to do "as one pleases at one's own pace" (Cordes and Ibrahim, 1999). Leisure is something that has liberat-ing qualities for the individual (Reid and van Druenen, 1995). In sum, leisure as personal experience or state of being is an internal state or con-dition that is self-defined and self-experienced by the individual.

CANADIAN-BASED RESEARCH ON THE CONCEPT OF LEISURE

Bob Ballantyne (Conestoga College):

> Leisure is "an emotional experience in which an individual: (1) acquires an in-ner feeling of personal satisfaction, (2) accomplishes an enriched sense of self-worth and well-being, (3) feels good about oneself and others, (4) experi-ences an inner calm due to an absence of anxiety often produced by stress and tension, and (5) achieves the joy of a re-creative experience" (Ballantyne, 1998: 2).

Ballantyne's definition of leisure closely links with the viewpoint of lei-sure as personal experience and state of being. Leisure is viewed as an individual condition that is case-specific. In order for one to experience leisure, a certain state of mind is necessary, and this is based on inner sat-isfaction. In this definition, no mention of time or time-restricting param-eters as a condition for leisure is made. Rather, Ballantyne chooses to concentrate primarily on the individual from within, indicating how lei-sure depends on the mindset of the beholder. Leisure is thus a self-deter-mined rather than a socially-determined experience.

Peggy Hutchison (Brock University) and Judith McGill (Consultant in Leisure Integration):

> Leisure is "a "state of mind"; a lifestyle; something that is entirely voluntary; something beyond the activity itself; something that gives life, balance and meaning (Hutchison and McGill, 1992: 5).

Hutchison and McGill's definition of leisure coincides with the leisure as personal experience and state of being viewpoint. The focus is on state of mind. It is as a result of one's state of mind that the leisure experience happens. Leisure is viewed as a condition that extends beyond the activ-ity of choice, and is determined by a freely chosen experience.

Leisure can be a time of inner peace, away from everyday stresses.

CULTURAL SPECIFICITY

The uniqueness of Canadian society, our political system, our social system, our ethnic cultures, and our historical roots and Aboriginal cultures make us who we are today. All of these factors combined, and more, help shape the definition of leisure in Canada today.

It should be noted that Hutchison and McGill also use the word lifestyle in their definition of leisure. For Hutchison and McGill, one's lifestyle conditions are closely linked to leisure. A sense of freedom and independence needs to be achieved in one's lifestyle so that the "state of mind" of leisure may be experienced.

John Farina (Wilfred Laurier University):

> Leisure is not time, leisure is not recreation, leisure is not necessarily activity, leisure is a state of being, it is a state of being free (Farina, 1969: 4).

> Leisure is characterized by freedom, a sense of freedom that is in the mind of man as differing from environmental or socially determined freedom. This freedom can be considered an opportunity to act as one pleases with the limits imposed by environment and social context (Farina, 1985 [page ref.]).

In both definitions, Farina emphasizes internal freedom. His focus is primarily on leisure as personal experience and state of being. Farina makes it clear in the first definition that leisure is not "discretionary time" and not necessarily "free time activity." He also makes it clear that leisure is not recreation, meaning that leisure is not restricted to activity alone.

For leisure to exist, one must be free from external and internal constraints. When this freedom is achieved, then one is in the right "state of being" to experience leisure. The experience of leisure is thus something that happens from within the individual. It is a personal experience.

Francis Bregha (University of Ottawa):

> Leisure is as much freedom to something as it is freedom from something.... Leisure, like freedom, is an end in itself. If perceived as a means, it should be called recreation – a worthwhile but quite utilitarian concept. We do not occupy our leisure in order to become healthier or more productive. Leisure allows us to be free, to be what we want to be (Bregha, 1985: 40-41).

For Bregha freedom is an essential condition of leisure. One has to be free from external and internal constraints to experience leisure. By finding leisure, and simply through the experience of leisure, one may be free. Leisure and freedom are two interrelated concepts.

For Bregha, leisure is based on personal experience and state of being. To truly be intrinsically free, a particular state of being is necessary. For Bregha, this state of being leads to the experience of leisure. Leisure is thus the state of condition that we all strive to achieve as we all want to be free.

Joseph Levy (York University):

> Leisure ... is both an activity and a state of mind.... [A]n activity [can be] anything that we choose to do during our non-obligatory time.... We all experience a state of leisure when our minds and bodies are functioning at optimum. When the skills, aptitudes and motivations that we possess are adequately challenged by our environment we feel very happy with ourselves (Levy, 1983: 13).

For Levy, leisure can be experienced by anyone at any time in any place as long as the right individual and social conditions exist. Leisure, for example, may be experienced during work if our state of mind allows it to happen and as long as the experience of work provides an adequate challenge. Thus leisure is closely linked to the personal experience and state of mind viewpoint.

Moreover, for Levy, leisure can also be activity engaged in during non-obligatory time. Leisure can be "free time activity." By highlighting "non-obligatory time," Levy indicates that leisure may be a time-specific activity. However, the experience of leisure is more likely to take place if a conducive personal and social environment exists during this non-obligatory time.

Thomas Goodale (University of Ottawa):

> Leisure means no more than free time; as in the phrase leisure time. In addition, the term has been resurrected from antiquity to refer to a state or condition; that is, where one is at. When one is at leisure one is in a relaxed, contemplative condition (Goodale, 1985: 44).

Goodale also highlights two viewpoints of leisure in his definition. In the first part of his definition his emphasis is on leisure as discretionary time. He does this by mentioning "leisure time" to explain what leisure is. In the second part of his definition, Goodale talks about contemplation, that is, a state of being. To this end, Goodale indicates that leisure is very much a personal experience and state of being.

Perhaps Goodale's intent is to link these two viewpoints of leisure. To experience leisure one must experience the necessary state of mind during a specific time period. It may be possible to experience this state of mind anywhere (including work) and during any time (including work and obligation time). So in this case, the two viewpoints of Goodale may not be mutually exclusive but, at times, may be intertwined.

Jill LeClair (Humber College):

> Leisure is "activity that is done outside the context of work and is fairly unstructured and not very competitive" (LeClair, 1992: 38).

For LeClair, leisure is activity that takes place during non-work time. LeClair does not emphasize an inner state of being or freedom as necessary conditions for the experience of leisure. Rather, leisure is the activity engaged in outside of work time. LeClair points out that the activity tends not to be serious, with few rules and little, if any, competition. It should be noted that, for LeClair, leisure is best compared to sport. The difference between leisure and sport is that sport has structure and rules, whereas leisure tends to be more loosely structured. Thus, for LeClair leisure is not only the opposite of work, but also extends to the type of experience enjoyed outside of work. This means that experiences such as taking out the garbage or doing laundry will probably not be classified as "leisure" although these are done outside of work time. It is therefore fair to state that LeClair's definition of leisure is largely determined by the experience of the activity.

Children actively experience both recreation and leisure while playing.

Photo: Health Canada.

PLEASURABLE PASTIMES

How Canadian Leisure Studies Students Define Leisure

The discipline of leisure studies is relatively young in Canada, as the first successful degree programs were not officially offered until the 1960s. It is thus no surprise that few Canadian researchers explore leisure and recreation or work on constructing definitions of leisure and recreation. Most literature that defines these concepts comes from American resources and Canadian leisure studies researchers tend to rely on American published research works.

To assist in enhancing the number of Canadian-based definitions of leisure and recreation, students enrolled in an introductory course on leisure in Canadian society were asked to construct definitions. Their definitions of leisure included the following:

- Leisure is free time with no family, social or institutional obligations.

- Leisure is a pleasurable pastime that involves one's likes and interests where one is relaxed or allowed to escape on a voluntary basis.

- Leisure is time left over after life's obligations have been complete; activities that give pleasure or satisfaction and internal rewards.

- Leisure is time available to pursue interest outside of work.

- Leisure is a relaxing, unstructured activity that differs for each individual.

The students' definitions of recreation included:

- Recreation is an organized form of activity that is geared towards the physical improvement of one's life.

- Recreation denotes the use of physical activity without strict guidelines, to pursue activities for the purposes of leisure and/or to connect with others who have similar interests.

- Recreation is an enjoyable activity that one takes part in to restore and refresh oneself.

Photo: Courtesy of Ted Temertzologu.

- Recreation is a voluntary physical activity that is done in the presence of others; is in contrast to work; and takes place during leisure time.

- Recreation is a socially acceptable activity that restores or refreshes you for work experiences during free time.

From the above definitions one could conclude that

- leisure is often viewed as a free-time activity or pursuit;

- leisure is pleasurable and enjoyable activity;

- leisure is self-chosen;

- leisure differs from person to person;

- recreation is activity;

- recreation is physical activity geared towards physical improvement;

- recreation takes place during free time or time outside of work; and

- recreation is an activity that helps re-create people for more work.

A CONCEPTUALIZATION OF LEISURE FOR CANADA

In Canada, we live in a society in which we can experience just about any activity or experience we please and call it leisure. Of course, we must take into consideration what is legally permissible, abide by the parameters of our Charter of Rights and Freedoms and take into consideration the health, safety and well-being of ourselves and others. So, with all this said and done, what is leisure in Canada? How can leisure be defined in Canadian society?

Consider the following definition: **Leisure** is any activity or state-of-mind experience that is freely driven or happens spontaneously during work time, obligation time and/or discretionary-time; and is permissible by the norms of society and is cultural-specific, meaning that it is derived according to the values, traditions or mores of a specific way of life or lifestyle of a particular cultural group(s) and Canada as a whole.

According to this definition, leisure can be anything for anyone at any time. However, the activity or the state of mind experience that is coined "leisure" is largely shaped by one's culture and society. In the case of Canada, our leisure is primarily determined by our cultural background, the makeup of society and by the opportunities that we are exposed to within our social system. There are certain things we can legally do. There are certain opportunities and activities that we are exposed to daily by Canadian media, by international media, through the Internet, by our institutions, and through our social and cultural groups and organizations. In addition, we live in a cultural mosaic with exposure to different values and traditions. The uniqueness of Canadian society, our political system, our social system, our ethnic cultures, and our historical roots and Aboriginal cultures make us who we are today. All of these factors combined, and more, help shape the definition of leisure in Canada today.

PURPOSE OF LEISURE IN CANADA

Minimal research exists in Canada on the purpose of leisure. It is often taken for granted that leisure is important in Canadian society, and thus is it is simply assumed that its purposes are self-explanatory. To a certain extent this may be true, yet it is of benefit to have a clear perspective of how Canadians, or Canadian-based research, describes the purpose of leisure.

Research conducted in Canada by Hutchison and McGill (1992) reports that the purpose of leisure is to build self-esteem and a sense of belonging in the community. It is through leisure that people discover that they: (1) have certain gifts and talents, (2) can contribute something to their communities, (3) are risk-takers and enjoy and even crave attention, (4) have a lot to teach others, (5) can master a certain skill, (6) can find some meaning to their life outside of work, (7) can express themselves in a creative way, (8) feel a sense of being connected to a larger group, and (9) have a feeling of accomplishment (pp. 4-5).

"RE-CREATION"?

Recreation, whether at work or outside of work, is activity and/or experience that "re-creates" the individual for more work. This "re-creation" is like recharging one's batteries to continue with more work or to take on life's obligations after work (e.g., cooking, cleaning and so forth) that are necessary for survival.

The Canadian *Report of the Study Committee on Environmental Resources* published by the Fitness and Amateur Sport Directorate in 1969 indicated that leisure has many purposes. This was made clear in the statement that "a leisure society will create the environment to allow satisfaction of personal needs including needs of: (1) health, (2) safety, (3) justice, (4) relaxation, (5) play, (6) challenge, (7) adventure, (8) variety of experience, (9) variety of opportunities, (10) fantasy, (11) beauty, (12) creativity, (13) esteem and recognition, (14) affection, (15) social interaction, (16) identity (with group, community), (17) involvement (social, political), and (18) participation in decision-making processes affecting one's everyday life" (p. 111). Thus, the purpose of leisure is to make life complete through the fulfilment of personal and social needs.

In addition to the aforementioned, recent research by McGill (1996) posits that a major purpose of leisure is to provide a unique context for learning about who we are and whom we might become. That is, by taking time for leisure we learn about ourselves and what we like to do. Thus, the purpose of leisure is to establish identity. In a young nation such as Canada, leisure can play a key role in firmly establishing a Canadian identity.

THE CONCEPT OF RECREATION

Recreation is a concept that is often perceived as being synonymous with leisure. However, when examined carefully, most researchers tend to agree that leisure and recreation are two very different concepts with similar underlying orientations. Recreation may be different from leisure when it is regarded as activity experienced during leisure time. Moreover, recreation may be considered as being the same as leisure when viewed as a personal experience much like that which commonly describes leisure. Thus, the concept recreation may be defined as: (1) activity and/or (2) personal experience (see Table 2.2).

Table 2.2: Two Viewpoints of the Concept Recreation

Viewpoint	Necessary Conditions
Recreation as Activity	The experience of activities defined by society as recreational. These activities are legal, enjoyable, active or passive and are engaged in during leisure time.
Recreation as Personal Experience	Extends beyond activity to include state of being and a way of life; an experience or activity that is self-defined and self-determined.

• Recreation as Activity

Recreation refers to the experience of activities that are defined by society as "recreational." These activities are legal, enjoyable, active or passive activities, and engaged in during leisure time. Moreover, **recreation as activity** tends to refer to activities that are structured and have some form of rules. Sports activities fall under this classification of recreation. However it is important to note that activities that have a lenient or no structure and rules (LeClair, 1992), such as arts and crafts, are also classified as recreation according to this perspective.

Recreation as activity also encompasses the provision of recreation services. The industry of recreation, including the sectors of recreation (public, commercial and voluntary), all provide recreation activities. The activities that are defined as recreation by society tend to be standard, meaning that they reflect a collective pool of activities characterized by society as being "recreation activities" experienced outside paid work and obligation time. Participation in these activities is voluntary and is motivated by a perception of the satisfaction that will be derived (Ballantyne, 1998).

• Recreation as Personal Experience

Recreation as personal experience is based on the understanding that recreation extends beyond activity to include a state of being and a way of life. Just like the personal experience and state of being viewpoint of leisure, recreation is an experience or activity that is self-defined and self-determined. Recreation is a personal experience that tends to be pleasurable. It may be structured, have a set of rules, and may be commonly defined by society as being a recreation activity (e.g., playing cards). However, the actual identification of an experience as "recreation" rests within the personal experience of the participant.

Recreation as personal experience is closely linked to state of mind. For a personal experience to be defined as "recreation," one must determine this to be the case based on inner feelings. These inner feelings may include pleasure, freedom, satisfaction and intrinsic motivation. Moreover, the identification of an experience as recreation is case-specific. Only the individual defines her or his experiences (including activity pursuits) as being recreation or non-recreation experiences. Thus, just like the personal experience and state of being conceptualization of leisure, recreation as personal experience can be "anything for anyone at any given time." Recreation as personal experience indicates that what we do for "recreation" largely stems out of the culture that we are a part of and the culturally specific values that we possess. That is, the culture that we belong to provides and encourages certain opportunities for recreation experiences while also instilling values within us to partake in cultural specific recreation pursuits. For instance, in multicultural Canada, we are encouraged to experience the ethno-cultural recreation activities of our ethnic roots.

MULTICULTURALISM PLAYS A PART, TOO

Recreation is a culturally determined activity by the host society and/or the ethnic culture; that is, recreation may be the cultural activities native to Canada (e.g., lacrosse or hockey) or the cultural activities brought to Canada from another land (e.g., the Scottish Highland games of Maxville, Ontario, or Italian bocce).

CANADIAN-BASED RESEARCH ON THE CONCEPT OF RECREATION

Peggy Hutchison (Brock University) and Judith McGill (Consultant in Leisure Integration):

> Recreation is "an activity that is undertaken during leisure time" (Hutchison and McGill, 1992: 5).

For Hutchison and McGill, the viewpoint of recreation as activity is used to define recreation. Recreation is activity that is pursued during leisure time, which means during discretionary time that is free from work and other obligations. The emphasis is on activity as an experience chosen during non-work and non-obligation time. This activity can be active or passive in nature.

John Farina (Wilfred Laurier University):

> Recreation is "activity indulged in voluntarily for the satisfaction derived from the activity itself and leading to revitalization of the mind, body or spirit" (Farina, 1969: [page ref.]).

Both viewpoints of recreation are included in Farina's definition. Recreation as activity is emphasized as it is clear that recreation is an activity that is voluntarily engaged in. Farina's definition goes on to talk about the effects that this activity may have on one's mind, indicating that recreation is also viewed as a personal experience. Nonetheless, it certainly does appear that the greatest emphasis by Farina is placed on the first viewpoint, that of recreation as activity.

Provincial Ministers Responsible for Recreation in Canada:

> [R]ecreation includes all of those activities in which an individual chooses to participate in his leisure time, and is not confined solely to sports and physical recreation programs, but includes artistic, creative, cultural, social and intellectual activities (National Recreation Statement, 1987: 5).

This government-released statement mentions recreation as consisting of a wide variety of activities. The key word used to describe recreation is "activities." The link is made here once again between recreation and leisure as free time. Recreation is viewed as activity, and this activity extends beyond sport and organized recreation programs to include passive and sedentary activities. Almost any activity can be defined as recreation. However, it should be noted that this statement is restricted to the word "activities" and does not mention the word "experience."

A CONCEPTUALIZATION OF RECREATION FOR CANADA

The most defining feature of Canadian society is that it is culturally diverse, consisting of a plethora of people from different ethnic backgrounds. In addition to the cultural pursuits of the original inhabitants of Canada, the Aboriginal Peoples, Canada is made up of different people from many lands who have brought with them their cultures, traditions and recreation activities, thus shaping how we define Canada today. For this reason, the following definition of recreation is based on the

Maurice ("Rocket") Richard.
Paul Taillefer/National Archives of Canada/PA 209768.

As a sport and recreational activity, ice hockey is a part of Canadian culture.

socio-demographic composition of Canadian society: Recreation is the freely chosen activities partaken within a time period free from all obligations for the end result of self-satisfaction. These can be structured, unstructured, based on ethnic cultural traditions or defined by the host culture as a part of the recreation industry.

This definition views recreation from an activity perspective and includes any activity that tends to be experienced outside of work and other obligations. Recreation may be a part of leisure, as recreation is the activity that is experienced during leisure time or non-obligation time. Recreation is a culturally determined activity by the host society and/or the ethnic culture; that is, it may be the cultural activities native to Canada (e.g., lacrosse or hockey) or the cultural activities brought to Canada from another land (e.g., the Scottish Highland games of Maxville, Ontario, or Italian bocce).

PURPOSE OF RECREATION

The purposes of recreation in Canada (as put forth by the Ministers Responsible for Recreation, 1974) are:

- to assist individual and community development,
- to improve quality of life, and
- to enhance social functioning.

It is also vitally important for the well-being of each and everyone of us.

PURPOSE OF RECREATION IN CANADA

The terms "recreation" and "sport" are often used together, as sometimes they mean the same thing. Depending on the context, various activities can be defined as sport and recreation. For instance, it is possible to define lacrosse as a sport activity and a recreation activity. Many definitions of sport and many definitions of recreation entail the essential elements of physical activities, competition and structure, and thus there is an overlap between the concepts of sport and recreation.

Historically in Canada, recreation and sport have often been viewed in the same light. Sport is often perceived as a part of recreation and vice versa (Vail and Carmichael, 1993). Various policies and practices put forth by governments make reference to recreation and sport as being intrinsically related. Also, recreation has often been incorporated in the mandate of Fitness and Amateur Sport directorates in Canada. This has led to national efforts by provincial fitness, sport and recreation directorates to construct a purpose statement for recreation.

In 1974, the provincial ministers responsible for recreation set forth the following purposes of recreation: (1) to assist individual and community development, (2) to improve quality of life, and (3) to enhance social functioning (*National Recreation Statement,* 1987). In 1987, the Ontario Ministry of Tourism and Recreation added a fourth purpose to this statement: to improve physical and mental health.

These purposes for recreation provide a picture as to the role of recreation in Canadian society. Recreation should help an individual to develop through the life stages, learn life skills and learn how to function within society. Recreation should also assist in the development of communities, through services and facilities catering to community needs. Recreation should also improve the quality of life as activities offer pleasurable, enjoyable experiences that help members of society reach a state of self-actualization. Moreover, recreation can help society build identity, harmony and cohesiveness through its social nature.

THE DEFINING ATTRIBUTES OF LEISURE

Working towards a Definition

Since the formation of leisure studies as an academic discipline, scholars have had a difficult time not only conceptualizing "leisure" but also agreeing on its definition. The difficulty arises from the fact that leisure, as an experience and in meaning, is culturally determined. Our ethnic and cultural backgrounds, the society that we are a part of, the institutions that educate and influence us and our families all shape our conceptualization of leisure.

In certain languages (e.g., Spanish and modern Greek) the word "leisure" does not exist. This is not to say that leisure does not exist, but rather that the term is not included in the national language of certain societies. Countries in which Spanish is the national language, such as Spain and Mexico, use the word *tiempo libre*, which means "free time." Furthermore, countries such as Greece and Cyprus that have modern Greek as their national language use the word *eleftheros chronos*, which also means free time.

In societies in which leisure studies has advanced as a discipline (e.g., the United States, United Kingdom and Australia), English is a national language. In bilingual Canada, the French word *loisir* directly translates to the English word "leisure." This has made the advancement of the discipline much easier in Canada than in other multilingual countries as the word leisure exists in both official languages.

Despite the existence of the word "leisure" in the English language, this notion is one that troubled scholars, particularly when it comes to agreeing on one universal meaning. Early research conducted by Joffre Dumazedier argued that leisure is activity, whereas Sebastien deGrazia postulated that leisure is a state of being. Contemporary research conducted in this discipline both in Canada and internationally argues that leisure is more than activity and state of being. In fact, the definition of leisure may be limited to activity and state of being or may indeed expand beyond these conceptualizations.

A Canadian Definition

How do Canadians define leisure? Do we agree on one definition of leisure? Do English-speaking and French-speaking Canadians agree on the same definition for *leisure* and *loisir*?

Forty fourth-year leisure studies students, both French- and English-speaking, were asked to identify key attributes that had appeared in the definitions of leisure they had encountered during their studies. It was found that the term "leisure" consisted of many different attributes that extended beyond activity and state of mind. The defining attributes identified by these students were as follows:

freedom	learning/knowledge
liberation	passion/desire
happiness	satisfaction
self-growth	freedom of choice
social	personal interaction
non-obligatory experiences	cleansing
experience	inner peace
flow	break from daily activities
relaxation	self-development
solidarity	sporting activity
strengthening mind	health
rejuvenation	healing/recuperation/ therapeutic
activity	relaxation
positive feelings	play
overall wellness	developing social skills
enhancing quality of life	observation
fun	peaceful
commitment	expressiveness
spare time pursuits	intrinsic meaning
pleasurable	positive state of mind

Research conducted by Richard Kraus (1997: 4) reveals a number of purposes of recreation for the individual participant. These are: (1) pleasure, (2) to address needs of excitement and challenge, (3) social acceptance and friendship, (4) feelings of accomplishment and self-mastery, (5) creative expression, and (6) improvement of physical and emotional health. Other research lists three purposes of recreation in Canada: (1) to aid in making the individual feel good about themselves, (2) to improve the quality of individual and social life, and (3) to fulfil our basic need of re-creation (for work and other obligations) (Karlis, 2002a: 2).

INTRODUCING THE CONCEPT OF PLAY

The **concept of play** is closely linked with recreation. The closeness of these two concepts is evident throughout the history of leisure and recreation in Canadian society. The "recreation movement" in Canada evolved primarily out of the "play movement" initiated by the National Council of Women, indicating that play may be a part of recreation, and recreation may be a defining feature of play. Moreover, as recreation is closely linked to leisure, play may also be a part of leisure and vice-versa.

Play can take place in the form of activity and/or experience. As activity, we often refer to sports as being playful when we claim to "play hockey" or "play squash." As experience, play may be viewed as being something pre-planned such as "playing Monopoly" or "playing Scrabble" or as a spontaneous experience such as "daydreaming." Play tends to be based on a number of specific elements such as competition, play-acting, and exploratory or creative behaviour (Kraus, 1994).

It is important to note that play usually consists of active involvement. Activities or experiences such as meditation, reading a book and attending lectures are more likely to be conceptualized as recreation than play. However, it should be noted that the beholder of the play activity or experience may choose to define the aforementioned sedentary pursuits as play. As is the case with leisure and recreation, the extent to which an experience or activity is defined as play may in some cases depend on the individual.

There are many elements of play that not only drive the player to engage in this activity or experience, but also help the player to experience play. According to Bishop and Jeanrenaud (1985), some elements of play that merit attention are: novelty, curiosity, exploration, assimilation or consolidation, and creativity. When one sits back and thinks about his or her own play activities and/or experiences, it is not difficult to understand the role these elements undertake in shaping our understanding of the concept play and the playful experience.

Although the word "play" does not regularly appear in this text, it is important to realize that play is closely linked with leisure and recreation. At times, leisure, recreation and play may be considered to mean the same thing; at other times, their meanings may be significantly different.

Creativity is an inherent part of play, and an important part of recreation programs.

Photo: Health Canada.

CONCLUSION

Leisure and recreation are two very similar, yet very different, concepts. They are similar from the activity perspective. They are also similar as both may require a certain state of being to be experienced, although this appears to be more common for leisure. Moreover, they are similar as both may consist of any experience at any time, yet once again this is more plausible for leisure than for recreation.

It is evident that little research exists in Canada that provides a conceptualization of leisure and recreation. The fact that leisure studies is still a relatively young field in Canada may justify this, but in all likelihood, the high reliance on the foundational concepts of leisure and recreation from American research is more likely the cause. Regardless, many researchers are critical of the lack of definitions. Peter Witt and Gary Ellis wrote almost twenty years ago that "our task in the future is to continue to sharpen our conceptualization of leisure" (1985: 116). This continues to be the case today as more research is needed in Canada on the conceptualizations of leisure and recreation.

Working definitions of leisure and of recreation have been presented, both specifically representative of Canadian society. In addition, both definitions help expand the limited Canadian-based research on the concepts of leisure and recreation.

CHAPTER 2: CONCEPTS OF LEISURE AND RECREATION

Study Questions

1. Why have the conceptual definitions of leisure and recreation evolved out of the United States?

2. List and describe the three viewpoints of leisure.

3. Explain Ballantyne's definition of leisure.

4. Why is freedom an essential condition of leisure for Bregha?

5. What does Levy mean by "we all experience leisure when our minds and bodies are functioning at optimum?"

Selected Websites

- **Leisure Information Network**
  http://www.lin.ca

- **Canadian Association for Leisure Studies**
  http://www.eas.ualberta.ca/elj/cals/home.htm

Key Concepts

- **Leisure**

- **Leisure as discretionary time**

- **Leisure as free time activity**

- **Leisure as personal experience and state of being**

- **Recreation**

- **Recreation as activity**

- **Recreation as personal experience**

- **Concept of play**

3

HISTORY OF LEISURE AND RECREATION IN CANADA

LEARNING OBJECTIVES

- To examine the early developments of leisure and recreation in Canada.

- To trace the historical evolution of the public, commercial and voluntary sectors for leisure and recreation in Canada.

- To examine the impact of social trends on the evolution of leisure and recreation.

- To explore the historical evolution of leisure and recreation activities and pursuits in Canada.

- To look at the impact government Acts have had on the development of leisure and recreation in Canada.

he history of leisure and recreation in Canada is broad and complex. It would take volumes to provide a detailed, thorough analysis of all the historical events that have evolved for leisure and recreation in Canada.

This chapter seeks to provide an overview of some of the key historical developments of leisure and recreation in Canada. It begins with a discussion of leisure and recreation prior to the Dominon of Canada, leisure and recreation in the infant years of Canada, and an overview of the Playground Movement in Canada. The early formation of municipal and voluntary leisure and recreation services in Canada is introduced, and the "golden age" of sport is examined. The impact of provincial government involvement and the effects of World War II are explored. The growth of services, opportunities and consumerism, and the boom in leisure and recreation are examined, followed by a description of the coming of age of higher education and research in leisure studies. The effects of government cutbacks on leisure and recreation are discussed, and the chapter ends with an examination of the increasing value of leisure and recreation.

"To be able to fill leisure intelligently is the last product of civilization."

— Bertrand Russell (1872-1970), British philosopher, mathematician. *The Conquest of Happiness*, ch. 14 (1930). "At present," Russell added, "very few people have reached this level."

LEISURE AND RECREATION PRIOR TO THE DOMINION OF CANADA

Historical research indicates that leisure and recreation in Canada began prior to Confederation. In fact, the first accounts of leisure and recreation, and physical activities can be traced back to the Inuit and the Aboriginal Peoples of southern Canada.

CANADA'S FIRST PUBLIC PARK

Perhaps the earliest park in Canada was established in Kingston, Ontario, in the late 1830s when Lord Sydenham established the Artillery Parade Ground for the purpose of locating Parliament at Kingston (Wright, 1983).

Traditionally, all aspects of life were integrated for the Inuit and Aboriginal Peoples of southern Canada. The activities and experiences of work, play, leisure, recreation and religion were all interconnected. Physical fitness was an important part of survival, and value was placed on the relationship between mind, body and spirit (Royal Commission on Aboriginal People, 1996).

The Inuit and the Aboriginal Peoples of southern Canada may have hunted and fished not only for survival, but also for pleasure. According to Searle and Brayley (2000: 15), the Inuit and the Aboriginal Peoples of southern Canada "played games, sang songs, played musical instruments, danced, and told stories for entertainment and amusement." Yet, Delorme (2000) notes that the only concern of the Inuit was survival and states that "they hunted the caribou seal and walrus herds and caught fish in order to feed and clothe themselves and make tools. Once the day's work was done, men, women and children would get together in igloos. Sometimes, they played games – simple ones, based mainly on hunting and fishing skills" (p. 17).

In contrast, despite the hazards of living in the Arctic, Ibrahim (1991) posits that the lifestyle of the Inuit was characterized by playfulness. The Inuit participated in a number of culturally significant games. *Agraoruk* was a game in which the contestant kicked a sealskin dangling from a pole. *Nalukatook* consisted of bouncing on a walrus hide held by others, similar to today's trampoline. *Ipirautaqurnia* was an activity that consisted of flipping a whip in an accurate fashion.

A popular team game played by the Algonquins and Iroquis was *baggataway* (Searle and Brayley, 2000). The Mohawks called this game *tewaarathon* (Cole, 1993). Today *baggataway* or *tewaarathon* is referred to as lacrosse, a name given to the game by the French settlers of Canada who perceived a resemblance between the curved netted stick and the bishop's crozier (Ibrahim, 1991).

Graeme Decarie, a history professor at Concordia University, claims that "lacrosse was invented by native peoples unknown centuries ago" (2000: 28). For the Aboriginal Peoples of Canada, lacrosse had multiple uses: "(1) the game was used for settling major conflicts as an alternative to armed conflict, (2) bestowing power on individuals or groups of people, (3) constituting a means of offering thanks to the Creator for allowing an elder or medicine person to remain with the people to continue sharing their richness of life with the youth, (4) developing maturity and respect among players, and (5) developing coordination, quickness and timing for the players" (Cole, 1993: 110). Bets were also placed on the outcome of lacrosse. As Decarie (2000) postulates, "native peoples bet heavily on lacrosse, so heavily that a losing team could sacrifice vast territories and suffer years of hardship" (p. 29).

Canadian historians tend to agree that the terrain and native inhabitants were significant determining factors in shaping the lifestyle, leisure and recreation forms of early European settlers (Horna, 1995). Early settlers to Canada were mostly peasants, craftsmen or fishermen, who adapted well to the native people's activity pursuits of hunting and fishing, as well as the sporting activities of the canoe, Inuit kayak, toboggan, snowshoe and lacrosse (ibid.). These early settlers also adapted some of their own pursuits such as dancing, horse racing, football and running (Howell and Howell, 1985). In addition, through the many military garrisons that were scattered in various parts of the country, English officers experienced equestrian sports and cricket, while early Scottish immigrants introduced curling in 1807 (Ibrahim, 1991).

The English settlers initially left lacrosse to native Canadians. In 1842, however, members of the athletic club of Montreal started to play lacrosse and compete with local native teams. This eventually led to the Western adaptation of the game with the implementation of rules, which also departed from the native pattern of year-round play (Baker, 1982).

In addition to the development of leisure, recreation and sports, the natural outdoors started to be appreciated as a leisure and recreation experience during the formative years of Canada. Research by Wright states that the earliest "public garden in Canada is linked to the settlement of St. John's, Newfoundland, the first overseas colonial government of Britain" (1983: 55). This piece of land called The Garden was full of wild roses, strawberries and various types of other fruits and provided a unique appeal and aesthetic appreciation to the people (England, 1975).

In the early settlement years, a number of public open space areas were used for recreational purposes. Wright (1983) describes five major types of open space areas that existed in Upper Canadian villages and towns in the early 1800s. The first is the *common,* which was land set aside for livestock, wood and fuel, and for exercise (Markham, 1980). One of the earliest examples of this type of open space was the Halifax Common established in 1750. The second type of open space is the *public square.* The intent of the public square was to provide an open space with pathways for strolling. One of the first squares in Canada was created in Montreal in 1821. The third type of open space, the *church plaza,* was the open space in front of churches used for religious ceremonies and public gatherings. The fourth type of public open space was *military lands* consisting of the square or parade ground adjacent to the barracks. The final type of public open space used for recreational purposes was *cemeteries.* Cemeteries were often used for walking and picnics.

Perhaps the earliest park in Canada was established in Kingston, Ontario, in the late 1830s when Lord Sydenham established the Artillery Parade Ground for the purposes of locating Parliament at Kingston (Wright, 1983). Today this area of land is referred to as City or Macdonald Park. This park, and other early parks established in Toronto and Hamilton, resulted out of elite leadership and were not the result of a common ideology or pressure by the general public.

According to Ibrahim (1991), the early settlers did not have much time or opportunity to devote to leisure and recreation, but rather occupied most of their time and effort building a nation. As a result, leisure and

A day in Stanley Park in Vancouver shortly after it opened in 1889.

Photo: City of Vancouver Archives/SGN 133.

recreation was secondary in importance. Shortly prior to Confederation, industrialization started to emerge. This became particularly evident in the 1850s as a population shift commenced from the countryside to the urban areas. New technology, new modes of transportation, urbanization and the influx of people to developing cities not only changed the nature of work and the structure of organizations of day-to-day living, but also introduced new opportunities for leisure and recreation.

The early English settlers of Canada participated in a ritualistic activity called "the bee." This activity consisted of "a co-operative communal effort to complete a harvest or to raise a barn" (Ibrahim, 1991: 150). This activity was a form of social recreation as it brought people together in a collaborative project. The host of this communal effort was to provide the food and drink (usually whisky) to the participants (ibid.).

By the mid-1800s sports such as cricket and curling brought by early English settlers to Canada started to expand in popularity, whereas many French settlers had to adapt their sports to the new social milieu. This was particularly evident in the Province of Quebec (Dauphinais, 1990). Despite the fact that the early French-speaking population of Quebec only came into contact with Anglophone settlers on a limited basis from 1840 to 1860, they had acquired an interest in sports, such as baseball and ice hockey, that required strength and individual effort (ibid.).

It was in 1844 that the "oldest series of international matches" in cricket commenced between Canada and the U.S. (Bowen, 1970). This was the start of a trend that later emerged, that of using international matches of sports to unify the country from within and to establish links within the Commonwealth and international communities (Redmond, 1989). The international attraction of cricket helped it to become one of the most popular pastimes of Canada prior to Confederation (ibid.).

In the 1850s, public parks were initiated in Ontario by the elite sector of society (Wright, 1983). Prior to Confederation, action was taken by Toronto City Council to provide public open space for recreational use with the establishment of the Committee on Public Walks and Gardens in 1851 (McFarland, 1970). In 1859 the chair of this committee "defended the preservation of public park areas before Council ... claiming that parks were of benefit to every social class in the community" (Wright, 1983: 85). Eventually, the *Recreation Grounds Act* was passed in Parliament in 1859 (Wright, 1984). Shortly after, in nearby Hamilton, Ontario, Gore Park was established (McFarland, 1970).

In the mid-1800s the need for commercial leisure and recreation started to become evident. One of the first private sport and athletic clubs was the Royal Canadian Yacht Club, established in Toronto in 1854 (Wright, 2000). The services offered by this club abided by many of the same principles of today's commercial sectors (e.g., the offering of a quality product for a cost). In addition, the third sector of leisure and recreation – the voluntary sector – also came into being. In the mid-1800s, the voluntary sector for recreation showed potential for expansion as one of the first voluntary sector recreation organizations in Canada, the YMCA, was founded in Montreal in 1851. This was the start of the expansion of YMCAs and other voluntary leisure and recreation services across Canada.

LEISURE AND RECREATION IN THE INFANT YEARS OF THE DOMINION OF CANADA

On July 1, 1867, the political union of four provinces (Ontario, Quebec, Nova Scotia and New Brunswick), consisting of approximately 3.5 million people, formed the Dominion of Canada. At that time only 12 percent of the population lived in cities or towns as most lived in rural areas (Lower, 1958). The impact of industrialization was soon to change this, however.

During the infant years of the Dominion of Canada (1867-99), social, political and cultural values started to change as the Puritan ethic towards leisure and recreation began to lose significance (Cross, 1990). It was also during this time that leisure and recreation needs and concerns emerged as Canadians experienced greater freedom, democracy and independence (McInnis, 1969). Labour unions started to increase as the rights of workers began to be conceptualized and the volunteer sector of recreation showed signs of growth and expansion with the founding of the YMCA in 1870 in Saint John, New Brunswick (Corporate Author, 2002a). This period also marked the time of the "beginning of change in the attitudes of men towards women" (Searle and Brayley, 2000: 16). It was during these years of renewed interest in recreation that some activities became "acceptable forms of public recreation for women. They included croquet, lawn tennis, golf, archery, roller skating, and ice skating" (ibid.).

Although its actual date of establishment was prior to Confederation, ice hockey started to blossom during the early years of the Dominion of Canada. A number of research accounts depict different sites as the birthplace of what has become Canada's game. Authors such as Tessier (1984), who claims that the first hockey game in Canada was played in Montreal at the corner of Bleury and Dorchester, have attributed a prominent French-Canadian role to the establishment of the game. Others, such as Searle and Brayley (2000), contend that hockey originated in Kingston, Ontario, in 1855 and credit British troops stationed in Kingston as being the first to introduce the game.

Gruneau and Whitson (1993), in *Hockey Night in Canada,* make reference to Captain James Sutherland as citing Kingston as the true birthplace of hockey in 1903. Other research purports that Nova Scotia, and more specifically Long Pond near Windsor, is the birthplace of ice hockey. Research by Vaughan (1996) finds that the Mi'kmaq, who called ice hockey *alchamadajk* or hurley-on-ice, first played the game with other participants in Nova Scotia.

HOCKEY'S EARLY BEGINNINGS

Although its actual date of establishment was prior to Confederation, ice hockey started to blossom during the early years of the Dominion of Canada.

THE BIRTHPLACE OF HOCKEY

Was It Really Windsor, Nova Scotia?

In 1994, the Canadian House of Commons proclaimed lacrosse and hockey, two sports with Canadian roots, as the national sports of Canada. However, hockey is a more high-profile sport than lacrosse. The people of Canada have come to recognize hockey as "Canada's game," and this is quite obvious in the value we place on winning international competitions and tournaments.

Despite the fact that hockey is "Canada's game," how much do we know about its history? When it originated? And where? Did it originate in Canada, and if so, where in Canada?

Tracing the historical roots of hockey is a difficult task. Some researchers such as Tessier (1984) give a prominent French-Canadian role to the establishment of hockey whereas others, such as Searle and Brayley (2000), claim that the game was introduced by British troops stationed in Kingston. Some research indicates that the first hockey game may have been played in Montreal in 1875 or Kingston in 1886, yet further research by Garth Vaughan (1994) makes the astonishing argument that the game originated neither in Montreal or Kingston but rather in Windsor, Nova Scotia.

This argument is made through a detailed, thorough historical overview by Garth Vaughan, a retired surgeon and lifelong follower of hockey, in a 1994 book entitled *The Puck Starts Here: The Origin of Canada's Great Winter Game*. In his book, Vaughan traces the historical evolution of the game from schoolboys at King's College in Windsor, Nova Scotia, to boys in Halifax and Dartmouth, then through soldiers and cadets who took the game to Montreal, Kingston and Ottawa.

Research by Vaughan claims that the game spread from east to west, starting with the boys of King's College, who had adapted the field game of hurley, brought to Canada by Irish immigrants, at around 1800. The game hurley was moved from the field to the ice and was originally played, according to Vaughan, on Long Pond in Windsor, Nova Scotia.

Vaughan claims that hockey sticks and skates were also introduced in Nova Scotia. The Mi'kmaq craftsmen of Windsor, Nova Scotia, were the first to carve hockey sticks from hornbeam trees in the early and mid-1890s. The Acme Club Spring Skate was invented by John Forbes and Thomas Bateman at the Starr Manufacturing Company in Nova Scotia in 1865, and this, according to Vaughan, revolutionized the game of hockey. Finally, Vaughan's research states that James George Aylwin Creighton introduced ice hockey, hockey sticks and the Halifax Hockey Club rules to the cities of Montreal and Ottawa in 1875 and 1884 respectively.

In addition to his compelling arguments regarding the roots of hockey, Vaughan presents facts and details relating to the early days of the game. For example, his research reveals that the word "hockey" is a centuries-old English word that is also a popular English surname. He discusses how some church clergy condemned hockey as a "desecration of the Sabbath." He also mentions that in the 1860s a man, referred to as the "dragon," was hired in Halifax to keep hockey players off ponds in order to protect skaters.

The detailed research put forth by Vaughan makes a strong case for Nova Scotia as having played the lead role in the origin of hockey in Canada.

Sources:

Searle, M.S., and Brayley, R.E. (2000). *Leisure Services in Canada.* (2nd Edition). State College, PA: Venture.

Tessier, Y. (1984). *Histoire du Hockey et des Sports.* Sillery, QU: Editions Tessier.

Vaughan, G. (1994). *The Puck Stops Here: The Origin of Canada's Great Winter Game Ice Hockey.* Fredericton, NB: Goose Lane Editions and Four East Publications.

Organized ice hockey as we know it today appeared in 1884 with the formation of the Montreal Hockey Club (Morrow, 1981). In its early years, ice hockey was a sport that was initially monopolized by the Anglophone elite (Dauphinais, 1990). It was not until 1895 that ice hockey started to become a highly popular sport of French Canadians. As the rapid development of hockey was becoming apparent, Lord Stanley donated hockey's trophy, the Stanley Cup, during his parting years as Governor-General in 1893.

As stated, Canada's climate played a significant role in the early development of leisure, recreation and sport, including the development of the commercial sector. This is most evident in Redmond's research in which he notes that "a perennial theme in emerging Canadian nationalism has been the idea that Canada's unique character was derived from the northern location, her severe winters and her heritage of 'northern races'" (1989: 198). Even George Beers, a Montreal dentist who was most responsible for the codification and promotion of the summer sport lacrosse, made continuous reference to the character-building effects of sport on ice and snow (ibid.).

The commercial sector of recreation expanded during this era as Canada became home to the first private golf club in North America, with the establishment in 1873 of the Royal Montreal Golf Club. In 1874, the Quebec City Golf Club was established (Reville, 1920; Wright, 2000). The commercial sector showed further signs of growth with the establishment of the London Curling Club in 1879 and the Ottawa Lawn Tennis Club in 1881, a sport that spread quickly from England.

The development of rails and waterways led to the expansion of regionalism (Betke, 1990). The expansion of the rail system also enticed the development of commercial recreation and tourism and the growth of the national park system. Moreover, the development of the cross-Canada railway system and the efforts of the Canadian Pacific Railroad company led to the establishment of Rocky Mountain Park (Banff) in 1885. The *Rocky Mountain Parks Act* received Royal assent on June 23, 1887, as land that was "reserved and set apart as a public and pleasure ground for the benefit, advantage and enjoyment of the people of Canada" (Lothian, 1976: 25). As a result of this Act, Glacier and Yoho parks were also established to make the mountain areas and British Columbia accessible to visitors (McNamee, 2002).

Further evidence of the emerging appeal of lacrosse in Canada was taking place as this sport started to challenge cricket as the most popular sport in Canada (Redmond, 1989). George Beers had a lot to do with this as he led two successful tours by Canadian lacrosse teams to Britain in 1876 and 1883.

One of Canada's first post-Confederation governors, Viscount Monck, set aside land on the west side of Rideau Hall, the Governor General's official residence, for cricket (Redmond, 1989). In subsequent years, this same area was transformed into a leisure playground as the

Long Pond, Nova Scotia, thought to be the birthplace of hockey.

facilities were used in the early 1900s for tobogganing, skating, ice hockey and curling (Hubbard, n.d.).

The *Public Parks Act of Ontario,* also entitled *An Act To Provide for the Establishment and Maintenance of Public Parks in Cities and Towns,* was passed in 1883. This Act provided for the establishment of a system of parks as well as the maintenance of existing parks (Wright, 1984). This Act not only encouraged the development of parks in Ontario but in other provinces as well and was instrumental in the eventual birth of Canada's national parks (ibid.).

In the 1880s, the middle class in Ontario started to assume greater responsibility for public parks as they began to be perceived as picturesque (Wright, 1983). Parks were viewed as idealized landscapes at the edge of the town, whose main purpose was the refreshment of mind, body and spirit through the experience of the outdoors and nature (ibid.). In fact, early parks were established in Ontario in several ways: "from the donation or sale of land to the municipality by the individual or family; by the acquisition of land by local government; or from the initiative of a group of citizens persuading the local council to acquire parkland" (Wright, 1984: 47).

By the 1890s, municipal parks had become a part of many municipalities in Canada. In fact, provinces such as Ontario and Manitoba had "passed enabling legislation laws empowering municipalities to establish parks and set procedures for acquisitions and standards for management" (Ibrahim, 1991: 157). In municipalities such as Winnipeg, for example, two "classes of parks" existed: (1) vacant green spaces that were free, open space used for recreational purposes, and (2) commercially operated parks that provided midway-style amusements (Macdonald, 1998).

McFarland (1970) posits that early parks in Canada were established as places of serenity for appreciation of the aesthetic beauty of nature. This made the parks of early Canada different from what they are today as park activities were limited to "walking, riding in one's carriage, botanical appreciation, and bird watching" (Searle and Brayley, 2000: 19). As Searle and Brayley note, "Do Not Walk on the Grass" signs clearly indicated that parks were meant to be passive areas (ibid.)

In 1893, Algonquin National Park was established (Eagles and Martens, 1997). This park was established out of the recommendation of the Royal Commission on Forest Reservation, "reserving a portion of the ungranted Crown domain to be set apart as a Forest Reservation and National Park" (Ministry of Natural Resources, 1974).

The rapidly developing cities in western Canada began to value public parkland in much the same way as the older cities in the eastern and central provinces. In 1888, only two years after the city of Vancouver was established, the city created a civic parks committee with a mandate to purchase and develop land for public parks. On September 27, 1889, Stanley Park was opened (Wright, 1984).

At the close of the nineteenth century, perhaps the most important development for leisure and recreation was the establishment of the **National Council of Women** in 1893 in Vancouver, Winnipeg, Toronto, Montreal and Halifax. The initial purpose of this council was to "unite in Dominion Federation for the betterment throughout Canada of conditions pertaining to the family and the state, all societies and associations of women interested in philanthropy, religion, education, literature, art or social reform" (McFarland, 1982). The National Council of Women played a leading role in the Playground Movement and in examining youth and leisure and recreation issues (McFarland, 1970). The focus of the National Council of Women was to promote the social welfare role of play and, more specifically, to encourage community leaders to establish playgrounds and sand gardens as aids to help build the social and moral character of children. As a result of the early efforts of the National Council of Women, the value of leisure and recreation pursuits were brought to the attention of the federal government, eventually leading to greater government roles in leisure and recreation (Ibrahim, 1991).

NATIONAL COUNCIL OF WOMEN

As a result of the early efforts of the National Council of Women, the value of leisure and recreation pursuits were brought to the attention of the federal government, eventually leading to greater government roles in leisure and recreation (Ibrahim, 1991).

By the end of the nineteenth century, it was evident that time for leisure and recreation was becoming available. The availability of this time created new opportunities and new potentials for leisure and recreation experiences. In his research, Michael Smith describes the state of condition of leisure and recreation in the late 1890s:

> In the late nineteenth century, as leisure time became more available, increasing numbers of men, women, and children, flocked to gymnasiums, to playing fields, to rinks, and they participated in a variety of recreational activities. They did this in the hope of not only achieving an exhilarating experience, but also to improving their health, fitness, and social accomplishments. Gymnastic exercises, outdoor recreations, and leisure activities are often touted as the best and easiest way to achieve a fit physique for men and a healthy and strong maternal future for women. By the beginning of the twentieth century, many people believed that their generation and civilization had surpassed all others; that the fittest indeed had survived. This view, a white, middle-class outlook, caused many to evaluate the leisure activities that dominated. Physicians, alternative medical practitioners, and educators carefully scrutinized all leisure pastimes. All too often supporters of physical culture and fitness feared that the thrill of competition, the push for success, and the lack of medical knowledge were driving participants to ignore cautionary reports, and to harm their physical, mental, and even moral, attributes. From the hazards of bicycling to the perils of excessive piano-playing, leisure activities were fraught with dangers. (1996: 267)

One of the first city councils to show an interest in the provision of recreation space was Ottawa City Council. In 1898 Mayor Bingham played a key role in influencing Ottawa City Council to set aside approximately eleven lots for leisure and recreation grounds to be used by citizens. These lots were referred to as "the Ottawa Ward Playgrounds" (Minutes of the Corporation of the City of Ottawa, 1899).

LEISURE AND RECREATION AS "DISCRETIONARY TIME"

In the early 1900s, leisure and recreation started to be viewed as pursuits that were dichotomous with work; that is, activities experienced during discretionary time.

Finally, in 1899, an Act of Parliament put forth the establishment of the Ottawa Improvement Commission (now known as the National Capital Commission). The commission became responsible for the management of the largest parks in Ottawa as well as federal government grounds. Through the Act of Parliament, the commission was granted authority for the purchase and acquisition of land in Ottawa for the establishment of public parks (Wright, 1984). Today, leisure and recreation continues to be an important part of the National Capital Commission. By this time, the cities of Toronto and Winnipeg had also established municipal park services to promote recreation involvement in the outdoors (Searle and Brayley, 2000).

1900-1909: THE PLAYGROUND MOVEMENT IN CANADA

The efforts initiated by the National Council of Women, and in particular, Mabel Peters, became evident with the establishment of the first playground in Saint John in 1906 (Searle and Brayley, 2000). At around the same time, a number of other cities, such as Regina, Vancouver, Winnipeg, Ottawa, Hamilton, Toronto and Montreal, all showed initiative towards the establishment of playgrounds, thus signifying the commencement of the **"Playground Movement"** in Canada. This movement is largely attributed to the efforts of the National Council of Women (McFarland, 1970). The rationale behind this movement was that the playground experience helped develop social and health benefits as well as provide places to play in crowded cities (ibid.).

The *Lord Day's Act* was proclaimed in 1907. According to Wetherall and Kmet (1990), this act led, to some extent, to the establishment of the "weekend." Mandatory time off work and holidays started to become popular. Leisure and recreation started to be viewed as pursuits that were dichotomous with work, that is, activities experienced during discretionary time.

The Ford Model-T automobile was introduced in 1908. This new means of transportation from one area to another allowed a freedom never experienced before. Recreation opportunities became vast and diverse as pleasure travel became popular (Wetherell and Knet, 1990). Weekend trips increased in popularity as did the spread of automobile travel for touristic purposes.

At the close of this decade, it was obvious that the American influence had begun to have an impact, particularly on physical fitness, physical recreation activities and sport activities in Canada (Lappage, 1985). This became evident through the adaptation of American football in Canada. In 1909, Earl Grey donated a trophy, the Grey Cup, for the Canadian football championship, thus helping to establish a Canadian identity with the game.

During this decade, women, men and children started to view leisure and recreation as activities that were not only important for physical and moral development, but also for social enhancement as well. Yet, during this decade the provision of leisure and recreation services continued to rest largely in the hands of individuals and voluntary groups such as the National Council of Women. The people of Canada had to play a key role in establishing, leading and providing necessary leisure and recreation services both for themselves and for society as a whole.

1910-1919: THE EARLY FORMATION OF MUNICIPAL AND VOLUNTARY LEISURE AND RECREATION SERVICES IN CANADA

Urban development plans started to be prepared in Toronto in 1911, in Calgary in 1912-1914, in Ottawa in 1915, and in Kitchener (formerly Berlin) in 1914 (Wright, 2000). The living patterns of Canadians started to change as masses of people relocated to cities from small towns and farming communities.

With an awareness of the trend towards urbanization, action was taken to provide leisure services in municipalities. In 1912 and 1913, at the annual meetings of the National Council of Women, emphasis was placed on the training and development of recreation leaders. More specifically, proposals were drafted for the training of playground teachers and supervisors. In addition, a proposal was also put in place for the establishment of a national organization (Markham, 1996). According to Markham (ibid.), these actions taken by the National Council of Women in 1912 and 1913 are the first recorded efforts to professionalize leisure services in Canada.

In June of 1913, the first full-time staff member for the implementation of a public recreation program was hired by the Toronto Parks Department. His name was S.H. Armstrong and his job title was Chief Supervisor of Playgrounds. Mr. Armstrong was a former vice-principal in the Toronto Board of Education (McFarland, 1970).

By 1915, "public parks were an accepted fact in town and city growth in Ontario" (Wright, 1983: 84). The "public parks movement" that took place between 1883 and 1914 brought to the forefront a general need for public recreational grounds and the enhanced development of public parks (Wright, 1984). By this time it had become obvious that urban development had engulfed the establishment of public parks.

In addition, this decade also witnessed the branching out of the voluntary sector of leisure and recreation in parts of Canada. In 1917, the expansion of the voluntary sector received a huge boost with the establishment of the Jasper Place Community League in Edmonton. The intent of community leagues was to assist in the organization and provision of recreation and sport services throughout the community. This community league started by using schools to hold recreational events. Programs offered included movie picture programs, concerts and socials (McFarland, 1970). Eventually, this community league played a key role in the establishment of municipal recreation through the promotion of playgrounds, parks, community centres and swimming pools (Kraus, 1984).

Photo: Cyril Jessop/National Archives of Canada/PA 30212.

Social and political activist Nelly McClung championed women's rights.

1920-1929: THE GOLDEN AGE OF SPORT

By the time the 1920s came along, most urban centres in Canada had established organized public parks and recreation systems (McFarland, 1970). The automobile was no longer a novelty as over twelve Canadian auto manufacturers now existed. In addition, most Canadians perceived the future with a confident, optimistic attitude while feeling secure and comfortable with the familiar (Craig, 1977). The majority of Canadians no longer lived on farms but in cities and small towns. In 1921, for example, 58 percent of Ontarians lived in cities or towns whereas only 42 percent remained in rural settings. The puritanical fervour that had dominated the Victorian era was replaced by a focus on urban problems and the "concerns of today." The economy had a turnaround after World War I with unemployment dropping to 8 percent in 1925. In most parts of Canada, seven statutory holidays were implemented in 1922: Christmas, Dominion Day, Labour Day, Victoria Day, Thanksgiving Day, Good Friday and New Year's Day. Tourism also started to develop as a major economic industry. The leisure and recreation activities of listening to radio and jazz were increasing in popularity. Municipal governments were starting to accept responsibility for society's need for leisure and recreation, as service clubs, churches and the YMCA played a key role in advocating for the need for recreation.

Table 3.1: Founding Dates for Canadian Sports

Organization	Date Founded
National Lacrosse Association	1867
became National Amateur Lacrosse Association	1880
Canadian Association of Amateur Oarsmen	1880
Canadian Wheelman's Association (bicycling)	1882
Amateur Athletic Association of Canada	1884
became Canadian Amateur Athletic Association	1898
became Athletic Union of Canada	1909
Canadian Lawn Tennis Association	1884
Canadian Rugby Football Union	1884
Canadian Lacrosse Association	1887
Canadian Cricket Association	1892
Royal Canadian Golf Association	1895
Canadian Canoe Association	1900
Canadian Amateur Swimming Association	1909
Dominion Football Association (soccer)	1912
Canadian Amateur Lacrosse Association	1914
Canadian Amateur Hockey Association	1914

Source: Metcalfe, A. (1987). Canadians Learn to Play: The Emergence of Organized Sport 1807-1914. Toronto, ON: McClelland and Stewart.

By the 1920s, the organization of sport had greatly evolved (see Table 3.1). The 1920s have been called the **"Golden Age of Sport"** in Canada as organized sports and sport leagues expanded (Wright, 2000). Popular sport activities of the day included ice hockey, golf and swimming. Private sport clubs also expanded rapidly as cities such as Hamilton and London had a few curling and lawn bowling clubs. Public outdoor athletic facilities, such as rinks, toboggan slides and swimming pools, were also found in cities and towns (ibid.).

During the 1920s, the influence of voluntary community associations and services clubs on the development of municipal recreation also started to unfold. The Gyro Club of Edmonton, a men's service club, much like the Jasper Place Community League, became actively involved in the supervision of playgrounds. In addition, the Gyro Club of Edmonton established carnivals to collect the funds needed to establish playgrounds. The activities of the Jasper Place Community League and the Gyro Club of Edmonton helped to illustrate the importance of community recreational services to public sector officials (McFarland, 1970).

Finally, it should be noted that during this decade the role of women in society started to change as women began to have the right to vote. "Women also demanded more equitable treatment for themselves as consumers of public recreation" (Searle and Brayley, 2000: 21). This decade signified the start of greater accessibility and opportunities for women in community leisure and recreation services.

THE ROARING TWENTIES

The 1920s have been called the "Golden Age of Sport" in Canada as the number of organized sports and sport leagues expanded considerably during this period (Wright, 2000).

1930-1939: PROVINCIAL GOVERNMENT INVOLVEMENT TAKES OFF

Mass forms of entertainment started to develop with the introduction of talking movies. By the 1930s, listening to the radio had become a popular leisure activity, particularly during the long, cold winter months (Wetherell and Kmet, 1990). Radio had an impact on the popularity of sports and, in particular, on hockey. Gruneau and Whitson (1993) eloquently describe the role radio played in Canada in the promotion of hockey by stating that "with the advent of national radio broadcasts Canadians began to follow NHL hockey with an almost religious fervour, and from the 1930s through the 1960s there was simply nothing in Canadian life that regularly brought so many Canadians from different parts of the country together to share the same cultural experience" (p. 275). Thus, radio may have contributed, at least in part, to the increase that eventually took place in live attendance at sport events such as hockey games.

In 1930, Canada's first *National Parks Act* was passed. This Act recognized that "neither could new parks be established nor existing parks be eliminated, nor their boundaries changed, without parliament's approval" (McNamee, 2002: 33). This Act also led to a change in name as the Dominion parks were renamed national parks. Thus, Canada's first national park, Rocky Mountain Park, was renamed Banff National Park (McNamee, 2002).

THE GREAT DEPRESSION ERA

The creation of new recreation services did not slow down during the 1930s. Indeed, it was during the Depression era that government involvement in recreation started to take off in Canada.

During the Great Depression of the 1930s, the establishment of new leisure service organizations did not halt. In 1933, McGill University's Dr. Arthur S. Lamb played a lead role in the establishment of the Canadian Physical Education Association (Gurney, 1983). Despite the fact that "recreation" was not included in the title of this organization, recreation was seen to be a part of its broader scope. This is clearly evident in research conducted by Markham (1996), who posits that "public recreation" and "professional organization" were subjects of focus in conference programs of the Canadian Physical Education Association in 1937 and 1939.

Physical recreation, during the years of the Great Depression and World War II, became a pressing concern of provincial and federal governments (Eisenhardt, 1945). A big reason for this pressing concern was that physical education had become popular within public school systems, and it was becoming widely recognized that physical education enhanced social, physical and moral well-being.

In 1934, a program called "Pro-Rec" was initiated by the Adult Education Division of the Department of Education of British Columbia. The first director of this public recreation program was Ian Eisenhardt. The intent of "Pro-Rec" was to offer all citizens of the province the opportunity to participate free of user fees in activities such as gymnastics, cricket, soccer, swimming, and women's classes for dancing. The original main objective of this program was to combat enforced idleness for unemployed young men. This objective was subsequently expanded to one of providing activity opportunities to all, including women and children over fifteen years of age. These activities took place in rented facilities such as community halls, school gymnasiums and armouries (Schrodt, 1984).

On November 9, 1934, the British Columbia Minister for Education, Dr. G.M. Weir, announced the creation of classes in recreational and physical education in British Columbia. These classes were created with the aim of building moral character in youth while battling idleness caused by unemployment (Annual Report of the Public Schools of the Province, 1934-1935).

In 1936, A.T. Whitaker, a commissioner of the Niagara Parks Commission, helped shape the Ontario Parks Association (Drysdale, 1970). The intent of this organization was to act as a voice for the parks movement within Ontario. In 1944 the name of this organization was changed to the Parks and Recreation Association of Canada (Drysdale, 1970; Markham, 1995). As noted by Markham (1996), the name change was based on two arguments: (1) that membership expanded outside of Ontario, and (2) that the organization was not confined to parks alone. The Parks and Recreation Association of Canada went on to adapt a new name in 1969, the Canadian Parks and Recreation Association, an organization that exists with the same name today.

Under the federal Department of Labour, *The Unemployment and Agricultural Assistance Act* of 1937 was passed. This was also known as the

Purvis Commission. The significance of this Act is that it marked the beginning of an era for federal-provincial programs in support of physical recreation and physical fitness. The intent of the Purvis Commission was to examine all aspects of unemployment across Canada. With reference to the work of Eisenhardt and "Pro-Rec," it was no coincidence that recreation became an important variable in the working of the Purvis Commission and in recommendations set forth to battle the problem of high unemployment.

The events of the 1920s and 1930s indicated a tremendous increase in the involvement of provincial government in recreation. These two decades also witnessed an increase in community involvement in recreation through the expansion of the Jasper Place Community League to suburban areas and the many development and construction projects of neighbourhood playgrounds (Bowler and Wanchuk, 1986). In fact, prior to the 1940s, "public-minded citizens who volunteered were totally responsible for all that happened in the neighbourhood and communities where they lived" (Minshall, 1984: 13).

1940-1949: THE IMPACT OF WORLD WAR II

The onset of World War II had a drastic impact on the economy, employment and social services, including leisure and recreation. Many leisure and recreational services in Canada were put on hold, or at least halted, with the exception of recreation activities and programs that were for the most part related to the war. In Saskatchewan, as was the case in many parts of Canada, recreation facilities were converted to housing services (Ellis and Nixon, 1986).

Research by Searle and Brayley (2000) indicates that leisure and recreation during the war years was not put on complete hold, but rather was reinforced due to the need for diversion as a means to maintain morale and psychological health. Furthermore, the introduction of camping and travel during the war, although not for pleasure, stimulated interest for post-war outdoors and tourism experiences.

In the early 1940s the problem of unemployment continued to be a primary concern for the federal government. In 1942, the *Vocational Training Coordination Act* was introduced with the intent "to fit any person for gainful employment or to increase his skills or efficiency therein" (Statutes of Canada, 1942). This Act allowed the Department of Labour to enter into an agreement with any province for the continuation of training experiences for youth. Thus, the physical training or physical recreation programs of some provinces received federal grants on a dollar-for-dollar basis for the provision of programs such as the "Pro-Rec" program of British Columbia.

On June 24, 1943, after several years of planning and preparation, the *National Physical Fitness Act* became law, and on March 31, 1944, this Act replaced the *Vocational Training Coordination Act* as the federal funding authority for provincial recreation projects. This Act helped provide the

Playground programs such as this one in Vancouver became common in the post-war period.

Photo: City of Vancouver Archives/CVA 11184-2662.

UPPER CANADA VILLAGE

Using Leisure to Explore Canadian History

Nations like Italy and Greece rely on historical sites such as the Roman Coliseum and the ancient theatre of Epidavros to attract tourists to their nations. In Canada, heritage parks such as Upper Canada Village not only provide visitors with an opportunity to learn about the past but also to experience it actively.

Upper Canada Village has been recognized as one of the top ten historical sites of North America. This is quite an accomplishment, considering the many North American historic sites, including those of Gettysburg, Pennsylvania, Colonial Williamsburg, West Virginia, and Citadel Hill, Halifax. It addition, Upper Canada Village was also the recipient of the Number One National/International Attraction Award in 2000 in Canada.

Photo: Courtesy of Upper Canada Village Heritage Park.

This re-created nineteenth-century village offers visitors a chance to experience historic dining, shopping, and horse-drawn wagon and tow scow rides. In addition, Upper Canada Village offers a number of special leisure activities and events for all ages including a heritage park, a children's activity centre, a photographic studio and the Queen Elizabeth Gardens.

The historic buildings and colourful characters who live and re-enact daily life as it once was add to the "leisure and learning" atmosphere of this heritage park. The artisans, trades people and farmers not only engage in the lifestyle of the nineteenth century, they also provide an entertaining means by which to learn. Visitors to Upper Canada Village witness: the spinning of wool in a log home; the grinding of wheat into flour in a steam-powered mill; and tradespersons demonstrating their skills by forging iron, shaping and soldering tin ware, crafting furniture and shoeing horses.

Leisure comes alive in Upper Canada Village. The experience of visitors is not only educational, it is also interactive. Visitors experience first-hand the daily life of the 1860s, while also learning about agriculture, communication, music, religion, transportation,

manufacturing and major events of the nineteenth century.

Upper Canada Village offers a number of beneficial experiences to visitors. These are: an opportunity to visualize life in the nineteenth century; an educational tour of village life around the time of Confederation; exposure to the leisure and recreation activities of the nineteenth century; an animated presentation of the daily routine of the people of Canada in the 1800s; and an outdoor recreational experience that contains aesthetic, natural and structural beauty.

Leisure in the 1860s

One of the popular leisure activities of the 1860s was music, and many individuals played musical instruments. In Upper Canada at the time, music was prominent in the home, the community and at church. Popular musical instruments of the nineteenth century featured at Upper Canada Village include pianos, violins, fiddles, guitars, bagpipes and flutes.

A number of other leisure activities were also experienced in the nineteenth century, such as sleighing, skating, horse racing, dancing and singing.

basis for the makeup of the National Council on Physical Fitness, which consisted of representatives from participating provinces. The mandate of this council was to: (1) assist in the extension of physical fitness, (2) assist in the extension of physical education, (3) encourage and develop activities related to physical development, (4) train physical education and physical recreation instructors, and (5) co-operate with provinces to carry out the provisions of the Act (Schrodt, 1984).

By 1943, the impact of community leagues, service clubs, local Councils of Women, the YMCA and other voluntary associations had come a long way in shaping the establishment of municipal recreation services. In Edmonton, for example, the Federation of Community Leagues, consisting of twenty-three member leagues, formed a strong lobby on behalf of the recreation interests of citizens. By 1944, the Edmonton Recreation Commission had been established (McFarland, 1970).

In addition to the efforts of the community leagues and service clubs, a number of other factors contributed to the development of municipal recreation in provinces such as Ontario. These factors included: urbanization, the recreation atmosphere of the 1940s, the provision of recreation services for the armed forces, involvement in post-war reconstruction projects including recreation centres and an awareness that those in charge of recreation for the armed forces would be seeking recreation opportunities in civilian life (McFarland, 1970).

The inauguration of provincial recreation services in Ontario took place in 1945 under the Physical and Health Education Branch of the Department of Education (Report of the Minister, 1945). By 1947, Ontario had one hundred municipal recreation communities (Skerrett, 1992). Also in Ontario, in 1948, the establishment of a ministry for recreation became closer when the Department of Education brought together the Adult Education Board and the recreation and fitness unit of the Physical and Health Education Branch into the Community Programs Branch, thus establishing a service organization. The intent of the branch was to assist communities within Ontario to plan and develop recreation activities (ibid.). Later, throughout the 1950s and 1960s, this branch supported: (1) the creation of municipal recreation departments, (2) the hiring of municipal recreation directors, (3) the development of resource materials in arts and crafts, music, drama, social recreation, physical recreation and sports, and (4) the establishment of English and citizenship classes for new Canadians (ibid.). Also, 1947-48 witnessed the first attempt by a Canadian university (the University of Western Ontario) to offer a recreation-related degree program (cancelled in 1955 as interest was not sufficient; McFarland, 1970).

The **Parks and Recreation Association** of Canada held its first annual congress in July 1946 in Montreal with 125 delegates (Markham, 1995). This was one of the first national events in Canada bringing recreation professionals together from coast to coast. This annual conference, as do subsequent ones, helped establish a national voice for leisure and recreation with a mission to address the needs of society in this area.

WARTIME RECREATION

The onset of World War II had a drastic impact on the economy, employment and social services, including leisure and recreation. Many leisure and recreational services in Canada were halted, or at least put on hold, with the exception of recreation activities and programs that were for the most part related to the war.

"The best estimate that can be made suggests that the field of research in Canada was born in the 1950s" (Burton, 1979: 15).

The Burrard Servicemen's Centre in Vancouver.
Photo: City of Vancouver Archives, CVA 1184-463.

Recreation facilities for former servicemen were established in the 1940s.

1950-1959: THE GROWTH OF SERVICES, OPPORTUNITIES AND CONSUMERISM

The 1950s was a decade of growth and conflict (Wright, 1984). According to Burton (1979: 15) "the best estimate that can be made suggests that the field of leisure research in Canada was born in the 1950s." The need for research in a field of leisure studies developed out of the emergence of municipal recreation departments within Canada. The need for research and professional training also became a concern for higher education systems. Two unsuccessful efforts, due to lack of enrolment, were made to offer university programs with an emphasis in recreation. The first effort was made by the University of Toronto, which offered a Bachelor of Social Work in Community Recreation in 1951-52. The second was by the University of Western Ontario, which attempted to offer a Bachelor of Physical Education degree with a recreation emphasis in 1955.

By the time the 1950s came around, the Canadian Physical Education Association, another strong national, provincial and municipal advocacy group for recreation, was here to stay. This organization that had been established by Dr. Arthur S. Lamb in the 1930s had now found a permanent home in the leisure industry. Eventually this organization

Table 3.2: Highlights in the Evolution of Voluntary Sector Leisure and Recreation Services Up to 1960

Dates	Highlights
1851	The founding of the YMCA in Montreal.
1893	The establishment of the National Council of Women in Vancouver, Winnipeg, Toronto, Montreal and Halifax. This organization played a key role in the playground movement and in examining youth and leisure and recreation issues.
1917	The establishment of the Jasper Place Community League in Edmonton. Its purpose was to assist in the organization and provision of recreation and sport services throughout the community.
1936	The creation of the Ontario Parks Association. Its purpose was to act as a voice for the park movement within Ontario. In 1944, the name of this organization changed to the Parks and Recreation Association of Canada. Its mandate was changed to address a national concern for parks and recreation.
1946	The Parks and Recreation Association of Canada holds its first annual conference in Montreal.
1950s	The Canadian Physical Education Association, the forerunner of the Canadian Association for Health, Physical Education and Recreation was here to stay. One of the objectives of this organization is to act as an advocacy group for recreation.

changed its name to the Canadian Association for Health, Physical Education, and Recreation.

In 1954 the *National Physical Fitness Act* introduced in 1943 was repealed. As a result, provinces were left on their own to support fitness and recreation initiatives (Westland, 1979). Not only did this change the relationship that had been established between the federal government and the provinces for recreation, but it also placed increased responsibility on the provinces for the implementation and provision of recreation services.

The 1950s was a decade of leisure growth in services, opportunities and consumerism. The demographical makeup of Canada in the 1950s had shifted towards youth. In 1951, the median age was 27.8 years, whereas in 1956 the median age was 27.4 years (McFarland, 1970). Along with demographic changes came activity changes. In the 1950s professional ballet and opera were introduced in Canada (Horna, 1987a). Television viewing became a popular pastime activity, and an increase in mechanized automobiles, motorboats, motorcycles and snowmobiles shaped the recreation interests of the time. By the 1950s, hockey had grown in popularity. In fact, as Gruneau and Whitson (1993) state, "the link between hockey and Canadian identity became taken for granted, a simple matter of common sense" (p. 275). However, hockey losses to European teams and the Soviets in the 1950s and 1960s "emerged as the primary threat to the pride taken in those identities" (ibid.).

1960-1969: THE LEISURE AND RECREATION BOOM

The 1960s were the boom years for leisure and recreation (Wright, 1964). Consumer spending and growth continued during this decade. The evolution of voluntary sector services in leisure and recreation had already established a rich history (see Table 3.2). During the 1960s, public leisure and recreation services, the commercial sector of leisure and recreation, the consumerism of leisure and recreation, and leisure and recreation education programs took off. It was at this time that Canadian society increased its concern for environmental conservation, the preservation of sites of historic value, pedestrian malls, and downtown revitalization and upgrading projects (Wright, 2000). Moreover, during the 1960s, an expansion of the public park and recreation system in Canada took place. In addition, a concern by the government and public decision-makers for physical fitness and quality of life started to emerge, particularly for youth (McFarland, 1970). The federal government also started to recognize the importance of hockey in the national culture (Gruneau and Whitson, 1993).

In 1961, to address the pressing concerns of the role of government in sport, recreation and leisure, the *Fitness and Amateur Sport Act* was passed. This Act was important as it did what had not been done since the repeal of the *National Fitness Act* in 1954; that is, to redefine the role of senior government in sport, recreation and leisure, and to help establish federal-provincial relationships (see Figure 3.1).

BABY BOOMERS

The 1960s were the boom years of leisure and recreation as the public, commercial and voluntary sectors expanded services. University and college education and research in leisure studies also rapidly developed.

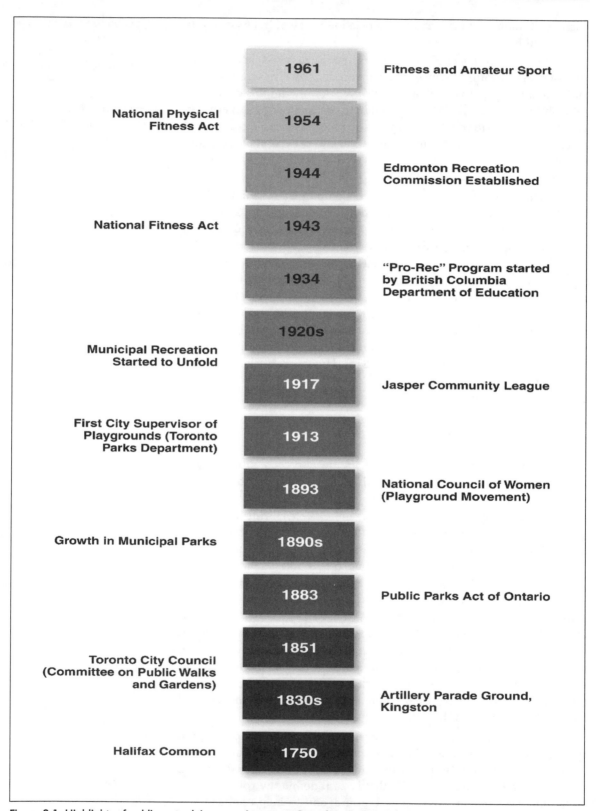

1961	Fitness and Amateur Sport
1954	National Physical Fitness Act
1944	Edmonton Recreation Commission Established
1943	National Fitness Act
1934	"Pro-Rec" Program started by British Columbia Department of Education
1920s	Municipal Recreation Started to Unfold
1917	Jasper Community League
1913	First City Supervisor of Playgrounds (Toronto Parks Department)
1893	National Council of Women (Playground Movement)
1890s	Growth in Municipal Parks
1883	Public Parks Act of Ontario
1851	Toronto City Council (Committee on Public Walks and Gardens)
1830s	Artillery Parade Ground, Kingston
1750	Halifax Common

Figure 3.1: Highlights of public sector leisure services up to Canada's Centennial.

By the early 1960s, Canadian rules football had begun to be viewed as an important part of national cultural identity. This became evident in 1962 when Parliament decreed that CBC and CTV, the two major Canadian television networks, make the transmission of the Grey Cup game available to each other. The Grey Cup final was thus used as an instrument to help establish Canadian identity through sport and leisure (Canadian Encyclopedia, 1985).

The 1960s was a period in which the offshoot of leisure research started to evolve. Research areas of focus in this new discipline in Canada focused largely on the leisure activities of youth (Burton, 1979) and on terminology issues such as the nature and uses of free time in Canadian society (Laplante, 1967). Most research in leisure studies at this time utilized univariate techniques deriving simple statistical forms such as frequencies, percentages and means (Burton, 1979). This increase in leisure research was largely enticed by the establishment of leisure studies or leisure studies-related degree programs in several universities and colleges. Throughout this decade, programs were established at the University of British Columbia, the University of Alberta, the University of Waterloo, the University of Ottawa, Mount Royal College, Lethbridge College and Centennial College (McFarland, 1970). Indeed, by the late 1960s, leisure studies had found a home in academia (see Figure 3.2).

In 1967, Canada experienced tremendous growth in the number of individuals and organizations conducting leisure research, the number of research studies conducted and the allocation of research funds (Burton, 1979). In fact, during the Centennial of Confederation and the decade that followed, both the federal and provincial governments sponsored and/or carried out a number of research studies on leisure behaviour. One of these research studies was Jack Knetsch's blueprint for the *Canadian Outdoor Recreation Demand Study* (CORDS).

The decade of the 1960s marked an increase in the number of government-subsidized programs for the development and establishment of recreation facilities. This trend was largely a result of the increasing number of people moving to the inner core of the city and the subsequent increased demand for a wider range of urban-regional recreational opportunities (Wright, 2000). Some of this money, although limited, was also put into facility operation or program planning (Searle and Brayley, 2000). Other money was put into enhancing research in leisure and recreation.

The increase in government involvement in leisure and recreation during the 1960s was not only financial but also structural and political. Most provincial governments established units, branches, or departments responsible for recreation. Many provincial sport organizations were formed as well (Inglis, 1994). The type of involvement, whether direct or indirect, varied from province to province.

Societal patterns played a key role in the selection of recreation activities during the 1960s. In general, Canadians preferred structured

ACADEMIC PURSUITS

The 1970s was a decade in which the leisure studies field emerged. Canadian-based academic journals in leisure studies were created such as *Recreation Review, Society and Leisure,* and the *Journal of Leisurability.*

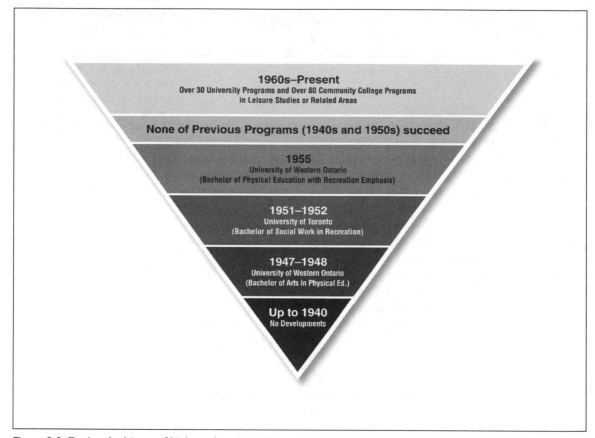

Figure 3.2: Tracing the history of higher education in leisure studies in Canada.

activities that were age-group specific and that were planned. Moreover, a preference existed for participation in formal social group activities and competitive activities. For the most part, society tended to prefer, or at least partake in, sedentary lifestyle activities (Wright, 2000).

Government support for recreation also expanded to support the dissemination of Canadian research in leisure studies. This was evident through the direct involvement of government in the organization of a research conference on leisure and recreation. From September 2-6, 1969, the Montmorency Conference on Leisure was held in Montmorency, Quebec. One of the planning committee members of this Conference was Cor Westland, who was on staff with the Fitness and Amateur Sport Directorate at the Department of National Health and Welfare Canada. In fact, the Department of National Health and Welfare Canada published the proceedings for this Conference.

In the late 1960s, research by Farina (1969) indicated that obligatory activities occupied a high proportion of non-work time of Canadians. For Farina, work-time reductions appeared to increase tasks of obligation during free time rather than increase involvement in leisure activities. Moreover, in this same piece of research, Farina reported that "a significant number of Canadians still equate the concept of leisure with idleness, sloth and sin" (p. 6). Thus, the benefits of leisure and recreation in Canada had yet to come of age.

In 1967, as a result of an amalgamation between the Youth Branch and the Community Programs Branch by the Department of Education in Ontario, a new branch with a mandate for recreation was established. This was called the Youth and Recreation Branch (Skerrett, 1992). The name change, to include recreation as one of its key terms, indicated greater awareness and increased importance placed on leisure and recreation services by the provincial government. It was not until the 1970s, however, that the mandates of provinces and territories for leisure and recreation started to unfold with the construction of policy statements.

1970-1979: HIGHER EDUCATION AND RESEARCH IN LEISURE STUDIES COMES OF AGE

The 1970s was a period of consolidation and conservation (Wright, 1984). In this decade it became apparent that the earth's resources were very much finite with renewable resources being subject to abuse (Johnson and McLean, 1996a). High energy costs as a result of the Arab oil embargo of 1973 had an impact, not only on travel and tourism, but also on the operation of recreation facilities and services. The end result for the actual provision of public services was that municipal recreation services became more facilitative and less involved in direct service provision (Searle and Brayley, 2000). The 1970s was a decade in which social, economic and technological changes altered society. The economy was altered from being "largely product based" to being more "service oriented" (Howard and Crompton, 1980).

Cor Westland, at the First World Conference of Experts on Leadership for Leisure Conference in September 1977, described the state of Canada in the 1970s as follows: (1) primarily an urban society with 1971 statistics indicating that 76 percent of Canadians live in urban areas, (2) a nation of immigrants, (3) an active policy on promoting bilingualism for two official languages (French and English), (4) acknowledgement by government of the multicultural nature of Canada, (5) an ageing society, (6) an increase in post-secondary education, (6) a post-industrial technologically advanced society, and (7) a society with a value for leisure and leisure behaviour as an important part of life (p. 193-198).

The 1970s was a significantly different period from the 1960s. The general public started to demand recreation as a basic right, as the value of leisure had started to be highly appreciated. Wright (2000) provides the following overview of the following changes that took place from the 1960s to the 1970s: (1) a shift in emphasis from highly structured activities with rules and regulations to non-structured activities allowing for less competition, flexibility and spontaneity in such endeavours; (2) an increase in the number of young adults through to the older age

NATIONAL RECREATION STATEMENT, 1978

In 1978, in Montreal, the Ministry of Fitness and Amateur Sport acknowledged the primacy of the provinces for recreation in Canada (National Recreation Statement, 1978).

categories continuing to participate in activities, both organized and as individuals (i.e., recreation hockey, biking, cross-country skiing); (3) the leading physical recreation activities for men and women were self-directed pursuits, spontaneous in nature such as walking or gardening; (4) most activities were participated in by one or two individuals, rather than being team oriented; (5) most activities engaged in were of the non-competitive type; (6) activities were experienced for personal self-fulfilment and growth; (7) the emphasis of activities highlighted a mix of physical, social and cultural interests; (8) activities engaged in were more of the informal, unstructured type; and (9) a growing concern for preventative health care with a significant increase in an active life-style, including walking and aerobic activities (p. 114-115).

Early in this decade, the growing need to understand special populations and therapeutic recreation better became evident with the establishment of the Therapeutic Information Centre at the University of Waterloo in 1970. In 1972, the Witt Report was released, which investigated the state of recreation services for persons with disabilities in Canada. During this same year, the first hiring of a therapeutic recreation consultant by the Province of Ontario took place (Hutchison and McGill, 1992).

In 1972 and 1975, Statistics Canada, on behalf of the Department of the Secretary of State, conducted national surveys on the levels of attendance of spectators at sports and cultural events. The *Ontario Recreation Survey* was conducted in 1974. The Fitness and Amateur Sport Directorate national survey of levels of participation in sport was implemented in 1976. Moreover, a series of annual surveys of tourism were conducted by the Government Office of Tourism in 1978. In total, in the latter part of the 1960s and in the early 1970s, there were as many as one hundred surveys on leisure and recreation carried out on behalf of municipal governments and other organizations in Canada (Ministry of State for Urban Affairs, 1973). Indeed, it had become evident that government had started to value leisure and recreation research.

Government was not the only part of society recognizing the importance of leisure research. The 1970s was a decade in which the leisure studies field emerged. Canadian-based academic journals in leisure studies were created, such as *Recreation Review, Society and Leisure* and the *Journal of Leisurability*. Leisure research centres were also introduced at Acadia University, the Université du Québec à Trois Rivières, and the University of Waterloo. By the time this decade came to a close, higher education studies and higher education research in leisure studies had become firmly established (see Table 3.3).

In the 1970s, a national, not-for-profit agency called **PARTICIPaction** was created. The intent of this organization was to encourage Canadians to take action and become more active. To fulfill this intent, PARTICIPaction relied on the media to relay its message. A national advertising campaign depicting a thirty-year-old Canadian as not being as fit as a sixty-year-old Swede was used to encourage

Table 3.3: The Early Evolution of Higher Education and Higher Education Research in Leisure Studies in Canada

Date	Event
1947-1948	The first attempt by a university in Canada to offer a recreation-related degree program by the University of Western Ontario, a Honors Bachelor of Arts in Physical Education with a recreation option in 3rd and 4th years.
1951-1952	The University of Toronto offers a Bachelor of Social Work program in Community Recreation.
1955-1956	The University of Western Ontario offers a Bachelor of Physical Education degree with a recreation emphasis.

Note: All three of the above programs were discontinued due to lack of enrolment and interest.

Date	Event
1960s	Leisure studies-related degree programs are successfully established at the University of British Columbia, the University of Alberta, the University of Waterloo, the University of Ottawa, Mount Royal College, Lethbridge College and Centennial College.
1969	The Montmorecy Conference of Leisure is held in Montmorecy, Quebec.
1970	*Recreation Review* (the forerunner of *Recreation Research Review*, the *Journal of Applied Recreation Research and Leisure/Loisir*) is established.
1974	*The Journal of Leisurability* is established.
1978	*Society and Leisure* is established.
1970s	The first Canadian Congress for Leisure Research is held.
1970s	Leisure research centres are introduced at Acadia University, the Université du Québec à Trois Rivières, and the University of Waterloo.

RECREATIONAL RETREAT

Constraints and efficiencies marked the decade of the 1980s for the creation and delivery of leisure services. This decade was defined by cutbacks in the public sector for leisure and recreation.

Canadians to take charge of their own lives and to strive to achieve physically fit lifestyles. As a result of the efforts of PARTICIPaction, the number of Canadians committed to physically active lifestyles increased tremendously, from 5 percent in 1972 to 37 percent in 1982 (Ferris, Kisby, Craig, and Landry, 1987).

In 1972, restructuring of the Ontario government departments led to the transferring of the Youth and Recreation Branch from the Department of Education to the new Ministry of Community and Social Services. In 1973, this branch was renamed the Sports and Recreation Bureau (Skerrett, 1992). It is relevant to note that, up to this point, the Province of Ontario had not "officially recognized recreation as a major social service and no clear, coherent provincial policy existed on leisure and recreation programs" (p. 3).

By 1974, Ontario, for example, had over six hundred municipal recreation committees. This number had grown tremendously in thirty years as in 1947 it was reported that only one hundred municipal recreation committees existed in the province (Skerrett, 1992). It was largely for this reason that the Sport and Recreation Bureau commenced to draft a leisure policy for Cabinet consideration in 1974 (ibid.). On December 17, 1974, the new Ministry of Culture and Recreation was established, uniting recreation-related programs such as Sports and Recreation, Citizenship and Multiculturalism, Cultural Affairs, and Heritage Conservation (ibid.). The Ministry of Culture and Recreation was thus responsible for three Acts affecting recreation: (1) the *Community Recreation Centres Act*, (2) Municipal Programs of Recreation (Regulation 200), and (3) the Certification of Municipal Recreation Directors and Arena Managers (Regulation 392/71).

PARTCIPaction had been planned and intentionally targeted to change the physical condition of Canadians through the use of the media. Another media event of that time appealed to the emotions of Canadians. This was the Canada-Soviet Summit Series of 1972. Canadians were glued to their TV sets watching this event as Canada sought to win the series and show the world that hockey was indeed a Canadian game. Canada almost lost the series as the Soviets, in preparing for the series, emphasized physical fitness. The value placed by the Soviet hockey players on physical fitness as compared to those who represented Canada was highlighted in the media. The difficulties Canada had in "winning at its own game," plus the comparisons of the two national teams, encouraged Canadians to take measures to enhance their own fitness levels. It was becoming evident that our physical conditioning was not at pace with the rest of the world.

Government involvement in leisure and recreation, and more specifically, the identification of mandates for leisure and recreation, continued to evolve during the decade of the 1970s. In Edmonton, in May 1974, the provincial government ministers responsible for recreation put forth a comprehensive definition of recreation, identifying it in the same light as other social services such as health and recreation. It was

Classroom fitness programs marked an increased awareness of active living in the 1970's.

Photo: Jon Easton/Ontario Ministry of Education.

resolved during a conference that the purpose of recreation in Canada should be: (1) to assist individual and community development, (2) to improve quality of life, and (3) to enhance social functioning (Skerrett, 1992). During a second conference of provincial ministers in Halifax in November 1974, an attempt was made to define the role of each of the sectors of government for recreation. It was recommended that municipalities have most of the responsibility for providing recreation. It was also put forth that the role of the provinces "was to provide incentive grants for new programs, support for capital construction and operation, leadership development, advice in special program areas, such as research, and assist in the exchange of information among communities" (ibid., p. 47). Furthermore, it was recommended that each province establish a policy for recreation and single departments to consolidate recreation programs, while also suggesting to the federal government that it establish a national policy on recreation.

In a subsequent conference held in 1978 in Montreal, the Minister of State for Fitness and Amateur Sport acknowledged the primacy of the provinces for recreation in Canada (*National Recreation Statement,* 1987) while also acknowledging "the federal government's withdrawal from the broad concept of recreation. Instead, Ottawa would concentrate on a more limited concept of fitness and physical recreation" (ibid., p. 81).

By the mid-1970s, the federal government had roughly seventy recreation-related programs with most of these falling within the Fitness and Amateur Sport Directorate of the Department of National Health and Welfare. In 1976, Iona Campagnola was appointed as the first Minister of State for Fitness and Amateur Sport, which consisted of two branches, Sport Canada and Recreation Canada (Skerrett, 1992).

In 1978 the **Lalonde Report**, also known as *A New Perspective on the Health of Canadians,* was published. This report was one of the first to acknowledge publicly that the health-care system was not the most important element in determining the health status of society. The Lalonde Report played a key role in the building of the National Health Promotion Directorate, leading to the fitness revolution that took place during the latter part of this decade (Wharf Higgins, 1995).

During March of 1978, a retreat of recreation professionals was sponsored by the Ontario Ministry of Culture and Recreation. The result was a document entitled **The Elora Prescription**. The intent of this document was to examine past and present social trends while trying to predict the future of recreation. A possible scenario for the future was presented, comparing the recreation and leisure services of society of 1975 with 1995. One of the main concerns addressed by *The Elora Prescription* was the number of problems in the recreation profession, such as too much specialization of recreation personnel and limited partnership between the service sectors. This report is significant as it showed a commitment on the part of the provincial government to predict future trends for recreation.

In 1979, a revised National Parks Policy was put forth by the federal government. The intent of this revised policy was to give first priority to ecological integrity. The revised Act also "committed the government to setting legislative limits to the size of downhill ski areas and the towns Banff and Jasper. Tourism facilities and overnight accommodation were to be located outside the parks wherever possible" (McNamee, 2002: 36).

The 1970s also witnessed an expansion in municipal recreation services for select populations. During this decade, and in particular during the latter part of this decade, leisure services provided for special populations by municipal recreation departments in Canada grew considerably (Lyons, 1981). In 1975 the Recreation Council for the Disabled in Nova Scotia was founded. In the same time period, other similar provincial organizations concerned with leisure and recreation began to be established across Canada (Hutchison and McGill, 1992).

1980-1989: LEARNING TO DO MORE WITH LESS

Constraints and efficiencies marked the decade of the 1980s for the creation and delivery of leisure services. This decade was defined by cutbacks in the public sector for leisure and recreation. Increasing costs in service provision and decreasing public funds signifies the condition of services during this decade. Changes in personnel were implemented as terms such as "downsize," "right size" and "flatten out" were used to describe the restructuring of recreation organizations (Harper and Johnston, 1992). Moreover, terms not previously utilized by public sectors providers, such as "marketing," "contracting out," "privatization," "customer service" and "community development," were also frequently used in the public sector milieu (ibid.).

A number of societal changes in the 1980s influenced the selection of and participation in recreation experiences. Major changes as presented by Wright (2000) are as follows: (1) a preference for more individualistic, small-group, non-organized, spontaneous activities; (2) a preference for less vigorous activities such as walking and nature appreciation; (3) a high value for quality of life, creativity and self-actualization, individualism, humanitarianism, community development, and an ecological ethic; (4) an increased use of "free" leisure activities such as public open space and pathways; (5) a gradual shift to less consumptive and expensive forms of recreation; (6) an ageing population with smaller households and more single-parent families; and (7) an increasing awareness of the link between preservation and protection of historic and cultural sites, natural areas and recreation (pp. 122-123).

Public recreation resources declined as a result of decisions made during the 1960s and 1970s (Ipson, 1993). Public recreation services were reduced during these economically inflationary times causing dissatisfaction for local recreation services (Davis and McKenzie, 1981). As a result, many public sector recreation agencies experienced the novel realization that essential service goals and basic recreation needs of the general public were not always fulfilled by public recreation services (Harper and Balmer, 1989).

During this decade, recreation departments at all levels of government tried to find different ways to increase revenues and reduce expenditures while increasing collaborative efforts. This decade also witnessed a renewed interest in community school recreation programs, tourism, consumerism, and commercial sector entrepreneurship. This trend continued into the 1990s and early 2000s.

In 1980, the Canadian Fitness and Lifestyle Research Institute was born. In 1981, this institute conducted the Canada Fitness Survey with the intent of assessing the fitness levels and physical recreation levels of all Canadians. A subsequent intent of this survey was to compare the fitness levels of Canadians with those of individuals from other societies.

In 1981, the Lyons Report, entitled *A Profile of Municipal Services for Special Populations in Canada,* was produced in order to provide an overview of the current condition of services for persons with disabilities. During the same year, the Canadian Federation of Sports for the Disabled was established (Hutchison and McGill, 1992).

Personal fitness programs became increasingly popular in the 1980s.

Table 3.4: History of Government Policies, Acts, Reports and Statements Related to Leisure and Recreation

Date	Policy, Act or Statement	Focus
1883	*Public Parks Act of Ontario*	Establishes a system of parks as well as the maintenance of existing parks.
1930	*National Parks Act*	Recognizes Parliament's approval for changes to existing parks and the establishment of new parks.
1937	*The Unemployment and Agriculture Assistance Act* (Purvis Commission)	Examines all aspects of unemployment and marks the beginning of federal-provincial programs in support of physical recreation and physical fitness.
1942	*Vocational Training Coordination Act*	Allows the Department of Labour to enter into an agreement with any province for the continuation of training experiences for youth.
1943	*Physical Fitness Act*	Establishes federal funding authority for provincial recreation projects.
1961	*Fitness and Amateur Sport Act*	Re-defines the role of senior government in sport, recreation and leisure, and helps establish federal-provincial relationships.
1978	Lalonde Report	The building of a National Program Health Directorate leading to a fitness revolution.
1979	Revised National Park Policy	Gives first priority to ecological integrity and the setting of legislative limits in park development.
1982	*Canadian Constitution Act*	The establishment of a charter for rights and freedoms, including freedom of association.
1983	Inter-Provincial Recreation Statement	Defines municipal and provincial roles for recreation.
1987	National Recreation Statement	Portrays the beliefs of government towards recreation.

It was during this decade that the *Canadian Constitution Act* (1982) and the *Multicultural Policy Act* (1987) were signed. These political actions led to a greater awareness of the diversity and pluralism in Canadian society. This increased awareness had an impact on leisure research. For example, the Ministry of Tourism and Recreation in Ontario launched a series of studies concerned with diagnosing the special leisure needs of ethnic individuals and groups (see Bolla and Dawson, 1989; Hall, 1988; Dembrowski, 1988).

During the 1983 meetings of the provincial ministers responsible for recreation and sport held in New Brunswick, a nineteen-page document entitled the *Inter-Provincial Recreation Statement* was issued. The intent of this document was to define provincial and municipal roles for recreation. In addition, this document laid out the foundation for inter-governmental and intra-governmental co-operation in recreation. It should be pointed out that this document was an agreement by the provinces and did not include a federal signatory.

Ottawa hosted the First International Conference on Health Promotion in 1986 (Wharf Higgins, 1995). This conference built on the foundation put forth by the Lalonde Report in 1974, and was intended to establish a relationship between health and lifestyle to the social and economic environment. Also in 1986, through the strong support and sponsorship of Fitness Canada, the Jasper Talks took place. The primary objective of this national forum was to discuss strategies for change in adapted physical activities (Hutchison and McGill, 1992).

In 1987 the *National Recreation Statement* was signed. This statement portrayed the beliefs of government towards the value of recreation (Searle and Brayley, 2000) and led to the establishment of provincial policies by the Ontario Ministry of Tourism and Recreation in 1987 and Alberta Recreation and Parks in 1988.

In 1988 the Campbell's Survey on Well Being was carried out to provide an update of the 1981 Canada Fitness Survey. The objectives of this survey were to: (1) describe changes in the physical recreation and physical fitness patterns of the Canadian population between 1981 and 1988; (2) identify a demographic profile of Canadians who increased, maintained, or decreased their activity patterns; (3) analyze the relationship between health status in 1988 and activity patterns from 1981-88; and (4) explore the existing relationship between activity patterns, motivations, incentives, barriers, and social circumstances for the period 1981-88. The results revealed that Canadians fifteen years of age and older were more active than in 1981.

Also in 1988, as a result of the growing international awareness of tourism, the first international conference on Tourism as a Vital Form for Peace was held in Vancouver. The mandate of this conference was to broaden awareness of the potential for tourism while: (1) contributing to mutual understanding, trust and goodwill among people of the world; (2) improving the quality of the environment; and (3) enhancing the awareness of sustainable development (D'Amore, 1990).

Fitness surveys showed that Canadians were becoming more active.

Photo: Courtesy of George Karlis.

In 1988, a comprehensive study by William G. Watson revealed that in the 1980s Canadians tended to be more active during their leisure time than they used to be. Most owned, at the very least, one colour TV; the number of hours worked had declined by almost 3 hours per week to a little over 38 hours since the 1950s; the number of Canadians engaged in commercial (as opposed to home) work had increased dramatically since World War II; the overall consumption of leisure had increased, with Canadians becoming more "goods-intensive"; standard holidays per year had increased and so had vacation time; and leisure activity involvement by Canadians had increased on a steady basis since the end of World War II.

1990-1999: THE INCREASING VALUE OF LEISURE AND RECREATION

Early in 1990, Canadian demographer David Foot published an article predicting that "growth in outdoor recreation is least likely to occur in winter activities and recreation sports" whereas "growth in outdoor recreation is most likely to occur in natural environmental and general recreation areas" (1990: 159). Foot argued that a shift would take place in the recreation service industry from facility-based recreation towards natural environment-based recreation.

The 1990s was a decade of environmental and ecological thrusts. Despite the poor performance of the Canadian economy, the need to understand, explore and experience leisure continued to grow. This became evident with the establishment of Fitness Canada's Active Living Alliance and its efforts in research and marketing, encouraging Canadians to be more active.

By the 1990s, leisure and recreation had evolved as an industry and as a part of life highly valued by society. Canada's national park system had become the largest in the world, and at 10.7 percent of total expenditure, Canada's expenditure on leisure pursuits ranked among the highest of all Western nations (Ibrahim, 1991). It had become evident that many communities in Canada were undergoing massive economic, social and structural changes resulting from factors such as the demise of traditional industries, shifting socio-demographic patterns, and lifestyle changes, including leisure and recreation (Wilkinson and Murray, 1991).

This decade witnessed the refusal of "the idea of benevolent paternalism" (Johnson and Mclean, 1996). The general public, as recipients of public recreation programs, no longer accepted the idea of having little choice but to participate in a limited array of public sector recreation services. It was during this decade that phrases such as "rights of the individual," "freedom of choice" and "empowerment" were more seriously considered by public recreation service providers to broaden the existing scope of leisure opportunities. The role of government in leisure and recreation was at the forefront as the Canadian Constitution was being discussed. The Canadian Parks and Recreation Association's board of directors decided to establish two goals to enter into the complex

Natural environment-based recreation became popular in the 1990s.

constitutional discussions. These were: (1) to ensure that the Canadian Constitution recognized and protected Canadians' rights to recreation and leisure, and (2) to increase awareness of the personal, social, economic and environmental benefits of recreation (Mirecki, 1992).

During the early 1990s, the First International Conference on Arts Management took place in August of 1991. This conference was organized by Ecoles des Hautes Commerciales de Montreal and the University of Ottawa and sixty-three papers were delivered on a diversity of topics related to arts and cultural organization management (Colbert and Mitchell, 1991).

In 1992, Fitness and Amateur Sport Canada put together a Task Force Report on Federal Sport Policy. This report, entitled *Sport: The Way Ahead*, suggested that community sport systems work closely together with municipal recreation departments to establish collaborative service provision systems. Furthermore, in 1992, the Parks and Recreation Federation of Ontario and the Ontario Ministry of Tourism and Recreation published *The Benefits of Parks and Recreation: A Catalogue*. This catalogue went on to become an example for the development of other benefit catalogues and handbooks in municipalities in Ontario and in other provinces such as Alberta. In 1999, the president of the Canadian Parks and Recreation Association, David R. Mitsui, referred to the "benefits movement" that was largely initiated by the creation of this catalogue as "perhaps the most significant development in the recreation and parks field in the last 10 years" (1999: 6).

Also in 1992, the Canadian Fitness and Lifestyle Institute conducted the National Workplace Survey. The main objective of this survey was to provide a detailed overview of the health promotion programs of companies. The results revealed that most large companies (one hundred employees or more) offered sport and recreation opportunities to employees while only approximately one-third of the companies had some kind of fitness program.

The 1990s witnessed an increase in fees and charges as a means to increase revenue for the provision of public recreation services (Connelly and Smale, 1999). In fact, during this decade, a growing need persisted for governments to become more efficient and spend less (Johnson and Johnson-Tew, 1999a). Public leisure service providers felt increased pressure to expand funding sources for the provision of recreation services, and sponsorship became a means to accumulate needed monetary resources (McCarville and Smale, 1996; Decke, 1991).

In 1998, Parks Canada became an official operating agency through the proclamation of the *Parks Canada Agency Act*. Also during this year, the Government of Canada affirmed that national parks in Canada would not be commercialized or privatized (McNamee, 2002).

In 1998-99, the Government of Ontario established the Ontario Government Business Plans for the Ministry of Citizenship, Culture and Recreation (Government of Ontario, 1998). The intent of this business plan was to incorporate business principles, models and service

THE IMPORTANCE OF THE RECREATION INDUSTRY TODAY

By the 1990s, leisure and recreation had evolved as a significant business sector in its own right as well as a part of life that was highly valued by Canadians.

marketing strategies to sustain provincial government involvement in the provision of recreation services.

Finally, the 1990s was a decade in which a new trend was observed in the general attitude towards the delivery of recreation services in Canada. Leisure and recreation started to be viewed as an "important contributor to the health of our nation and of individuals" (Searle and Brayley, 2000: 28). Leisure and recreation began to gain recognition as an important avenue for health-care prevention and the reduction of health costs.

CONCLUSION

The history of leisure and recreation in Canada can be traced from the early activities of the Inuit and Algonquin peoples. After the arrival of the early settlers in Canada, the leisure and recreation pursuits of the people of pre-Confederation Canada became shaped through interaction between the Aboriginal Peoples and the European newcomers. For instance, lacrosse and canoeing were activities introduced by the Aboriginal Peoples, whereas curling and "the bee" were activities introduced by the early settlers.

The history of public recreation in Canada begins with the provision of public open spaces for parks such as the Halifax Commons, public squares in Montreal, and Gore Park in Hamilton, Ontario. Concern for the urban poor and for children led to the playground movement and the eventual establishment of many volunteer organizations and municipal recreation in Canada. After World War II, the provinces along with the federal government became more actively involved in the provision of recreation services with the passing of the *National Fitness Act* in 1943.

Since the 1950s, leisure and recreation services has experienced a steady growth in Canada. The local, provincial and federal governments have all played a key role in shaping policies and services for leisure and recreation (see Table 3.4). Despite economic constraints, the public sector in Canada continues to be actively involved in the provision of leisure services, although the past two decades have witnessed significant developments in the provision of programs and services in the commercial and voluntary sectors. Perhaps the most important recent historical development of the 1990s was the creation of the *Benefits of Parks and Recreation: A Catalogue* by the Parks and Recreation Federation of Ontario and the Ontario Ministry of Tourism and Recreation in 1992. This catalogue is currently used extensively throughout various parts of Canada and provides a solid foundation for the future development of leisure and recreation services in Canada.

CHAPTER 3: HISTORY OF LEISURE AND RECREATION IN CANADA

Study Questions

1. What were the multiple uses of lacrosse for the Aboriginal Peoples of Canada?

2. List and describe the three culturally significant games of the Inuit?

3. Describe the five major types of open space areas that existed in Upper Canada.

4. What was the intent of the National Council of Women?

5. What was the objective of the community leagues?

Selected Websites

- **National Library of Canada (Backcheck: A Hockey Retrospective)**
  http://www.nlc-bnc.ca/hockey

- **Early Canadiana Online**
  http://www.canadiana.org/eco/index.html

- **The British Columbia History Internet/Website**
  http://victoria.tc.ca/Resources/
  bchistory-contents.html

- **Canadian Archival Resources on the Internet**
  http://www.usask.ca/archives

- **Canadian Confederation (National Library of Canada)**
  http://www.nlc-bnc.ca/2/18/index-e.html

Key Concepts

- **National Council of Women**

- **Playground Movement**

- **Golden Age of Sport**

- **Parks and Recreation Association**

- **PARTICIPaction**

- **LaLonde Report**

- **The Elora Prescription**

The clock tower at the Halifax Citadel. Photo: Canadian Tourism Commission.

4

THE PUBLIC SECTOR

LEARNING OBJECTIVES

- To examine the relationship between government, politics, leisure and recreation.
- To articulate the relationship between the Canadian Constitution, leisure and recreation.
- To explore the levels of government and their roles for leisure and recreation.
- To view the quest for a national policy on leisure and recreation.
- To examine "the right to recreation services."

In Canada, as in all nations of the world, a close link exists between government, leisure and recreation. In fact, government not only helps shape our viewpoint of leisure and recreation but also our leisure and recreation lifestyles. The government of a nation determines the stance that a particular society takes towards leisure and recreation services and the leisure and recreation industry. Canadian society is perceived by many nations as the ultimate model of democracy. In fact, many non-Canadian researchers of leisure studies often comment on the positive influence the democratic principles and the public sector have on the provision on leisure and recreation services.

This chapter describes the relationship between government, the public sector, and leisure and recreation in Canada. It begins with a description of government in Canada, followed by an examination of the relationship between democracy, leisure and recreation. The delivery of leisure services by different levels of government is introduced and former and current quests for a national policy on recreation are examined. The concept of recreation as a basic right is discussed, and the chapter ends with an overview of what is required to maintain public sector leisure and recreation in Canada.

"Like every other good thing in this world, leisure and culture have to be paid for. Fortunately, however, it is not the leisured and the cultured who have to pay".

— Aldous Huxley (1894-1963), British novelist. *Mr. Scogan, Crome Yellow*, ch. 22 (1922).

GOVERNMENT IN CANADA

In the 1990s, the main political parties in Canada were the Progressive Conservatives, the Liberals, and the New Democratic Party. Today, the face of politics in Canada has changed dramatically with the downfall of the Progressive Conservative and New Democratic parties and the creation of two strong new parties, the Canadian Alliance and the Bloc

THE SWEEPING EFFECTS OF GOVERNMENT

We cannot work, or eat or drink; we cannot buy or sell or own anything; we cannot go to a ball or a hockey game or watch TV without feeling the effects of government.

— Forsey, 1987: 7.

Quebecois. Changes such as these have had an impact on leisure and recreation and its future as two of the three parties that traditionally defined government in Canada have been replaced by two new parties, bringing with them their own political philosophies, beliefs and directions.

Despite changes in political parties, the intent of politics and government in Canada remains the same. In simple terms, governments in democracies such as Canada "are elected by passengers to steer the ship of the nation. They are expected to hold it on course, to arrange for a prosperous voyage, and to be prepared to be thrown overboard if they fail in either duty" (Forsey, 1982: 1).

Canada is a federal state with its self-governing provinces and territories controlled by a central government. A federal state by definition is "one that brings together a number of different political communities with a common government for common purposes and separate 'state' or 'provincial' " or 'cantonal' governments for the particular purposes of each community" (Forsey, 1982: 7). This means that "we cannot work, or eat, or drink; we cannot buy or sell or own anything; we cannot go to a ball game or a hockey game or watch TV without feeling the effects of government" (ibid., p. 1).

DEMOCRACY, LEISURE AND RECREATION

The word **democracy** comes from the root Greek words *demos* (people) and *kratia* (rule). Democracy, in its truest form, is thus concerned with people ruling. The concept democracy is people-driven, whereby people (all people) live in an equal society with equal say in the decision-making process. Since politics and government are concerned with the decision making of a society, democracy is a philosophy that entails direct access to the decision-makers.

Canada is a representative democracy. It is a society in which all people have an opportunity to vote for a political representative who will be directly involved in the making of societal decisions. By definition, a representative democracy is "that political system in which the governors who make decisions with the force of law obtain their authority directly or indirectly as a result of free elections in which the bulk of the population may participate" (Jackson and Jackson, 1990: 24).

The Canadian Constitution shapes and limits political power. Thus, Canada is also a constitutional democracy. "The documents and behaviours which comprise the Constitution limit the powers of the government by specifying the form of involvement of elected representatives and the division of authority among the partners in the federation" (Jackson and Jackson, 1990: 25). The Canadian Constitution identifies the power given to those who govern us.

By being a representative democracy and a constitutional monarchy, the political model of Canada represents a system in which people do in fact have a chance to be heard and, at the very least, an opportunity to influence decision-makers. The people of Canada may choose to vote and be represented by someone who has similar political and leisure philosophies. The elected Members of Parliament may in turn present the leisure and recreation concerns of their constituents to government and lobby for these needs to be fulfilled through policy.

THE CANADIAN CONSTITUTION, LEISURE AND RECREATION

In 1982 the Canadian Constitution was officially signed (Forsey, 1982: Ministry of Supply and Services, 1982). The Canada Constitution presents the **Charter of Rights and Freedoms**. This Charter of Rights and Freedoms does not mention leisure or recreation. It is assumed by convention by the federal government of Canada, however, that leisure and recreation are basic rights and freedoms of all Canadians.

By not mentioning leisure and recreation in the Charter of Rights and Freedoms, one may question the importance of leisure and recreation in Canadian society. The section of the Charter of Rights and Freedoms that most closely relates to leisure and recreation is the fourth fundamental freedom stated as "freedom of association." Freedom of association is closely linked to leisure and recreation as it allows individuals to come together to form groups and associations to fulfill basic leisure and recreation needs. An argument may also be made that two of the other three fundamental freedoms also relate to leisure and recreation. The first two fundamental freedoms are linked to the "state of mind" or "state of being" conceptualization of leisure as leisure is an intrinsic experience, meaning that it can be anything for anyone. These two fundamentals freedoms are: (1) freedom of conscience and religion, and (2) freedom of thought, belief, opinion and expression, including freedom of the press and other media of communication.

LEVELS OF GOVERNMENT AND THE DELIVERY OF LEISURE SERVICES

In Canada, there are three levels of government: federal, provincial and municipal. Each of these levels has its own mandate for leisure and recreation. Furthermore, each of these levels of government is concerned with the provision and delivery of leisure and recreation services to the people of Canada (see Table 4.1).

The public sector in Canada has as its primary intent the communal good of society. It is for this reason that each level of government is directly involved with leisure and recreation. Leisure and recreation is viewed as a necessity for society, in particular for the good of society (see Table 4.2).

Leisure and recreation departments, at all levels of government, exist for a number of reasons, such as, yet not limited to, the following: (1) to provide recreation that because of its nature inculcates values/ideals to the user; (2) to provide opportunities for recreation to disadvantaged clients: the poor, persons with physical or mental disabilities, and so forth,

Traditional changing of the guard at Fort Anne, Annapolis Royal, Nova Scotia.

Photo: Canada Tourism Commission.

Table 4.1: A Comparison of Public Recreation Involvement of the Three Levels of Government

Level of Government	Authority	Mandate	Primary Clients
Federal	Convention	To promote health and well-being through recreation and sport.	National sport and recreation associations
Provincial	Convention	Varies, but may include the following: To promote health and well-being through recreation To promote preservation, protection and enjoyment of natural resources To preserve cultural heritage To promote citizenship To stimulate economic development through the leisure industry	Municipalities Provincial sport and recreation associations
Municipal	Enabling Legislation	Usually akin to the following: To encourage the development of recreation programs and facilities To act as a catalyst for recreation development in the community	The general public Local sport and recreation associations Local special interest groups

Source: Searle, M.S., and Brayley, R.E. (2000). *Leisure Services in Canada*. (2nd Edition). State College, PA: Venture.

Table 4.2: The Public Recreation Sector

Nature of Service	Usually Free; Necessary for Society
Service Orientation	Good of Society; Needed Service
Financial Base	Tax Revenues; User Fees
Originating Authority	Three Levels of Government (Federal, Provincial, Municipal)
Focus Clientele	General Public

and (3) to provide those opportunities deemed valuable by society that, because of their nature (e.g., cost compared to potential income generation), would not be provided by the private sector such as an urban park or open space (Johnson and Mclean, 1996b: 21).

FEDERAL GOVERNMENT

The federal government in Canada "has power to make laws for the peace, order and good government of Canada, except for subjects assigned exclusively to the legislatures of the provinces" (Forsey, 1982: 19). Although recreation falls within the constitutional responsibility of the provincial governments, the Government of Canada has a role in recreation that primarily includes those activities that are national and international in scope (Ontario Ministry of Tourism and Recreation, 1987). The federal government receives its authority by convention and has a mandate "to promote health and well-being through recreation and sport" (Searle and Brayley, 2000: 90). The primary clients of the federal government are national sport and recreation associations (ibid.).

In a way, the federal government takes a back-seat approach when it comes to leisure and recreation as legislative authority falls within the hands of the provinces. The former Minister responsible for Saskatchewan Culture, Multiculturalism and Recreation, Colin Maxwell, in an interview with Shelley Vandermay, makes this point evidently clear in stating that "we are definitely seeing a void that has been created by the federal department responsible for Sport and Recreation. They are, in my view, asking the provinces to pick up and fill the void" (Vandermay, 1990: 11).

Perhaps a back-seat approach is indeed taken by the federal government towards leisure and recreation, yet this is not to say that the federal government has a complete hands-off approach. In addition to the shaping of policies and legislation, a number of federal government departments and agencies are directly or indirectly involved with leisure and recreation. Three federal government departments and agencies are directly involved: (1) Canadian Heritage, (2) Industry Canada, and (3) Parks Canada.

The intent of **Canadian Heritage** is to: (1) foster cultural participation, (2) encourage active citizenship and participation in Canada's civic life, and (3) strengthen connections among Canadians. Canadian Heritage is responsible for national policies and programs that promote Canadian content. Its mission strives to move towards a more cohesive and creative Canada.

Canadian Heritage is directly involved with leisure and recreation as it houses Sport Canada. The mission of Sport Canada is to support the achievement of high performance excellence and the development of the Canadian sport system to strengthen the unique contribution that sport makes to Canadian identity, culture and society. Sport Canada's focus is on:

FEDERAL INVOLVEMENT

Although recreation falls within the constitutional responsibility of the provincial governments, the Government of Canada has a role in recreation that primarily includes those activities that are national and international in scope (Ontario Ministry of Tourism and Recreation, 1987).

• enhancing the ability of Canadian athletes to excel at the highest international levels through fair and ethical means,

• working with key partners to enhance coordination and integration to advance the Canadian sport system,

• advancing the broader federal government objectives through sport, position sport in the federal government agenda and promoting the contribution of sport to Canadian society and

• increasing access and equity in sport for targeted under-represented groups.

Industry Canada is also viewed as having a direct relationship with leisure and recreation as tourism is a part of its mandate. The mission of Industry Canada is to foster a growing, competitive, knowledge-based Canadian economy. The objectives of Industry Canada are to: (1) improve conditions for investment, (2) improve Canada's innovation performance, (3) increase Canada's share of global trade, and (4) build a fair, efficient and competitive marketplace.

The program areas of Industry Canada include, yet are not limited to, the following: (1) developing industry and technology capability, (2) fostering scientific research, (3) setting telecommunications policy, (4) promoting investment and trade, (5) promoting tourism and small business development, and (6) setting the rules and services that support the effective operation of the marketplace. The Canadian Tourism Commission (see Chapter 10), the agency that has the primary mandate for tourism in Canada, reports directly to Industry Canada.

Parks Canada is responsible for national parks, national historic sites and other heritage places. Its purpose is to ensure the long-term integrity of the aforementioned while also encouraging public understanding and appreciation of Canada's heritage and history. The mandate of Parks Canada is as follows: "On behalf of the people of Canada, we protect and present nationally significant examples of Canada's natural and cultural heritage and foster public understanding, appreciation and enjoyment in ways that ensure their ecological and commemorative integrity for present and future generations."

Other federal government departments, agencies and corporations that are indirectly involved with leisure and recreation include: (1) the Canada Council for the Arts, (2) the Canadian Science and Technology Museum Corporation, (3) the Canadian Broadcasting Corporation, (4) the Canadian Museum of Civilization, (5) the Canadian Museum of Nature, (6) the Canadian Radio-Television and Telecommunications Commission, (7) the National Archives of Canada, (8) the National Arts Centre, (9) the National Film Board of Canada, (10) the National Gallery of Canada, (11) the National Library of Canada, (12) Telefilm Canada, and (13) the National Capital Commission.

It should be mentioned that the federal government recognizes the significant role that the activities of lacrosse and hockey have played in the history of Canada, and continue to play in shaping Canada's identity

THE CANADIAN HEALTH NETWORK

Leisure, Health and Government in Canada

Many leisure studies researchers posit that leisure makes up one-third of our lives; that is, if we devote eight hours to work and eight hours to sleep, the final eight hours of our daily time is given to leisure. If we are to stay healthy, and maintain physical, social, mental and spiritual health we must make good use of our eight hours of leisure time.

To enhance our awareness of healthy living, Health Canada (a federal government depart ment) has established the Canadian Health Network, with the intent of assisting Canadians in finding information on how to stay healthy and prevent disease. The Canadian Health Network seeks: to maintain health information as a public good; to not re-create existing health information; to present quality, credible and practical information from multiple perspectives; to be socially inclusive and respective of diversity; and to exemplify ethics and integrity.

This national, non-profit, bilingual web-based service focuses on a number of topics, such as: active living, cancer, complementary and alternative health, determinants of health, environmental health, health promotion, the health system, healthy eating, HIV/AIDS, injury prevention, mental health, relationships, sexuality/reproductive health, substance abuse/addictions, tobacco, violence prevention and workplace health.

Issues that are presented focus on the following select populations: Aboriginal Peoples, children, ethnic groups, men, people with disabilities, seniors, women and youth.

Recent Health Promotions Program of the CHN

The Canadian Health Network has recently introduced a new interactive resource entitled "Stairway to Health." The intent of Stairway to Health is to encourage Canadians to take the stairs rather than the elevator. The focus of this program is primarily on Canadians in the workplace, as it is argued that 15 million Canadians spend more than half their waking lives at work. Thus, work, which can be a sedentary activity, may be used as an environment in which to exercise simply by changing the means used to get from one floor to another.

What Makes Leisure Healthy?

- Many leisure activities are active (e.g., playing tennis, walking).

- Sedentary leisure activities exercise the mind (e.g., reading, watching TV).

- Leisure enhances social functioning (i.e., community programs and services bring people together).

- Leisure assists individual development (i.e., learning new skills at different stages in life).

- Leisure is educational (i.e., it helps us learn and appreciate diversity and pluralism).

- Leisure offers opportunities for spiritual growth (e.g., through the attendance and involvement in religious services).

- Leisure gives us balance in life (i.e., it compensates for the aspects of work that are boring and monotonous).

- Leisure enhances our self-esteem (i.e., it helps us feel good about ourselves).

- Leisure helps us achieves our goals.

- Leisure provides us with identity and helps us feel and become a part of a group.

Source: <http://www.canadian-health-network.ca>.

PROVINCIAL MANDATES

The mandates of provincial and territorial governments for leisure and recreation vary for each respective province and territory.

and the quality of life of Canadian people. For this reason, the House of Commons was informed on May 12, 1994, by the Acting Speaker, Mrs Maheu, that the Senate passed Bill C-212 recognizing lacrosse and hockey as the national sports of Canada (House of Commons Debates, May 12, 1994).

PROVINCIAL AND TERRITORIAL GOVERNMENTS

Like the federal government, provincial and territorial governments also receive their authority by convention. The mandates of provincial and territorial governments for leisure and recreation vary for each respective province and territory. Searle and Brayley (2000: 90) identify the following five functions that may appear in the mandates of provinces and territories for leisure and recreation: (1) to promote health and well-being through recreation, (2) to promote preservation, protection and enjoyment of natural resources, (3) to preserve cultural heritage, (4) to promote citizenship, and (5) to stimulate economic development through the leisure industry. In addition, Searle and Brayley list two groups of primary clients for leisure and recreation for provincial and/or territorial governments. These are: (1) municipalities and (2) provincial sport and recreation associations.

Provincial and territorial legislatures have power over subjects such as the following: (1) direct taxation in the province, (2) natural resources, (3) prisons (except penitentiaries), (4) charitable institutions, (5) hospitals (except marine hospitals), (6) municipal institutions, (7) licenses for provincial and municipal revenue purposes, (8) incorporation of provincial companies, (9) solemnization of marriages, (10) property and civil rights in the province, (11) the creation of courts and the administration of justice, (12) fines and penalties for breaking provincial laws, (13) matters of local or private nature in the province, (14) education, and (15) recreation.

A detailed overview of the mandate of each province and territory in Canada is impossible to present in this text. Therefore, the Province of Ontario and the Province of Alberta will be highlighted as examples of the role of provincial governments in recreation.

In 1987, the Province of Ontario put forth a Community Recreation Policy Statement. The intent of this policy was two-fold: it identified the Ministry of Tourism and Recreation as the Ministry in Ontario representing and coordinating the interests and programs of recreation, and it provided direction for municipalities for the future development of community-based recreation. The objective of this policy was to emphasize the development of co-operative planning, service creation and the delivery of recreation services in the community (Reid, 1989). This objective is clearly spelled out in the following Community Recreation Policy Statement:

> Governments at all levels are not and should never be the primary providers of recreation services. The primary role of government is to assist and enable the provision of the wide range of recreation services to meet the needs and

interests of their constituent citizens. Voluntary organizations and many non-profit and commercial agencies will continue to be the major deliverers of recreation/leisure opportunities (Ontario Ministry of Tourism and Recreation, 1987).

In Canada, recreation falls within the constitutional responsibility of the provinces and territories. Yet, as indicated in this policy statement, the provincial government is not the primary provider of recreation services but rather assists and enables the municipalities, commercial and voluntary sectors to provide ample recreation opportunities and services. It should also be noted that, in the case of Ontario, the provincial government may have primacy for recreation services yet this does not mean exclusivity; that is, other provincial departments may also include recreation in their mandates (Ontario Ministry of Tourism and Recreation, 1987).

Similar to Ontario, the Province of Alberta's Sport and Recreation Branch emphasizes collaboration with communities for the provision of leisure and recreation services. However, the "core business of the branch is to support participation in community sport and recreation to help individuals, families and communities improve the quality of life in Alberta" (website at: <http://www.cd.gov.ab.ca/building-communities/ sport_recreation_recreation branch>).

MUNICIPAL GOVERNMENTS

In Canada, municipal governments are established by provincial legislatures. The powers given to the municipal government is that which provincial legislatures see fit to give them. The election of municipal officials (i.e., mayors, city councillors and so on) is based on the process and system prescribed by the provincial legislature (Forsey, 1982).

For municipalities to exist in Canada, the province has to have enabling legislation that permits this to happen. Municipal departments, such as those dealing with leisure and recreation, must be based on appropriate legislative authority. Municipal governments receive their authority through enabling legislation. "Enabling legislation is that which allows, but does not necessarily require, something to happen" (Searle and Brayley, 2000: 89). Thus, municipalities exist only if allowed or permitted by a province or territory.

For example, in Ontario, municipalities are created through *The Municipal Act* and *The Ministry of Tourism and Recreation Act* (Ontario Ministry of Tourism and Recreation, 1987). Moreover, in Ontario, "Municipal Recreation Committees mandated under the Ministry of Tourism and Recreation Act, authorized by a supporting municipal by-law and operating under a Municipal Council have contributed to the significant growth of recreation services and facilities across Ontario" (Ontario Ministry of Tourism and Recreation, 1987: 6).

The mandate for involvement in leisure and recreation by municipalities usually consists of the following: to encourage the development of

Community parks such as the one above are managed by municipal governments.

Photo: Toronto Parks and Recreation Association.

recreation programs and facilities, and to act as a catalyst for recreation development in the community (Searle and Brayley, 2000: 90). The primary clients of municipalities for leisure and recreation are the general public, local sport and recreation associations, and local special interest groups (ibid.).

The municipal level of government, it may be argued, is the level in which the recreation needs of the general public are directly addressed through the offering of recreation services. Thus, the role of this level of government is pivotal, as it is here that the bulk of public leisure services are delivered (Dawson, Andrew and Harvey, 1991). The provision of recreation opportunities such as crafts, outdoor programs and access to museums, libraries, parks, heritage resources, performing arts and sports are examples of the diverse mandates of municipal recreation departments (Ontario Ministry of Tourism and Recreation, 1987). Indeed, municipal recreation departments are "closest to the people and most able to respond to the needs of the community in matters of recreation" (ibid., p. 8).

MUNICIPALITIES: DIRECTLY SERVING THE NEEDS OF THE PEOPLE

The Management Information System (M.I.S.) used by the City of Halifax is a tool that provides a quantitative and qualitative data bank of information containing the types of recreation services provided to the general public and measuring the efficiency and effectiveness of the City of Halifax's Parks and Recreation Department (Murray and McGrath, 1990). As a result, municipal decision-makers are in a position to evaluate, suggest and implement change to better serve and address the recreation program needs of Halifax residents.

Another example of how municipalities work directly with the people to address general recreation needs is through the use of advisory committees. One such committee, the Parks and Recreation Advisory Committee, exists in the City of Ottawa. The mandate of this advisory committee is two-fold: to advise on all aspects of the provision of leisure and recreation services in the City of Ottawa, and to promote and maintain communication with the public on parks and recreation needs. This committee provides a forum for citizens to raise issues and concerns regarding parks, recreation and leisure issues so that advice and guidance can be provided to Ottawa City Council for the provision of policies, programs and practices.

It should be noted that no two municipalities use identical services for the provision of recreation programs. The reason is that no two municipalities have identical social, political, economic and demographic characteristics (Davis-Jamieson, 1990). After all, many municipal leisure and recreation departments have developed as a result of pressure applied by local citizens expressing recreation needs and concerns. It is pressure imposed by the people (i.e., special interest groups) that leads to the

Photo: Canadian Tourism Commission.

Halifax's "Public Gardens," still a major attraction for local citizens, dates back to 1836.

establishment of municipal recreation services (ibid.). This is a primary reason why municipal recreation services include the direct provision of services in their stated mandates.

Commencing in the 1990s, municipal governments, as agents of provincial governments, were called upon to endure a greater demand for recreation services (Glover, 1999). Despite the understanding that municipal governments, such as the case of those in Ontario, tend to be fiscally healthier than other levels of government (Siegal, 1997), the reduction of transfer payments and the downloading of responsibilities imposed fiscal restraints on municipal recreation departments in the 1990s (Johnson and Johnson-Tew, 1999). Also, increased expectations, accountability, competition, rationalization and technology have restructured the traditional approach used by the public sector to provide leisure services (Harper, Mahon, Foreman and Godbey, 1999). As a result, municipal governments have begun to incorporate a more business-like approach (Smale and Frisby, 1990) in the provision of recreation services by adopting market strategies and using alternative service delivery approaches (Walsh, 1995; Glover and Burton, 1998). Glover (1999) refers to these strategies as "reinventing government movement" and claims that this poses new challenges for public sector leisure professionals in the provision of public sector leisure services.

The success of a municipal recreation department greatly depends on its ability to establish and sustain a good working relationship with the other service sectors of recreation (Davis-Jamieson, 1990). It is the task of municipal recreation leaders to work closely with local volunteer groups and private sector organizations to ascertain that the recreation needs of municipal residents are met. This function has become increasingly important as decreased funding has been allocated to municipal government for the funding of leisure services (Whyte, 1992; Crompton and McGregor, 1994).

In addition, the success of municipal recreation departments also rests on the extent to which public sector-operated residential community centres and services fulfill the recreation needs of the people in a fair and equitable fashion. Since direct service provision takes place at the local level, it is particularly important for community members to become actively involved in expressing desired needs (Karlis, 1994a: 10). It is equally important for municipal recreation leaders to explore the recreation needs and trends of their respective community to best provide necessary recreation services.

One example of a municipality that has taken measures to ascertain that its recreation services and opportunities are distributed in a fair and equitable fashion is the City of Ottawa. In August 2001, the City Council of the City of Ottawa approved a recreation and culture service mandate. The goals of the City of Ottawa recreation service mandate are to support community access, and to support participation and overall health and well-being through recreation and culture programs (Stewart, 2002a).

MUNICIPAL GRASSROOTS

The municipal level of government is the level in which the recreation needs of the general public are directly addressed through the offering of recreation services.

LOCALIZED SERVICES

No two municipalities use identical services for the provision of recreation programs as no two municipalities have identical social, political, economic and demographic characteristics (Davis-Jamieson, 1990).

Another example of a municipality committed to equity in recreation services provision is the City of Toronto. In May 2003, Toronto Parks and Recreation launched an initiative to include its residents in the establishment of a strategic plan for the goals and direction of Toronto Parks and Recreation up to 2010. By asking for input from the community, Toronto Parks and Recreation affirmed its commitment to providing quality recreation services for all (http://www.city.toronto.on.ca/parks/parks_future.htm).

YESTERDAY'S QUEST FOR A NATIONAL POLICY ON RECREATION

One of the biggest criticisms of the Canadian political system made by Canadian leisure and recreation professionals is that Canada does not have a national policy on recreation. For years, Dr. E.H. (Ted) Storey has argued that a national policy is needed and that it is simply not enough for the federal government of Canada to assume by convention that leisure and recreation is important and is a basic right and freedom of all Canadians.

In 1990, Dr. Storey published a paper entitled "The Quest for a National Policy on Recreation: A Brief History." In this article, Storey states that one of the major problems facing the leisure and recreation service industry is that a national policy does not exist. Storey discusses that a national policy on recreation has been close to being complete, particularly during the late 1970s and early 1980s, yet in each case failed to become a reality. A change in government from the liberals to the conservatives put this on hold.

Lloyd Minshall (1984) also eloquently argues for the formulation of a national policy on recreation. Minshall states that it is a problem for the recreation industry that no national policy is in place. According to Minshall, the formulation of a national policy will provide program direction and continuity to the recreation service sector throughout Canada.

Research by Westland (1985) depicts how efforts put forth in the 1970s made it appear as if the federal government might have been prepared to work towards the development of a national policy for recreation. The creation of the Recreation Canada Directorate in 1973 indicated that a national policy was close to being established. Moreover, the following letter provided evidence of the quest for a national policy for recreation. This letter, dated July 12, 1978, and addressed to the President of the Canadian Parks and Recreation Association from the then Prime Minister of Canada, Pierre Elliot Trudeau, indicated that a shared jurisdiction between the federal government and the provinces was necessary for recreation.

I believe recreation services to be the domain of no single government jurisdiction. Recreation is a very personal activity which demands the same recognition, respect and encouragement as is afforded to all other basic social concerns. No one jurisdiction can fully provide for all the recreation services required by the citizens and no jurisdiction can operate effectively without some impact on recreation.

A further event in the late 1970s enhanced optimism that a national policy for recreation was close to being developed. Trudeau's administration had a process of policy formation using draft discussion papers referred to as "White Papers" and "Green Papers." In 1977, it released a Green Paper entitled *Toward a National Policy on Recreation.* This paper depicted the roles of the individual, the community, municipal government, provincial organizations, provincial government, national organizations and the federal government for recreation. However, a number of major problems were not resolved in this document such as the impact of a withdrawal of the federal government from recreation and the process by which federal and provincial documents for recreation would be used for joint decision making (Skerrett, 1992).

By October 1983, after no further progress had been made to finalize a national policy on recreation, the provincial Ministers responsible for recreation and sport decided to take action and implement an *Interprovincial Recreation Statement.* This statement put forth that, as with other social services in Canada, recreation lies within the jurisdiction of the provinces. At this point in time, the quest for a national policy on recreation had ceased.

Although the quest for a national policy on recreation had halted in 1983, there was renewed hope for a future national policy with the establishment of the National Recreation Statement. The **National Recreation Statement** (1987) articulates that the primacy of recreation is in the hands of the provinces and territories, yet a clear and necessary role exists for federal government in recreation. The federal government's role is to complement the provincial and/or territorial governments in the development of recreation through: (1) assisting in the development of recreation services so that all can participate through the provision of resources and support to the national recreation organizations and agencies, (2) ensure international and domestic representation in recreation services that serve a shared objective, and (3) establish and distribute promotional and resource materials encouraging participation in leisure activities.

The National Recreation Statement (1987) also presents key functions for provincial/territorial governments in recreation. These were stated as follows: (1) to develop and implement a public policy on recreation as well as associated programs; (2) to support municipal and educational administrations and local governments in the delivery of leisure services, (3) to influence the education system so that all students can acquire skills, knowledge, attitudes and a recreational philosophy, and (4) to meet regularly with other recreation jurisdictions, including the federal government, to plan, coordinate and share best practices.

NATIONAL RECREATION STATEMENT, 1987

The National Recreation Statement of 1987 asserted that the primary responsibility for recreation lies with the provinces and territories but that an important role also exists for the federal government in complementing the work of the provinces and territories in this work.

PROVINCIAL/TERRITORIAL POLICY STATEMENTS ON RECREATION

By the People, for the People?

What value do the provincial and territorial governments of Canada place on leisure and recreation? To address this question one needs to look no further than the recreation policy statements utilized by this level of government.

Despite the fact that responsibility for the provision of recreation services falls within the hands of the provincial governments, few provinces or territories have constructed policy statements for recreation. One of those to do so is the Province of Ontario, which in 1987 put forth the following Community Recreation Policy Statement:

> Government at all levels are not and should never be the primary providers of recreation services. The primary role of government is to assist and enable the provision of the wide range of recreation services to meet the needs and interests of their constituent citizens. Voluntary organizations and many non-profit and commercial agencies will continue to be the major deliverers of lei-sure/recreation services.

Photo: Hamilton Conservation Authority/Canadian Tourism Commission

This policy can be used as an example of how provincial governments may view recreation. The Ontario Ministry of Tourism and Recreation policy statement commences by stating that "all" government levels "are not" and "should never" be the "primary providers" of recreation services. The opening phrase of this statement makes it clear that federal, provincial and/or territorial and municipal governments are and probably never will be responsible for providing recreation services. Despite the fact that we pay a considerable amount of taxes, the government, in turn, states that it is not responsible for meeting our recreation needs.

The policy statement goes on to state that the voluntary, non-profit and commercial sectors "will" continue to be the major deliverers of leisure/recreation services. The government identifies the other sectors of the service industry as being the primary deliverers of leisure and recreation services. Although citizens do not pay taxes to the voluntary, non-profit and commercial sectors, the government expects these service sectors to provide the needed social services of leisure and recreation.

When a government organization uses a policy statement to deny responsibility and to assign it to someone or something else, it appears as those it is concerned only with its own benefit. In defence of government, however, one must ask if it is feasible to expect government to make a statement claiming that it has the main responsibility for providing leisure and recreation services. After all, Canada has more than 30 million people who have many social service needs, of which leisure and recreation make up only a small part. Can we reasonably expect a provincial or territorial government to fulfill all of our diverse and pluralistic leisure and recreation needs?

So who benefits most from the Ontario Ministry of Tourism and Recreation policy statement? Is it government, the people, or both?

TODAY'S QUEST FOR A NATIONAL POLICY ON RECREATION

Storey claimed in 1990 that it was time to implement a national policy as the leisure industry was experiencing significant changes resulting from the changing structure of the public sector. Indeed, unlike the affluent 1960s and 1970s, the 1990s experienced a dramatic decrease in public sector investment in leisure services. Storey posited that a national policy was needed to follow the policy-formation lead that had been implemented by various Canadian provinces and territories.

Perhaps now really is the time for a national policy on recreation to be put into place as a move away from mass participation in recreation programs has been promoted by the federal government (see Karlis, 2002b; Vandermey, 1990). The implementation of such a policy would ease the minds of those who are concerned about the future of recreation services in Canada. This uncertainty in the provision of public sector leisure services would without doubt be eased if the federal government took the initiative to construct a national policy on recreation.

In the past four decades some effort has been made by the federal government to put together a national policy related to recreation. With the exception of the National Recreation Statement of 1987, it appears, however, that sport rather than recreation has been the driving force beyond the shaping of a national policy.

Most recently, after two years in the making, on May 24, 2002, the federal, provincial and territorial Ministers responsible for Sport, Fitness and Recreation finalized the **Canada Sport Policy**. In putting this policy together, the Ministers were all driven by the collective goal of making the sport system more effective and inclusive. More specifically, this policy challenges all stakeholders to enhance participation, excellence, capacity and interaction in sport. The vision of the Canada Sport Policy is to have, by 2012, "a dynamic and leading-edge sport environment that enables all Canadians to experience and enjoy involvement in sport to the extent of their abilities and interests and, for increasing numbers, to perform consistently and successfully at the highest competitive levels." The stated goals of this policy are: (1) enhanced participation for Canadians from all segments of society in quality sports activities at all levels and in all forms of participation, (2) enhanced excellence for Canadian athletes and teams to achieve world-class results at the highest levels of international competition through fair and ethical means, (3) enhanced capacity for an athlete/participant-centred development system, and (4) enhanced interaction for the components of the sport system to be more connected and coordinated as a result of committed collaboration and communication among the stakeholders.

It is relevant to note that, for the most part, with the exception of the mention of leisure time as the period in which to experience sport, the term "recreation" is omitted from the Canada Sport Policy. It is stated, however, in the introduction of the Canada Sport Policy that this policy builds on the National Recreation Statement of 1987. Moreover, this

CANADA SPORT POLICY, 2002

With the exception of "leisure time" as the period in which to experience sport, the term recreation is omitted from the Canada Sport Policy of 2002.

Photo: Louis Ducharme/Canadian Tourism Commission).

The Ice Hotel in Quebec City is made of over 12,000 tons of snow and ice.

policy maintains the existing alignment of government responsibilities as operationalized in the National Recreation Statement of 1987.

The current federal-provincial and/or territorial agreement on mutual roles and responsibilities in recreation and the National Recreation Statement of 1987 are probably the closest that we have come to the establishment of a national policy on recreation.

RECREATION AS A BASIC RIGHT

Canada has often been described as a social welfare society. Although the Canadian Constitution does not mention recreation, it is basically assumed by convention by the federal government that recreation is important for the social welfare of the people in Canada. If recreation is viewed as being an important avenue for the social functioning of society, then recreation is a basic right and recreation services should, at least in part, be provided by government. The question that needs to be addressed, however, is the following: Is recreation a basic right in Canada?

According to Johnson and McLean (1996a; 1996b), recreation in Canada has developed and has become more accepted as a "right" by the people of Canada. In addition to being a right, recreation is also perceived as being an "entitlement." By viewing recreation as a "right," the people of Canada have continued to place demands on the public sector to maintain or expand municipal recreation services (ibid.).

The reality of the new millennium is that municipal public sector recreation services are rationing services due to high costs. Another reality for municipal recreation services is the growing number of publicly operated services charging user fees (Johnson-Tew, Havitz and McCarville, 1999). Nonetheless, recreation continues to be viewed as a social need or good in Canada. The demand for the provision of municipal recreation services continues to exist, even at the basic level, and through the continuation of public recreation services, it certainly does appear that recreation is very much a basic right.

However, as fiscal restraints continue, the provision of leisure and recreation services becomes more limited. In a traditional social welfare society such as Canada, the concepts of right, equity, justice and respect are highly valued. All individuals have the right to be respected and treated as equals. The public sector has historically recognized that recreation is a basic right through the many policies and Acts implemented by all levels of government and the active role of the voluntary sector. The partnership between the public and voluntary sectors will continue to play a key role in determining the "basic right" of recreation and "equality" in the provision of its services, but this is not to say that a national policy for recreation is not needed. After all, as Westland (1985: 393) argues, the purpose of recreation policies should be "the creation of conditions under which all citizens can develop their full potential as humans"; that is, to ensure that all citizens have the right to recreation.

THE MAINTENANCE OF PUBLIC SECTOR LEISURE AND RECREATION IN CANADA

It is evident that the public sector played a major role in the evolution of leisure and recreation in Canada (see Chapter 3). The public sector took action to establish parks, community centres, government departments at all levels addressing leisure and recreation, and provincial and federal policies related to leisure and recreation.

Times change, people change and needs change. The following list of what is required to ensure that public sector leisure and recreation continues to exist in Canada in the future is based on past and current trends.

• An Active Voice from the People of Canada

Historically, municipal leisure services in Canada evolved out of the efforts of community groups such as the National Council of Women and the Jasper Place Community League. It was the efforts of community groups and their voices that brought leisure and recreation concerns to

PUBLIC SECTOR SERVICES

In Canada, the public sector is
involved with leisure and
recreation as it:

- establishes, maintains and
  conserves national parks;
- establishes and operates
  community centres;
- operates government
  department at all levels;
- creates
  federal/provincial/municipal
  policies; and
- implements federal/
  provincial/municipal policies.

the forefront of society and to the attention of public sector service
providers.

The voice of the people in democratic Canada is powerful. Not only
do we have the right to vote for the political candidate who will best
address our interest, but by coming together in association with others
with similar leisure and recreation needs, we can approach the decision-makers of society and express our concerns. This may in turn lead
to sustainability in the provision of public sector leisure and recreation
services in Canada.

• Continued Participation

The demand for a service must be there for it to continue to exist. If
Canadians continue to participate in public sector leisure and recreation
services, the supply of these will continue to be maintained. The basic
"supply-demand" principle extends beyond economics to include social
needs as well.

Many of us, at one time or another, have registered in a leisure program at our local municipal community centre only to find out later that
the program has been cancelled due to a lack of participants. Have you
ever stopped to wonder what would happen to municipal community
centres if no one registered in their programs or activities? Not only
would the community centre cease to operate, but the spillover would
have an impact on all levels of public sector services. If people do not
participate in public sector leisure and recreation services, public sector
leisure and recreation services would soon stop being offered. To sustain
the maintenance of public sector leisure and recreation services at all
levels of government, people must continue to participate.

• A Sound Economy

Public sector subsidies are needed not only to provide leisure and recreation services, but to provide all other social services such as health
care and sanitation. During periods of fiscal restraint, leisure and recreation services are often cut when a choice has to be made regarding the
allocation of limited public subsidies. No one can argue that the provision of health-care services, for example, should not receive precedence
over leisure and recreation services.

The decade of the 1990s commenced with a recession. The economy
improved, but with the onset of the new millennium, the Canadian economy once again faces turbulent times. This trend of bad economic times,
followed by good, then bad, is nothing new in Canada. In fact, since the
energy crisis of the early 1970s, Canada's economy has gone through a
number of ups and downs. As a result, public sector leisure and recreation has not had the opportunity to develop over a sustained long
period of time. A sound and stable economy would help public sector
leisure and recreation services not only to be maintained, but also to
evolve.

• A National Policy for Recreation

A national policy for recreation has been close to becoming a reality on a number of occasions, yet has failed to materialize. The only way for leisure and recreation to fully blossom in Canada is for the federal government to implement a national policy for recreation that not only sets governmental direction, but also solidifies the stance the government takes towards leisure and recreation. If leisure and recreation are indeed basic rights of the people, a national policy should exist justifying that this is so.

Currently, the federal government in Canada assumes by convention that leisure and recreation are important services in Canadian society. A national policy for recreation would take public sector leisure and recreation to the next level as the federal government would come out in strong support of leisure and recreation. If our federal government shows strong support through the passing of a national policy, public leisure and recreation services in Canada would continue to exist for years to come.

• The Establishment of a Federal Government Department or Branch for Leisure and Recreation

If a national policy for recreation is put forth, it would justify the formation of a federal government department or branch for leisure and recreation. The establishment of such a department or branch would give leisure and recreation a presence at the senior governmental level. Moreover, the establishment of such a department or branch would provide a base for provincial and municipal leisure and recreation services to grow through the direct assistance of the senior government.

A federal government department or branch would help steer the course of action for public sector leisure and recreation on a national scale. Yet, the establishment of a federal government department or branch for leisure and recreation would also go one step beyond directing public services; that is, it would acknowledge to society that leisure and recreation is a valued service of the Government of Canada. This would help maintain public sector leisure and recreation services in Canada for years to come.

CONCLUSION

Change in the provision of public sector recreation services is determined by government funding or government policy (Johnson and Johnson-Tew, 1999a). Over the past twenty years, there has been increasing cuts in public funding for the provision of recreation services. However, research by Johnson and Johnson-Tew (ibid.) indicates that, from 1988 to 1998, on average, public sector leisure opportunities in Canada have actually increased.

In 1985, Cor Westland constructed six reasons justifying why government should be involved in the recreation field: (1) government has a

FEDERAL LEADERSHIP REQUIRED

The only way for leisure and recreation to fully blossom in Canada is for the federal government to implement a national policy for recreation that not only sets government direction, but also solidifies the stance the government takes towards leisure and recreation.

responsibility to all citizens, in contrast to a private agency or club that, by its nature, limits its services to membership; (2) government has the required financial, physical and personnel resources or, if needed, the means to acquire them through taxation, expropriation or other legal means; (3) government has continuity, thus ensuring a degree of permanence in the provision of services, a permanence often lacking in private agencies that frequently depend on the efforts of a limited number of dedicated people; (4) government has the potential to provide services more economically than the private sector is able to do; (5) government possesses the mechanism needed for the planning, administration and management of its services; and (6) the public has come to expect and demand government services (Westland, 1985: 392).

The roles of leisure and recreation are recognized by the public sector in Canada. In 1987 the Ontario Ministry of Tourism and Recreation constructed ten guiding principles for the future of recreation. It is relevant to conclude this chapter with a presentation of these guiding principles as they provide an understanding as to how the public sector views leisure and recreation. These guiding principles are stated as follows:

- Recreation is a fundamental human need for persons of all ages and is essential to a person's physical and social well-being and to overall quality of life.

- Recreation services play a significant role in the creation of cohesive and quality communities.

- Recreation services should comply with the intent and spirit of the Charter of Rights and Freedoms and human rights legislation and should provide opportunities for both genders, all age groups, all ethnic groups and special interest groups.

- Recreation services should be commensurate with individual and collective interests and serve the need of the total community.

- The primary responsibility for identifying and meeting recreation needs rests with the individual.

- The responsibility for the provision of recreation opportunities beyond those supplied by the individual, is shared by all levels of government and many public, private and voluntary organizations.

- The geographic community is the focal point for recreation activity.

- The effective delivery of recreation services is dependent upon citizen participation and the commitment and capability of the community volunteers.

- The partnership between volunteers and professionals is an integral part of the recreation delivery system.

- Each municipality has the responsibility to ensure the availability of the broadest range of recreation opportunities for every individual and group consistent with available community resources and needs (p. 12).

CHAPTER 4: THE PUBLIC SECTOR

Study Questions

1. Although leisure and recreation do not appear in the Canadian Charter of Rights and Freedoms, it may be argued that certain fundamental freedoms relate to leisure and recreation. List these and explain how they may relate to leisure and recreation.

2. List three reasons why leisure and recreation departments exist in all levels of government.

3. Compare and contrast the primary clients for the three levels of government.

4. What is the focus of Sport Canada?

5. List five federal government departments, agencies and corporations that are indirectly involved with leisure and recreation.

Selected Websites

- **Manitoba Culture, Heritage and Tourism**
  http://www.gov.mb.ca/chc/rrs

- **Government of Canada**
  http://www.canada.gc.ca

- **Parliamentary Internet**
  http://www.parl.gc.ca

- **Environment Canada**
  http://www.ec.gc.ca

- **Ontario Ministry of Tourism and Recreation**
  http://www.tourism.gov.on.ca

Key Concepts

- **Democracy**
- **Charter of Rights and Freedoms**
- **Canadian Heritage**
- **Industry Canada**
- **Parks Canada**
- **National Recreation Statement (1987)**
- **Canada Sport Policy**

2004 Fishing & Outdoor Super Show, National Trade Centre, Toronto.
Photo: Courtesy of Ted Temertzolgu.

5

THE COMMERCIAL SECTOR

LEARNING OBJECTIVES

- To define commercial recreation.
- To describe the commercial recreation sector in Canada.
- To present trends in commercial recreation.
- To depict examples of types of commercial recreation organizations in Canada.
- To overview the positive and negative impacts of commercial recreation.

L eisure products and services are among the most important goods produced in the economy. If the true measure of economic activity is its ability to produce utility, then the commercial recreation sector plays a key role in Canada's economy.

This chapter introduces the commercial recreation sector. It commences with definitions of commercial recreation and proceeds to present trends in commercial recreation. Types of commercial recreation organizations are examined, followed by the presentation of the positive and negative impacts of commercial recreation. The chapter ends with a description of the basic principles necessary for the continued supply of commercial recreation in Canada.

"The superficiality of the American is the result of his hustling. It needs leisure to think things out; it needs leisure to mature. People in a hurry cannot think, cannot grow, nor can they decay. They are preserved in a state of perpetual puerility."

— Eric Hoffer (1902-1983), U.S. philosopher. *The Passionate State of Mind*, aph. 172 (1955).

DEFINITIONS OF COMMERCIAL RECREATION

Commercial recreation is the concept used to describe the services provided by the commercial sector of leisure and recreation. Simply put, commercial recreation refers to the provision of leisure and recreation services at a cost, with the ultimate intent to make a profit. Commercial recreation is a "business-oriented approach" used to offer leisure and recreation products and services to society.

The literature defines commercial recreation as "recreation for which the consumer pays and for which the supplier expects to make a profit" (MacLean, Peterson and Martin, 1985: 220). Moreover, commercial recreation has also been defined as "the provision of recreation-related products or services by private enterprise for a fee, with the long-term intent of being profitable" (Crossley and Jamieson, 1993: 6). Crossley and Jamieson (1993) go on to state that the definition of commercial recreation includes two key points: that of "recreation-related," meaning

Table 5.1: The Commercial Recreation Sector

Nature of Service	Cost Profit-Oriented
Service Orientation	Consumer Desire
Financial Base	Fees Revenue Corporate Sponsorship
Originating Authority	Individual/Corporation Initiative
Focus Clientele	Specific Market Group General Public

that it must include any product or service that supports a leisure, travel or tourism pursuit, and that of "long-term" intent, recognizing that if a service is not making a profit it will fail and cease to exist.

In both definitions, emphasis is made on investing money for personal profits. The business of commercial recreation is about achieving profits for financial gain and organizational survival (Johnson and Johnson-Tew, 1999; Karlis, 1995). Commercial recreation is "business about livelihoods, competition and survival" (Scott, 1998: 8). To guarantee its success, commercial recreation must provide a quality product and service to attract customers and/or a specific market group (Scott, 1998).

Commercial recreation is based on the willingness of the consumer to pay a price for a service. The provision and operation of commercial recreation services very much depends on consumer demand. For the commercial recreation industry to survive, the consumers of society must be willing to pay and must have a desire to consume a quality product. Moreover, the commercial recreation enterprise must utilize the necessary management, marketing and business means not only to best provide the needed services, but also to understand leisure trends at given time periods so as to ensure organizational survival.

TRENDS IN COMMERCIAL RECREATION

Crossley and Jamieson (1993) list five factors that have an impact on commercial recreation: (1) international, national, regional and local economic conditions affect the ability of people to spend for recreation and leisure; (2) demographic changes underlie significant changes in the market for recreation and leisure; (3) energy availability affects all forms of commercial recreation; (4) foreign policy, war and terrorist activity alters tourists' choices of destinations; and (5) new technology continually improves travel and recreation products, and entirely new concepts and/or products emerge.

The commercial recreation sector is a major part of the leisure industry, and throughout the history of Canada, it has witnessed tremendous growth. At certain times, this growth has been more rapid than in others. In general, however, growth in commercial recreation can be attributed to a number of trends, including social and economic trends.

During the infant years of the Dominion of Canada, the commercial sector of recreation was rooted in the establishment of local sporting clubs, such as rowing, golf and lawn tennis. On a broader, more national scale, commercial recreation began to expand with the establishment of Rocky Mountain Park. Enhanced accessibility to this natural area via rail led to the creation of a hotel to cater to the needs of travellers (Searle and Brayley, 2000). It was this expanded means of travel and the advent of the new aesthetic park with hotel facilities that enticed Canadians to pursue the luxuries of commercial recreation.

Commercial recreation tends to increase in popularity when people have free time, discretionary income and access to leisure services and products. After World War II, the number of hours worked by Canadians decreased, holiday time increased, and mass production of leisure products such as the television and automobile led to an increase in commercial recreation (Watson, 1988).

Commercial recreation such as travel and tourism decreases during times of economic uncertainty, energy crises and unsafe environments. For example, the energy crisis of the 1970s was accompanied by escalating fuel costs, thus reducing air and automobile travel. However, a study by Johnson and Johnson-Tew (1999a) reveals that, from 1988 to 1998, the number of commercial recreation opportunities increased in Canada, meaning that the recession of the early 1990s did not have much of an impact on the number of available commercial recreation opportunities. In fact, during this time period, it appears as though a steady growth took place in respect to the availability of commercial recreation opportunities (ibid.). Thus, economic uncertainties may not always decrease the willingness of citizens to pay for the services of commercial recreation.

In 1987, for example, the Ontario Ministry of Tourism and Recreations policy statement identified the private (commercial) sector as a key player in the future provision of leisure and recreation services. This has transpired in the leisure industry as the public sector has pulled away from holding the major responsibility for leisure and recreation, thus providing an expanded milieu for commercial recreation growth.

The 1980s and 1990s witnessed public sector cutbacks leading to the downsizing of recreation services. These changes also led to the contracting out of previously public sector-operated services such as ski resorts and golf courses to commercial recreation enterprises (Karlis, 1998b). During the past two decades, commercial recreation has experienced tremendous growth not only in its traditional stream of operations but also as a result of the contracting out of facilities and services.

Park Safari African" in Hemmingford, Que. Photo: Courtesy of James Karlis.

Widespread automobile use led to unique commercial leisure activities.

THE CANADIAN MUSIC INDUSTRY

The Business of Leisure and Recreation in Canada

Although we are geographically situated beside the United States, a nation that has historically produced a high number of popular musicians, Canadian musicians have also done well. A large number of music stars have developed and evolved out of Canada. Indeed, the commercial leisure and recreation sector has benefited tremendously from Canadian musical talent.

The music business is a multi-billion dollar commercial leisure and recreation industry. Music, whether live or recorded, is a popular form of entertainment enjoyed daily by almost all Canadians. Listening to music or being a part of the audience at a concert or music hall not only makes us feel good, but it also provides us with a diversion from the routine of our day-to-day lives. To achieve the "leisure state" provided by music, we, the consumers, are prepared to spend money, sometimes large sums of money, to be entertained by Canadian music and musicians.

Like all industries, the music business consists of entrepreneurs and consumers. The entrepreneurs are the musicians, the music writers, the producers, the recording companies, the radio stations, the stage crews and production companies, and all other individuals involved in putting together the music product and show. The consumers are the majority of over 30 million Canadians who listen to music daily.

Canadian musicians tend to receive a tremendous amount of support from Canadian radio and television stations and Canadian websites through the promotion of music tracks and compact discs. In turn, this leads to the exposure of Canadian talent and aids in the growth of the Canadian music industry.

The biggest income earners in the music business appear to be the performers. For example, we are willing to pay top dollar (well over $100 for a decent seat) to watch Celine Dion perform. Her talent has made her one of the most famous, and wealthiest, of all time. Her royal-like glamour awes Canadian citizens, as was evident by the fans who waited outside the Montreal Cathedral to catch a glimpse of her extravagant wedding.

Website for the 2004 Juno Awards.

The Juno Awards

In 1970, the Gold Leaf Awards, organized by Stan Klees and Walt Grealis, were held in the St. Lawrence Hall in Toronto. In 1971, the Gold Leaf Awards were re-named the Juneau Awards. This change was in honour of Pierre Juneau who was, at that time, the head of the CRTC. It was under Pierre Juneau that the Canadian Content Regulations were implemented in 1971. The spelling of the name of the awards then changed from "Juneau" to "Juno," the name of the mythological chief goddess of the Roman pantheon.

Today, more than thirty years later, the Juno Awards continue to recognize Canadian music and the achievements of Canadian musical artists. The media plays an active role in promoting the awards and the Canadian stars that partake in the award ceremonies.

Sources: <http://www.junoawards.ca>; <http://schwinger.harvard.edu/~terning/Canadians/musisians.html>.

Commercial recreation has expanded by promoting fads and trends through mass communication The television, radio, and most recently the Internet have been used as avenues to promote and encourage the use of commercial recreation services and products. Since the late 1990s, almost all Canadian households have had access to the Internet. It is not only a commercial recreation product in itself but is also a mass communication tool for the advertisement and promotion of commercial recreation services and products.

Another reason for growth in commercial recreation is that we are currently living in a consumer-oriented society (Foot, 2000; Karlis, 1998b). The media is constantly bombarding us with the latest trends, fads and services of leisure and recreation. Innovations in facility and equipment and improvements in the quality of products lead us, as consumers, to want to have the latest and the best. The commercial sector of leisure and recreation recognizes consumer-oriented needs and strives to provide a quality service and product for a price, often an expensive one. The commercial sector has responded to the "business opportunities" of leisure and recreation, and has recognized the need for innovative leisure and recreation goods, supply and services.

A further reason for growth in commercial leisure and recreation is the increase in the number of small businesses. In a study of three women operating a small business related to the leisure and recreation field (e.g., personal training, organizational development, transportation demand management, and alternative health), it was found that self-entrepreneurship helps in "reducing barriers in our lives," "reducing barriers in society," and "reducing barriers to success" (Rehman, 1999: 25-26). Thus, the desire to work for oneself and to be free from organizational bureaucracies has enticed individuals to establish small businesses and many of these are related to leisure and recreation.

The history of leisure and recreation in Canada reveals that it has not been long since Canadians have come to value leisure. Research by Farina (1969) indicates that, in the 1960s, some Canadians continued to have a negative viewpoint of leisure, equating it to idleness. The PARTICIPaction movement of the 1970s and more recently the introduction of the document *The Benefits of Parks and Recreation: A Catalogue* in 1992 by the Parks and Recreation Federation of Ontario and the Ontario Ministry of Tourism and Recreation helped change this negative image and enhance the value Canadians placed on leisure and recreation. Mass media and its portrayal of leisure and recreation as having "glamour" and as part of the "good life" have also helped increase its value. Its increased value has led to an increase in the number of services and products provided by the commercial recreation sector.

The nature of the commercial recreation sector in Canada very much stems from the entertainment business. In fact, "society reserves its highest pay for those who structure our leisure time" (Scott, 1998: 5). High fees and salaries are demanded and given to musical artists such as Celine Dion, Shania Twain and Bryan Adams, and athletes such as Jose

SUPPLY MEETING DEMAND

The commercial sector has responded to the "business opportunities" of leisure and recreation, and has recognized the need for innovative leisure and recreation goods, supplies and services.

BIGGER BUSINESS

For better or worse, the broad leisure industry, and more specifically commercial recreation, is now a major contributor to the creation of capital, resources and wealth within our society.

Theodore of the Montreal Canadians and Ed Belfour of the Toronto Maple Leafs. The reason why entertainers and athletes such as the afore-mentioned receive such large sums of money is that we are willing to pay top dollar to be entertained by these stars. Leisure, and more specifically, commercial recreation, is big business and helps boost the flow of capital within society.

The terrorist attacks of September 11, 2001, have had a dramatic impact on commercial recreation, in particular those services related to travel and tourism. Consumers are reluctant to fly or to travel to certain destinations. As the fortunes of businesses such as restaurants, entertainment and lodging are closely linked to travel and tourism, the impacts of the terrorist attacks have been felt by many industries in the commercial recreation sector.

TYPES OF COMMERCIAL RECREATION ORGANIZATIONS

Research on commercial recreation has attempted to provide classifications of the **types of commercial recreation** organizations yet the classifications vary from researcher to researcher.

According to Bullaro and Edginton (1986), commercial recreation services consist of five classifications: (1) travel and tourism, (2) entertainment services, (3) leisure services in the natural environment, (4) hospitality/food services, and (5) retail activities. For McIntosh and Goeldner (1984), there are four basic components: (1) transportation, (2) accommodations, (3) shopping, and (4) activities. For Crossley and Jamieson (1993), there are four types of commercial leisure and recreation services: (1) the travel/transportation industry, (2) the hospitality industry, (3) the local commercial recreation industry, and (4) facilitators (e.g., travel agencies, travel schools, and so forth).

For Ellis and Norton (1988), there are also four parts: (1) tourism, (2) local commercial recreation, (3) retail sales, and (4) manufacturing. Tourism is made up of destinations, activities and travel facilitation. In the case of Canada, destinations refer to a visit, for example, to the Parliament Buildings and the nation's capital. Activities refer to experiences such as those at theme parks (e.g., Canada's Wonderland north of Toronto), and travel facilitators refer to different transportation modes (e.g., Air Canada, Via Rail) and travel agents (e.g., services offered by the C.A.A.).

Local commercial recreation is divided into three types of services: outdoor commercial recreation, indoor commercial recreation, and clubs. Outdoor commercial recreation includes golf courses, ski resorts, fairs and carnivals, and theme and sport parks that are owned and operated by local residents. Indoor commercial recreation includes movies, plays, musicals, concerts, ballet facilities and banquet halls. Finally, "clubs" consists of three categories: (1) social, (2) health, and (3) sport and racquet clubs. Social clubs are restaurants and night clubs that are locally owned and operated. Health clubs are fitness clubs such as

Goodlife Fitness. Sport and racquet ball clubs are those that build on the health club concept and offer services such as tennis and racquetball courts.

Retail sales is a broad category of the commercial recreation sector. It includes sporting equipment such as C.C.M., clothing such as ROOTS, and larger items such as motor homes and recreation vehicles. Also included under retail sales are retail outlets such as department stores, catalogue shopping and Internet shopping.

Finally, manufacturing is a part of the commercial recreation industry as it includes the production of items such as hockey sticks, hockey pucks, motorcycles and recreation vehicles used in the commercial recreation sector.

In Canada, the commercial recreation sector is vast and diverse. It is made up of services such as travel and tourism, nightclubs and bars, music concerts and concert halls, fitness and health facilities, bowling lanes, tennis and racquetball clubs, yoga and aerobic studios, and golf courses and driving ranges. By no means is this list all-inclusive.

POSITIVE AND NEGATIVE IMPACTS OF COMMERCIAL RECREATION

Whenever a service such as leisure and recreation is provided for a price, positive and negative impacts exist. The "business" of leisure and recreation involves the flow of capital, usually in large sums. The cost for leisure and recreation services and/or products may thus have positive implications for some, yet negative for others.

Positive impacts of commercial recreation include: (1) increase in employment opportunities; (2) stimulation of local economies through increased commerce; (3) attraction of outside capital (new businesses, new investors for existing businesses); (4) increased property values; and (5) increased recreation opportunities for local residents (Crossley and Jamieson, 1993).

Negative impacts of commercial recreation include the following: (1) many types of commercial recreation have high failure rates and/or short life cycles, thus resulting in unemployment and decreased economic contribution to the local community; (2) crime can increase as tourists can be easy prey; (3) increased land values can backfire on young residents wishing to buy property for the first time; (4) natural resources can be overused to the point of ruining the attraction; and (5) local culture in rural or remote areas can be harmed (Crossley and Jamieson, 1993).

The goal of commercial recreation is to enhance the positive impacts while reducing the negative. Those seeking to operate a successful commercial recreation enterprise need to consider current social and economic trends and the barriers to participation for prospective clients (e.g., expense, lack of time, physical conditions, lack of interest, lack of skills, lack of companions, lack of knowledge, lack of safety and lack of transportation) (McIntosh and Goeldner, 1984; Epperson, 1977).

Photo: Sunshine Water Park, Toronto.

The "Sunshine Water Park" offers water-based activities for children and families.

Moreover, good management skills are of utmost importance in the commercial recreation sector as the leisure industry is people-based: managers must get the most out of people in order to provide the most to people (Scott, 1998).

THE BASIC PRINCIPLES FOR THE CONTINUED SUPPLY OF COMMERCIAL RECREATION IN CANADA

In Canada, the commercial recreation sector was based historically on the principle of providing a quality product for a quality price to those who could afford to pay. Early commercial recreation services in Canada such as the Royal Montreal Golf Club (1873), the Quebec City Golf Club (1874) and the London Curling Club (1879) were all established to provide leisure and recreation services of superb quality for a price.

Today, commercial recreation services rest on the same basic principle, but the challenges for these services are much more complex than they were in the late 1800s. First, the number of commercial recreation enterprises in Canada has expanded tremendously, thus making competition intense. Second, the growth in public sector leisure and recreation services has provided an alternative choice for participation at a lesser cost. Third is the rapid growth of the largest sector of the leisure and recreation industry; that is, the voluntary sector.

To enhance their probability of survival, a number of basic principles need to be maintained by commercial recreation enterprises in Canada. What follows is a description of some of these principles.

• Provide a quality product

Commercial recreation in Canada has survived historically through the provision of a quality product. The oldest and some of the more contemporary commercial recreation services in Canada have survived or continue to survive because they offer a quality product.

We all enjoy partaking in a quality leisure and recreation product, whether it is a fine dining experience or playing tennis on top quality tennis courts. In tough economic times, commercial recreation enterprises may attempt to reduce costs by providing a product that is not of top quality. Canadians have supported commercial recreation enterprises in the past because quality products have been offered. To sustain its survival, it is paramount that the commercial recreation sector continues to provide a quality product.

• Focus on service

Recreation is a service industry because it consists of the provision of a service with the end goal of satisfaction. Both people and products (e.g., computers, fitness equipment) provide recreation services. In the case of products, the people who manufacture, design and produce them

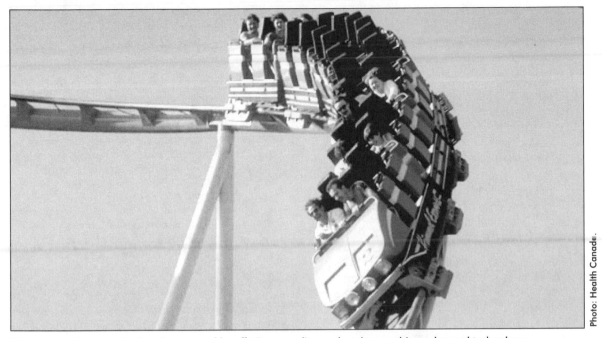

Photo: Health Canada.

Theme parks have survived and prospered by offering a quality product that combines play and technology.

for use in commercial sector enterprises need to produce quality goods that will provide a quality service.

Of utmost importance for the survival of commercial recreation services in Canada is the quality of people-oriented services. Leisure and recreation is a people-oriented profession, and when people are paying top dollar to be served, they expect "top-dollar" service in exchange. Commercial recreation enterprises that have survived in Canada are those that focus on people-oriented service. Goodlife Fitness, for example, offers its clients qualified personal trainers to help them achieve their personal fitness goals. Having someone provide you with a service goes a long way in determining whether or not you are satisfied with your commercial recreation experience. "Focus on service" has made Goodlife Fitness a long-term successful Canadian commercial recreation enterprise.

• Remain competitive

When the Royal Montreal Golf Club was established in Montreal in 1873, it had one big advantage – no competition. This club was the only one of its kind, not only in Montreal, but in North America. Today, however, hundreds of private golf clubs exist in Canada and North America.

To survive today, commercial recreation enterprises in Canada must be competitive. They must underprice the competition while offering a comparable quality product and service. Goodlife Fitness, one of the

COMMERCIAL RECREATION

Are We Prepared for the Future?

In the 1980s the once vibrant public sector in Canada began to face financial restraints and constraints. Unlike the 1960s and early 1970s, the federal government encountered a different scenario, one which led to the reduction and changing structure of the public sector.

The public sector has continued to downsize, reduce and do more with less, meaning that the commercial and voluntary sectors have had to compensate for the reduction in public sector leisure and recreation services. If this trend continues, leisure studies students will have to be prepared to face a changing leisure industry, one that relies on commercial recreation for service provision.

Below are two sets of suggestions to assist in preparing for the future of commercial recreation.

Suggestions for University and Community College Leisure Studies Curricula

- The commercial recreation sector has become one of the largest sectors in the leisure industry, and it is time to enhance the knowledge base passed on to students regarding this sector.

- Increasing the number of leadership courses in both university and college leisure studies curricula would help to prepare students for careers in commercial recreation.

- Aspiring leisure administrators in the leisure service industry, including commercial recreation, should take as many administration courses as possible in the school of business.

- Academic programs of leisure studies in both university and college would benefit greatly from hiring academic staff with practical experience in the commercial recreation industry.

- Internship coordinators must become aware of this need and increase the number of commercial sector student intern placements.

Suggestions for University and Community College Students

- Courses that are useful and extend beyond the basic knowledge given in "administration in leisure services" courses include strategic planning, human resource management, personnel management, micro-economics, budgeting and macro-economics.

- Volunteering in a commercial enterprise during your student years is a great way to acquire job skills, learn about the commercial sector, make professional contacts, "get your foot in the door" of an organization and gain valuable work experience.

- A part-time position in this area will provide benefits beyond the financial; it will help you to gain valuable "paid-work experience" in the commercial recreation industry.

- By going that extra mile and doing research (library, Internet, media), you will discover different means to succeed in this service sector while learning about the successes and failures of specific commercial recreation enterprises.

- Volunteering is only one means of networking and making contacts. Other means include presenting research at conferences, attending conferences and workshops, paid employment and introductions from friends, family and so forth. You will be surprised how many contacts you will make simply by exchanging cards and becoming more actively involved in the community.

oldest, biggest and most competitive health and fitness facilities in Canada, has remained competitive by offering promotions and special incentives (e.g., reduced initiation fees and membership rates) for new and existing members. These incentives help Goodlife Fitness maintain membership and remain competitive with other health clubs.

• Remain affordable

One of the biggest problems facing the sustained survival of many commercial recreation industries in Canada is cost efficiency. For example, both the Ottawa Senators and the Calgary Flames Hockey Clubs have experienced financial difficulties in recent years. Despite these difficulties, these clubs have made efforts to remain affordable commercial recreation experiences for fans by offering special ticket prices and promotions for various games throughout the season.

Remaining affordable is key to the success of many Canadian commercial recreation enterprises. Unlike public and voluntary sector organizations, commercial sector organizations rely heavily on sales. The price of a product needs to be carefully set so that it not only garners a profit for the commercial recreation business, but also remains affordable to the general public. By remaining affordable, commercial recreation organizations such as the Ottawa Senators and Calgary Flames Hockey Clubs increase their probability of survival.

• Be unique

Commercial recreation enterprises that are unique are often successful and therefore survive. Being unique means not only being different, but also offering an incentive that is attractive to users. One example of a commercial recreation enterprise in Canada that is unique is Putting Edge in St. Catharines, Ontario. This indoor mini-golf facility offers a "glow in the dark" mini-golf experience. To make this experience even more unique for participants, packages are offered that include pizza and all-you-can-drink soft drinks for the affordable price of $20.

Being unique means being able do something that the competition is not doing, or, at the very least, to be the first to offer something original. The desire to experience something unique can be used as a lure by the commercial recreation sector to attract participants away from more traditional leisure and recreation services offered by the public and voluntary sectors.

• Recognize leisure and recreation trends and fads

In recent years, the annual Canadian Parks and Recreation Association National Trade Show and Conference has been attracting more and more delegates from the commercial recreation sector. The reason for the increased appeal of this trade show and conference is the chance to learn and be first to find out about current leisure and recreation trends

SELLING RECREATION

- Quality products/services
- Unique products/services
- Prestige in participation
- Social networking
- Political and employment creation
- Media promotion

and fads. Through the exhibits of the trade show, commercial recreation entrepreneurs explore, first-hand, new ideas, equipment and services that could aid their organizations in providing up-to-date services.

The leisure and recreation needs of society are changing more rapidly than ever before. Mass communication devices, such as television and the Internet, constantly bombard us with new leisure trends and fads. In addition, we seem to grow bored sooner with our leisure and recreation experiences than we did in the past, perhaps as a result of knowing that alternative leisure and recreation choices exist. For commercial recreation enterprises to survive, they must remain ahead of the game by recognizing these fads and acting to fulfill them.

• Be cognizant of societal trends

In order for commercial recreation to survive, the provider must be familiar with the social trends of society, including demographics. To be cognizant of social trends means to know what has happened, to recognize what is currently happening, and to make a sound, educated guess as to what may happen.

Social trends tell us a number of things, such as the availability of discretionary income, work trends and living patterns. Demographics indicate the service and activity preferences of different age groups. For instance, we know that those born during the baby boom era are now approaching retirement with a greater leisure ethic, more knowledge and more money than previous generations. By being cognizant of societal trends, the commercial recreation sector helps to ensure its future survival.

CONCLUSION

Commercial recreation has become one of the largest sectors in the leisure and recreation industry. A number of factors have contributed to this growth, such as an increased value on leisure and recreation, consumerism, and the mass promotion of quality leisure and recreation products, services and activities through the media.

Prior to the terrorist attacks of September 11, 2001, tourism had developed as the prime commercial recreation service in Canada, but these events have had a drastic impact as travel to Canada has decreased tremendously. Although the Canadian Tourism Commission is optimistic of a full recovery for the Canadian tourism industry, it will take time.

Commercial recreation is a volatile business. Its success depends on recognizing leisure and recreation needs, and providing a quality service to address these needs while also making a financial profit. The success of commercial recreation enterprises is also affected by the state of the economy and workforce, the availability of discretionary income, and global events.

CHAPTER 5: THE COMMERCIAL SECTOR

Study Questions

1. Define commercial recreation.

2. List five factors that have an impact on commercial recreation.

3. What social factors have enticed an increase in commercial recreation in Canada?

4. What social trends have caused a decrease in certain forms of commercial recreation in Canada? Please explain.

5. Describe the three types of local commercial recreation presented in this chapter.

Selected Websites

- **Transportation Sector in Canada**
  http://canadaonline.about.com/cs/transportation

- **Starting a Sports or Recreation Business**
  http://www.entrepreneur.com/Your_Business/
  YB_SegArticle/0,4621,304291,00.html
  (Article from *Entrepreneur's Start-Ups Magazine*,
  November 2002, by Geoff Williams.)

- **Resort and Commercial Tourism Association**
  http://www.r-c-r-a.org

Key Concepts

- **Commercial recreation**

- **Types of commercial recreation**

- **Positive impacts of commercial recreation**

- **Negative impacts of commercial recreation**

6
THE VOLUNTARY SECTOR

LEARNING OBJECTIVES

- To overview voluntary sector terminology.
- To examine the nature of the voluntary sector and volunteerism in Canada.
- To explore the relationship between leisure studies and the voluntary sector.
- To present examples of voluntary leisure organizations in Canada.
- To introduce the Accord between the Government of Canada and the voluntary sector.

As a result of the reduction of public sector services in the 1980s and 1990s, a renewed interest in and need for voluntary sector leisure and recreation developed in Canada. As yet, despite this trend, little research exists on this sector of leisure and recreation in Canada.

This chapter examines the voluntary sector of leisure and recreation in Canada. The first part introduces the terminology used by the voluntary sector. The nature of the voluntary sector is explored, followed by an examination of volunteerism in Canada and the composition of the voluntary sector. The relationship between leisure studies and the volunteer sector is overviewed and the different types of voluntary leisure and recreation organizations are described. The chapter ends with a discussion of the Accord between the Government of Canada and the voluntary sector and a description of what is required for the survival of voluntary sector leisure and recreation organizations in Canada.

"The basis on which good repute in any highly organized industrial community ultimately rests is pecuniary strength; and the means of showing pecuniary strength, and so of gaining or retaining a good name, are leisure and a conspicuous consumption of goods."

— Thorstein Veblen (1857-1929), U.S. social scientist. *The Theory of the Leisure Class*, ch. 4 (1899).

VOLUNTARY SECTOR TERMINOLOGY

Research in the field of leisure studies reveals a lack of consensus regarding terminology in this field of inquiry. Terms such as "voluntary," "non-profit," "third sector" and "non-governmental organization" are often used interchangeably to describe voluntary leisure and recreation organizations. The reason for this lack of consensus is that the voluntary sector has been explored in different fields of study, and thus the terminology used to describe it has roots in different academic disciplines (Lohman, 1992; Thayer Scott, 1997).

THINKING LOCALLY

The voluntary sector is the leisure service sector that has the closest ties to local communities, as voluntary sector organizations are operated primarily by local volunteers.

The concept "voluntary sector" evolves out of the field of sociology, particularly studies of voluntary associations in British literature. The term "non-profit" comes from economics and reflects a model of market economics in which profits cannot be distributed to owners or share-holders. "Third sector" is a notion with origins in political science: government is the "first sector," the private sector is the "second sector" and the remainder of organizational life is referred to as the "third sector." The final term, "non-governmental organizations (NGOs)," evolves out of the international development community and social economy (Hall and Banting, 2000). Non-governmental organizations is a concept frequently used in Europe and Quebec (Jenson and Phillips, 2000).

The term used in this text is the "voluntary sector," because this term, as compared to the others, is more closely associated with social inquiry.

THE NATURE OF THE VOLUNTARY SECTOR

The **voluntary sector** is the area of service that has the closest ties to local communities, as voluntary sector organizations are operated primarily by volunteers. A large number of voluntary sector organizations are governed by volunteer boards and rely on the day-to-day services of volunteers to maintain and sustain services and operations. Voluntary sector organizations are thus about people providing a service for each other, for their respective organizations and for the community as a whole. The characteristics of voluntary sector recreation organizations are presented in Table 6.1.

Voluntary organizations range from formally operated organizations with written constitutions and elected and/or appointed officials to informal networks of individuals that come together to address specific needs and concerns (Arai, 2000/2001). The following examination of the nature of the voluntary sector focuses on five key features extracted from the **International Classification of Non-Profit Organizations (ICNPO)**, which was developed through a twenty-two nation comparative study by the John Hopkins Comparative Nonprofit Sector Project (Hall and Banting, 2000). These five key features are: (1) organized, (2) private, (3) non-profit distributing, (4) self-governing, and (5) voluntary.

"Organized" refers to the fact that the organization must, to some extent, be institutionalized. That is, the organization must have some degree of internal structure with set goals in order to give it a degree of organizational permanence. The organization must have a mandate, a vision and a target population.

"Private" is a term used to distinguish this type of organization from a governmental one. When an organization is "private," it is non-governmental; that is, "private" means distinct from the instrumentalities of government and the exercising of government authority.

The third feature, "non-profit distributing" is central to the nature of the voluntary sector. Simply put, "non-profit distributing" means that

Table 6.1: The Characteristics of Voluntary Recreation Sector Organizations

Nature of Service	Profit-Making for Sustaining Services
Service Orientation	Good for Selected Populations Good for Society/Community
Financial Base	Membership; Donations User Fees; Fundraising Corporate Sponsorships
Originating Authority	Individuals/Groups
Focus Clientele	Select Populations Local Communities General Public

the organization does not return generated profits to its owners or directors. Rather, registered profits are put into sustaining and maintaining the operation.

By being "self-governing," an organization is equipped to control its own activities. "Self-governing" means that the voluntary sector organization is autonomous and that decision making comes from within. The process of self-government means that the organization controls its own destiny.

The final feature, "voluntary," assumes that the organization has a significant degree of voluntary participation in the conduct of its activities (program volunteers) and/or the management of its affairs (voluntary members of the board of directors).

VOLUNTEERISM IN CANADA

Today, more so that ever, volunteerism has become essential for the delivery of leisure and recreational services in Canada. In an Ontario study, Larsen, Montelpare and Donovan-Neale state that "volunteers are an essential component in the delivery of many community leisure services" while "making a significant contribution in providing opportunities for leisure" (1992: 131).

But who are volunteers? For Morris (1969), volunteers are persons who undertake unpaid work for the community or for its individual members. For Sheard (1986), volunteering refers to unpaid activities people undertake of their own free will for the benefit of family, friends and the community. For Parker (1992), volunteering is about helping others, meaning the betterment of society and the enhancement of the quality of life of the individual doing the volunteer work. For Stebbins (2000/2001), volunteering, especially when it is a chosen activity, could be leisure.

WHY VOLUNTEER?

- Because most employers ask for work experience in addition to a degree/diploma in leisure studies. Volunteering is a good means to acquire this work experience.
- To get to know professionals in the industry while also providing professionals with an opportunity to get to know you, your skills, your talents, and your credentials.
- To acquire practical skills and knowledge that formal education do not provide.

The recruitment of volunteers and the actual sustaining of volunteer services is a difficult task. Volunteers need not only to be pleased with what they do but also be empathetically attached to the volunteer position and the organization offering the volunteer experience (Karlis, 2003). But what motivates people to volunteer? And what is the makeup of volunteerism in Canada? A study conducted by the Volunteer Centre of Ottawa-Carleton (1992) lists a number of incentives identified by volunteers who were involved in volunteer work. These include: (1) achievement, (2) recognition and feedback, (3) personal growth, (4) giving something back, (5) bringing about social change, (6) family ties, and (7) friendship.

Volunteerism in Canada is composed of a number of different groups of people. Research by Minshall (1984) describes seven types of volunteers (seniors, unemployed, teenagers and students, youth, families, persons with disabilities and law-breakers) and also indicates the reasons for volunteering on the part of each group. Seniors tend to volunteer in daytime programs and activities as volunteer work tends to fill time that was once "paid-work time." Persons who are unemployed may volunteer to regain self-esteem. Teenagers and students are often motivated to acquire new skills and education. Youth, particularly those who are from broken homes, may volunteer with seniors to substitute for missing grandparents. Families tend to volunteer to work together on community projects of interest. Persons with disabilities may volunteer to gain more active participation in the community. And law-breakers may volunteer to fulfill court orders of community service.

In 1987, over 5 million adult Canadians volunteered their services. In 1997, it was estimated that almost a third of the Canadian population engaged in volunteer work (Hall, Knighton, Reed, Bussiere, McRae and Bowen, 1998). More recently, figures released in 2001 by the Government of Canada's Voluntary Sector Initiative revealed that over 7.5 million Canadians volunteer.

In a recent article on patterns of volunteering over the life cycle of Canadians, Selbee and Reed (2001: 6) stated that "married individuals volunteer more than those who are single, divorced, widowed or separated. Individuals with children five years and under volunteer the least, those with children six and over volunteer the most, and those without children fall somewhere between." Moreover, Selbee and Reid (ibid.) mention that students and part-time workers volunteer more often than full-time workers and unemployed individuals. Students and part-time workers engage in volunteer work as they tend to have a different daily time schedule than full-time workers. In addition, students and part-time workers may have certain personal goals that they wish to fulfill as a result of volunteer work. These personal goals, may include, yet are not limited to the following: (1) getting "foot in the door" of a company or organization, (2) making professional and employment contacts, (3) building on personal resume, (4) gaining work experience, and (5) providing a service to society.

THE MAKEUP OF THE VOLUNTARY SECTOR IN CANADA

The voluntary sector in Canada is of diverse scope and size, with over 180,000 incorporated not-for-profit groups. The easiest way to determine its makeup is according to the primary types of goods or services provided. The International Classification of Non-Profit Organizations distinguished twelve types of voluntary sector organizations. These twelve types of voluntary sector organizations are shown in Table 6.2 and provide an overview of the voluntary sector in Canada.

In Canada, no central registry exists for voluntary organizations that are not registered charities. Therefore it is difficult to say how many of these organizations exist, how many are a part of the "culture and recreation" category, and what resources they depend on.

As the data that does exist on the voluntary sector is derived primarily from registered charities, this information does not provide a detailed comprehensive overview of the voluntary sector. However, it does provide some useful information. For instance, according to Revenue Canada (June 1999), there were 77,926 charities registered in Canada. Moreover, according to Hall and Macpherson (1997), only 3.9 percent of all registered charities are leisure and recreation organizations.

Most voluntary sector leisure and recreation organizations in Canada are not registered, and for this reason we cannot rely upon Revenue Canada or any other government department to provide details on them. What we do know about voluntary sector leisure and recreation organizations in Canada comes mostly from literature in the field of leisure studies.

LEISURE STUDIES AND THE VOLUNTARY SECTOR

Canadian-based research in leisure studies focusing on voluntary organizations has expanded tremendously during the recent past. There are articles that describe the condition of voluntary organizations, research depicting the use of different management approaches in voluntary organizations, and studies that focus on the volunteer and his or her role within the voluntary organization.

One study discusses how Management By Objectives (MBO) can be a useful approach for the sustainable process of operation for the future management of voluntary organizations (Karlis, 1989a). It argues that voluntary organizations operated by volunteer staff members may benefit from this approach as MBO offers access to decision making. MBO is presented as system of management in which unpaid staff of a voluntary recreation organization can become actively involved in shaping the course of action of the volunteer. In turn, it concludes that more active involvement in management decisions by volunteers will lead to a closer personal relationship between the organization and the individual. Thus, in small leisure and recreation organizations, a democratic approach to management consisting of input from both volunteers and management may be useful (Karlis, 1998).

Table 6.2: International Classifications of Non-Profit Organizations

Culture and Recreation: Includes organizations and activities in general and specialized fields of culture and recreation.

Education and Research: Includes organizations and activities administering, providing, promoting, conducting, supporting and servicing education and research.

Health: Includes organizations that engage in health-related activities, providing health care, both general and specialized services, administration of health-care services and health support services.

Social Services: Includes organizations and institutions providing human and social services to a community or target population.

Environment: Includes organizations promoting and providing services in environmental conservation, pollution control and prevention, environmental education and health, and animal protection.

Development and Housing: Includes organizations promoting programs and providing services to help improve communities and promote the economic and social well-being of society.

Law, Advocacy and Politics: Includes organizations and groups that work to protect and promote civil and other rights, advocate the social and political interests of general or special constituencies, offer legal services and promote public safety.

Philanthropic Intermediaries and Voluntarism: Includes philanthropic organizations and organizations promoting charity and charitable activities, including grant-making foundations, voluntarism promotion and support, and fundraising organizations.

International: Includes organizations promoting cultural understanding between peoples of various countries and historical backgrounds and also those providing relief during emergencies, and promoting development and welfare abroad.

Religion: Organizations promoting religious beliefs and administering religious services and rituals; includes churches, mosques, synagogues, temples, shrines, seminaries, monasteries and similar religious institutions, in addition to related organizations and auxiliaries of such organizations.

Business and Professional Associations, Unions: Includes organizations promoting, regulating, and safeguarding business, professional and labour interests.

Groups not elsewhere classified.

Source: Hall, M., and Banting, K.G. (2000). The nonprofit sector in Canada: An introduction. In K.G. Banting (Ed.) *The Nonprofit Sector in Canada.* Kingston: School of Policy Studies, Queens University. (pp. 1-28)

A subsequent study discusses how a centralized system of management may be useful for voluntary organizations. In a centralized approach, organizational goals are set by management and fulfilled by management and their employees. Large voluntary organizations, those consisting of over five hundred members and employees, tend to benefit more from a centralized approach to management than from a decentralized system of management (Karlis and Lithopoulos, 1991).

With respect to the differing approaches used to manage voluntary organizations, a further study mentions that managers in voluntary organizations must be fully aware of displacement principles and practices. Research of a voluntary ethnic community organization reveals that today, more than ever, recreation administrators must become cognizant of the changing recreation needs of a rapidly evolving society. Recreation managers must be prepared to implement the displacement of services rapidly and promptly (Karlis and Gravelle, 1997).

In his research on serious leisure, Stebbins (1982) presents volunteerism, amateurism activities and hobbyist pursuits as three types of serious leisure. Volunteerism is a form of serious leisure as it is undertaken with the intent of bettering society and the individual; that is, it is driven by altruistic, self-interested motives and freedom. Serious leisure is the voluntary activity that "captivates its participants with its many challenges and inherent complexity" (Stebbins, 2000/2001: 314).

Arai (2000/2001) describes the role volunteers play in community building in Canada. In her research she describes three **types of volunteers** in the leisure industry. The first type is called citizen volunteers. This group is characterized by individuals who become interested because of citizen concerns (e.g., healthy communities and poverty) and thus volunteer their efforts. The second type, techno volunteers, refers to individuals who have been recruited by organizations to accomplish specific tasks using a specific skill (e.g., fundraising, computer skills). The third type, labour volunteers, are directly involved in the provision of services in voluntary organizations (e.g., events and program planning, activity coordinator).

Recent research examined the levels of satisfaction for volunteers at the Francophone Games. The results indicated that individuals who volunteered were extremely satisfied with the experience. Moreover, volunteers at these games were interested in maintaining their volunteer involvement and claimed that they could identify with the experience (Larocque, Gravelle and Karlis, 2002).

Although volunteers give their time and efforts freely, voluntary organizations incur a number of organizational costs for things such as logistical support, developmental costs to recruit volunteers, training and development, and appreciation rewards and incentives (Sutherland, 1990). Labossiere and Gemmell (1989) present a series of increasing challenges that voluntary sector leisure and recreation organizations will need to address to attract volunteers and maintain survival. These challenges include understanding the trends in volunteering, anticipating future trends, recognizing effective techniques to manage volunteers, and understanding the nature of short-term, task-specific volunteer opportunities.

A further challenge facing volunteer organizations is the establishment of partnerships for sponsorships and funding. Research by McCarville, Flood and Froats (1996: 189) indicates that "interest in sponsorship is pervasive in the sport and leisure literatures." Sponsorship has

VOLUNTEERING JUST FOR FUN

Volunteerism is a form of serious leisure as it is undertaken with the intent of bettering society and the individual; that is, it is driven by altruistic, self-interested motives and freedom (Stebbins, 2000/2001).

CANADIAN PARKS AND RECREATION ASSOCIATION (CPRA)

The Canadian Parks and Recreation Association (CPRA) is the national voice for a vibrant grassroots network with partnerships that connect people who build healthy, active communities, and impact the everyday lives of Canadians.

The association was founded in 1945 as the Parks and Recreation Association of Canada (PRAC). PRAC was formed in a time of concern to deal with the changes and challenges expected after the Second World War, including the need to provide parks and recreation services. Twenty-five years later the association's name was changed to the Canadian Parks and Recreation Association.

Over the years the association has changed significantly. It has responded to changes in the social, economic and political climate in the past and will continue to do so in the future. It is an association driven by the interests of parks and recreation in Canada and by doing so, will change itself according to societal changes as they occur.

become an important means of acquiring needed resources, including financial support. Volunteers are called on to establish contact with corporations (e.g., McDonald's, Coca Cola and so forth) to solicit sponsorships. Usually corporations, in exchange for funds and donations, obtain the right to advertise at the event or volunteer centre. In most cases, however, the types of organizations that obtain sponsorships are those that offer sport rather than leisure events (Kindel, 1993).

Volunteerism has become a sophisticated activity requiring serious commitments by both the volunteer and the voluntary organizations. The voluntary leisure and recreation organization, and more specifically the recreationist within it, needs to recognize the dynamic characteristics of volunteers so that volunteerism can operate effectively (Larsen and Montelpare, 1990).

TYPES OF VOLUNTARY LEISURE AND RECREATION ORGANIZATIONS

A document put forth by the Ontario Ministry of the Attorney General (2000) provides a detailed classification of four broad categories of non-profit, non-charitable corporations: (1) athletics and sports, (2) arts, (3) business and professional groups, and (4) community.

The athletics and sports category consists of the following types of organizations: (1) aquatics, (2) athletics clubs, (3) curling, (4) fishing and hunting (rod and reel) clubs, (5) flying, (6) golf, (7) health clubs, (8) hockey, (9) riding, (10) skating, (11) snowmobiling, (12) swimming, and (13) yachting. The arts category consists of dance, theatre, literary, music, and photography clubs. The business and professional groups category is made up of businesswomen and businessmen fellowship clubs, employees' associations, merchants' associations, professional associations and trade associations. The largest of all categories, the community, is made up of fifteen types of organizations: (1) community associations, (2) community centres, (3) community clubs, (4) conservation, (5) ethnic, (6) fraternity/sorority, (7) historical, (8) home and school associations, (9) lobbying, (10) research and/or scientific, (11) residents, (12) service clubs, (13) social clubs, (14) social service organizations, and (15) women's affairs.

The aforementioned report reveals the depth and magnitude of the voluntary leisure and recreation sector in Canada. What follows is a brief overview of a few such organizations.

• The Canadian Parks and Recreation Association (CPRA)

In 1945 the Parks and Recreation Association of Canada was founded. This association was the forerunner of the **Canadian Parks and Recreation Association (CPRA)**, a voluntary leisure service organization that acts as a national voice for leisure professionals, practitioners and participants throughout Canada's provinces and territories.

The intent of the CPRA is to bring together Canada's people in order to build healthy, active communities to better the day-to-day lives of Canadians. The mission of the CPRA is to: (1) act as a national voice for parks and recreation in Canada, (2) build and nurture partnerships in the recreation industry, (3) advocate for parks and recreation as being essential for individual, family and community health and well-being, (4) communicate and promote the many benefits and values of parks and recreation throughout Canada, (5) address the diverse and changing needs of members, and (6) provide educational opportunities to enhance our understanding of parks and recreation.

• The Canadian Fitness and Lifestyle Research Institute

The **Canadian Fitness and Lifestyle Research Institute** is a registered not-for-profit applied research organization that has existed since 1980. The intent of this organization is to create and communicate knowledge on physical activity, the determinants of physical activity, and the outcomes of physical activity. The end goal is to provide relevant research that will assist individuals, professionals and policy-makers in improving the lifestyles of Canadians, thus resolving health, societal and economic issues.

As an applied research organization, the activities of the Canadian Fitness and Lifestyle Research Institute are as follows: (1) the monitoring of change in the physical activity and health status of Canadians, (2) the development of research priorities and recommendation strategies to increase physical activity levels for reducing the public health burden of sedentary living, (3) assisting governments in policy development and the setting of goals for enhancing the physical activity and fitness levels of the Canadian populations, (4) increasing individual awareness of the benefits of an active lifestyles through the synthesizing and interpreting of research knowledge, (5) helping health, fitness and well-being related agencies to establish effective policies and programs, and (6) identifying needs for further research while also developing the scientific understanding of physical activity.

• The Canadian Association for Health, Physical Education, Recreation and Dance (CAHPERD)

Unlike the previous two national organizations, the **Canadian Association for Health, Physical Education, Recreation and Dance (CAHPERD)** focuses on youth. The primary objective of this national, charitable, voluntary-sector organization is to enhance physically active and healthy lifestyles for Canadian children and youth. The mission of CAHPERD centres on advocating and educating for quality physical and health education programs within supportive school and community environments.

The Canadian Parks and Recreation Association believes parks are essential to well-being.

Photo: Toronto Parks and Recreation Association.

SIZE AND IMPACT OF THE VOLUNTARY SECTOR

It may be argued that the voluntary sector is the largest of the three service sectors in Canada. In the volunteer sector, a great many different types of organizations directly or indirectly offer leisure and recreation services and opportunities.

• The Canadian Association for Leisure Studies (CALS)

The **Canadian Association for Leisure Studies (CALS)** was established in 1981 during the Third Canadian Congress on Leisure Research at the University of Alberta in Edmonton. The intent of CALS is to act as an avenue for international and Canadian scholars and practitioners for the sharing of leisure and recreation research. CALS has three main purposes: (1) the awarding of the triennial *Canadian Congress on Leisure Research*, (2) the maintenance of an electronic mail discussion list for the exchange of information among leisure and recreation scholars and practitioners, and (3) the dissemination of research through the publication of the peer-reviewed journal *Leisure/Loisir*.

• Parks and Recreation Ontario (PRO)

Parks and Recreation Ontario (PRO) is a not-for-profit corporation formed in 1995. PRO is concerned with enhancing the quality of life, health and well-being of the people of Ontario. The goals of PRO are: (1) to promote the value and benefits of parks and recreation, (2) to influence public policy and legislation for parks and recreation, (3) to provide the services of professional and volunteer development to members, and (4) to provide members with an opportunity to address common interests and opportunities.

• The Ontario Research Council on Leisure (ORCOL)

The **Ontario Research Council on Leisure (ORCOL)** was founded in 1975 to promote and disseminate research on recreation, leisure, sports, fitness, culture and tourism. At that time, ORCOL's major reason for being was "the support, promotion, and publication of applied recreation research" (Heywood, 2000/2001: 9). In the early years of the organization, the Government of Ontario played an active role in encouraging it to address the needs of the practice and the practitioner through research that related to the applied settings of recreation.

Today, ORCOL has become largely self-reliant. Its membership consists of leisure and recreation scholars and practitioners concerned with the advancement of leisure research throughout Ontario and Canada. One of its major tasks is to co-operate with the Canadian Association for Leisure Studies in the development of the journal *Leisure/Loisir*.

• The Chebucto Boys and Girls Club (Nova Scotia)

The Chebucto Boys and Girls Club has existed since 1996. Its objective is to help children build self-esteem and to develop strong social skills through various recreational and educational programs. More specifically, the mission of the club is to work with families and young adults so that youth can be offered opportunities to develop skills, knowledge and values. Programs include school programs, day camps, sports nights and youth drop-in evenings.

• **The Hellenic Orthodox Community of Calgary**

The Hellenic Community of Calgary has existed since 1957, with the intent of providing religious, recreational and philanthropic services to its members of Hellenic and non-Hellenic descent. This ethnic community organization strives to promote Hellenic culture within Canada through its many recreational and non-recreational services. As with other ethnic community organizations in Canada, its goal is to provide services, including recreation, to the needs of immigrants and their descendants while helping to preserve ethnicity in this multicultural society. Ethnic community organizations such as this one play a vital role in contributing to the voluntary sector of leisure and recreation (Burnet and Palmer, 1988).

THE ACCORD BETWEEN THE GOVERNMENT OF CANADA AND THE VOLUNTARY SECTOR

In December 2001, the Government of Canada and the voluntary sector in Canada worked together to establish the basis for a framework agreement referred to as the Accord. The Accord has been established in the context of the **Voluntary Sector Initiative** whose long-term objective is "to meet the challenges of the future and to enhance the relationship between the sector and the federal government and their ability to serve Canadians" (Corporate Author, 2002a: 34).

The major focus of the Accord is to bring together the public and voluntary sectors. Today, as government has legislated a greater mandate for the provision of recreation services to the voluntary sector, the Accord assists to bridge the gap between these two sectors so that a collaborative relationship can be formed. More specifically, the Accord "documents shared values, principles and commitments that will shape future practices, including the right of each to independence, including the voluntary sector's right, within the law, to challenge public policy and advocate for change" (Corporate Author, 2002a: 34).

The Accord is based on the guiding principles of: (1) independence, (2) interdependence, (3) dialogue, (4) co-operation and collaboration, and (5) accounting to Canadians. Moreover, it offers the voluntary sector: (1) a stronger voice than in the past for expressing concerns and needs, (2) streamlined government rules and regulations, (3) more opportunities to engage in public policy development, and (4) increased access to new technologies, training and research.

The Accord affirms the importance of what has traditionally been known as the "third sector" of society. By collaborating in the creation of this Accord, the Government of Canada recognizes that the voluntary sector, the sector in which the greatest number of leisure and recreation organizations exist, is critically important for addressing the needs of society, including leisure and recreation. Its creation also indicates how future leisure and recreation needs of Canadians will increasingly be addressed by the voluntary sector.

ONTARIO RESEARCH COUNCIL ON LEISURE (ORCOL)

The Ontario Research Council on Leisure was founded in 1975. It promotes and disseminates research articles on a number of topics concerning recreation and leisure including sports, fitness, culture and tourism.

The council is composed of researchers in the leisure field from government, academe and consultancies to other agencies. The council draws its members from a wide range of people who are interested in leisure and recreation research.

The council is responsible for the publication of the *Journal of Applied Recreation Research* and *Recreation Research Review.*

A PROFILE OF CARIBANA

By: Patrick Shepperd

Caribana began as the dream of enthusiastic individuals from diverse backgrounds but with a common West Indian heritage. They called their organization the Centennial Committee. On July 28, 1967, it was formally incorporated as the Caribbean Committee for Cultural Advancement, but later changed to the Caribbean Cultural Committee-Caribana (January 15, 1969). Their dream was the construction of a monument of goodwill, a confirmation of Caribbean culture and a statement of belonging to their adopted land, Canada.

This dream was forged in the heady days of 1967, when Canada was celebrating its Centennial and the West Indian community was asked to make a contribution which would enhance the celebrations of Expo '67. It took the form of a colourful parade down Yonge Street. George Bancroft, former executive director in the Ministry of Culture and Recreation, wrote in Caribana's 1980 *Souvenir Magazine*:

Caribana celebration.

> I saw the first [parade] in 1967. It was spontaneous, exuberant and a lot of fun. This was organized, I believe, by Dr. Al Liverpool and his colleagues. I recall this first venture was made to coincide with the celebration of our Canadian Centenary. I remember the groups assembling on Bloor Street outside the Varsity Stadium . . . and proceeding east along Bloor to Yonge, then down Yonge Street. It was one of the first grand public statements of the West Indian presence in Canada.

The dream persists today for over 200,000 revellers, well-wishers and patrons, who celebrate in the parade down University Avenue or on Olympic Island in late July and early August each year.

Caribana's struggles over the last seventeen years are part of the painful learning experiences of a non-profit organization endeavouring to stage one of Canada's major tourist attractions. These experiences would have been sufficient to daunt the spirit of most volunteer organizations and to cause their early demise. However, Caribana has tenaciously survived throughout these years. The survival and success of Caribana is the story of the men, women and children in the community who have played a role in its support.

What were the guiding principles of the organization, and how were these principles followed? What aims were enunciated and how successful was Caribana in achieving them? As stated by Romain Pitt, a Toronto lawyer born in Grenada who was one of the founding directors:

> "The most important thing to remember was that there were three features in designing the organization. We wanted a large board of directors. We decided, on the basis of the history of failures of other organizations, it was important to have enough people to do the job. As a result of that decision, the odds were that we could attract highly skilled (and influential) people to the Board.
>
> The Board had to be apolitical. By virtue of its decision not to take political sides, it would be possible to have people of many different persuasions working together. Membership was voluntary. The Letters Patent state that the directors shall serve . . . without remuneration, and no director shall directly or indirectly receive any profit from his position.
>
> Because of the size of the Board, there would always be a core of dedicated and unselfish people to call on."

Photo: Canadian Tourism Commission.

The organization has consistently maintained these principles throughout the years even though a twenty-one-member board has been unwieldy at times. In October 1983, through constitutional amendment, the number was reduced to fifteen.

The committee's first aim was the promotion of Caribbean culture. Culture is loosely defined as the manifestation of a people's heritage through the spoken and written word, song, dance and works of art. In this area Caribana has been eminently successful in planning, organizing, promoting and displaying the best available components of West Indian artistic talent in Toronto. The second aim was to acquire, maintain and operate a community centre. Other aims refer to the recognition and support of similar organizations; the sponsorship of events of a social or recreational nature; the acquisition and use of gifts in the furtherance of these aims and the undertaking of financial endeavours in the pursuit of its objectives. However, the objectives were more difficult to achieve than originally anticipated. The difficulties experienced resulted partly from the nature of the organization, its structure and its role in the community.

The form and function of the organization changed considerably over the years. What was originally conceived as a celebration for a single event in 1967 became a continuing program. Liverpool—a medical practitioner at Doctor's Hospital in the College-Spadina Avenue area—was the driving force behind the formation of the Centennial Committee. He and his group contacted various West Indian island governments to obtain their support in the venture. The response was tremendously positive. Local Toronto businessmen and community groups were also extremely excited by the prospect of participating in this event. Al's drive and infectious enthusiasm were helpful in attracting support.

The committee's tasks were made easier by the excitement generated by the commitment of local and West Indian governments, airlines, tourist boards, artists and interested individuals. For the first time in Canada a West Indian exposition of cultural events that would parallel Canada's main event, Expo '67 in Montreal, was going to be staged in Toronto. As a result of the strong, positive community response, the Centennial Committee decided with the support of Metropolitan Toronto and the City of Toronto

Councils to hold the event on Olympic Island for one week. The Centennial Ball at Casa Loma and the parade of costumed bands down Yonge Street began the show. Eric Lindsay, a lawyer and founding director, said:

> We are pleased that the West Indian governments were prepared to contribute artistic talent and to pay for the transportation of the artists from Trinidad, Jamaica, etc. Local businessmen, individuals and groups also gave unstintingly of their resources of time, money, expertise and products. Contributions of plants, straw hats, food, posters, advertisements, promotions, were happily made. We had good help, plenty of it and at little or no cost.

The 1967 celebrations were successful in terms of impact on the community—the demonstration of the capability of a volunteer group with no prior experience to orchestrate one week of intense activity and the satisfaction of the participants in the celebration of a national event. The success of the 1967 celebrations was due in large measure to the donations, assistance and contributions of the emerging Black community and the active participation of mainstream Canada in a colourful and happy affair.

In 1968 Caribana harnessed the energy and drive that was built up with the momentum of 1967. The focus was placed on doing something for the West Indian community, which created changes in the growth of the organization. The Cultural Committee felt that in the emerging West Indian community—composed mainly of graduates, students, businessmen and recent immigrants—there was a need to provide social services such as assistance with immigration matters.

In addition to Caribana shows, the committee pursued its social objectives by sponsoring interpretative dance classes in 1969 and 1970, together with a drama group that presented two plays by Caribbean playwrights, the formation of a steel band, and the provision of practice facilities and the sponsorship of lectures and seminars for new immigrants from the Caribbean to aid their understanding of and adjustment to Canadian life. From October 1970 to April 1971, the committee offered temporary accommodation to the Black Youth Organization, whose primary purpose was to assist underprivileged Black youth.

Non-West Indians who were previously active in the organization and in the development of the festival became onlookers. The organization, now called the Caribbean Committee for Cultural Advancement, was structured around a board of directors, whose executive committee was responsible for the formal administration of the organization. The remaining six directors contributed ideas, suggestions and advice through ad-hoc subcommittees. The main subcommittees dealt with business, social and cultural activities, research, public relations and recreation. A Carnival subcommittee, composed of members and band leaders, was formed to organize and plan the Caribana parade, which was increasing in size and complexity. Like most volunteer organizations, the committee relied on assistance from members and supporters to perform the many functions associated with staging such an event, from the development and distribution of print material to the erection of stage lights. Archibald Bastien, a founding director and a professional engineer, worked closely with city officials in providing electric power to Olympic Island. Individuals, such as Peter Marcelline, a City Planner and long-standing founding member, donated their vacation time to perform many functions from the collection of tickets to the dispensing of beer.

In 1967 community support for Caribana was given in time, money and expertise. However, in the ensuing years, this same support was left to the organization itself. The expense of renting halls, an office, equipment, booths, island ferries, chairs and tables and providing for artists' fees, prize monies, printing, advertising, security and insurance was increasingly difficult to meet. The organization was forced to appeal to the provincial government for assistance. This situation deteriorated to the extent that in 1974 the chairman, Mr. Elmore Daisy, presented to the province a brief in which he wrote:

> The Caribana festival is our major source of revenue. While we can justifiably claim that the past six Caribana events have been culturally successful, we have been able to realize only minimal amounts of net revenue. The 1970 Extravaganza experiment left us with a deficit of some $16,000 which we have reduced to some $2,500 total indebtedness. In brief then, net profit from each year's function was barely sufficient to enable the organization to keep functioning on a year-round basis.

> We therefore request that you consider favourably this application for a grant of $25,000 in support of general activities and to finance in part our planned community activities on a continuing basis.

The grant request was denied. Shorn of support in 1974, without viable assets and already committed to the event, directors signed personal loan guarantees to obtain the needed funds. Two years later, the province awarded a rival group of Carnival band leaders, called the Carnival Development Association, $20,000 to stage a Carnival parade scheduled for Caribana week. At that time, the committee received only a permit for the same event.

For the next five years, 1976-81, the future of the organization was in doubt. Other groups captured the essence and spirit of Carnival and built upon the concept to stage various summer productions. George Lowe, the first treasurer and a member of the Centennial Committee, said in reference to the Centennial parade: "It was the first time that West Indians had given anything to Canada. You can now see the effects in other parades where the costumes are much more colourful and people seem to enjoy themselves more on the street."

While the impact of colour was indeed significant in other street festivals in Toronto, it was not until the expected summer Caribana festival was threatened, because of increasing deficits in 1982 and 1983, that provincial grants in excess of $7,500 were made available to the group.

The present organization looks to a future bright with hope. New directions are being pursued with a more efficient organization. The Ministry of Citizenship and Culture has committed its support together with the assistance of the Metropolitan Toronto Police Force. Caribana's place in the history of the city as a multicultural centre is assured.

───────
Source:
<http://www.coconutpalmz.com/caribana/history.htm>.
From: Polyphony Summer 1984, pp. 135-139; © 1984 Multicultural History Society of Ontario. Reproduced by permission of the Multicultural History Society of Ontario.

THE SURVIVAL OF VOLUNTARY SECTOR LEISURE AND RECREATION ORGANIZATIONS IN CANADA

Almost any association can be classified as a leisure and recreation organization, regardless of whether or not leisure and/or recreation appears in the name of the organization or in its mission statement. All voluntary sector leisure and recreation organizations have one thing in common, however – a reliance on the efforts of members and volunteers for sustained survival.

Below are suggestions that may sustain voluntary sector leisure and recreation organizations in the future.

• Rely on members

Membership is the "backbone" and "heartbeat" of voluntary sector leisure and recreation organizations. These organizations rely on their membership not only to carry out day-to-day tasks, but to provide volunteer work whenever necessary. Membership is also a source of funds in the form of membership fees and donations.

In the case of the YMCA/YWCA, active membership has not only helped this organization expand throughout Canada, but to survive for over 125 years. Its members make their contributions through volunteer work and membership, and they also have an opportunity to participate in deciding which types of leisure and recreation activities need to be offered.

• Know your membership

What has helped the YMCA/YWCA survive is that the administration of this organization understands the needs of its members. With the changing of generations, leisure and recreation needs also change. The YMCA/YWCA has managed to keep pace with changing times and has altered services to cater to the leisure and recreation needs of today's membership.

The administrative bodies of ethnic community organizations may face the greatest challenge in knowing their membership. Many of Canada's immigrants who arrived between 1950 and 1970 have been the founding members of many of the ethnic community organizations in Canada, and they continue to be a part of their administrative structures. If these organizations are to survive, the elder administrative officers must know the needs of their younger members and potential members to provide better services.

Moreover, volunteer-operated interuniversity organizations such as chess or badminton clubs often experience a change in membership from year to year. The challenge for clubs such as these is to continue to address the needs of members while "knowing" and "recognizing" the unique participation goals of new members year after year.

WITHOUT THEM, NOTHING

All voluntary sector leisure and recreation organizations have one thing in common – a reliance on the efforts of members and volunteers for sustained survival.

- **Invest in leisure and recreation.**

Leisure and recreation experiences and opportunities attract individuals to become members in voluntary sector leisure and recreation organizations. For voluntary sector leisure and recreation organizations to survive, leisure and recreation must come to the forefront of their agenda. In the case of ethnic community organizations, administrators would be wise to incorporate leisure and recreation in mission statements and organizational constitutions.

- **Invest in the future**

Voluntary sector leisure and recreation organizations invest in their future by maintaining membership and by seeking to bring in new members. By recognizing the changing demographic makeup of a voluntary organization, action can be taken. This action can lead to a number of outcomes such as the establishment of new facilities and resources. For instance, many ethnic community organizations in Canada, such as the Hellenic Community of Ottawa and District, have established seniors' recreation centres as a means of investing in their future.

A classic example of investing in the future is the Canadian Soccer Association. Since 1912 this organization has continued to grow steadily by investing in the future through the analysis of participation trends. Today, more than twenty board directors continue to strive to address the needs of future soccer players in Canada.

- **Fundraising**

Fundraising is an ongoing task for all voluntary sector leisure and recreation organizations as its survival and the continuous expense of operating it depends on capital at hand. For this reason, many such organizations are operated like a business, having a few paid staff members (e.g., secretaries, community centre managers, custodians, and so on), and a financial reserve.

In addition to its membership drives, donation campaigns, bake sales and so forth, the Hellenic Community of Ottawa and District offers the largest Greek Festival in Canada each August. This ten-day event is put together by volunteers who prepare Greek food, entertain with Greek folk dances, and present their talents in cultural works of arts and displays. This fundraising event attracts thousands from the Ottawa area and elsewhere and has become the biggest annual fundraising event of this organization.

Perhaps the best example of fundraising happens on the doorsteps of Canadian households every Saturday as young girls and boys sell raffle tickets or chocolate bars to collect money for team travel and tournaments. Not only do these young athletes depend on this fundraising, but the organizations rely on it to keep membership fees to a minimum.

VOLUNTEERS—THE KEY TO SUCCESS

Ethnic Community Festivals

One of the major challenges that ethnic community organizations face is the generation of revenue. Despite the fact that Canada is a multicultural society, ethnic community organizations rely primarily on the fund-raising efforts of volunteers for income generation, as minimal assistance, if any, is received from government programs.

In order to accumulate funds, ethnic community organizations have traditionally relied on membership fees, donation campaigns within membership, bake sales, craft sales, luncheons and cultural dances. All of these means of generating income are fine, yet the returns are barely enough to ensure survival of the organization.

Case Study — Greek Festival

For ten days each August, the Hellenic Community of Ottawa holds one of the most successful ethnic community festivals in North America. In fact, this festival has been referred to by many Greek-Canadians as being the most successful Greek festival in Canada. "Success" for this festival is defined in three ways: (1) its contribution to the multicultural fabric of Canada and the City of Ottawa, (2) the degree of satisfaction for both Greeks and non-Greeks, and (3) the generation of income for the ethnic community.

After recognizing that more funds were required to guarantee survival and to expand its services, the Hellenic Community of Ottawa decided to turn its one-day Greek Festival into a ten-day event. Volunteer members planned, coordinated and implemented activities and also placed their efforts in providing a quality product for both Greeks and non-Greeks alike.

Volunteer members start food preparation months in advance for this ten-day event. In addition, each year a different volunteer festival chairperson is assigned to oversee and direct the entire event. A volunteer recruitment campaign within the community membership commences three months before the festival to make sure that all necessary volunteer positions needed to successfully run the festival are filled.

Volunteers are at the heart of ethnic festivals such as the Greek festival in Ottawa.

Photo: Ccourtesy of James Karlis.

The recruiting, scheduling and assignment of volunteer positions is also coordinated by volunteer members. With the exception of paid security and custodial help, the Hellenic Community of Ottawa's Greek Festival is operated by volunteer members, which translates into greater financial profit for the organization.

This festival is a classic example of "working for leisure through leisure." Volunteer members who devote time to this festival always appear to be enjoying themselves throughout the ten-day event. Volunteer members also enjoy the monetary gains that this festival generates for their ethnic community as the past few years have witnessed the renovation and expansion of the community hall and the creation of a seniors' recreation centre.

• Seek public sector assistance

In the past, public sector departments such as Heritage Canada have provided grants to voluntary sector leisure and recreation organizations. Today, however, public sector subsidies are under restraint and less and less financial assistance is available. This trend, however, may change. Administrators of voluntary sector leisure and recreation organizations would be wise to keep informed about grant programs or other forms of assistance that may be offered through the public sector.

• Establish an organizational culture

Voluntary sector leisure and recreation organizations that continue to exist, such as the YMCA/YWCA and the Canadian Parks and Recreation Association, have done a great job in establishing membership identity. People are proud to say that they are members. This identification with the organization goes a long way towards shaping the culture of the organization as the culture of the individual becomes a part of the organization's culture.

An organization that has established a strong organizational culture is more likely to survive. The "way of life" offered by such organizations becomes well known and potential members may be attracted to join.

CONCLUSION

The voluntary sector is the service sector that has the closest ties to the community. The voluntary sector relies on volunteers for the provision and operation of leisure and recreation services and is based on "people serving people"; that is, on volunteers serving the leisure and recreation needs of the community and themselves.

The voluntary sector in Canada consists of over 180,000 incorporated non-profit groups and is the sector in which the bulk of leisure and recreation organizations are housed. Despite this, little research has been conducted in leisure studies in Canada in this area. To better understand the role the voluntary sector plays in the leisure industry, more research is required.

There are many types of voluntary leisure and recreation service organizations in Canada. This chapter provided only a brief overview of a few of these organizations. Of these, the Canadian Parks and Recreation Association plays a major role in bringing leisure and recreation professionals together to address leisure and recreation concerns in Canada.

CHAPTER 6: THE VOLUNTARY SECTOR

Study Questions

1. Why does a lack of consensus exist in voluntary sector terminology?

2. List and explain the characteristics of voluntary sector leisure organizations.

3. List and explain the five key features of the John Hopkins Comparative Nonprofit Sector Project.

4. Briefly describe the makeup of the voluntary sector in Canada.

5. What do the findings of Selbee and Reed's study reveal?

Selected Websites

- **Parks and Recreation Ontario**
  http://www.prontario.org

- **Recreation Nova Scotia**
  http://www.recreationns.ns.ca

- **Saskatchewan Parks and Recreation Association**
  http://www.spra.sk.ca

- **Alberta Recreation and Parks Association**
  http://www.sport.ab.ca

- **British Columbia Parks and Recreation Association**
  http://www.bcrpa.bc.ca

Key Concepts

- **Voluntary sector**

- **International Classification of Non-Profit Organizations (ICNPO)**

- **Volunteerism**

- **Types of volunteers**

- **Canadian Parks and Recreation Association (CPRA)**

- **Canadian Fitness and Lifestyle Research Institute**

- **Canadian Association for Health, Physical Education, Recreation and Dance (CAHPERD)**

- **Canadian Association for Leisure Studies (CALS)**

- **Parks and Recreation Ontario (PRO)**

- **Ontario Research Council on Leisure (ORCOL)**

- **Voluntary Sector Initiative**

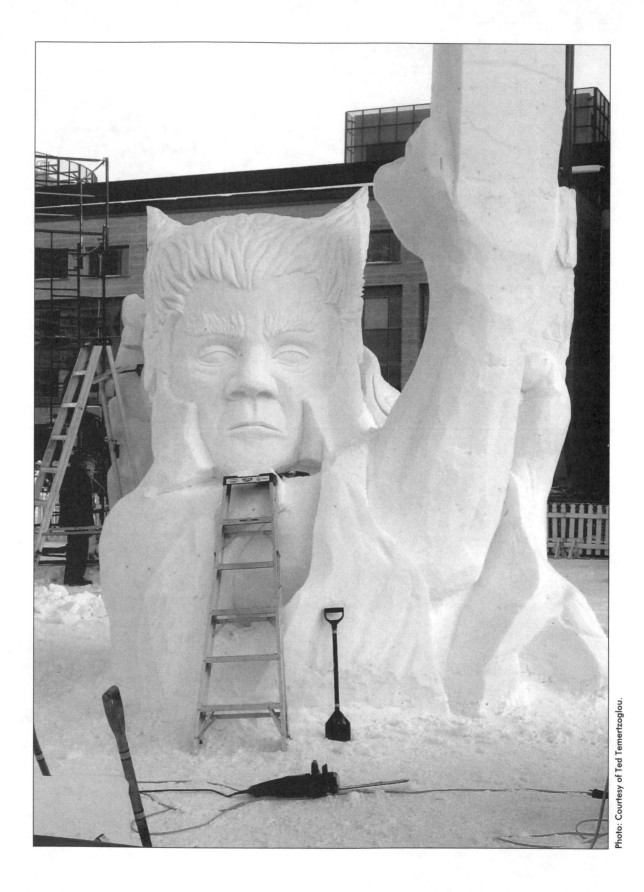

7

LEISURE, RECREATION AND COMMUNITY DEVELOPMENT

LEARNING OBJECTIVES

- To present the relationship between leisure, recreation and community development.

- To provide definitions of community development in leisure studies.

- To review Canadian-based literature on leisure, recreation and community development.

- To overview the types of community development in leisure and recreation.

- To examine community development experiences in leisure and recreation services in Canada.

Leisure and recreation are experiences that help build self-esteem, enhance quality of life and instil a sense of belonging to one's community. In addition, leisure and recreation opportunities offered through community services not only help to enhance the value of a residential community but also help to increase property values.

"The more we do, the more we can do; the more busy we are, the more leisure we have.

— William Hazlitt (1778 - 1830), one of the great masters of English prose style.

This chapter examines leisure, recreation and community development in Canada. The chapter begins by introducing the meaning of community and community development, followed by common definitions of the term "community development" in the field of leisure studies. It then provides an overview of the evolution of community development in Canada and the types of community development in leisure and recreation. Citizen participation is examined, followed by a description of community development experiences in leisure and recreation services in Canada. The chapter concludes by presenting the benefits of community development, including its ultimate purpose, that of creating healthy individuals and communities.

THE MEANING OF COMMUNITY

To understand community development and its relationship to leisure and recreation, one must first explore the meaning of community. "Community" tends to be viewed as an association or grouping of

DEFINING "COMMUNITY"

The concept "community" can be defined as an association or grouping of people that consists of two or more people.

people that consists of two or more people. However, a review of literature in the social sciences and in leisure studies indicates that the concept of community extends beyond the basic exploration of the makeup of association or grouping of people.

For Edwards and Jones (1976), there are four components of community. These are: people, location in geographical space, social interaction and common ties. That is, the meaning of community is two or more people with common characteristics, values and traditions who are a part of a community and interact socially. A community is formed simply through the existence and social interaction that takes place between and among a collective group of people in a specific locale.

According to Poplin (1972), a community derives from people's degree of locality identification and from the commitment shown by the people towards a common core of values. For Zentner (1964), a community is: (1) a group structure that is shaped around goals, (2) a collective grouping that has some collective identity, (3) a group of people who maintain an occupied space or community centre, and (4) a gathering of people who have a degree of local autonomy and responsibility.

Active Living Canada (1993) has defined community as "any group of people who share something in common: geography (e.g., town, city, province, reserve), interests (e.g., fitness, wilderness tripping, politics, travel), status and life experiences (e.g., age, culture, socio-economic status), or affiliations and relationships (e.g., workplace, schools, unions, clubs)." According to this perspective, each of us can belong in more than one community, and it is thus possible for each of us to play a key role in the shaping and organization of more than one community.

Research in leisure studies has also focused on defining the concept of community, as a close link exists between the analysis of communities and the operation of leisure and recreation services. For Hutchison and McGill (1992), the fact that leisure plays a key role in building self-esteem and a sense of belonging in the community is ample proof that this relationship exists. Hutchison and McGill (1992: 120) mention that there are four preferred ways of understanding community. These are: (1) psychological sense of community, (2) community as a spatial or geographical concept, (3) community as social networks, and (4) associational perspectives of community. For these researchers, a community is understood according to the way it is perceived, its location or situation, and its social potential and opportunities.

Hutchison (1990) also presented findings from a series of workshops on community development. The intent of these workshops was to brainstorm the attributes of an ideal community. The results revealed the following attributes: (1) relationships, (2) neighbourhoods, (3) networking, (4) interdependence, (5) sharing, (6) co-operation, (7) participation, (8) integration, (9) working together, (10) full membership, (11) union with others, (12) inclusion, (13) equal opportunity, (14) commitment, (15) familiarity, (16) contributing, (17) diversity, (18) belonging, (19) services, (20) friends, (21) self-help, and (22) acceptance.

COMMUNITY DEVELOPMENT

Despite its broad conceptualization, certain attributes are prevalent in helping to determine a collective understanding of the meaning of the term **community development**. These attributes include people, change, process, improvement and time. One of the biggest problems with conceptualizing community development is that the concept is often used interchangeably with "community-based services." In reality community development differs in scope and meaning from community-based services. This is clearly articulated in research by Labonte (1993), which illustrates that community development consists of a process of change driven by the social relations of the people of the community, whereas community-based services are driven primarily by actions for change initiated by the administrative body of the community.

The 1970s was a period in which the conceptual nature of community development exploded as this new area of inquiry started to evolve rapidly in academic research. As a result, this decade witnessed the development of many definitions of the term. One of these definitions was by Ploch (1976) who presented community development as "the active voluntary involvement in a process to improve some identifiable aspect of community life; normally such action leads to the strengthening of the community's patterns of human and institutional interrelationships" (p. 8). More specifically for Ploch, community development is a process taken within the community through self-determination and collective action by interested parties. The intent of community development is to enhance human existence and collective interdependence.

For Roberts (1979), community development refers to a system whereby individuals gather together to address a problem(s), issue(s), or need(s). Community development has "certain underlying propositions: that people are capable of both perceiving and judging the condition of their lives; that they have the will and capacity to plan together in accordance with these judgments to change that condition for the better; and that they act together in accordance with these plans" (p. 15).

Community development is a process that: (1) focuses on educating and motivating people for self-help, (2) leads to the establishment of local leadership, (3) brings forth a sense of citizenship, (4) helps solidify democratic action at the grassroots level, (5) entices growth through self-generating and self-sustaining means, (6) allows people with an environment to build co-operative and harmonious relationships, and (7) leads to gradual, harmonious change (Khinduka, 1975). Community development is a "process in which the people of a community attempt a collaborative effort to promote what they consider to be the well-being of their community" (Edward and Jones, 1976: 138). Furthermore, community development is an action-oriented process that tends to consist of the following six steps: (1) recognition of need for action, (2) initiation of action, (3) study and diagnosis of the need for action, (4) selection of the goal and the plan for action, (5) goal achievement, and (6) institutionalization of the achieved goal (ibid., p. 148).

DEFINING "COMMUNITY DEVELOPMENT"

Certain attributes are prevalent in helping to determine a collective understanding of the term "community development." These attributes include people, change, process, improvement, and time.

Photo: Health Canada.

Local teams aid in community development by fostering a sense of solidarity and pride.

ONTARIO HEALTHY COMMUNITIES COALITION

In Canada, few organizations are directly involved in community development. One of these few is the Ontario Healthy Communities Coalition (OHCC), a registered charity that was established in 1992. Below is an extract from the OHCC's website describing this organization's profile, membership, mission and services.

"The OHCC assists in organizing Healthy Communities initiatives. The OHCC provides bilingual services, educational resources and support to communities that pursue local healthy community goals. This is made available to community organizations through regional Community Animators who have expertise in community development and facilitation. They work closely with community groups and coalitions to identify and provide their training and development requirements."

Below is a selection of definitions of community that also appeared in the literature in the 1970s. It is relevant to note that most of these definitions continue to be relied on as a basis for the establishment of theories and models in community development, as well as for implications of practical use in applied settings.

- Community development is "the deliberate attempt by community people to work together to guide the future of their communities, and the development of a corresponding set of techniques for assisting community people in such a process" (Bennett, 1973: 59).

- Community development is "an educational approach which would raise levels of awareness and increase the confidence and ability of community groups to identify and tackle their own problems." (Darby and Morris, 1975: 43).

- Community development is a "series of improvements which take place over time as a result of the common efforts of various groups of people. Each successive improvement is a discrete unit of development. It meets a human want or need" (Dunbar, 1972: 43).

- Community development is about "finding effective ways of helping and teaching people to adapt new methods and to learn new skills. This process is, however, done in such a way as to retain community control and community spirit" (Frederickson, 1975: 97-98).

- Community development is a "process of creating special community organizations throughout society which will be responsible for chanelling demands to centers of power, to distributors of benefits" (Hammock, 1973: 18).

According to these definitions, the key characteristics of community development appear to be people, change, collective action and process-driven. The more contemporary definitions of community development are similar. For instance, Christenson, Fendley and Robinson (1989) define community development as "a group of people in a locality initiating a social action process (i.e., planned intervention) to change their economic, social, cultural, and/or environmental situation" (p. 14). The focus of this definition is on people working together to carry out change. The change agents are the people who are most affected by the social and economic factors of their immediate environment.

Perhaps the most comprehensive definition of community development is one put forth by the United Nations. This classic definition states that community development is "a process designed to create conditions of economic and social progress for the whole community with its active participation and the fullest possible reliance on the community's initiative" (United Nations, 1955: 6). Thus, community development is a concept that entails the appropriate use of society's human and material resources to enhance self-help, participatory democracy and social support.

The aforementioned research on the meaning of community development evolves primarily out of the fields of community development, resource development, social work and sociology. Despite the multidisciplinary origins of the conceptualization of community development, the underlying assumptions are similar; that is, community development is about people working together to improve not only their living conditions but also their quality of life. These assumptions have also served as a basis for the definition of community development in leisure studies.

DEFINITIONS OF COMMUNITY DEVELOPMENT IN LEISURE STUDIES

As little research exists regarding leisure, recreation and community development, few leisure studies researchers have attempted to define community development from a leisure and recreation perspective. American leisure scholars define community development as "the method of organization in which the role of the professional is one of assisting individuals in the change process, rather than intervening with programmes to bring about desired change" (Edington, Compton and Hanson, 1980: 37).

Canadian-based leisure studies research by Muriel Kerr, Jim Ward and Don Hunter define community development from a leisure and recreation perspective. For Kerr (1990) community development is defined as "the ability to work as part of one's community with various sectors, to build community involvement, endorsement and commitment. The ability to be a catalyst, a motivator, an example" (p. 34). For Ward (1986) "community development is not about imparting expert knowledge. It is about acting as catalyst to start the ball rolling" (p. 8). Whereas, for Hunter (1986) community development is defined as the "enhancement of the quality of life in a particular community through the active involvement and participation of citizens and concerned agencies within a coordinated approach" (p. 18).

In a study on community recreation and community development, community development is defined as a "process which consists of people with common concerns coming together. It is a process in which the grouping of people with common ideas helps increase the probability that common needs will be fulfilled" (Karlis, 1994a: 10). The study posits that, in the case of leisure and recreation, community development takes place when needs are expressed and requests to fulfill these needs are brought to the attention of decision-makers of community services. The process can be said to consist of three general steps: "(1) finding others with similar recreation needs; (2) grouping with others with similar recreation needs; and, (3) expressing your recreation needs as a group to the recreation programmers and planners of the community center" (ibid.).

Further Canadian-based research in the leisure and recreation field by Pat Hunt (1994) defines community development as the "enhancement of the quality of life of a community through the active involvement and participation of citizens and concerned agencies within a coordinated approach" (p. 1). For Hunt, community development in leisure and recreation is not a passive exercise but comes out of active involvement and collaborative efforts of service providers and participants. In general, Hunt (1995) posits that there are five key characteristics in defining community development in leisure and recreation settings: (1) community participation, (2) partnerships, (3) shared power and decision making, (4) empowerment, and (5) belief in the value of collective action.

For Hutchison and McGill (1992), community development is a human service approach for the provision of leisure and recreation services. That is, the community development approach in leisure and recreation extends beyond the parameters of leisure and recreation services. The community development functions are centred on helping identify needs and concerns, acting as a resource, and supporting in the establishment and implementation of programs. More specifically, for Hutchison and McGill (1992) community development focuses on

- bringing people in the community together to increase collaboration and co-operation;

- building the confidence of community groups to be more self-reliant;

- building a strong sense of community by strengthening groups;

- working to achieve consensus on a range of issues for action;

- assuming that those in power are willing to work with community groups (p. 166).

Finally, leisure studies research by Herchmer (1996) notes that community development is about emphasizing "the attainment of goals" (p. 27). For Herchmer, community development in leisure and recreation services is concerned with helping participants achieve their goals while not relying on traditional leadership approaches. It is about enabling participants to "assume more responsibility, power and ultimately control" (ibid.).

THE EVOLUTION OF COMMUNITY DEVELOPMENT IN CANADA

In Canada, community development evolved out of the social work discipline. Community development that took place in the twentieth century was precipitated by the need for people to work together collectively to address the social concerns of the community. The 1930s is often viewed as the decade that brought together community development and leisure (Karlis, 2002a). In the 1930s, community-owned leisure and recreation increased in popularity in Canada with the success of community leagues in Jasper and the Gyro Club in Edmonton. The impact of the Playground Movement and a philosophy geared towards "keeping kids of the streets" enticed citizens at the grassroots level to come together (Hunt, 1994: 2).

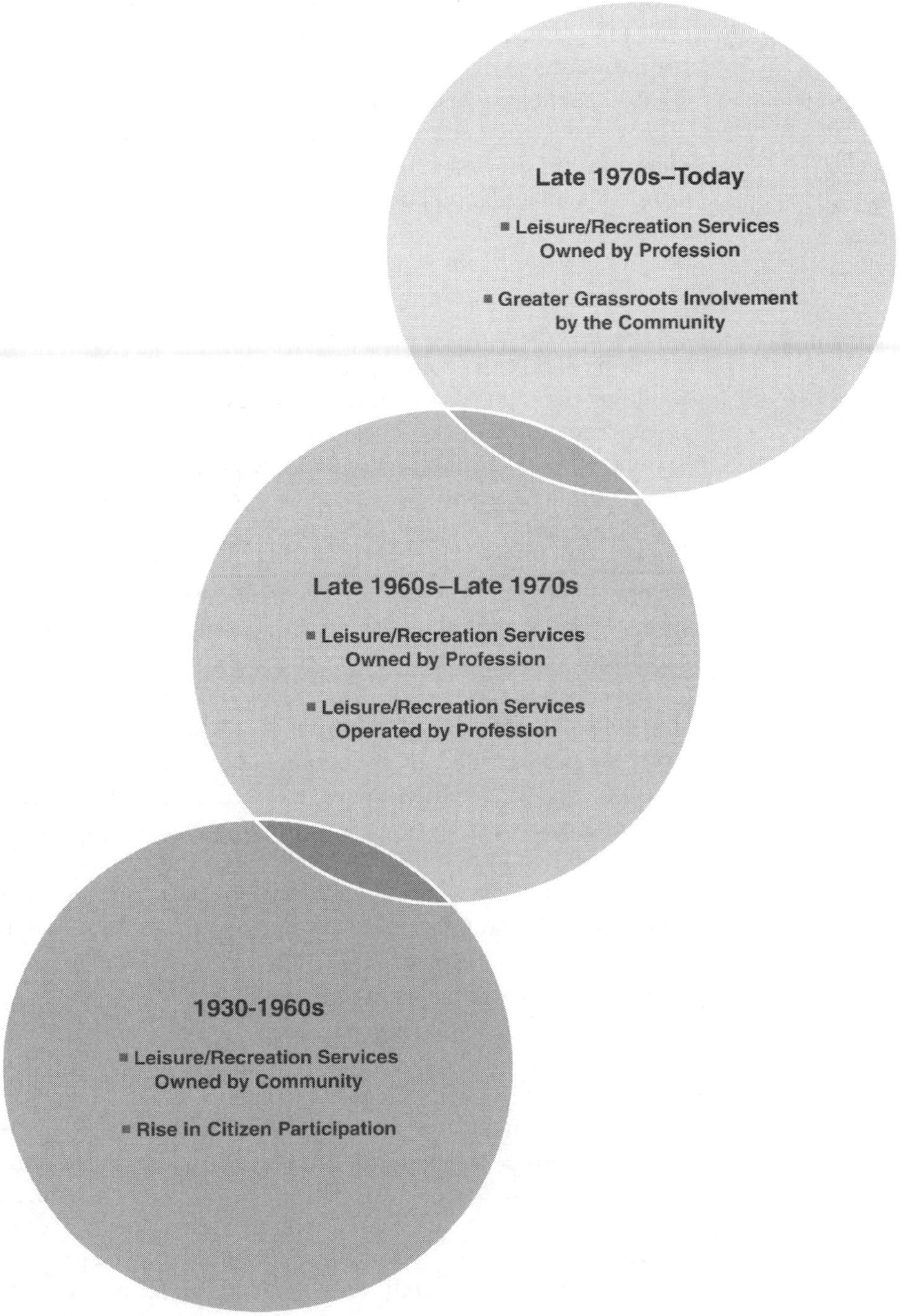

Late 1970s–Today

■ Leisure/Recreation Services
Owned by Profession

■ Greater Grassroots Involvement
by the Community

Late 1960s–Late 1970s

■ Leisure/Recreation Services
Owned by Profession

■ Leisure/Recreation Services
Operated by Profession

1930-1960s

■ Leisure/Recreation Services
Owned by Community

■ Rise in Citizen Participation

Figure 7.1: The evolution of community development in leisure and recreation services.

UNITED NATIONS' DEFINITION

Community development is defined as a "process designed to create conditions of economic and social progress for the whole community with its active participation and the fullest possible reliance on the community's initiative." (United Nations, 1955: 6).

From the 1930s until the late 1960s, a number of citizen participation events took place in Canada that led to the evolution of community development. In 1930, St. Francis Xavier University established an extension department that focused on the self-help approach to change. In 1945, a Citizen's Forum was initiated between the Canadian Association for Adult Education and the Canadian Broadcasting Corporation that promoted active citizenship in Canadian society. In 1954, local citizens were provided with the opportunity to partake in the decision-making process in the construction of the St. Lawrence seaway. And in 1968, Algonquin College of Applied Arts and Technology in Ottawa was given a grant by the Canada Council on Urban and Regional Research to explore the relationship between community colleges, community development and citizen involvement throughout the change process.

In the 1960s, the coming of age of the baby boomer cohort led to a building boom in leisure and recreation services, including a change in focus from community development. In the 1960s and early 1970s, for example, four leisure and recreation community centres were built in cities such as Toronto, Montreal and Vancouver. Focus thus started to shift from leisure and recreation services owned by the community to leisure and recreation services owned and operated by the profession (Hunt, 1994). Public sector involvement took a direct role in the provision of leisure and recreation services resulting in decreased input and involvement at the grassroots level of the community.

In the latter part of the 1970s, focus shifted once again to a greater involvement at the grassroots level (See Figure 7.1). Increased attention by community leisure and recreation personnel on "listening to the community" was initiated as it was realized that communities were not responding as well to a direct leisure and recreation provision approach (Hunt, 1994). It became apparent that a community development approach allowing for input and decision making by community members was the most effective means for the provision of community leisure and recreation services (ibid.).

In the 1980s and the 1990s, the trend of increasing demand for community development in municipal leisure and recreation services continued (Allen, 1991; Connelly, 1992; McCormick, 1991). Leisure and recreation services in municipalities across Canada increased their focus and reshaped mandates to include community development. Despite this trend, however, a concern still persists that a limited understanding of the concept of community development is held by leisure and recreation researchers and practitioners (Swan, 1990; Hutchison and Nogradi, 1993). Despite a trend in the leisure service sector to an increasing demand for community development, few leisure studies university and college graduates have completed a course on community development. In fact, few universities and colleges offer community development courses in leisure studies curricula. One of the universities leading the movement towards the expansion of community development in leisure studies curricula is Brock University in St. Catharines, Ontario.

LEISURE STUDIES RESEARCH IN COMMUNITY DEVELOPMENT

The 1970s was the decade in which leisure studies research in community development in Canada started to expand. One of the first studies, conducted by D'Amore (1977/1978), presented community development as being perhaps the only appropriate means for the delivery of leisure services.

The 1980s saw minimal advancements in leisure studies research in community development in Canada. Some studies tended to focus primarily on the programming nature of leisure and recreation to community development (see Bella and Lanthier, 1984; Hunter, 1986) whereas others examined the impact of community integration on leisure lifestyles (see Anderes and Fortier, 1987; Sandys and Leaker, 1987; Kaminski-Morris, 1987).

Two 1980 studies need to be highlighted as these present a picture of the public sector trend of the late 1980s towards enhanced community involvement in the provision of leisure and recreation services. In the first study, Don Hunter (1986) addressed the then current state of the municipal role in community development by pondering the philosophical issue of enabler versus provider. For Hunter, both enabler and provider philosophies can co-exist within the same delivery system, yet be used in different situations. The co-existence of both enabler and provider approaches helps enhance the delivery of leisure and recreation services in municipal settings for staff and volunteers. For this reason, Hunter argues that "the ideal system is one where volunteers and staff use their collective strengths to focus on a common purpose – serving the public effectively" (p. 21).

The second study focused on community development and municipal leisure and recreation services. Ward (1986), a community services administrator in the City of Toronto's Department of Parks and Recreation Department, posited that community advisory councils could be effective mediating structures for the establishment of leisure and recreation services. Ward went on to address the issue of whether or not effective community development could be initiated by municipal leisure and recreation departments. He concluded by stating that "if local government, via its municipal recreation departments, is flexible enough to feel comfortable in a world of participatory democracy, where people run their own lives, and if it is willing to support the notion of community advisory councils as effective mediating structures between itself and the private lives of those who live in the city's neighborhoods, then it can be the appropriate employer of community development workers" (p. 14).

Photo: Health Canada.

One possible forum for community involvement is how to deal with crowded beaches.

The 1990s was the decade in which the greatest expansion of leisure studies research in community development took place in Canada. In the early 1990s, focus turned to the conceptualization of community development within a leisure and recreation context (see Connolly, 1992). Furthermore, the publishing of a theme issue on community development by *Recreation Canada* in 1993 revealed the growing need within the industry to expand research that focused on community development.

Although community development, in theory and practice, has existed for many years in the leisure and recreation industry in Canada, minimal focus has been placed in this area in leisure studies research. The expansion of such research in recent years in Canada is largely attributed to such researchers as Peggy Hutchison (Brock University), Allison Pedlar (University of Waterloo), Susan Arai (University of Guelph) and Don Reid (University of Guelph).

In a special two-volume theme issue of the *Journal of Applied Recreation Research* on "community development and recreation practice," guest editor Peggy Hutchison (1996) posited that "there has been a lack of information on this topic" (p. 3). Indeed, the intent of putting together the two issues was to "fill the gaps that have existed in the literature" as well as to provide "new and exciting ideas for supporting the community development process in our communities" (ibid.).

In these two issues on community development, seven Canadian-based articles were published. In her paper, Pedlar explores the concepts of communitarianism and community development with respect to leisure and recreation. She argues that, since the importance of leisure and recreation for the enhancement of quality of life becomes more critical during times of economic distress, it is important to re-think the intent of community development. To this end, Pedlar suggests that recreation be "seen more clearly as praxis rather than product" (Pedlar, 1996: 5).

Arai presents the findings of a series of qualitative interviews conducted in the Township of Woolwich in southwestern Ontario. The interviews revealed that "citizen participation contributes to the development of personal empowerment" (Arai, 1996: 42), indicating that the benefits of citizen participation in empowering individuals need to be taken into consideration in a leisure and recreation industry that continues to be dominated by "programming for service delivery and the treatment of people as consumers rather than citizens" (ibid.). In other words, greater focus needs to be placed on the abilities and capabilities of people in leisure and recreation organizations to not only implement change but to also carry out change.

Research by Reid and van Dreunen illustrates that community development is an effective delivery mechanism when leisure is regarded as a means to advance citizenship and assist in the social evolution of society. Thus, leisure is a "vehicle for community development, not the focus" (Reid and van Dreunen, 1996: 58). These authors conclude that leisure, and ultimately recreation, may be a positive force in the social transformation of neighbourhoods and communities.

In their article, Hutchison and Nogradi (1996) explore the conceptualization of community development in leisure and recreation services and settings. In this qualitative study of academics, practitioners and citizens, the analysis of data by Hutchison and Nogradi revealed the

following: (1) community development, an alternative to traditional recreation programming, focuses on a process of involving citizens in decision making, and results in changes in their lives and in the local
community; (2) the intent of community development is to educate and
involve citizens in a process of individual empowerment and community change; (3) most people believe the scope of issues to be addressed
must be broad; (4) involving a range of different stakeholders is central
to understanding community development; and (5) the meaning of community development is reflected in the numerous roles demanded of the
practitioner (p. 93).

Research by Karlis, Auger and Gravelle (1996) illustrates how community development may be implemented in leisure and recreation service organizations using different approaches. The argument put forth is
that the means and process used to implement community development
in leisure and recreation service organizations depends largely on the
nature and size of the organization. Organizations that have greater
resources and are larger in size may benefit more from having external
change agents implement community development. Conversely, leisure
and recreation organizations with limited social and financial resources
that are small in size tend to benefit more from an internally driven community development approach.

Stroick's research explores the development of community associations and federations. Through the use of survey research, Stroick com-
pares the mandate, funding, operating structure, programs and services
of the Federation of Calgary Communities to other similar organizations
across Canada. It was concluded that each Canadian community association federation surveyed has a "dual continuum of internal organizational development and external participation in decision-making
processes" (Stroick, 1996: 182).

The final article in the special two-volume issue on community development presents the practitioner's view. In this article, Godin (1996)
explores the current relationship that exists between community development and the arts. The author, through illustrative examples from the
City of Calgary, overviews the process used by Calgary to fuse together
community development and the arts. This process is referred to as
"community cultural development" in exploring the impact the arts may
have in community building. The conclusion is that community cultural
development, the integration of community development with the arts,
can be beneficial as it may bring together the arts and recreation at the
grassroots level.

In addition to the aforementioned special issue of the *Journal of Applied
Recreation Research*, a number of other Canadian-based studies on leisure,
recreation and community development were published in the 1990s by
Herchmer, Hunt and in *Active Living Canada*. In a study conducted by
Herchmer (1996), focus was placed on identifying the broad tasks of
community developers working in leisure and recreation settings. In
conclusion, Herchmer (1996) lists the following four broad categories of

WORKING TOGETHER

Community development that
took place in the twentieth
century was precipitated by the
need for people to work
together collectively to address
the social concerns of the
community.

TOOLS OF THE TRADE

The "tools of the trade" of community development (Hunt, 1995) are:

• Advocacy
• Developing your knowledge
• Communication
• Leadership
• Program planning

responsibilities that leisure and recreation community development workers must possess when working in leisure and recreation settings:

• Know and Be Known in Your Community
• Facilitate the Development of Community Groups
• Assist Community Groups
• Facilitate the Development of Strategic Alliances (p. 37).

Research by Hunt (1995) argues that community development in leisure studies is important as it helps to build leaders. By passing on the "tools of the trade" of community development to leisure and recreation professionals, these individuals are in a better position not only to understand community development but to also function as leisure and recreation leaders. These "tools of the trade" are: (1) advocacy, (2) developing your knowledge, (3) communication, (4) leadership, and (5) program planning.

Advocacy refers to taking a stand for a certain issue, point of view, perspective, or activity provision. Developing your knowledge means that you need to learn about the processes, approaches and functions of community development. Communication is concerned with being able to express points of view and information in a clear, concise and unbiased way while overcoming expressive and receptive blocks. Leadership entails recognizing the actions to be taken to carry out change and implementing the process of change. Finally, program planning is concerned with outlining the community development plan from start to finish while identifying each step that needs to be fulfilled throughout the entire process.

In a document entitled "Active Living Communities," *Active Living Canada* (1993) discusses the interchangeable use of the terms "community development," "community mobilization," "community organizing," "community action" and "community participation." In fact, each of these terms is presented as a community-driven approach. According to *Active Living Canada*, there are five key characteristics necessary for the functioning of a community-driven or community development approach: (1) community participation, (2) partnerships, (3) shared power and decision making, (4) empowerment, and (5) belief in the value of collective action. When these five characteristics are experienced, democratic action takes place.

In addition to the studies published in the 1990s, research on leisure, recreation and community development has continued to evolve in the new millennium. An article by Parson (2002) highlights the implementation of Industry Canada's Smart Communities initiative in the City of Charlottetown. The focus on Industry Canada's Smart Communities initiative is to use information and communication technology to empower residents, institutions and regions. In his research, Parsons illustrates how the City of Charlottetown is building an Internet portal with eight other community stakeholders while focusing on "community inclusion." Information and communications technology are identified as a means to successfully implement community development among community groups.

Finally, research by Fowler and Cohoon (2002/2003) describes how community development has been used as a tool for building neighbourhood-based partnerships. In their study, Fowler and Cohoon use the City of Moncton's Community Services Department as an example of an organization that is oriented towards facilitation. This department consists of a full-time community development staff of four individuals that come up with the ideas for programs and arrange for the provision of public subsidies, but leave the operation of the programs up to neighbourhood groups. As a result, Fowler and Cohoon conclude that community development through municipal and neighbourhood partnerships is an effective means to address the needs of the participants of community leisure and recreation services.

APPROACHES OF COMMUNITY DEVELOPMENT

Although many different approaches to community development appear in research in the disciplines of community development and social work, it is possible to classify all into two general types: (1) self-help, and (2) technical assistance. Each of these approaches evolves out of social interaction that takes place between two or more persons. In fact, citizen participation is primary for each of these approaches as both rely on the efforts of change agents and the group or community that is the focus of change.

• Self-Help

The self-help approach of community development assumes that all people have the ability and capability to be change agents; that is, to: (1) come together, (2) examine their situation, (3) design strategies to deal with various aspects of their environment, and (4) implement plans for improvement (Christenson, 1980).

The self-help approach is based on the premise that people are both willing and capable of helping each other to fulfill not only individual needs but also collective wants. According to this approach, the change agents are those who will be directly affected by the change (i.e., the people of the group or community). These individuals not only diagnose what needs to be changed, but also lead and direct the effective implementation of the change. This means that people acting as self-help change agents must fully comprehend the culture and environment in which the change will be implemented.

The underlying assumption of the self-help approach is that those who want change are those who understand how best to carry it out, rather than an external change agent who is not fully cognizant of the setting for change or a part of the targeted change environment. This approach stresses co-operation and sound communication between,

Canada's "Snowbirds" bring a national spirit to many local communities.

Photo: Courtesy of Geogre Karlis.

EXPANDING HORIZONS

Research on leisure, recreation and community development has continued to increase in the new millennium.

within and among group members (Horton, 1992) and relies extensively on "citizen participation."

• Technical Assistance

The technical assistance approach of community development is a "direct form of assistance" in which those requiring change rely on outside help to implement community development. Technical assistance is concerned with "transferring the responsibilities for both diagnosis and change from the hands of organizational members to the hands of change agents external to the organization" (Karlis et al., 1996: 134).

The basic assumption behind the technical assistance approach is that change is best carried out when implemented by professionals. In other words, external change agents trained in community development are the most qualified to implement change. These agents not only possess the skills and tools to diagnose what needs to be changed but also have the means to carry it out effectively.

The technical assistance approach focuses on the provision of services by the change agents to the target population. "Citizen participation" takes place as members of the target population are called upon to participate by helping the change agents conceptualize the nature and environment of the target population and the issues that need to be changed. However, the actual implementation of the process of community development rests largely within the hands of the change agents who guide, direct and implement the process.

Perhaps the best way to understand the technical assistance approach is to view change agents as consultants. They are hired from outside of the group or organization requiring change, and like consultants, they provide their expertise for a cost to the group or organization.

TYPES OF COMMUNITY DEVELOPMENT IN LEISURE AND RECREATION

Although the community development approaches of self-help and technical assistance evolve from research in the disciples of community development and social work, both approaches are used by the leisure and recreation service sectors. In the leisure and recreation industry however, including research in leisure studies, it is uncommon to refer to these approaches using these terms. Rather, three types of community development approaches tend to be utilized by the leisure and recreation industry and in leisure studies research: (1) direct services, (2) indirect services, and (3) self-sufficiency (Hunt, 1994).

• Direct Services

The **direct service approach** is closely linked to the technical assistant approach as it is based on the hiring of instructors and/or consultants to provide the service. In the case of leisure and recreation services, most community programs are provided as direct services (e.g., cross-country ski programs, swimming programs, and seniors aerobics). Instructors tend to be hired on a contract basis for the provision of the program and are not full-time employees of the community providing the service. Similarly, consultants who are hired to act as change agents or to implement community development are hired externally and are not full-time employees of the leisure and recreation organization.

• Indirect Services

The **indirect service approach** has increased in popularity since the late 1970s. It offers the members of the community the opportunity to experience "self-help" in the provision of leisure and recreation services; that is, members of the community work in conjunction with the community association (e.g., municipal leisure services or recreation community centres) to operate a desired service.

The indirect service approach requires a partnership between the community association and the citizens of the local community. For instance, the municipality may provide the community centre, leisure and recreation staff, and the needed supplies, while the citizens of the community provide the leadership, planning, organizing, directing and controlling of the required leisure and recreation service.

• Self-Sufficiency

The **self-sufficiency approach** is often used synonymously with self-help, as the citizens needing to fulfill leisure and recreation needs take action to address these concerns. Not only is the leadership and direction initiated by the people, but the building and securing of resources is also carried out by them. Unlike the "indirect services" approach, the self-sufficiency approach is one in which citizens have to rely on their own personal resources to implement community development.

The self-sufficiency approach to community development is commonly used by voluntary sector leisure and recreation organizations (e.g., ethnic community organizations). Volunteers run the entire show from start to finish. Volunteers who implement the self-sufficiency approach usually have little if any training in community development.

• Economic and Demographic Factors

Although it is possible for all leisure and recreation organizations to engage in direct service, indirect service or self-sufficiency community development, economic and other social factors such as size and demographics may determine the type experienced (see Table 7.1). Commercial sector leisure and recreation organizations tend to be large in size, consist of affluent memberships and have access to the necessary economic resources to afford direct service community development. The

Self-sufficiency leads to creative programs and fosters community development.

Photo: Courtesy of James Karlis.

availability of financial capital makes it possible for many commercial leisure and recreation organizations to hire trained experts, consultants, or instructors to carry out the community development process and subsequently implement desired change.

Public and voluntary sector leisure and recreation organizations tend not to have the same economic luxury of hiring external change agents. Change is thus often initiated from within the organization and often voluntarily through volunteer (unpaid) efforts. The types of community development that take place are indirect services and self-sufficiency.

In some cases, a municipality or a voluntary organization may consist of affluent members who have the economic means and are willing to contribute to initiate the direct services approach to change. The likelihood of this happening is much greater in larger organizations as the chance of having economically affluent membership increases as does the likelihood of having more organizational resources (e.g., community funds).

CITIZEN PARTICIPATION

Citizen participation is defined as the "process by which individuals increasingly take part in decision-making within the institutions and environments that affect them" (Arai, 1996: 27-28). Citizen participation is concerned with the actions taken by groups of individuals to address their concerns directly or to find assistance to do so. It is thus concerned with increasing the desire among people to carry out change; more specifically, it is concerned with achieving a state of personal empowerment.

For Rothman, Erlich and Teresa (1981), citizen participation is a purposeful activity that is initiated with action in mind. It is an activity that is initiated by the individual(s) in an attempt to fulfill personal and social goals through collective action and direct input in the decision-making process. Moreover, citizen participation is concerned with the re-distribution of power; that is, granting the power for decision making to those who previously did not have this power (Arnstein, 1969).

Citizen participation is an opportunity for all people, be they administrators or not, to take part in the decision-making process. Citizen participation is a form of "participatory democracy" where all have a say in the decisions that directly affect them. For citizen participation to exist, "citizens must be given adequate opportunity to articulate needs, express preferences about proposed activities, assist in the selection of priorities and otherwise participate in the development of application" (Community Services Administration, 1978: 101)

For citizen participation to take place, those who will be affected either directly or indirectly by change need to experience empowerment. **Empowerment** is concerned with who is going to give power, who is going to get power, and how power is going to be balanced out fairly. Citizen participation is thus concerned with the fair and equal allocation of power in order to enhance the democratic action of the decision-making process.

In research on citizen participation, Rosener (1975) presents a process in planning and implementing citizen participation. Rosener's process commences with management or decision-makers permitting citizen participation to take place. Rosener's nine-step citizen participation process is as follows:

(1) Identification of individuals for participation.

(2) Selection of policy process rules.

(3) Articulation of participation goals and objectives.

(4) Identification of participation methods and techniques.

(5) Analysis of required resources.

(6) Matching alternative methods to objectives considering available resources.

(7) Selection of appropriate methods to attain objectives.

(8) Implementation of chosen participant activities.

(9) Evaluation.

The leisure and recreation service industry is about people serving people. Similarly, the notion of community development also entails a focus on people, in particular, on people coming together to serve collective needs. Citizen participation may thus be critical for the successful implementation of any community development approach in any leisure and recreation service organization.

An article published in the *World Leisure and Recreation Journal* lists a number of directions that may assist managers of public and non-profit leisure and recreation organizations to implement citizen participation:

• Understand what citizen participation is, its processes, and what its benefits are for participants.

• Determine the individuals or areas of the organization that will benefit from citizen participation.

• Make contact with participants who show leadership, initiative and drive.

• Express encouragement for joint efforts in the decision-making process.

• Believe in the abilities and capabilities of participants (Karlis, 1998c: 39).

COMMUNITY DEVELOPMENT EXPERIENCES IN LEISURE AND RECREATION SERVICES IN CANADA

In 1996, Hutchison and Campbell sent out a survey to thirty communities across Canada. Of the fourteen communities that responded, ten were found to be engaged in substantial community development.

Community events demand leadership and initiative on the part of the organizers.

Photo: Health Canada.

BROADENING CITIZEN PARTICIPATION

"Since recreation is a service industry, the primary intent of recreation services, particularly those in the public and non-profit sectors, is to provide a satisfying service to participants. The opportunity to practice citizen participation may thus enhance the probability of participants being satisfied with recreation services" (Karlis, 1998: 37).

These communities were: (1) Saanich, British Columbia; (2) Calgary, Alberta; (3) Regina, Saskatchewan; (4) Saskatoon, Saskatchewan; (5) Brantford, Ontario; (6) Kitchener, Ontario; (7) Cambridge, Ontario; (8) Mississauga, Ontario; (9) Burlington, Ontario; and (10) Niagara Falls, Ontario.

The main findings of Hutchison and Campbell (1996) revealed the following:

- All fourteen settings reported having a significant community development component.

- All but one community used a combination of direct service provision and community development.

- Agencies had officially been using the community development approach for anywhere from one to forty years.

- Community development was initiated for three reasons: response to Master Plan, a commitment to community development, or tradition of community development.

- The structure(s) for community development included: neighbourhood associations, geographical lines, zone boards, liaisons with groups, advisory committees, and partnerships.

- Agencies varied in the number of staff officially working as paid community developers from three to forty.

- Most departments had a working definition of community development which included concepts such as: sharing skills and resources, enabling citizens to identify and respond to own needs, acting as an enabler, and partnerships.

- Nine communities had written policies which supported the community development approach.

- The top six priorities in community development included: group development and support; building partnerships; citizens planning and operating programs; community assessment; policy development with community groups; and networking with citizens (p. 138).

In May 1989, the City of Saskatoon, Saskatchewan, introduced a series of forums that brought together the arts, heritage and multicultural communities. These forums, entitled Burning Issues, were organized so that a grassroots approach to development could be implemented (Haensel, Bliss, Brownridge and Twardochleb, 1991). These forums abided by the following guiding principles: (1) recognizing the organic nature of the forums growing and changing according to group needs, (2) honesty in stating of personal needs to groups needs, and (3) willingness to set aside personal administrative agenda while facilitating the needs of the groups agenda (Haensel et al., 1991: 34). The purpose of the forums was to network, identify common concerns, discuss key issues and initiate planning for the cultural future of Saskatoon (ibid.).

The community development approach that was used for the Burning Issues forum is closely related to the "indirect services" approach. The process of community development allowed the various leaders of community groups to lead and direct for change while using municipal resources to provide services. The process of the forums consisted of the following steps:

- The organizing committee meets and discusses the expressed needs of the groups.

- An agenda is developed, preparatory letters and packages sent out.

- A brochure with registration information is prepared and sent out.

- The forums are free to participants and generally include refreshments.

- Often a special person or activity acts as a drawing card.

- We provide a chance for small group discussion and we choose and train our facilitators well.

- A follow-up letter is sent out after the session that summarizes the proceedings for those who attended as well as those who could not attend.

- We pay attention to feedback and try to make changes or provide for the needs as expressed (Haensel et al., 1991: 35).

The results of the grassroots experience of community development in Saskatoon reveal that input by citizens in the decision-making process has made municipal administrators aware of community needs and wants. Haensel et al. (1991: 35) state the following reasons why this grassroots approach has been successful is leading towards the implementation of change: (1) the members of the cultural community in Saskatchewan are ready and willing to participate in these kinds of discussions; (2) the organizing committee is broadly based and draws on different sectors of the community (e.g., arts, heritage, multicultural); (3) the organizing committee is willing to pay attention to what the groups need (follow-up and feedback); and (4) the organizing committee is committed to showing results.

A further study by Kerr (1990) highlights the experiences of two leisure and recreation communities that have successfully implemented community development approaches in helping to establish healthy communities. These two communities are Vancouver's Mount Pleasant Healthy Communities Committee and the Port Alberni Parks and Recreation Commission and Healthy Communities, both situated in British Columbia.

Vancouver's Mount Pleasant Healthy Communities Committee used a self-sufficiency approach to initiate the change process. This commenced when one of the city's community health nurses acted to

Photo: Health Canada.

Grassroots community development needs to address the real needs of real people.

FORCES OF CHANGE

The process of community development rests largely within the hands of the change agents who guide, direct and implement the process.

address the negative aspects visible in the community (e.g., drugs, prostitution and lack of park space) by calling a meeting of fifty Mount Pleasant residents and community workers. These individuals viewed a film on healthy communities and brainstormed ways to help Mount Pleasant to become a healthy community. The end result was that the committee decided to empower and encourage citizens to work together. The goal was to involve and encourage all community organizations and associations to lend a hand in changing the face of Mount Pleasant into a healthy community.

Leisure and recreation was seen as vital to implementing the community development process in Mount Pleasant. In addition to encouraging citizen decision making for the establishment of more parks, emphasis was also placed on the development of leisure and recreational services. A "natural link" was viewed as existing between leisure, recreation and making Mount Pleasant a healthy community (Kerr, 1990: 33). This meant that all organizations and agencies involved in leisure and recreation could assist through the establishment of festivals, fundraising events and leadership development.

In the case of the Port Alberni Parks and Recreation Commission, community development has been implemented primarily from an indirect services approach. In a 1990 interview with Anne Morrison, the Community Services Division Coordinator of Port Alberni Parks and Recreation Commission, Kerr makes it clear that citizens are encouraged to assist themselves when it comes to the provision of leisure and recreation. The facilities, services and staffing are made accessible by the Port Alberni Parks and Recreation Commission, but it is up to volunteers and citizens of the community to take lead roles in addressing the needs and providing the direction for the provision of leisure and recreation services (Kerr, 1990).

THE BENEFITS OF COMMUNITY DEVELOPMENT

What follows is a brief overview of the benefits of the implementation of community development in leisure and recreation services and organizations.

• Opportunity to Engage in Dialogues at the Grassroots Level

Community development is a "people-friendly" approach to implementing change. It provides opportunities for all, including those at the grassroots level, to engage in participatory democracy. Since those at the grassroots level are often most affected by changes in services and activities, the opportunity for them to engage in community dialogues is important. In leisure and recreation, it is the grassroots participants that keep services and programs operating, and it thus makes sense for administrators to provide community members with the opportunity to dialogue.

• **Contribution to the Decision-Making Process**

The opportunity to engage in dialogues at the grassroots level also holds the potential to contribute to the decision-making process. Community development is an approach that offers participants a voice in this process, particularly in decisions that directly affect them. By bridging the gap between those at the grassroots level and those in administrative positions (those responsible for decision making), those at the grassroots level can express their needs, wants, concerns and suggestions directly. In the case of leisure and recreation, this means that people who experience the services and activities of an organization will have a direct impact on the decision-making process.

• **Development of Personal Leadership Skills**

The potential to contribute to decision making, and the opportunity to work together with others in a decision-making capacity leads to an environment conducive to the development of personal leadership skills. Community development, in theory and practice, offers an environment for self-help to evolve, particularly at the grassroots level. The development of leadership skills for those at the grassroots level in leisure and recreation, however, may not be a complex task. Many employees or volunteers in this field have leadership training and skills, no matter the level to which they belong in the administrative hierarchy of the organization.

• **Enhancement of Community or Organizational Pride**

Establishing a dialogue for change, engaging in the decision-making process and developing personal leadership skills enhances pride in the community or organization. Individuals at the grassroots level begin to identify more with the culture of the community or organization and want to contribute in enhancing its "image." A sense of community or organizational pride develops simply through establishing an open relationship, not only among its members, but between the members and its administrative hierarchy.

• **Building of Self-Identity and Self-Esteem**

Being actively involved in a group setting goes a long way in helping one to develop leadership skills, yet it also permits one to develop intrinsically. Actively contributing in one's group or community allows an individual to feel good about himself or herself. It contributes to self-identity while enhancing self-esteem. As with community development, one of the intents of leisure and recreation is to help one feel intrinsically good.

• **Provision of Volunteer Experience**

Community development as a whole, in particular the self-help approach, provides volunteer experience. The participant tends to enter the community development experience out of her or his free will and offers free service, without financial compensation, throughout the entire process. The voluntary sector is a key part of the leisure and recreation industry as most leisure and recreation organizations are classified as voluntary or non-profit organizations. Similarly, most leisure and recreation organizations (pubic, voluntary and even some commercial) rely on volunteers for the provisions of services. Just like the community development movement, the leisure and recreation movement in Canada is largely dependent on the efforts of volunteers and the volunteer experience.

• Development of a Team Atmosphere

The community development experience brings together people with collective needs in an effort to address these needs through mutual efforts. Those involved in the community development process enter a situation that may potentially develop into a team effort to strive to achieve common goals. Community development is a "team-oriented" approach with the underlying assumption that the probability of fulfilling individual leisure and recreation needs increases when these are pursued collectively by a team lobbying to decision-makers.

• Opportunity to Contribute to Group Development

Community development allows for an environment of collective action, which in turn leads to organizational development. As a result, internal relationships are established. Organizational structures (e.g., units and divisions) evolve not only out of the experience but also the decisions of community development. Thus, without individual contributions, group development would be shaped by the concerns of a selected few decision-makers rather than a democratic group of collective decision-makers.

• Enhancement of Social Functioning Opportunities

The community development process and experience is social in nature, as it depends on people coming together, expressing their collective needs and desires, establishing a plan to fulfill these needs and desires and taking action to address them. The community development process and experience not only provides a social forum, but it also enhances social functioning opportunities.

• Contribution to Development of Culture and Image of Group or Organization

The individual who partakes in the community development process and experience not only assists in carrying out goals and objectives leading to change, but also helps to shape the cultural fabric of the group or organization. Each and every individual who engages in community development in a group or organization brings a part of her or his culture (e.g., perceptions, values, beliefs) to it. Since the individual plays an active role in the shaping of the group or organization, elements of her or his culture may become defining characteristics of the culture and image of the group or organization.

HEALTHY INDIVIDUALS AND COMMUNITIES: THE ULTIMATE PURPOSE OF COMMUNITY DEVELOPMENT

The ultimate purpose of leisure and recreation is to assist in making individuals and communities healthy. Similarly, the ultimate purpose of community development is to enable individuals and groups to function in a healthy community and environment.

In the late 1980s, the idea of "healthy communities" was adapted in Canada after reflection on the experiences of several European cities (Berlin, 1989). As a result, the Canadian Healthy Communities Project was sponsored by the Canadian Institute of Planners, the Federation of Canadian Municipalities and the Canadian Public Health Association. This project had its focus at the municipal level, with the intent of enticing local and residential communities to be become healthy places for individuals to develop and grow. The objective of the Canadian Healthy Communities Project is based on the understanding that "the fundamental conditions and resources for health are peace, shelter, education, food, income, a stable ecosystem, sustainable resources, social justice and equity" (Ottawa Charter for Health Promotion, 1986: 1). Two main factors play a vital role in ensuring that communities are indeed healthy: community involvement and partnerships (Kerr, 1990).

The Canadian Healthy Communities Project established a process in the late 1980s that was deemed to fulfill its intent. This process was put forth as a set of guidelines to participating communities interested in making their community a healthy one:

- A Council resolution expressing political commitment to a Healthy Communities approach;
- The development and implementation of a specific municipal policy, or strategy for a healthy community;
- An inter-sectoral process – that is, an interdisciplinary, public/private, co-operative approach;
- A meaningful community participation process at every stage of the project – including, but not solely defined by – grassroots membership in a Healthy Communities Steering Committee;
- The development and use of appropriate evaluation methods for the local project(s); and
- Sharing of information with other municipalities and the national network (Berlin, 1989: 12).

Photo: Courtesy of Ted Temertzoglou.

Promoting fishing expeditions in Labrador – an example of a local community initiative.

PEOPLE SOFT

Community development is a "people-friendly" approach to implementing change. It provides opportunities for all, including those at the grassroots level, to engage in participatory democracy.

The Canadian Healthy Communities Project is based on the principles of community development, as it incorporates the efforts of citizens in decision making and program implementation. It is also closely linked to leisure and recreation as the opportunity and potential to experience leisure and recreation helps to enhance the "level of healthy-ness" of the community. Greater opportunities and potential to experience leisure and recreation in one's community leads to wellness (Hills, 1989), including the enhancement of one's quality of life.

CONCLUSION

An increasing number of municipal leisure and recreation departments are utilizing community development approaches in service provision (Ward, 1991; Reid, 1993a). Community development often involves citizen participation in all leisure and recreation service organizations, particularly public (municipalities and voluntary) organizations. Citizen participation is an approach "by which individuals increasingly take part in decision-making within the institutions and environments that affect them" (Arai, 1996: 27-28).

Despite its widespread use in leisure and recreation organizations during the past thirty years, little focus has been placed on the relationship between leisure, recreation and community development in Canada. In addition, minimal research has been conducted in Canada on understanding the conceptual nature of community development from a leisure and recreation perspective. The time has now come to expand leisure studies research on the concept, types and process of community development as "to many practitioners, community development is already an accepted strategy for doing business. For others, it may sound rather intimidating. But, if we want to make sure we maximize the delivery of the personal, social, economic and environmental benefits of parks and recreation, community development is the only way to go if we are committed to ensuring first things first" (Herchmer, 1996: 42).

CHAPTER 7: LEISURE, RECREATION AND COMMUNITY DEVELOPMENT

Study Questions

1. How does Active Living Canada (1993) define community?

2. Compare and contrast the community development definitions of Muriel Kerr, Jim Ward, and Don Hunter.

3. List the three steps of Karlis's (1994) process of community development.

4. Briefly describe the evolution of community development in Canada.

5. Summarize Pedlar's research entitled "Community development: What does it mean for recreation and leisure?"

Selected Websites

* **Alberta Community Development**
  http://www.cd.gov.ab.ca

* **Human Resources Development Canada**
  http://www.hrdc-drhc.gc.ca

* **Community Development Corporation of Peterborough**
  http://www.cdc.on.ca

* **Community Development Corporation Prescott-Russell**
  http://www.sdcpr.on.ca

* **Southeast Manitoba Community Futures Development Corporation**
  http://www.seed.mb.ca

Key Concepts

* **Community development**

* **Direct service approach**

* **Indirect service approach**

* **Self-sufficiency approach**

* **Citizen participation**

* **Empowerment**

8

CANADIAN CULTURE, MULTICULTURALISM AND ETHNICITY

LEARNING OBJECTIVES

- To define culture and, specifically, Canadian culture.
- To overview Canada's Multicultural Policy and its implications for leisure and recreation.
- To examine the impact that leisure and recreation services of ethnic community organizations have on multicultural Canada.
- To explore the relationship between culture, diversity and equality in service provision.
- To overview research on leisure and ethnicity.

Canada is a diverse and pluralistic nation consisting of many different people from many different societies. The multi-ethnic fabric of Canada makes our society interesting, not only in cultural makeup but also in its cultural practice, of which leisure is an important part.

This chapter examines Canadian culture, multiculturalism, ethnicity and leisure in Canada. It begins by defining culture in general, followed by a closer look at Canadian culture. It examines the makeup of Canadian society and the effects of multicultural policy and practice. Ethnic community organizations are introduced. The concept of equal opportunity and equal recognition through leisure and recreation services is explored. The chapter ends with a discussion of ethnicity and the selection of leisure and recreation activities.

"Canada will be a strong country when Canadians of all provinces feel at home in all parts of the country, and when they feel that all Canada belongs to them."

— Pierre Elliott Trudeau, Prime Minister of Canada. Address to Liberal Convention, Ottawa, 5 April 1968.

DEFINING CULTURE

To understand Canadian culture, it is helpful to first examine the concept of culture in general. Although we constantly "live culture," it is not a concept that is easily defined. Literature reveals that there are many different meanings and many different perspectives of the concept culture. In fact, there are so many different definitions and perspectives of culture, it is difficult to argue that one is right and the other is wrong. Each definition of culture provides an understanding as to what this complex notion means.

Table 8.1: Classifications of Ethno-Cultural Specific Leisure Pursuits

Classification	Types of Activities
Social	Ethno-Cultural Dances Ethno-Cultural Religious Celebrations, Festivals and Events Ethno-Cultural Coffee Shops Ethno-Cultural Social Clubs
Media	Ethno-Cultural Newspapers Ethno-Cultural Websites Ethno-Cultural Radio Programs
Arts	Ethno-Cultural Theatrical Performances Ethno-Cultural Art Displays Ethno-Cultural Mosaic Displays Ethno-Cultural Academic Presentations

According to Fox (1994) culture is a construct. Culture signifies "the way we interpret and experience social life" (p. 23). This means that culture is a concept that reflects our overall behaviour. The way we act, the way we talk and the way we socialize are all patterns of behaviour that signify the culture that we have been raised in and to which we belong. Culture, therefore, according to Fox, refers to our everyday life behaviour.

For Hoffman (2002) culture is the lens of the microscope by which we view ourselves within a particular society. This means that we all have a different viewpoint of our culture despite having one identifying label. According to Hoffman, we can say that we are "Canadian," yet the way that we define Canadian culture varies depending on our individual perspective. The fact that we are all "Canadian" means that culture is something shared and agreed upon, if only from a labelling perspective.

What makes defining culture difficult is that we may perceive attributes of culture differently. It is true that everything that makes up a society is a part of its culture. It is also true that some things are collectively agreed upon by all people of a society as being a part of its culture (e.g., national flag, national anthem). Not all things, however, are collectively agreed upon; they depend on the perspective of the beholder. For example, the governments of most countries do not have nationally proclaimed sports. While many citizens of soccer powerhouse nations (e.g., Germany and Brazil) will define the sport as a major part of their culture, not all individuals in Germany and Brazil would agree that soccer is their national sport.

Research presents culture as consisting of three attributes: (1) religion, (2) language, and (3) social, media and arts activities (See Table 8.1). This research argues that many cultures have a national religion. The national religion of a society is often signified on its flag through a religious symbol (e.g., the cross on the flag of Greece; the star of David on the flag of Israel). Culture is also defined by the national language or languages of the state (e.g., French and English in Canada; English in Great Britain). Furthermore, culture is also defined by the social activities and behaviours of the people of a society, including its media and arts activities (e.g., CBC and hockey in Canada; BBC and soccer in Great Britain, Royal Winnipeg Ballet in Canada). Media and arts activities are developed by the people of a particular culture to address their specific cultural recreation needs (Karlis, 1993a). In fact, culture and leisure are inseparable concepts (Heron, 1990) as recreation, as a part of leisure, is an essential attribute of culture.

From the above review of literature, we can conclude that **culture** can mean anything and everything. Culture is a construct determined and defined by society, yet it is a concept that contains an individual perspective. Culture influences "the selection as to what needs are to be fulfilled and to what degree" (Abrams, 1969). What makes defining culture interesting is that it reflects the way of life of people. Culture is important in our understanding of the behaviours, attitudes and mindset of the people that constitute a given society. Since all people are different and have different viewpoints, culture is not easily defined and not collectively agreed upon.

UNDERSTANDING DIVERSITY

Culture is important in our understanding of the behaviours, attitudes and mindset of the people that constitute a given society.

CANADIAN CULTURE

What is Canadian culture? Students studying leisure in Canadian society tend to define Canadian culture as: (1) a multicultural one, (2) hockey, (3) Molson beer, (4) a bilingual society, (5) a country made up of immigrants from all over the world, (6) a society with a rich Aboriginal history, (7) beaver tails, (8) maple syrup, (9) Tim Horton Donuts, and (10) the Grey Cup. These students tend to define Canadian culture according to their perceptions of the attributes of Canadian society.

Most of these students do not agree on all the aforementioned attributes as being defining elements of Canadian society. Many argue that beaver tails, for example, are a fancy "Canadianized" version of crepes and do not define Canadian society. Others argue that not all Canadians like or drink Molson beer and that this is not a reflection of Canada. Others argue that hockey is an international sport played in many different nations and thus does not identify Canada alone.

Most of these students were born and raised in Canada, yet, for the most part, they cannot agree on what Canadian culture is. This is not uncommon, however, given Hoffman's (2002) argument that the culture of a society depends on the definition given to it by the members of the society. A further reason why these students may not all agree on the

CANADA'S UNIQUENESS

Canadian culture expands beyond traditionally defined cultural attributes to those activities that reflect the uniqueness of Canadian society.

meaning of Canadian culture is that Canada is a young nation with a young history, and its culture is still very much in a formative stage.

Researchers from all disciplines of the social sciences, arts and humanities have attempted to define Canadian culture from a number of perspectives: geographical, political, demographic, social and cultural.

Grace (2001) associates Canadian culture with geographical location. She posits that, "despite our continual lament that the north is not valued or understood as important, indeed, essential to the Canadian identity, to what makes us a distinct imagined community, and to the geopolitical reality of Canada as a circumpolar national state, a very great deal of attention has in fact been paid to the North" (p. 74). Hillier (2000) argues that Canada is often defined according to its demographic composition; that is, the multi-ethnic makeup of the Canadian population. Moreover, Hillier describes Canada as a bilingual, bicultural society in stating that "Canadian society is that of 'two solitudes' or 'two nations warring within one bosom'" (p. 178).

Descriptions of **Canadian identity** are also based on people uniting socially and culturally through leisure pursuits. Pierre Burton (1987) describes Canadian culture by comparing it with American culture. Burton states that, "as for culture we [Canadians and Americans] don't even speak the same language. You think of culture in terms of opera, ballet and classical music. To us, it covers everything from Stompin' Tom Connors to Hockey Night in Canada" (p. 9). Thus Canadian culture expands beyond traditionally defined cultural activities to those activities that reflect the uniqueness of Canadian society.

For Matheson (1997), Canadian identity may be reflected through our national symbols, for instance, the national colours of the flag, the maple leaf and the beaver. Others may argue that Canadian identity is largely determined by our political makeup; that is, a constitutional monarchy implementing a representative democratic practice (Jackson and Jackson, 1999).

THE MAKEUP OF CANADIAN SOCIETY

According to Schmidt, "the face of Canada is constantly changing" (1996: 8). Each year thousands of immigrants arrive bringing their homeland traditions with them. These ethnic homeland traditions become fused into the way of life of Canadian society. As a result, the makeup of Canadian society is constantly evolving as a cultural mosaic.

The Canadian population comprises many different ethnic groups while immigration is a consistent feature of the growth of Canadian population (Butler, 1990). For the first sixty years of the past century, most immigrants came from European nations, such as the United Kingdom, Italy, Germany and the Netherlands, including the United States (Statistics Canada, 2003a). A large number of immigrants came to Canada between 1951 and 1971, a period of thrust in European migration (Karlis, 1993a). In the 1980s, most immigrants arrived from Africa, Central and

Photo: Secretary of State Canada.

The many faces of Canada represent a cultural mosaic.

South America, and Southeast Asia (Whelan, 1987). This trend continues today. However, tougher immigration policies have made immigration to Canada much more difficult than it was prior to the 1990s.

The largest single origin group reported by Statistics Canada (1996a) was "Canadian origins" (5,326,995). The second largest group was "European origins" (3,742,890), and the third largest group was for those of "British Isles origins" (3,269,520). It should be noted however, that these statistics do not take into account the generations of ethnic groups. For example, an individual born in Canada to Italian-born parents may have identified with "Canadian origins" whereas his or her brother may have classified himself under the heading "European origins."

The fifth round of the 2001 Census of Population released on January 21, 2003, indicates that the proportion of foreign-born is the highest it has been in seventy years as 5.4 million people or 18.4 percent of the total population were born outside of Canada. Immigrants who came to Canada in the 1990s came mostly from Asia and the Middle East. In fact, 58 percent were born in Asia and the Middle East, 20 percent in Europe, 11 percent in the Caribbean, Central and South America, 8 percent in Africa, and 3 percent in the United States (Statistics Canada, 2003a).

MULTICULTURALISM: POLICY AND PRACTICE

In the late 1950s and early 1960s, the face of Canada started to change dramatically as immigration was at its peak. At that time, Prime Minister John Diefenbaker took a stance in support of the rich resource that Canada had in its ethnically diverse population in stating that Canada was "a garden into which has been transplanted the hardiest and brightest flowers from many lands, each retaining in its new environment the best of the qualities for which it was loved and prized in its native land" (Secretary of State of Canada, 1987: 7).

On October 8, 1971, Prime Minister Pierre Elliot Trudeau made an official statement in the House of Commons proclaiming Canada as a multicultural society (House of Commons Debates: Official Report, Volume VIII, October 8, 1971). Indeed, many agree today that it was Prime Minister Trudeau's statement on October 8, 1971, that led to an expanded opportunity for Canadians to preserve their ethnic heritage while living in multicultural Canada.

It was not until July 21, 1988, that the **Multiculturalism Act** became law. This Act "commits the Government of Canada to assist communities and institutions in bringing about equal access and participation for all Canadians in the economic, social, cultural and political life of the nation" (Multiculturalism and Citizenship Canada, 1990).

In the late 1980s, Prime Minister Brian Mulroney reaffirmed the richness that Canada had as a multi-ethnic society. More specifically, Mulroney made reference to multiculturalism as a determining factor of Canadian culture. For Mulroney, "multiculturalism is an affirmation of our commitment that Canadians of all ethnic and racial backgrounds have the right to equal recognition and equal opportunity in this country. This multiculturalism lies at the very heart of the idea of Canada, of our sense of country. As with our official languages, it reflects where we have come from and where we are going" (Secretary of State of Canada, 1987: 1-2).

ETHNIC COMMUNITY ORGANIZATIONS

To fulfill the leisure and cultural needs of ethnic community groups in Canada, Canada's multiculturalism policy allows the basis for the establishment of **ethnic community organizations**. Indeed, most ethnic groups in Canada have established their own community organizations. These organizations fulfill a number of roles, such as providing a place for social contact, the maintenance of ethnic ties and the maintenance of cultural and linguistic traditions (Butler, 1990). Ethnic community organizations are a means to strengthen ethnic identity in Canada (Breton, Reitz and Valentine, 1980) through religious structures (e.g., churches, synagogues, mosques, temples), and social centres and recreation facilities to address the spiritual, intellectual and social needs necessary to practice ethnic heritage.

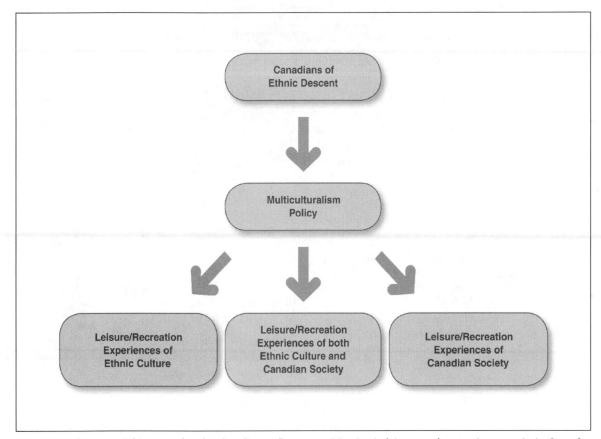

Figure 8.1: The potential impact of multiculturalism policy on participation in leisure and recreation pursuits in Canada.

It is in ethnic community organizations that Canadians of ethnic descent practice their ethnic heritage (Karlis, Gravelle and Pawlick, 1997). It is also in these organizations that Canadians of ethnic descent participate in the ethno-cultural specific recreation activities (e.g., cultural dances) of their homeland culture (Karlis, 1998d; 1991b). Thus, ethnic community organizations play a key role not only in the promotion but also the maintenance of ethnic culture in multicultural Canada.

It is through ethnic community organizations that Canada's multiculturalism policy is fully experienced. They exist and operate through provisions made possible by Canada's commitment to being a multicultural nation. In fact, the Government of Canada provides a number of financial incentives (e.g., grants) to help support the existence and sustainability of these organizations and their cultural-specific programs and recreational activities. Heritage Canada has, for example, offered grants to help establish services within ethnic community organizations. In addition, a number of matching grant programs have existed, such as Wintario (Ontario Lottery Corporation), that encourage these organizations to double their fundraising efforts through government-provided grants.

THE "B & B" COMMISSION

The Formation of Multicultural Policy in Canada

In the mid-1960s Canadian society experienced increased difficulties with English-French relations. As a result, the federal government designated a Royal Commission on Bilingualism and Biculturalism not only to examine the nature of these difficulties, but to also suggest recommendations to alleviate the tension. The Royal Commission on Bilingualism and Biculturalism explored the situation from coast-to-coast and, as a result, implemented the *Bilingualism and Bicultural Act* of 1969.

During their coast-to-coast interactions with many different Canadians, the Royal Commission on Bilingualism and Biculturalism received feedback on more than just difficulties with English-French relations; they were also introduced to the hardships of members of ethnic groups. Representatives of ethnic community groups from all areas of Canada argued that Canada's system of ethnic assimilation was not only unfair, but also unjust. The argument presented by representatives of ethnic groups was that, although their background was not English or French, their contributions to Canadian society were significant and, as a result, the multilingual and multicultural aspect of Canada should be encouraged rather than discouraged through an assimilation policy.

The Royal Commission on Bilingualism and Biculturalism agreed with the representatives of the ethnic communities and presented to the federal government a recommendation for cultural pluralism. This led to Canada's first multiculturalism policy introduced by former Prime Minister Trudeau in 1971. In 1982, multiculturalism became law, yet it was not until 1988 that the *Multiculturalism Act* (Bill C-93) was passed.

Multiculturalism

Multiculturalism is a process that allows for the existence of a cultural mosaic. It encourages the maintenance of ethnic cultural identities while upholding common Canadian values. Multiculturalism is about choice, it is about freedom to be, and it is about identifying yourself with the

Quebec separatist march in the 1960s.

Photo: Malak/National Archives of Canada/C5306.

culture of your choice while also being Canadian. Multiculturalism in Canada makes it possible for someone of Lebanese heritage to identify herself or himself as Lebanese born in Canada, a Lebanese-Canadian, a Canadian of Lebanese descent, or a Canadian.

Our neighbours in the United States have a different philosophy towards cultural pluralism. This philosophy has been named "The Melting Pot" after the title of a play that was performed in Washington in 1908. This play, written by Israel Zangwell, portrayed the ideal that all immigrants can be transformed into Americans.

Even today, when an immigrant becomes an American citizen, she or he becomes naturalized, and is encouraged to identify solely as "American."

Although Canada's multiculturalism policy provides the legal basis for their existence, it is up to the members of the ethnic community organizations to sustain operations. Members (immigrants and their descendants) work together mostly through volunteer efforts to organize, operate and implement the ethno-cultural specific services of their respective ethnic community organization (Karlis, 1998d; Karlis and Dawson, 1990; Karlis and Bolla, 1989). Most of these individuals have little, if any, formal training or education in leisure studies and the provision of leisure services (Karlis, 1990a).

Canada's multiculturalism policy stresses equal opportunity and recognition for all ethnic groups to maintain ethnic cultural traditions and leisure activities. However, the impetus for the maintenance of ethnic culture and leisure services falls primarily within the hands of the members of ethnic groups and their ethnic community organizations. It is up to the members of these organizations to work together to maintain their ethnic traditions and leisure activities to ensure that Canada is a truly multicultural society. In essence, it is the responsibility of Canada's ethnic population to fully implement Canada's multiculturalism policy.

Multiculturalism in policy and practice has contributed to the diverse and pluralistic nature of leisure and recreation services in Canada both within and outside of ethnic community organizations. Canada's multiculturalism policy has contributed to the substantial growth of ethnic ensembles, song and dance groups, folk art, and other extracurricular activities found in the leisure domain (Horna, 1987b). Indeed, Canada's multiculturalism policy has made it possible for Canadians to participate in the leisure and recreation activities of their ethnic and Canadian culture (see Figure 8.1).

EQUAL OPPORTUNITY AND RECOGNITION THROUGH LEISURE SERVICES

A question that has often been raised about Canada's multiculturalism policy deals with the issue of "equal opportunity and equal recognition." A number of factors make some ethnic community organizations more powerful and more likely to maintain ethnic community traditions. Size, time period in Canada, lobbying strength and geographical location are determining factors for the experience of the traditions of ethnic heritage. Larger, more established ethnic community groups such as the Greeks, Italians, and Jewish groups of Toronto have not only had the time in Canada to establish distinct ethnic communities, but have also formed strong lobby groups to encourage the provision of their ethno-specific activities. More recent ethnic groups such as the Somalians and Ethiopians have been at a disadvantage mainly due to their limited time in Canada.

Although no perfect policy exists to deal with multi-ethnic societies, Canada's multiculturalism policy does at the very least encourage equal opportunity and recognition of ethnic groups. This means that all individuals of ethnic descent are encouraged to participate in the ethnic

MELTING POT VERSUS MULTICULTURALISM

Which Approach Is Better for Leisure and Recreation?

The biggest criticism of multiculturalism has been presented in a controversial book by Neil Bissoondath entitled *Selling Illusions: The Cult of Multiculturalism in Canada*. In this book, Bissoondath argues that, through time, a Canadian may hyphenate six or seven different ethnic identities. The end result is that people in this situation may be confused as to who they actually are. The argument is, if immigrants are encouraged to identify only as "Canadian," through time, this identify confusion would not happen for the next generations.

Bissoondath goes on further to state that multiculturalism entices discrimination, and the maintenance of ethnic identities separates groups into the "we" rather than uniting all Canadians as the "us."

Which Approach Is Best for Leisure and Recreation in Canadian Society?

Canada is still a relatively young nation. Children of immigrants from the big European thrust of the 1950s to 1970s now have descendants who are becoming third-generation Canadians. Also, today, the immigration rate is the highest it has been in the past seventy years with over 18 percent of Canadians indicating that they are immigrants. It is thus obvious that a large number of Canadians probably maintain close relations with their ethnic homelands. This means that the leisure and recreation needs and interests of many Canadians may be ethno-cultural specific.

The mere fact that Canadians of ethnic descent have the opportunity to identify with their ethnic culture entices not only the formation of ethnic groups but also the establishment of volunteer-operated ethnic community recreation centres. This is not to say that similar organizations do not exist in the United States, as they do, but perhaps what makes multiculturalism a good approach for the provision of ethnic recreational services is that its philosophy encourages ethnic cultural maintenance, and ethnic cultural recreation activities are a means to preserve ethnic cultural identity in mainstream society.

Photo: Health Canada.

In addition, multiculturalism may be the best approach for immigrants to experience leisure as it brings people with different ethnic backgrounds together through "common identity." By being encouraged to identify with one's ethnic cultural background, individuals with the same backgrounds not only come together to form interest groups to address needs, they also establish ethnic lobby groups to influence decision-makers to fulfill ethno-cultural needs (including leisure and recreation).

Perhaps the most compelling argument for multiculturalism is that it allows for greater access to government resources. Heritage Canada and the various multicultural policies at all levels of government send a clear message to all Canadians that it is okay to be who you are; it is okay to practice ethnic cultural leisure and recreation experiences; and we will help you through policy formation and government programs but you must also help yourself to ensure that you address your diverse ethnic leisure and recreation needs.

cultural traditions and leisure activities of their ethnic homeland. Simply knowing that their host nation supports ethnic diversity is often more than enough for Canada's ethnically diverse population to experience a diversity of leisure and recreation opportunities reflective of both their ethnic homeland and Canadian culture.

ETHNICITY AND THE SELECTION OF LEISURE AND RECREATION ACTIVITIES

Since the 1970s, research in leisure and ethnicity has continued to grow (Karlis, Bolla and Dawson, 1992; Karlis, 1990b). One of the first attempts to kick-start research in this area was a study conducted by Malpass (1973) positing that the "total" community included the ethnic group. Another study conducted by the Ontario Ministry of Tourism and Recreation in 1984 discussed how recreational services did not adequately address the cultural differences of society. These initial studies prompted the awareness among leisure studies researchers that more research was needed to better understand the people of Canada's cultural mosaic and their recreation needs and behaviours (Karlis, 1990b).

Canadian researchers such as Pat Bolla, Don Dawson and myself at the University of Ottawa, Jarmila Horna from the University of Calgary, and Susan Tirone at Memorial University have taken a lead role in conducting research in this area. They have published a number of studies indicating that ethnicity represents a critical dimension in the selection of the recreation experiences for Canada's immigrants and their descendants.

A recent study of Canadian teens of South Asian descent reveals that leisure preference is determined by adherence to South Asian cultural traditions (Tirone, 1999/2000). This study revealed that a need and preference exists for young Canadians to experience the leisure activities of their ethnic roots. Thus, participation in specific ethno-cultural activities is not only a need of immigrants to Canada but, in some cases, a preference for their children as well. Another series of studies also found this to be the case (Karlis 1999; 1997a; 1989b; 1987).

A study of the Greek Community of Toronto found that immigrants from Greece not only prefer but also tend to participate in leisure activities that are classified as "Greek." While comparing the preference and participation towards Greek and non-Greek social, media and arts activities, it was discovered that, in each of these categories, a strong preference to participate in the leisure activities of the ethnic culture exists (Karlis 1993a).

Research by Bolla and Dawson (1990) also justifies the need and preference of Canada's ethnic populations to experience the leisure activities of their homeland culture. In a study of the Lebanese, Chinese, Italian, Polish and Jamaican communities of Ottawa, Bolla and Dawson found that members of these ethnic community organizations strive to fulfill leisure needs through involvement in ethno-cultural leisure

Photo: Courtesy of Ted Temertzoglou.

While sports such as basketball attract people of all ethnic backgrounds, more localized leisure and recreational activities are often intended for particular social and ethnic groups.

pursuits. In fact, the ethnic community organization plays a vital role in fulfilling this need and preference.

A 1995 study published in *Canadian Ethnic Studies* shows that the inadequate use of the concept "ethnicity" poses conceptual problems as well as programming problems for research on ethnic groups. In many studies, the concepts of ethnicity, race and nationality are used interchangeably. As these concepts differ in meaning, researchers need to first conceptualize the concept "ethnicity" and distinguish it from other related concepts. By doing so, they will be in a better position not only to contribute to the body of knowledge but to help create useful programming approaches for Canada's ethnic population (Karlis and Dawson, 1995a).

In a study on Indo-Canadian women, Tirone and Shaw (1997) found that leisure was perceived as not important. Other factors such as family tended to be central to the lifestyle of these women. Pawlick and Karlis (1998) argue that leisure is important for immigrant women in Canada but that cultural and religious restrictions limit participation. Pawlick and Karlis recommend that the leisure industry cater directly to the needs of immigrant women to ascertain accessibility to leisure services.

Statistics Canada reported in 1996 that 27 percent of the population aged sixty-five and over were immigrants. As Canadian society continues to age, the number of senior immigrants will continue to be high. Leisure service providers in Canada will need to identify this target group and identify its unique leisure needs.

Research on the Polish community of Ottawa revealed that more leisure services were needed for senior women members (Bolla, Dawson and Karlis, 1991). For Bolla et al., the ethnic community needed to identify more clearly the unique leisure needs of this selected population. McCue (1986), however, argues that the lack of leisure involvement by aged immigrants is the result of language and communication barriers. McCue goes on to state that "older individuals will not accept easily intolerant attitudes to values they cherish and will not participate in recreation programs if they feel there is a bias toward them or the life experiences they hold dear" (p. 16). Nonetheless, lack of opportunity and limited accessibility to leisure services is the primary obstacle that aged immigrants face in the pursuit of leisure (Karlis, 1990a)

In a study of two immigrant groups in western Canada, Horna (1980) examined the role leisure plays in re-socialization; that is, a change in the leisure patterns of immigrants is explored as a result of both environmental and socio-economic factors. This change is presented as consisting of four basic shifts: (1) a decrease in the quality of discretionary time, (2) a lesser diversity of leisure activities, (3) a change in the meaning of and satisfaction with leisure activities, and (4) a transfer of the central locus of leisure and of the composition of participants to the family.

Finally, Tirone (1999/2000) presents children of immigrants as having two distinct yet overlapping needs for recreation services. In her research, Tirone posits that South Asian children prefer and actually participate in the activities of their ethnic origin. Preference and participation for non-ethno-cultural specific leisure activities were also reported by members of this South Asian group. However, an earlier study argues that most children of immigrants tend to be assimilated into the mainstream culture and to participate mostly in its leisure activities (Karlis, 1987).

CONCLUSION

Leisure and recreation activities can "minimize differences based on gender, race or language and ... emphasize the development of meaningful relationships based on shared interests" (Vail, 1994: 11). Furthermore, a study by Horna (1987c) reveals that ethnicity, together with cultural, socio-economic and psychological factors, influences the selection of recreation activities. Yet, not enough is known about the leisure needs of Canadians of ethnic descent as little research has been conducted in this area (ibid.).

The lack of research on leisure and ethnicity in Canada has not helped in eliminating the constraints to leisure faced by Canada's ethnic population. This sector experiences a number of constraints in the pursuit of leisure including lack of knowledge of programs and limited comprehension of French and English. Public sector recreation practitioners can assist in alleviating these constraints through an understanding of ethnic groups and an adaptation of selected recreation activities that caters to the needs and values of ethnic individuals (Karlis, 1993b).

In a study of South Asian teens in Canada, Tirone (1999) found that leisure pursuits are shaped by traditional cultures and by the cultural norms of Canadian society. Individuals who identify with two cultures tend to experience the recreation activities of both societies collectively (Karlis 1989). Persons of ethnic descent are often found to have "one foot in the ethnic homeland" and "one foot in Canada" when it comes to the selection of recreational experiences.

"If recreation is a basic human need, it is incumbent upon recreation professionals to take action and strive towards fulfilling the recreation needs of all, including the diverse and pluralistic populations of society" (Karlis, 1994b: 42). However, in Canada, most of the recreation services offered, particularly by the public sector, tend to be geared towards the values and traditions of the dominant culture (Karlis, 1991/1992). Canadians of ethnic descent rely largely on ethnic community organizations to fulfill specific ethno-cultural recreational needs.

The following recommendations for recreation practitioners are made to enhance the scope of the service industry so as to address the recreation needs of Canada's multicultural populations more effectively: (1) have an understanding of the notions of multiculturalism, pluralism and diversity; (2) have a general understanding of the nature of the ethnic cultures that shape their respective multicultural society, and an even better understanding of the specific ethnic culture of the recreation participant; (3) have an understanding of the values of the ethnic participant; (4) have a good understanding of the recreation resources available within the public, commercial and volunteer sectors of society; and (5) be empathetic to the needs and situation of ethnic clients (Karlis and Kartakoullis, 1992).

In sum, to serve the ethnic leisure needs of multicultural Canada, the leisure service provider must understand the "cultural context" of the leisure participant or potential participant (Fox, 1993). By following the above recommendations, recreation practitioners can assist in maintaining Canada as a multicultural society, as recreation may be critical for the preservation of ethnic identity in Canada (Karlis and Kartakoullis, 1996).

CHAPTER 8: CANADIAN CULTURE, MULTICULTURALISM AND ETHNICITY

Study Questions

1. List and describe the three attributes of culture.

2. Explain Hoffman's definition of culture.

3. Define Canadian culture. How does your definition of Canadian culture compare to the literature presented in this chapter?

4. What implications do you feel the 2001 Census of Population will have on the programming of leisure and recreation?

5. Briefly describe the evolution of Multiculturalism Policy in Canada.

Selected Websites

- **Halifax Info – The Cultural Mosaic of Nova Scotia**
  http://www.halifaxinfo.com

- **Nova Scotia Multicultural Festival**
  http://www.halifaxinfo.com

- **Saskatchewan Culture, Youth and Recreation**
  http://www.cyr.gov.sk.ca

- **Canadian Heritage-Multiculturalism**
  http://www.pch.gc.ca/multi

- **Canadian Multiculturalism**
  http://www.culturecanada.gc.ca

Key Concepts

- **Culture**
- **Canadian identity**
- **Canadian Multiculturalism Act**
- **Ethnic community organizations**

9

LEISURE, RECREATION AND CANADA'S ABORIGINAL PEOPLES

LEARNING OBJECTIVES

- To introduce the study of leisure, recreation and Canada's Aboriginal Peoples.

- To examine the relationship between the Canadian government, Canada's Aboriginal Peoples, and leisure and recreation.

- To overview the Report of the Royal Commission of Aboriginal Peoples and its implications for leisure and recreation.

- To explore tourism in Aboriginal communities and the relationship between social issues, leisure and recreation.

- To present the National Recreation Roundtable on Aboriginal/Indigenous Peoples.

Like all people in Canada, Canada's Aboriginal Peoples have unique and distinct leisure needs and services that are cultural specific. This chapter examines leisure for, among and by Canada's Aboriginal Peoples.

The chapter opens with an overview of Canada's original inhabitants, followed by an examination of the relationship between the Government of Canada, Canada's Aboriginal Peoples, and leisure and recreation. Leisure and recreation on and off reserve are described, as is the effect of tourism in Aboriginal communities. The relationship between social issues and leisure and recreation is explored, and the chapter ends with a discussion of the National Recreation Roundtable on Aboriginal/Indigenous Peoples.

"The bow cannot always stand bent, nor can human frailty subsist without some lawful recreation."

— Miguel De Cervantes (1547-1616), Spanish writer. the Canon, in *Don Quixote*, pt. 1, bk. 4, ch. 21 (1605), trans. by P. Motteux.

ORIGINAL INHABITANTS

Canada's Aboriginal population is diverse and pluralistic. Its **Aboriginal Peoples** come from a diversity of First Nations, each possessing their own culture. In general, there are three broad cultural groups that distinguish the Aboriginal Peoples of Canada: First Nations, Inuit and Métis (Thornton, 2001; Mitsui, 2000). Part II of Canada's 1982 *Constitution Act* defines "aboriginal peoples of Canada" as including the Indian,

UNIQUE IDENTITIES

Not all Aboriginal People in Canada have the same cultural background and traditions, meaning that variations exist for leisure needs and participation patterns within and amongst the various groups of Aboriginal People in Canada.

Inuit and Métis people of Canada. Many of these groups have their own language and cultural ideals. In addition, each aboriginal culture in Canada has evolved uniquely as a result of differing traditions.

In this text, Canada's Aboriginal Peoples will be examined as a distinct dimension within Canadian society. The reader should keep in mind, however, that not all Aboriginal Peoples in Canada have the same cultural background and traditions and that variations exist in leisure needs and participation patterns within and among the various groups. In addition to being referred to as the "Aboriginal Peoples of Canada," other terminology is also used, including: Aboriginal, Native or First Nations people (Fox, Ryan, van Dyck, Chivers, Chuchmach and Quesnel, 1998). In this text, the term "Aboriginal Peoples" will be used to refer to this group of people and its collection of communities and tribal affiliations (e.g., Mohawk, Cree, Ojibwe, Métis).

In an interview with Harold Cardinal, an active member of the Assembly of First Nations, Malloy (1991) notes a number of collective values that are representative of all the groups of Canada's Aboriginal Peoples. These include a focus on children, and respect for the elders of communities. Cardinal emphasized that Canada's Aboriginal Peoples tend to associate spirituality with nature and in particular with the connection between humans and the earth. In this regard, a deep appreciation for ecology, the environment and the outdoors exists.

Canada's Aboriginal Peoples, as reported by Statistics Canada in 1996, neared 800,000 persons (1996b). Moreover, Statistics Canada reports that, from persons registered under the *Indian Act*, 227,285 lived on-reserve, whereas 260,755 lived off-reserve (1996c). On January 21, 2003, the fifth round of data of the 2001 Census of Population showed that the total number of Aboriginal Peoples in Canada was 976,300, an increase of 22 percent from 1996 (Statistics Canada, 2003a). In fact, people who identify themselves as "Aboriginal" account for 3.3 percent of Canada's population.

Census data provides the following information on the Aboriginal Peoples of Canada: (1) the Aboriginal share of the total population is on the rise; (2) the Aboriginal population is much younger than the non-Aboriginal population, but is ageing,; (3) one-quarter of Aboriginal persons could conduct a conversation in an Aboriginal language; (4) Aboriginal children are less likely to live with both parents; (5) the highest concentrations of Aboriginal population is in the North and on the Prairies; and (6) about one-half of Canada's Aboriginal persons live in urban areas (Statistics Canada, 2001a).

The mere fact that Canada's Aboriginal Peoples are not a homogeneous group should make it clear that their leisure and recreation needs and participation patterns are not the same. In addition to having their own language and cultural ideals, the needs and interest of this population differ according to geographical region. Those in eastern, central and western Canada will have somewhat different participation patterns than those living in the remote cold-climate areas in the territories.

THE CANADIAN GOVERNMENT, CANADA'S ABORIGINAL PEOPLES, AND LEISURE AND RECREATION

Although Canada's Aboriginal Peoples are the original inhabitants of Canada, it was not until the 1982 Canadian *Constitution Act* that law was implemented recognizing their rights. Part II, Section 35 of the 1982 Act laid the foundation for the recognition of existing Aboriginal and treaty rights and land claims agreements, while acknowledging that Aboriginal and treaty rights are guaranteed equally for both genders.

As a result of the 1982 Constitution Act, Canada's Aboriginal Peoples have authority to undertake certain decisions and to partake in the decision-making process with various levels of government on issues of direct concern. A collaboration exists between the Government of Canada and Canada's Aboriginal Peoples for the designation and protection of Aboriginal land for national parks while considering their traditional land use. This leads to preferential economic and tourism opportunities for members of Aboriginal communities from land areas used for touristic purposes (Auger and Karlis, 2000).

The Canadian government has also taken an active role in assisting in the establishment and development of recreation programs for Canada's Aboriginal Peoples. For example, in 1989, the Ministers of Northern Affairs and Culture, Heritage and Recreation actively participated in the Remote Communities Recreation Conference to pledge support for recreation programming in Aboriginal communities. This support was the result of need expressed by Aboriginal community leaders for greater government involvement in Aboriginal community recreation programs.

In 1985, the Government of the Northwest Territories approved the establishment of a Community Recreation Leaders Program to provide leadership training and educational opportunities for persons of Aboriginal descent. This multi-million dollar program proved to be effective in providing the foundation for leadership preparation. Unfortunately, not all Aboriginal communities in Canada have benefited from this program as it focused solely on Canada's Arctic (Legaree, Schofield and Hayden, 1994).

Various levels of government assist in the provision of recreation services for Canada's Aboriginal Peoples, although this tends to happen only after a need is expressed by the decision-makers of Canada's Aboriginal communities. Henhawk (1993) posits that the obvious lack of recreation directorships in Aboriginal communities must first be recognized by the Ontario Aboriginal Recreation Council before receiving financial support for program establishment by the Ontario Ministry of Culture, Tourism and Recreation. This may also be the case for other provinces and territories in Canada.

Many of Canada's national and provincial parks were designated as such prior to the 1970s with minimal consideration to the Aboriginal Peoples and their rights. After Berger's 1977 pipeline enquiry, Parks Canada became more empathetic to the concerns of the Aboriginal

Traditional activities are common in northern Aboriginal communities.

Photo: Nunavut Tourism.

THE CANADIAN ABORIGINAL FESTIVAL

A Profile

The Canadian Aboriginal Festival is one of Canada's most successful festivals. Offered each year in Toronto, Ontario, it is the largest Aboriginal festival in Canada, both in the number of events and activities offered and the number of people who attend.

The Canadian Aboriginal Festival is a presentation of Indian Art-I-Crafts, a non-profit Aboriginal organization.

The Canadian Aboriginal Festival is a unique opportunity to share and learn about North America's Aboriginal Peoples. The Canadian Aboriginal Festival offers activities for all, including shopping, food, dancing, lacrosse, contemporary music and visual arts. In 2003, the Canadian Aboriginal Festival celebrated its tenth anniversary at the SkyDome in Toronto.

The main events at the Canadian Aboriginal Festival are as follows: pow wow, music awards, education day, market place, fashion show, lacrosse competition, traditional teachings, film festival, visual arts, performing arts and workshops.

Although all the above activities are important for the preservation of Aboriginal culture, two stand out as being extremely relevant for its maintenance: the pow wow, and the Canadian Aboriginal Music Awards.

Pow wows are "thanksgiving ceremonies." They have traditionally been dedicated to warriors while also giving thanks to the Creator and Mother Earth for all that she has provided for her people. The pow wow is one of the oldest and most important Aboriginal ceremonies. Each begins with a Grand Entry where all the dancers enter the dance circle for the first time. The pow wow is considered to be the "centrepiece" of the Festival as visitors from Canada and abroad come to witness this ceremony.

The Canadian Aboriginal Music Awards honour the top musical artists of Aboriginal communities. Its mission is to acknowledge and honour the keepers, teachers, promoters, creators and performers of Aboriginal music; to continue to develop and promote the diversity of Aboriginal music; to celebrate the excellence of Aboriginal music; and to recognize the unique vision of the musicians and encourage this rich cultural voice.

Source: Extracted from: <http://www.canab.com>.

Photo: CGTB/Canadian Tourism Commission.

Peoples. As a result, in 1979, Parks Canada Policy addressed the idea of the joint management of parks by Aboriginal Peoples and government. Today, "land claim settlements and Aboriginal treaty rights ... play as great a part as National Park Policy or legislation in determining the role of aboriginal peoples in planning for and managing national parks" (Peepre and Dearden, 2002).

THE ROYAL COMMISSION ON ABORIGINAL PEOPLES

The **Royal Commission on Aboriginal Peoples** was formed in 1991, with the intent of building a new relationship between Canada's Aboriginal and non-Aboriginal Peoples. In 1996, following years of public inquiries and more than 350 research studies, published reports and roundtable sessions, the Royal Commission's Final Report was finalized. This Final Report consists of five volumes totalling 3,956 pages.

A CD-ROM entitled *For Seven Generations: An Information Legacy of the Royal Commission on Aboriginal Peoples* supplements the Final Report. This CD-ROM contains more than 200,000 pages of research, testimony and reference information accumulated by the Royal Commission. It is the most comprehensive collection of information ever put together on Canada's Aboriginal Peoples (Public Works and Government Services Canada, 1996).

The Royal Commission on Aboriginal Peoples, its Final Report and the supplementary CD-ROM consist of: (1) submissions to the Royal Commission by Aboriginal Peoples, (2) a collection of commissioned studies, (3) research reports, (4) submissions from Aboriginal communities, and (5) transcripts from public hearings and Royal Commission deliberations.

The Royal Commission on Aboriginal Peoples, its Final Report and the supplementary CD-ROM make mention of recreation, but one has to dig through the Final Report and the supplementary CD-ROM to pinpoint information directly and indirectly related to leisure and recreation. Information is found in the public hearings, tabled hearings, roundtable reports and research studies, yet these are not provided under a distinguishable separate heading. Nonetheless, a number of contemporary issues in recreation and leisure for Aboriginal Peoples in Canada can be extracted.

A feature article in the *Journal of Leisurability* identifies the following five contemporary issues in leisure and recreation for Aboriginal Peoples in Canada from the material compiled by the Royal Commission: (1) tourism, (2) substance abuse and crime, (3) cultural maintenance, (4) education, and (5) land use planning and wildlife management. Tourism is discussed as a resource that provides economic, social and cultural opportunities for all members of the Aboriginal community. As for substance abuse and crime, recreation is viewed as an avenue for crime prevention and for therapeutic use. An argument is put forth for the

ROYAL COMMISSION ON ABORIGINAL PEOPLES

The Royal Commission on Aboriginal Peoples, its Final Report and supplementary CD-ROM mention recreation, yet one has to dig through these materials to pinpoint information directly or indirectly related to the leisure and recreation needs of Aboriginal Peoples in Canada.

POW WOWS

While exploring the leisure and recreation participation patterns of members of the Kitigan Zibi reserve in Quebec, it was found that cultural leisure and recreation pursuits offered on reserve (e.g., pow wows) played a vital role in reinforcing cultural self-awareness.

existence of a symbolic relationship between Aboriginal leisure and cultural viability with regard to cultural maintenance. Education through recreation is discussed as a means for individual and social development. And land use planning and wildlife management are not only recreational but also cultural concerns of the Aboriginal Peoples in Canada. (Dawson, Karlis and Georgescu, 1998).

Dawson et al. (1998) conclude their study by stating that these five issues "emerge as the most salient from the unprecedented compilation of documentation assembled in support of the Royal Commission's deliberations" (p. 8). The role of leisure and recreation and its impact on Canada's Aboriginal Peoples are not fully exhausted in the five aforementioned issues. To expand an appreciation of the relationship between leisure and recreation for Canada's Aboriginal Peoples, focus needs to be placed on leisure and recreation both on- and off-reserve.

LEISURE AND RECREATION ON- AND OFF-RESERVE

It has been said that Canada's Aboriginal Peoples live within two cultures, the dominant Euro-North American and the Aboriginal culture (Fox et al., 1998). As with all cultural groups, the Aboriginal population also consists of cultural sub-groups such as the Cree, Iroquis and Algonquin. Members of these groups live within the aforementioned cultures while also experiencing their own unique cultural traditions reflective of their ancestry.

With this general assumption, a series of studies have been conducted to explore culture and the impact it has on the leisure and recreation preferences and participation patterns of Aboriginal Peoples. A few of these studies have been conducted in Canada. Studies that exist tend not only to explore cultural leisure and recreation preferences and participation patterns, but also cultural identity as well.

One study discovered that Aboriginal Peoples living on-reserve had greater access to the leisure and recreation opportunities that reflect Aboriginal culture. While exploring the leisure and recreation participation patterns of members of the Kitigan Zibi reserve in Quebec, it was found that cultural leisure and recreation pursuits offered on-reserve (e.g., pow wows) played a vital role in reinforcing cultural self-awareness. More specifically, this study found that Aboriginal culture-oriented activities accessible on-reserve were instrumental in the maintenance of the Aboriginal culture of its members (Karlis, 1995b). Indeed, traditional leisure and recreation activities offered on-reserve engender and reflect interpersonal relationships (Wellman, 1987) while enhancing social cohesion.

Aboriginal Peoples living off-reserve were more likely to be integrated in the mainstream culture. A series of interviews of members of an Ottawa-area reserve revealed that members living in Ottawa engaged less frequently in Aboriginal cultural leisure and recreational activities than their on-reserve peers (Karlis, 1995b). In fact, members of this

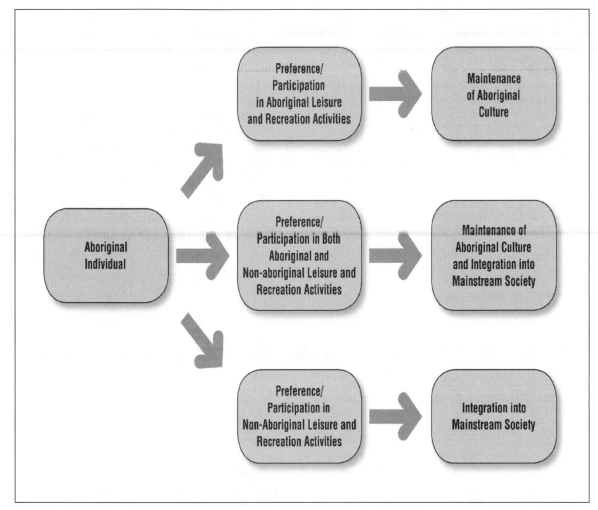

Figure 9.1: The potential impact of leisure and recreation activity involvement on the maintenance of Aboriginal culture.

community showed a preference for leisure and recreation activities classified as "non-Aboriginal" (e.g., football and soccer).

Subsequent research reveals that members of an Algonquin native community near the Ontario-Quebec boarder tend to value leisure and recreation for its social potential. Moreover, surveyed members of this community indicated that leisure and recreation is a means to find compensation from work. Further findings revealed that Aboriginal culture leisure and recreation (dance, songs, games and special events) contributes to cultural maintenance (Karlis and Dawson, 1996). Indeed, it may be that preference for and participation in Aboriginal culture-specific leisure and recreation activities helps enhance the maintenance of Aboriginal culture in Canada (see Figure 9.1). Other factors such as family, education and community involvement may also help in its maintenance.

ON- AND OFF-RESERVES

Research conducted by Malloy, Nielson and Yoshioka (1993) supports the view of the Ontario Chiefs, arguing that differences exist in leisure and recreation service administration practices available to Aboriginal People living on- and off-reserve.

Like all groups subject to the influences of a dominant mainstream culture, preserving cultural traditions is vital for the Aboriginal Peoples of Canada. For this reason, in 1991, the Ontario Chiefs expressed concern at their annual conference at the inadequacy and lack of leisure and recreation programs and services in Aboriginal communities. It was argued that the lack of leisure and recreational opportunities was one of the contributing reasons for the breakdown of the cultural fabric of Aboriginal communities (Henhawk, 1993). Indeed, through participation in leisure and recreation activities provided in Aboriginal organizations, the likelihood of Aboriginal cultural maintenance is enhanced (Saskatchewan Senior Citizens' Provincial Council, 1988).

Research conducted by Malloy, Nilson and Yoshioka (1993) supports the views of the Ontario Chiefs, arguing that differences exist in the leisure and recreation service administration practices available to Aboriginal Peoples living on- and off-reserve. In fact, accessibility and leadership training appear to be the main differences. For this reason, Henhawk (1993) calls for increased public sector involvement for the provision of facilities on-reserve.

The unique leisure and recreational needs of Aboriginal Peoples living on-reserve are not only culture specific, they are also value oriented. For example, there is a great deal of social interaction between elders and the younger members of the community. This in itself is an important social leisure and recreational activity (Harold Cardinal in Malloy, 1991), but the elders also emphasize the relationship between humans, nature, the environment and the earth (Harold Cardinal in Malloy, 1991). Outdoor leisure and recreational opportunities (e.g., festivals, lacrosse, etc.) are thus highly valued and considered to be an important part of Aboriginal cultural traditions.

Reid (1993b) indicates that most Aboriginal communities "have neither a minimum acceptable level of economic nor leisure activity which results in extreme social and psychological problems for numerous individuals" (p. 88). In a field research study consisting of a sample of Ontario Aboriginal communities, Reid found that the social development and cultural benefits of leisure and recreation were perceived to be important. This importance falls into five categories: (1) the joy of pure participation, (2) relaxation, stress reduction and improved health, (3) relief from boredom, (4) a tool for individual rehabilitation and social development, and (5) cultural expression. Despite their importance, this study postulated that most Aboriginal communities experience a number of constraints to the development and delivery of leisure and recreation services, such as planning and organizational development, the adequacy of structures, the development of the training of volunteers, and leadership. Indeed, the result of Reid's study leads one to believe that increased public sector involvement in the provision of services on-reserve would be of great assistance to Aboriginal communities. The type of help that would probably be most welcomed is leadership training, program development, program implementation and activity planning.

Not all Aboriginal reserves have organized leisure and recreation administrative bodies to serve the needs of its members. In fact, leisure and recreation may be perceived as activity for the young. Standup (2000), in research conducted at the Kahnawake Mohawk Territory, states that when many residents hear the words "sport and organized recreation," they "think of small children playing a game or sport" (p. 27). Standup goes on to posit that the words "sport and organized recreation" tend to be associated with two activities played by the young, hockey and lacrosse. Research reveals that many traditional games of Aboriginal Peoples living on-reserve have been adopted or adapted from colonialistic lifestyles. Cole (1993), while examining the leisure and recreation practices of the Stoney of Alberta and the Mohawks of the Six Nation Confederacy, found that wrestling, tug-of-war and tewaarathon have become acculturalized and incorporate the rules and regulations of the dominant society.

Moreover, research by Condon (1995) describes how leisure and recreation acculturation has taken place in Inuit communities throughout the Canadian Arctic. The younger generation in these communities have begun to play non-Inuit games (e.g., hockey, basketball, baseball, and volleyball). The increased involvement in these activities reflects a decreased participation level in the traditional games of the Inuit.

A trend in Aboriginal communities is to bring Aboriginal Peoples together through sport. For example, Manitoba Aboriginal Sport and Recreation Council plays a key role in enhancing the sporting life of Manitoba's Aboriginal communities by sponsoring softball and hockey tournaments, organizing the Manitoba Indigenous Summer Games and helping prepare Team Manitoba for the North American Indigenous Games (Lamirande, 2000). Through the experience of non-traditional sporting activities, cultural cohesion and social interaction by participants is enhanced.

It is evident that more is needed to fulfill the social and cultural leisure and recreation needs of Aboriginal Peoples living on-reserve. For those living off-reserve, Aboriginal social and cultural leisure and recreation opportunities are offered at Native centres such as the Odawa Friendship Center in Ottawa, yet, these are not enough. In 1991, the Ontario Chiefs identified two major cultural leisure and recreational concerns wanted and needed by Aboriginal Peoples living on and off-reserve: committee development and facility development (Henhawk, 1993). Both of these needs have to be addressed.

Aboriginal programs foster cultural expression, such as the unique Inukshuk.

The City of Winnipeg is an example of a municipality that has taken measures to address directly the leisure and recreation concerns of its Aboriginal population. Winnipeg has the largest Aboriginal population of all cities in Canada, with almost 50,000 Aboriginal persons. As this number is expected to grow to over 75,000 by 2016, the Community Services Department has taken measures to ensure that the unique leisure and recreation needs of this population are fulfilled today and for years to come. Two new Aboriginal positions have been established by this

THE ODAWA NATIVE FRIENDSHIP CENTRE

Establishing Social Cohesion and Providing Social Services Off-Reserve

In Canada, most Aboriginal persons live off-reserve. Access to cultural-specific leisure activities is thus limited for this group as the leisure and recreation activities offered by society tend to be, for the most part, representative of mainstream activities. Seldom will one encounter an Aboriginal cultural-specific leisure or recreation activity offered at a local community centre or municipal centre.

Research on culture and society identifies the importance of participating in cultural-specific leisure and recreation activities, not only for satisfaction, but also for cultural maintenance. For most Aboriginal persons living off-reserve, there is a risk of assimilation through recreation involvement.

One organization that offers Aboriginal cultural leisure opportunities outside of the reserve is the Odawa Native Friendship Centre in Ottawa, Ontario.

Mission

The mission of the Odawa Native Centre is to enhance the quality of life for Aboriginal people in the Capital region; to maintain a tradition of community, an ethic of self-help and development, as well as to provide traditional teachings from our elders. These are important values which we will continue to reinforce in the next millennium.

Odawa is Committed to...

• reinforcing Aboriginal cultural development and creating greater awareness and interaction with other cultures; this includes the Annual Summer Odawa POW WOW, which is a celebration of Aboriginal culture, enjoyed by 18,000 visitors – Aboriginals and non-Aboriginals from across North America;

• promoting positive Aboriginal images, self-respect and expression through a variety of cultural programs and activities;

• facilitating the development of skills, knowledge and leadership in Aboriginal youth that

will allow them to successfully participate in the surrounding community; and

• continuing to offer a range of services that meet the special needs of Aboriginal people who require assistance to adapt to an urban environment.

Events and Programs

• The Odawa Native Friendship Centre offers a full calendar of events including programs for all age groups and needs, cultural events and social/recreational activities. Staff welcome suggestions and support from the community in expanding services. These include:

• Aboriginal Family Support Program
• Aboriginal Pre-Natal Nutrition Program
• Aboriginal Healthy Babies Program
• Parents as Teachers
• Programming for Early Parenting Support
• Sweetgrass Home Child Care Activity
• Healing and Wellness Program
• Life Long Care Program
• Employment Referral Training Program
• Dreamcatchers Youth Program
• Aboriginal Responsible Gambling Research Project

Services

1. Recreation. Odawa offers a wide variety of recreational activities such as sporting events, tournaments and social gatherings.

2. Cultural awareness. All Odawa services emphasize cultural awareness. The Annual Odawa POW WOW and Traditional Winter POW WOW also increase cultural awareness among both Native and non-Native people in the region.

3. Support/information referral. The Friendship Centre provides information and referral service to all who require assistance in some way.

Source: Extracted from: <http://www.odawa.on.ca>.

Department. The Community Resource Coordinator (Aboriginal Community) is responsible for the development of the Aboriginal Services portfolio. The Recreation Coordinator (Aboriginal Services) has a mandate to develop and implement culturally appropriate programs and service delivery (Grey and Johnson, 2000). Winnipeg serves as an excellent model of how the leisure and recreation needs of this select population can be better addressed at the municipal level.

Not all Aboriginal Peoples have the luxury of having leisure and recreation programs delivered on- and off-reserve. In the Northwest Territories, for instance, only one Aboriginal reserve exists. Thus, in the majority of communities, leisure and recreation services are provided to Aboriginal and non-Aboriginal residents collectively, and service providers must be aware of the makeup of this group. They need to recognize the distinctness of Aboriginal Peoples through an understanding of history, language differences and traditional games (Shauerte, 2000).

TOURISM AND ABORIGINAL COMMUNITIES

The Aboriginal Peoples of Canada possess a rich history, and Aboriginal communities are a principle tourist attraction of Canadians and international visitors. These visitors seek to learn about Canada's Aboriginal Peoples and their ways of life (Auger and Karlis, 2000).

One of the main attractions offered to visitors in Aboriginal communities is the opportunity to witness Native festivals. In a study of Native festivals in Canada, Hinch and Delamere (1993) found that many benefits are experienced not only by the Aboriginal community and its people, but also by the tourist as well: the community benefits as its social and cultural traditions are reinforced, and the tourist benefits by gaining knowledge of the ways of life and traditions of the community.

Tourism is a form of cultural exchange and growth (Epitropoulos, 2002). Some touristic opportunities offered by Aboriginal communities concentrate on further reinforcing its cultural values and traditions. For example, on Herschel Island, off the north coast of the Yukon territories, the Elder/Host Junior Park Ranger Program has been established to provide young people of Aboriginal descent with a chance to learn about their roots and become accustomed to Aboriginal values and traditions (Duncombe, 1998). Elders, who act as cultural ambassadors and cultural leisure and recreation promoters, lead in activities such as caribou hunting while at the same time sharing cultural stories with the Junior Park Rangers.

Photo: Nunavut Tourism.

Elders play an important role in promoting Aboriginal art and culture.

A similar type of tourism takes place in Northern Quebec, but the emphasis is placed on integrating non-Aboriginal Peoples into the daily leisure and recreation lifestyles of local Aboriginal Peoples through activities such as hunting and dog-sledding (Auger and Karlis, 2000). This type of cultural tourism is effective as it brings together Aboriginal and non-Aboriginal Peoples in a learning experience.

RESEARCH AGENDA

More research is needed in exploring the relationship between leisure, recreation and culture within Aboriginal communities.

Similarly, research by Colton (1999) on the Little Red River Cree First Nation indicates that economic, socio-cultural and political-environmental themes are motivations for indigenous tourism development in Canada. In fact, it may be that the primary motivation for tourism development in Aboriginal communities is job creation, wage employment and greater economic diversification. Yet as Colton states, the benefits of tourism for Aboriginal communities are more than just economic; they extend to social and cultural benefits, such as bringing people back to their roots, and to political benefits, in helping in the creation of strategies for the control over their land.

A further study by Osawabine (2000) reports that in the Manitoulin/Sagamok region of Ontario, culture, tourism, heritage, recreation and parks are all interrelated. This community offers visitors a wide array of natural and cultural leisure and recreation opportunities. Visitors can experience the past and enjoy the present with such offerings as pow wows, canoe trips and state-of-the art heritage museums. The ability of the people of the Manitoulin/Sagamok region to utilize natural and cultural resources for touristic purposes has benefited this community both socially and economically. Many Aboriginal businesses exist that rely on tourism, such as bed-and-breakfast inns, campsites, restaurants and a book store specializing in Aboriginal books and music (Osawabine, 2000).

According to Colton (2002), many Aboriginal communities "recognize that tourism development can stimulate change in social, cultural and environmental dimensions" (p. 68). Despite this understanding, not all Aboriginal communities have fully explored the potential of tourism. For Colton (2002), tourism development should be placed at the forefront of broader community goals. Traditionally in Aboriginal communities, tourism development has been initiated and controlled by external organizations rather than by members of the community (Ofori and Hammer, 2002).

Finally, in a study of the Rolling River First Nation community, it was found that little comprehension of the Aboriginal culture is possessed by leisure and recreation decision-makers, thus limiting the potential of marketing a tourist site around the needs of this select group (MacKay, 1996). Indeed, as MacKay (1996) concludes, more research is needed on exploring the relationship between leisure, recreation and culture within Aboriginal communities.

SOCIAL ISSUES, AND LEISURE AND RECREATION

In 1996 the Report of the Royal Commission on Aboriginal Peoples reported that leisure and recreation could be used as a means to alleviate crime patterns and other social problems within Aboriginal communities. Leisure and recreation is recognized as a means to combat criminal involvement by youth, teen pregnancy, alcohol abuse, family violence and unemployment.

Photo: Nunavut Tourism.

Recreation services can play a vital role in sustaining small communities in the North.

Reid (1993c) argues that leisure and recreation is an excellent means for Aboriginal communities to battle social and domestic problems within their communities. Their appropriate provision can benefit community members in a number of ways. One of these ways is to fill the free time of youth by enticing them to playgrounds and helping to keep them off the streets.

Moreover, a paper published by Morinis (1982) reveals that alcohol and drugs are destructive activities or criminal activities engaged in by "Skid Row Indians" of Vancouver. In fact, the use of alcohol has become a problem in many Aboriginal communities. Leisure and recreation may be a means used to overcome problems such as alcohol abuse (Dawson, Karlis and Georgescu, 1998).

A greater emphasis needs to be put on leisure and recreation service provision within Aboriginal communities, which may in turn help alleviate some of their social and domestic problems.

THE NATIONAL RECREATION ROUNDTABLE ON ABORIGINAL/INDIGENOUS PEOPLES

From the 2000 *Parks and Recreation Canada* theme issue entitled "Together with Aboriginal Peoples" an excerpt was adapted from the Draft Report on the National Roundtable on Aboriginal/Indigenous Peoples. This excerpt highlighted the intent of the roundtable, the preamble, and the declaration. Below is an overview of what was presented.

The **National Recreation Roundtable on Aboriginal/Indigenous Peoples** was held on the Four Nations Reserves at Hobbema, Alberta, on February 17-20, 2000. It was hosted by Health Canada, the Inter-Provincial Sport and Recreation Council, and the provincial and territorial governments. It attracted one hundred delegates from all over Canada, including government officials from all levels, Aboriginal governments, and representatives from Aboriginal and non-Aboriginal non-governmental organizations of leisure, recreation and related fields.

The focus of the roundtable was on "integrating the physical, mental, emotional and spiritual aspects of life-fundamental to Aboriginal cultures" (Corporate Author, 2000: 32). Its purpose was to adopt a holistic approach through an understanding of traditional lifestyles while determining how active living can be used to enhance quality of life.

The preamble and declaration (see sidebar) accurately portray the role of leisure and recreation for Canada's Aboriginal Peoples. The delegation of the roundtable recognized that leisure and recreation is vital for the well-being of Canada's Aboriginal Peoples. Leisure and recreation is not only a means to promote physical, mental and spiritual well-being, but also a way to address social issues encountered by Aboriginal communities.

MASKWACHEES DECLARATION — PREAMBLE:

"We, the delegates of the National Recreation Roundtable on Aboriginal/Indigenous Peoples, held in Maskwachees, February 2000, are deeply committed to improving the health, wellness, cultural survival and quality of life of Aboriginal/Indigenous Peoples, through physical activity, physical education, sport and recreation.

"We affirm that the holistic concepts of Aboriginal cultures, given by the Creator, and taught by the elders, promote balance through the integration of the physical, mental, emotional and spiritual growth of the individual.

"We recognize that many social issues including poverty; health concerns such as type II diabetes, heart disease, and fetal alcohol syndrome; rates of incarceration; substance abuse; harassment and racism; and a sedentary lifestyle have contributed to poor health and a low quality of life for many Aboriginal/Indigenous Peoples.

"We recognize that Canada's endorsement of Article 3 of the United Nations Declaration on the Rights of Indigenous Peoples and the recommendations from the Royal Commission on Aboriginal Peoples dealing with recreation, sport and active living."

**MASKWACHEES
DECLARATION:**

*"We declare that sustainable
commitment and investment in
active living, physical activity,
physical education, recreation
and sport are essential to
promote health and address
social issues facing
Aboriginal/Indigenous Peoples
in communities across Canada.
And therefore we call on all
Governments, Non-Government
Organizations, communities and
individuals in Canada to endorse
this Declaration."*

CONCLUSION

Canada's original inhabitants engage in leisure and recreation activities on-reserve and off-reserve. Leisure and recreation is a means of preserving Aboriginal culture, particularly through the pursuit of traditional activities such as powwows and tug-of-war. However, leisure and recreation may also lead to acculturation as most Aboriginal Peoples live off-reserve and tend to engage in the leisure and recreation activities of mainstream society.

Leisure and recreation has a number of benefits for Aboriginal communities ranging from economic (tourism) to social (combating social problems). Nonetheless, literature reveals that Aboriginal communities tend to lack the needed leisure and recreation resources necessary to provide comprehensive leisure and recreation services (Karlis and Dawson, 1995b). To enhance the provision of leisure and recreation services in Aboriginal communities, Nielson (1993), with reference to the Royal Commission on Aboriginal Peoples, suggests that leisure and recreation professionals: (1) encourage and support Aboriginal Peoples to develop their own recreation delivery system; (2) promote Aboriginal Peoples to speak for themselves about recreation to all levels of government, and to participate at all levels of the recreation delivery system; (3) recognize and celebrate cultural differences and promote recreation activities specific to Aboriginal Peoples; (4) promote professional and technical training and recreation studies and ensure these opportunities are available within aboriginal communities; and (5) promote the inclusion of culturally sensitive leadership training materials in existing national training programs, and take a strong stand on racism (p. 34).

CHAPTER 9: LEISURE, RECREATION AND CANADA'S ABORIGINAL PEOPLES

Study Questions

1. Briefly describe the makeup of the Aboriginal Peoples of Canada.

2. What are the six information trends on the Aboriginal Peoples of Canada as presented by Statistics Canada 2001?

3. Provide a brief summary of the findings of the Royal Commission on Aboriginal Peoples for leisure and recreation.

4. Research by Dawson, Karlis and Georgescu (1998) identifies five contemporary issues in leisure and recreation for aboriginal peoples in Canada. What are these issues?

5. Describe the impact that preferences and participation patterns in Aboriginal cultural leisure activities may have on the maintenance of Aboriginal culture.

Selected Websites

*   **Aboriginal Canada Portal**
    http://www.aboriginalcanada.gc.ca/

*   **Aboriginal Peoples Television Network**
    http://www.aptn.ca

*   **Indian and Northern Affairs Canada**
    http://www.ainc-inac.gc.ca

*   **Turtle Island Native Network**
    http://www.turtleisland.org

Key Concepts

*   **Aboriginal Peoples**

*   **Royal Commission on Aboriginal Peoples**

*   **National Recreation Roundtable on Aboriginal/ Indigenous Peoples**

10

CANADIANS, LEISURE AND RECREATION

LEARNING OBJECTIVES

- To examine the leisure and recreation participation patterns of Canadians.

- To present research on the leisure and recreation participation patterns of selected provinces within Canada.

- To review Canadian-based research on leisure and recreation for leisure studies students, the homeless, youth, women, the aged and special populations.

- To examine the leisure and recreation constraints and barriers experienced by selected populations in Canada.

- To overview the current state of condition of leisure and recreation services for selected populations in Canada.

Leisure and recreation preferences and participation patterns are largely culturally determined. What we prefer and actually participate in is largely influenced by the values, beliefs and traditions of the society that we are a part of. But, what do Canadians do for leisure and recreation? Do we play hockey and lacrosse, participate in pow wows, or engage in multicultural dances and festivals?

This chapter examines what Canadians do for leisure and recreation while exploring the leisure and recreation activities of selected populations within Canadian society. It begins with an overview of the leisure and recreation activities of Canadians, following by a look at the activities of the following selected groups: leisure studies students, the homeless, youth, women, the aged and special populations.

"Conspicuous consumption of valuable goods is a means of reputability to the gentleman of leisure."

— Thorstein Veblen (1857-1929), U.S. social scientist. *The Theory of the Leisure Class*, ch. 4 (1899).

THE LEISURE AND RECREATION ACTIVITIES OF CANADIANS

With over 31 million people living in Canada, it is impossible to depict the specific leisure needs, preferences, behaviours and participation rates of each member of this society. In addition, the multicultural fabric of Canada, and the fact the Canada is still a relatively young country, makes it virtually impossible to state that Canadians have a unique identity based solely on specific leisure and recreation activities.

Table 10.1: Most Popular Sports, 1998

	Total*		Male		Female	
	000s	%	000s	%	000s	%
Population aged 15 years and older	**24,260**		**11,937**		**12,323**	
Golf	1,802	7.4	1,325	11.1	476	3.9
Hockey (ice)	1,499	6.2	1,435	12.0	65	0.5
Baseball	1,339	5.5	953	8.0	386	3.1
Swimming	1,120	4.6	432	3.6	688	5.6
Basketball	787	3.2	550	4.6	237	1.9
Volleyball	744	3.1	394	3.3	350	2.8
Soccer	739	3.0	550	4.6	189	1.5
Tennis	658	2.7	434	3.6	224	1.8
Skiing, downhill/alpine	657	2.7	342	2.9	315	2.6
Cycling	608	2.5	358	3.0	250	2.0
Skiing, cross-country/ Nordic	512	2.1	208	1.7	304	2.5
Weightlifting	435	1.8	294	2.5	140	1.1
Badminton	403	1.7	199	1.7	204	1.7
Football	387	1.6	347	2.9	40	0.3
Curling	312	1.3	179	1.5	133	1.1
Bowling, 10 pin	282	1.2	132	1.1	150	1.2
Softball	210	0.9	118	1.0	92	0.7
Bowling, 5 pin	200	0.8	78	0.7	122	1.0
Squash	163	0.7	X	X	X	X
Karate	129	0.5	81	0.7	48	0.4
Figure skating	121	0.5	46	0.4	75	0.6
Rugby	104	0.4	X	X	X	X
Ball hockey	91	0.4	X	X	X	X
Snowboarding	81	0.3	X	X	X	X
In-line skating	70	0.3	X	X	X	X
Racquetball	58	0.2	X	X	X	X
Other Sports	323	1.3	1.8	1.8	104	0.8

"X" indicates that data is unavailable, not applicable or confidential.
* Persons frequently play more than one sport.
Source: Statistics Canada, General Social Survey, 1998.

A number of studies, federal, provincial and municipal, have been conducted to try to understand better what Canadians do for leisure and recreation. Most research has been commissioned by the federal government of Canada, more specifically, Statistics Canada. In addition, the **Canadian Fitness and Lifestyle Research Institute** also conducts a series of studies such as the Physical Activity Monitor. The Canadian Fitness and Lifestyle Research Institute, in its 2001 Physical Activity Monitor, reported the five most popular physical activities of Canadians as found in the 1998/1999 National Population Health Survey. These five, in rank order of highest reported popularity, are: (1) walking, (2) gardening, yard work, (3) home exercise, (4) swimming, and (5) bicycling.

As far as passive leisure activities are concerned, television is one of the most popular in Canada. Statistics Canada (1998b) presents that, on average, men eighteen and over watch 20.9 hours of television per week, whereas women watch 25.5 hours per week. Furthermore, a provincial breakdown indicates that women and men in Quebec, whose primary language of household is French, average the greatest number of hours of television viewing per week with 30.1 and 23.2 respectively.

Further statistics that give us an understanding of what Canadians do for active leisure pursuits are those that present the most popular sports in Canada. Statistics Canada (1998c) presents golf as being the most popular sport in Canada. Hockey, one of Canada's two national sports, was the second most popular sport. It is interesting to note that lacrosse, Canada's other national sport, was not ranked as a "most popular" sport in Canada by Statistics Canada in 1998 (see Table 10.1).

Moreover, further statistics illustrate the involvement of Canadians in cultural activities. According to Statistics Canada (1998d) the three most frequently participated cultural activities of Canadians are all reading-oriented activities. These activities are (in rank order according to most frequent participation): reading a newspaper, reading a magazine and reading a book. The fourth most frequently engaged in cultural activity is "use of library services," whereas the fifth is "going to a movie" (see Table 10.2).

The 2001 version of the Canadian Fitness and Lifestyle Research Institute's Physical Activity Monitor reveals that 57 percent of adults aged eighteen and older are not active enough for optimal health benefits. In fact, more than half of the Canadian population is physically inactive. On its twentieth anniversary in 2000, the Canadian Fitness and Lifestyle Institute reported that slightly more than one-third of Canadians are sufficiently active, as compared to 1991, when only 21 percent of Canadians were active enough to achieve desired health benefits.

In addition to national statistics, various provinces such as Nova Scotia, Alberta and Ontario have conducted leisure surveys of their citizens. In the case of Nova Scotia, a study was commissioned by the Nova Scotia Sport and Recreation Commission in collaboration with Decima Research. The results of this study, as presented by Robertson and Singleton (1996), indicate the following activities as being engaged in more

CANADIAN FITNESS AND LIFESTYLE RESEARCH INSTITUTE

Based in Ottawa, the Canadian Fitness and Lifestyle Research Institute is a national research agency concerned with advising, educating, and informing Canadians and professionals about the importance of leading healthy, active lifestyles.

The institute is directed by a board of directors comprised of eminent scholars and professionals in the areas of public health, physical education, sport sciences, recreation and medicine, as well as universities and federal and provincial levels of governments.

Established in September 1980, in recognition of the need identified by national organizations, federal and provincial governments, and Canadian universities, the institute is the leader in bridging the gap between knowledge on physical activity and its use. As a primary source of knowledge and through its network of national and international scholars, the institute provides a comprehensive range of services required for evidence-based decision making to governments at all levels as well as national and private sector organizations.

Source:
<http://www.cflri.ca/cflri/pa/index.html>.

Table 10.2: Participation in Culture Activities by Sex, Canada, 1998

	Both Sexes		Male	
	000s	%	000s	%
Population aged 15 years and over	**24,260**	**100.0**	**11,937**	**100.00**
Read a newspaper	19,851	81.8	9,915	83.1
Read a magazine	17,264	71.2	8,166	68.4
Read a book	14,881	61.3	6,478	54.3
Use library services	6,688	27.6	2,845	23.8
Borrow materials	6,036	24.9	2,432	20.4
Use Internet	583	2.4	296	2.5
Do research	1,898	7.8	964	8.1
Attend a program	277	1.1	81	0.7
Other	107	0.4	49	0.4
Go to a movie	14,340	59.1	7,216	60.5
Watch a video on VCR	17,690	72.9	8,921	74.7
Listen to cassettes, records, CDs	18,625	76.8	9,166	76.8
Use Internet	7,171	29.6	4,117	34.5
Communicate	5,478	22.6	3,081	25.8
Research	5,412	22.3	3,248	27.2
Read a newspaper, magazine, book	2,322	9.6	1,432	12.0
View video, film, TV, listen to music	1,204	5.0	799	6.7
View art or museum collections	1,011	4.2	611	5.1
Create artistic compositions, designs	983	4.1	601	5.0
Electronic banking	1,437	5.9	942	7.9
Download software, other	2,714	11.2	1,864	15.6

Source: Statistics Canada, General Social Survey, 1998.

frequently during free time: walking (34 percent); outdoor chores (34 percent); outdoor activities (e.g., picnicking and hiking) (20 percent); hobbies and crafts (20 percent) and reading (19 percent). In 1992, the Alberta government conducted the Alberta Recreation Survey. The intent of this survey was to monitor opinions, preferences and participation patterns. The results revealed that the "top five" favourite leisure or recreational activities were as follows (presented in rank order): walking for pleasure, camping, golf, bicycling and fishing.

In 1989, Hall and Rhyme examined the leisure behaviours and recreation needs of Ontario's ethno-cultural populations. The results revealed the following: (1) reading for pleasure was reported by the greatest number of respondents to be a favourite activity while walking for pleasure was chosen second; (2) significant variations in the types of activities chosen by some ethno-cultural groups exist (e.g., the favourite activity of the Chinese is "watching television" whereas the favourite activity of the Italians is "spending time with family"); (3) Chinese, South Asians and others indicated that participation in their favourite activities would increase if they had more opportunity to do so with people of their own ethno-cultural background; and (4) volunteer and service organizations (e.g., ethnic community organizations) were most often identified as providing assistance in addressing recreation needs through services.

Furthermore, a study by Horna (1995) discusses the impact of Canada's cold climate on the leisure and recreation pursuits of Canadians. It is argued that Canadians adapt their leisure and recreation to the environment. Horna (1995) finds that the leisure and recreation styles of Canadians consist of three patterns: (1) the passive and interactive core found in most parts of the world; (2) the warm season's peripheral pursuits that consist of sports carried out, to a large extent, outdoors; and (3) the outdoor "cold" activities and the "warm" activities of the indoors. For Horna, the passive and interactive core activities refer to watching television, reading a book, playing a sport or doing physical exercise (e.g., jogging or lifting weights). The warm season peripheral pursuits refer to everything from playing soccer to hiking and fishing, whereas the outdoor "cold" activities refer to activities such as snowshoeing, snowmobiling and cross-country skiing. Thus, Canadians have access to the best of both worlds through seasonal-oriented leisure and recreation pursuits as most places in Canada experience the beauty of four full seasons of differing climate and varying leisure and recreation opportunities.

Statistics and studies such as the aforementioned give us some indication as to who the people of Canada are and the leisure and recreation behaviours they prefer and experience. For the most part, however, these statistics explore the population of Canada either as a whole or as homogeneous groups – that is, minimal information is presented on the leisure and recreation participation pattens of selected groups within Canadian society. The question that therefore unfolds is: Do specific select populations within Canadian society have specific leisure and recreation needs, preferences and activity opportunities?

Photo: Health Canada.

Bicycling is increasingly a popular recreational activity for young families.

LEISURE STUDIES STUDENTS

Leisure studies students are not your typical selected population. However, this group might be of interest to the primary readers of this book. A limitation, however, is that little research exists exploring the leisure and recreation pursuits of leisure studies students.

A study by Auger, Dawson, Gravelle, Karlis, Pageot and Zalatan (1999) examines the interest for and participation in cultural leisure and recreation activities for leisure studies students at the University of Ottawa. For Auger at al., cultural leisure and recreation activities are defined as reading for pleasure, buying works of arts and crafts, attending theatre performances (plays) and attending music recitals (concerts). The results of the study reveal that the favourite leisure and recreation activities for undergraduate leisure studies students are: sports, socializing with family and friends, and watching TV and movies. It is interesting to note that very few of the 135 students examined mentioned cultural leisure and recreation activities as favourites, yet female respondents read magazines more than male respondents. Approximately half of the students "rarely" read books other than textbooks required for classes.

THE HOMELESS

This group consists of those who have been homeless for a long period of time, homeless for a moderate period of time, or homeless during one specific time (Dail, 1990). In Canada, homelessness is a growing problem. More than 14,000 Canadians are classified by Statistics Canada (2001b) as being in shelters. A large number of these individual are seniors, persons with mental disabilities, single mothers with their children, or immigrants. These individuals, like all members of society, have specific needs that must be fulfilled, and one of these needs is leisure and recreation. But where do the homeless turn to meet this need? What do the homeless in Canada do for leisure and recreation?

In Canada, time away from work (free time) is viewed as a necessary prerequisite for leisure and recreation. However, there are a number of individuals in our society who do have time away from work, yet for one reason or another cannot classify this as leisure time. One of these groups is the homeless.

Leisure and recreation for the homeless tends to be offered in shelters, yet even this is something new. Thanks to social service providers, homeless shelters have begun to expand their focus beyond temporary housing to leisure and recreation activities and services to enhance self-esteem (Harrington and Dawson, 1996). Today leisure and recreation activities for Canada's homeless are viewed as "an important avenue for normalization and reintegration" (p. 99). These activities assist persons who are homeless not only to enhance their quality of life but also to re-establish themselves into a non-homeless lifestyle.

To understand what homeless people do for leisure and recreation, one needs to recognize where members of this group can be found and who provides the leisure and recreation services. According to McLaughlin (1987), four types of shelter systems exist in Canada: (1) private sector permanent housing, (2) government-subsidized housing with conditional tenure, (3) temporary and emergency shelters, and (4) the streets.

For their part, those who provide leisure and recreation service activities in shelters tend to be either paid or volunteer employees with little, if any, professional training in the leisure and recreation field. Moreover, these leisure and recreation service providers may employ one of several approaches for leisure and recreation service provision such as leisure education, leisure counselling and community recreation.

The year 1987 was designated as the International Year of Shelter for the Homeless, which brought an increase in global awareness of homelessness. As a result, many municipalities in Canada identified this group as a distinct one requiring special leisure and recreation services. For instance, initial action for this inclusion was taken in 1989 by the City of Ottawa and in 1991 by the City of Gloucester (see City of Ottawa, 1989; City of Gloucester, 1991).

In the case of Ottawa, on November 7, 2002, a report on Ottawa's Community Action Plan to Prevent and End Homelessness (2002-2005) was submitted by Jocelyn St. Jean, the General Manager of the People Services Department to the Health, Recreation and Social Services Committee and Ottawa City Council. This Community Action Plan consists of four components: (1) increasing the supply of affordable and appropriate housing; (2) preventing individuals and families from becoming homeless, and assisting people while they are homeless; (3) achieving legislative and policy changes to end homelessness; and (4) ensuring a coordinated, comprehensive and accountable community response to homelessness.

In 1998, in an attempt to find a solution to aid homeless people, the former Mayor of Toronto, Mel Lastman, took part in a three-day trade mission with former New York Mayor Rudolf Giuliani. The focus was on sharing ideas as to how to bring homeless people off the streets and into warm shelters (Lackey, 1998). For the most part, leisure and recreation appears to have been overlooked in their discussions.

Perhaps the most difficult part of providing leisure and recreational services for the homeless is that this group of individuals is not a homogeneous one. To be able to best serve the recreation needs of this group, leisure and recreation service providers must first be able to recognize the demographic makeup of this population and, second, explore the leisure and recreation needs and preferences of these individuals as well as the specific benefits to be gained. Once this research is done, the recreation providers of Canada will be in a better position to address the issue of leisure, recreation and homelessness.

HOMELESSNESS

Homelessness in Canada is a serious problem, and this is particularly evident in the largest cities of Toronto, Montreal and Vancouver. Homeless shelters in these cities have a primary concern to ascertain the well-being of these individuals through the provision of warm shelters during the cold winter months.

Inside these shelters, little is offered in the form of structured leisure and recreation services.

THE COALITION OF ACTIVE LIVING

Promoting Active Healthy Living for Canadians

The 1960s and the 1970s were decades in which the federal government became more concerned with the fitness levels of Canadians. During these decades, it had become evident that Canadian athletes were not faring well in international competition. The concern was that other nations were doing a better job of promoting and encouraging their citizens to live actively and be physically fit.

In the 1970s a program called PARTICIPaction was introduced. A subsequent program called Active Living was introduced in the 1980s. The intent of both of these programs was to encourage Canadians to become more active, to live active lifestyles, and eventually to increase the level of fitness of Canadian citizens.

It appears that both of these programs did work, as the fitness levels of Canadians have increased. Yet, as reported by the Canadian Fitness and Lifestyle Institute, more needs to be done in regards to encouraging Canadians to live actively.

To continue to help in the evolution of a "fit Canada," the Coalition of Active Living was founded in November 1999 in Ottawa. Below is an overview of the Coalition for Active Living.

What Is the Coalition of Active Living?

The coalition is made up of hundreds of groups, organizations and individuals committed to making sure that the environments where we live, learn, work and play support regular physical activity. The coalition is working to achieve this goal by advocating for public policies that support physical activity.

The members, partners and supporters of the Coalition for Active Living represent a wide range of sectors, working at the local, provincial/ territorial and national levels in a variety of ways to advance physical activity in Canada.

Mission

The members of the Coalition work together to develop, implement and evaluate the outcomes of joint actions that will enable physical activity to be integrated into the lives of Canadians.

Vision

The vision of active living in Canada is one in which Canadians value and integrate regular physical activity into their daily lives.

Goals

The Coalition is committed to making sure that the environments where Canadians live, learn, work, and play support regular physical activity.

Policy Platform

Preamble: In order to determine the issues that the Coalition for Active Living could address, nationwide consultations were held from December 2000 to January 2001. Some 200 active living leaders across Canada were asked to identify

- the most critical national issues relating to physical activity,
- some effective and realistic solutions to these issues, and
- the special actions that the CAL could take in the short term.

The consultations affirmed the need for a strong national voice and an identification of five national issues:

1. Infrastructure
2. Access
3. Children and Youth
4. Diversity
5. Communication

Source: Extracted from: <http://www.activeliving.com>.

YOUTH

The United Nations proclaimed 1985 as the International Year of the Youth. The United Nations defines "youth" as those who are from thirteen to twenty-four years of age. In the 1986 Canada Census, the term "youth" comprises "young adolescents" who are from ten to fourteen years of age, and "older adolescents" who are from fifteen to nineteen years of age.

Research in the area of youth, leisure and recreation in Canada has increased dramatically since the early 1990s. During this decade a number of studies (Guy, 1993; Kent, 1993; Trottier, 1990) were published in *Recreation Canada* while an entire issue of the *Journal of Leisurability* in Spring 1991 was devoted to youth and leisure. The Canadian Parks and Recreation Association put together a **National Policy on Youth** consisting of the following ten policy statements (Pavelka and Godin, 1994: 26-27):

- Input from youth in program development and evaluation should be the cornerstone to program development.

- Program/service infrastructures need to be designed in such a way that they ensure consistent satisfaction of needs but are flexible in order to be responsive to ever-changing environments.

- Programs/services should be designed to empower youth to make meaningful decisions with an end to realizing outcomes.

- Programs/service providers should have constant awareness and consideration for constraints to participation.

- Staff who work directly with youth need to be well trained and empowered to make decisions to ensure a high degree of responsiveness.

- Staff who work directly with youth need to have regular access to the organization's decision-makers to ensure proper communication of results and requirements.

- Youth servicing organizations need to involve "quality of life" stakeholders in the community.

- Youth serving organizations need to develop evaluation mechanisms that meet the needs of all potential stakeholders and the public at large.

- Youth serving organizations need to measure success in relation to the goals of the greater community.

- Youth serving organizations need to develop and/or maintain mechanisms for the sharing of youth program/service-related information with other local, provincial and national contacts.

The National Policy on Youth has served as a basis for a greater focus on addressing the leisure and recreation needs of youth through programs and services. Since this policy was put forth, Canadian-based

Photo: Jon Easton/Ontario Ministry of Education.

School programs for youth can foster active lifestyles that will last a lifetime.

research on youth, leisure and recreation has also expanded. Some of the focus of this research has been on increasing participation, overcoming constraints to participation, and understanding and serving youth-at-risk.

The Canadian Fitness and Lifestyle Research Institute's 2001 Physical Activity Monitor presents the results of the National Population Health Survey of 1998-99. One of the categories of this survey is devoted to youth. It reveals, in rank order for highest popularity, that for youth aged from twelve to nineteen years of age, the five most popular physical activities are: (1) walking for exercise, (2) bicycling, (3) swimming, (4) jogging/running, and (5) basketball. Statistics Canada in its 1998 General Survey identified soccer, swimming and hockey as the three most popular sports among children aged from five to fourteen (Statistics Canada, 1998c).

Subsequent research on youth, leisure and recreation shows that leisure provides youth with both risk and opportunity (Robertson, 1993; Kent, 1993; Caldwell and Smith, 1996). Furthermore, research postulates that leisure and recreation helps youth adjust from the developmental stages of young adulthood to adulthood. For instance, Larson and Kleiber (1993) suggest that leisure and recreation activities (e.g., hobbies and arts) are positive factors in shaping youth development. Moreover, participation in leisure and recreation is viewed as being "protective" in that it mediates involvement in problem behaviour (e.g., substance abuse, vandalism, crime and physical violence) (Caldwell and Smith, 1996). Research also shows that leisure is instrumental in the career development of youth as it helps in the development of a life-span perspective (Munson, 1996). In a subsequent study of Grade 10 youth in Ontario, Shaw, Kleiber and Caldwell (1993) found that leisure and recreation activities can be both beneficial and detrimental to the identity formation of adolescents depending on the type of activity and the gendered nature of the activity. Finally, recent research by Mannell, Zuzanek and Schneider (2002) reveals that busyness and time pressure, largely as a result of extracurricular leisure and recreation activities, positively and negatively influence the psychological well-being of youth. Thus, the "right time-balance" is needed so that leisure and recreation experiences remain consistently positive for youth.

WOMEN

Women experience a number of constraints in the pursuit of leisure and recreation. Similar to men, women may face constraints such as scarce resources and lack of time (Leith and Shaw, 1997). However, women tend to face a number of additional constraints such as limits of choice; lack of a sense of entitlement and the presence of an ethic of care (Harrington, Dawson and Bolla, 1992); body image (Frederick and Shaw, 1985) and lack of cultural specific activities (Pawlick and Karlis, 1998).

Harrington and Dawson (1993) note that the effects of motherhood and gender roles pose constraints on leisure and recreation for women. Research by Zuzanek and Mannell (1993) also suggests that gender roles have an impact on women's leisure and recreation, particularly for mothers who work full time and have to catch up with domestic obligations on weekends. Further research by Shaw (1992) reveals that work is unequally divided between men and women, thus impacting the leisure and recreation of women. Subsequent studies by Shaw, Bonen and McCabe (1991), Hunter and Whitson (1991), and Jackson and Henderson (1995) indicate how constraints imposed by the social structures and cultural interpretations of society (e.g., gender, family, and lifestyle) can limit the leisure and recreation of women.

A study by Rublee and Shaw (1991) examines how immigrant women experience constraints to physical and social mobility. Community and leisure participation is identified as a constraint central to the integration process of the thirteen Latin American women they examined in Halifax, Nova Scotia. Leisure and recreation opportunities offered by society tend to overlook the needs of this select group, thus creating a barrier to community involvement.

The simple provision of leisure and recreation activities is insufficient to cater to the specific needs of this select population. "At issue is that simply offering the opportunities is not enough. Outreach, advocacy and special measures are required to create the appropriate environment for effective change" (Friars, 1994: 27). Only if such measures are taken will equality be fully incorporated.

Research in 1985 by Susan Shaw was instrumental in laying the foundation for expanding Canadian-based research on women, leisure and recreation. In her study, Shaw describes how issues related to women, leisure and recreation merit serious attention in Canada, as "unpaid work" undertaken by women was not structured and was thus not distinguished by a set leisure time as compared to men who work. In Shaw's study it was clear that women did not have the same leisure and recreation opportunities as men.

The 1990s witnessed a tremendous increase in research on women and leisure resulting in large part from an enhanced focus on women by organizations throughout the leisure and recreation service sector. Organizations such as the Inter-Provincial Sport and Recreation Council, the Canadian Association for Health, Physical Education and Recreation, and Active Living Canada all incorporate gender equity policies. The intent of **gender equity policies** is to address the issues of fairness and equity in the provision of leisure and recreation services. The Canadian Parks and Recreation Association has taken measures towards acting on a national scale for the promotion of gender equity. To help facilitate this process, Friars (1994) recommends that the Canadian Parks and Recreation Association create partnerships with the Canadian Association for the Advancement of Women in Sport, Canadian Sports Council, Canadian Association for Health, Physical Education and Recreation, Canadian Intramural Recreation Association, and the Canadian Fitness and Lifestyle Research Institute. In addition to the establishment of gender equity policies, federal government organizations such as Sport Canada have established policies to ensure that women receive fair and equitable treatment in the allocation of services. The intent of the Sport Canada Policy on Women and Sport (1986) is to ensure that the needs of women in sport are identified, promoted and supported.

A further study by Tirone (1995) on women who have immigrated from India found that "North American concepts used to define leisure have little relevance in the lives of the immigrant women" (pp. 2-3). Tirone posits that these women "are not inclined to have a social life that is apart from their children, husband and extended families. These women are not interested in having time to themselves" (p. 3). To this end, a constraint to leisure and recreation may be imposed on leisure and recreation administrators simply through a lack of understanding of the unique needs of immigrant women. This may also be the case for other groups of women.

Increased research in the area of women, leisure and recreation has led to the ongoing development of leisure and recreation opportunities and programs for girls and women. Programs such as "Women and Action" in Toronto, "Females Active in Recreation" in London, Ontario, and "On the Move" in British Columbia seek to establish equality and fairness in the provision of leisure and recreation services (see Friars, 1994). However, more effort by all sectors of society is needed to help eliminate barriers and constraints experienced by women in pursuit of fair and equitable leisure and recreation opportunities.

THE AGED

In 2000 roughly 3.8 million people in Canada were reported to be sixty-five years of age or older. In fact, seniors constitute one of the most rapidly growing population groups in Canada due to the massive population explosion in Canada between 1946 to 1965, called the baby boom. As a result of the ageing of this large population cohort, Statistics Canada forecasts that by 2016, 17 percent of all Canadians will be seniors and that by 2041, 23 percent of Canadians will be sixty-five and older (Canadian Centre for Justice, 2001a).

Today, many of these baby boomers have started planning leisure and recreation opportunities for their senior years, including activities that will help maintain longevity and good heath. David Foot, a Canadian demographer from the University of Toronto, argues that ageing baby boomers in Canada will have different leisure and recreation needs than those of previous generations as they will age with a leisure ethic, more discretionary income and a greater need for active-oriented leisure and recreation pursuits (Foot, 2000). Indeed, early research in the 1990s indicated that ageing seniors were seeking, more so than in the past, an active lifestyle (McLeod and Wright, 1992).

A study conducted in 1983 by Marc-Andre Delisle on the elderly of Quebec found that they are not only more active than their predecessors, but they also have more discretionary income and retire earlier from work. Delisle's findings reveal that all the above factors have re-shaped the way seniors perceive and participate in leisure and recreation experiences. Rates of participation in physical, cultural, educational, volunteer activities, and in travel and tourism were found to have increased for this generation.

Little research exists, however, on the needs of the ageing boomers. In a recent study of the 1992 Ontario Senior Games, Levy, Losito and Levy (1996) reported that major barriers for participation for seniors are "transportation" and "financial." Moreover, "lack of skill" is also presented as being a constraint to senior involvement. Despite research supporting the importance of fitness activities for seniors (Mobily, Nilson, Ostiguy and MacNeil, 1993), this group confronts a number of barriers in the pursuit of fitness activities.

Canada's ageing seniors will be better educated, healthier, expected to live longer, retire earlier, and embrace a more relaxed attitude towards the puritan work ethic (Gravelle, Wood and Karlis, 1995). In response to these trends, Gravelle et al. argue that leisure and recreation practitioners must play a leadership role in instilling an active living philosophy in all seniors. To assist leisure and recreation practitioners to better serve the needs of Canada's growing senior population, Gravelle at al. (1995: 11-12) have recommended that leisure and recreation practitioners:

- become aware of active living and its applicability to the aged;

More than ever before, seniors are pursuing a variety of leisure activities.

Photo: Health Canada.

MALL WALKING: A GROWING TREND

An Alternative to the Treadmill and the Gym?

Photo: Courtesy of Rowan Thompson.

Statistics Canada presents walking as being the recreation activity most frequently experienced. You may say that of course this is so, as we walk to get from point A to Point B almost every minute of every day. But does this walking constitute a recreation activity? Does a difference not exist between walking simply to do things and walking for recreation purposes?

For the most part, walking for recreation purposes refers to going for a leisure stroll in your neighbourhood, power-walking for exercise, or even walking for pleasure. Walking for recreation purposes, however, can be difficult in many parts of Canada as cold and icy conditions make it difficult to experience this popular recreation activity in the outdoors for a big part of the year. It is not uncommon to have wind-chill factors and frost-bite warnings in many parts of Canada throughout the winter months.

Mall walking is a growing trend in Canadian society. It is extremely popular with seniors and ageing baby boomers who love to walk for exercise but do not want to walk in the freezing cold. Mall walking is an alternative to the treadmill or the gym. It is a relatively inexpensive form of exercise as mall walkers do not have to pay membership and user fees in health clubs but rather use the corridors and facilities of local shopping malls to do their walk.

Mall walking is "working out" indoors. In fact, this activity has become a trend not only in cold Canada, but also in places with warmer clients that are sometimes unbearable in the summer (e.g., Florida). Shopping malls in Canada and throughout the world have opened their doors to mall walkers as this opportunity is viewed as being beneficial for the entire community.

Reasons Why Mall Walking Has Become a Trend

1. *Out of hot, cold and humid conditions.* When walking in a mall, mall walkers do not have to worry about dressing for varying weather conditions. In addition, mall walkers do not have to worry about snow, wind-chill factors, ice, freezing rain, wind, rain, heat and the sun.

2. *Out of harm's way.* Mall walkers do not have to worry about inhaling the pollutants of automobiles, crossing dangerous intersections, being splashed by automobiles, or noisy and busy street traffic.

3. *Restrooms, food and water readily available.* All malls provide these services.

4. *Security available.* Mall walking provides people with safety as they walk with others. In addition, shopping malls also have security personnel on patrol.

- become aware of the fact that Canada is an aging society, and that Canadians are retiring to recreation and active living rather than from it;

- should act as leaders in educating and instilling an active living philosophy in all seniors and ageing Canadians;

- should encourage and support the development of programs and services oriented towards active living for seniors; and

- at the public, private and non-profit levels, should work closely with Fitness Canada's Active Living Department to assure that the needs of senior Canadians are met.

The findings of Gravelle et al. build on a previous study conducted by Thornton and Collins in 1986. In a study of 119 older adults in Canada, Thornton and Collins found that, although activity and leisure counts decreased with age, the decrease was not as sharp as one might assume. In fact, it was concluded by this team of researchers that some seniors do not disengage from activity and leisure involvement throughout the ageing years. Thus, as research by Horna (1987c) and Colley (1985) suggests, the spillover of leisure and recreation choices continues to be consistent throughout the life stages.

Further research reveals that aged immigrants have become forgotten clients in the provision of leisure and recreation services in Canada. Aged immigrants rely on their ethnic communities to fulfill their ethno-specific leisure and recreation needs. In smaller cities and towns, these ethnic communities do not exist. If they do exist, these communities do not have the appropriate facilities or trained leisure and recreation personnel to address their needs (Karlis, 1990a). This is not the case for all ethnic communities as larger ethnic groups such as the Greeks and the Jews have established senior centres for their members in larger cities such as Toronto and Montreal. However, public leisure and recreation services are also needed (ibid.), as Dembrowski (1988) also argues.

Some seniors in Canada have the economic means to retire in communities that offer a choice of public leisure and recreation and park services. Research by Backman and Backman (1997) reveals that, for ageing seniors, the availability and accessibility of recreation-oriented resources is a retirement community preference. An example of such a community is the City of Kingston, Ontario, which has attracted a number of retiree residents from Ontario and the rest of Canada.

Research on leisure, recreation and the aged has continued to expand in the past thirty years. This research focuses mostly on providing an understanding of what the aged do for leisure and recreation and their leisure and recreation constraints and opportunities. Almost thirty years ago, an article by Douse (1974) argued that the aged are one of the greatest challenges for leisure and recreation service professionals as health

Table 10.3: Words with Dignity

Instead of...	Use...
Disabled, handicapped, crippled	Person with a disability, People with disabilities
Crippled by, afflicted with, suffering from, deformed	Person who has... or, Person with...
Lame	Person who has a mobility impairment
Confined, bound, restricted to a wheelchair	Person who uses a wheelchair
Deaf and dumb, deaf mute, hearing impaired	Person who is... Deaf... or hard of hearing
Retarded, mentally retarded	Person with an intellectual disability
Spastic (as a noun)	Person with cerebral palsy
Physically challenged	Person with a physical disability
Mental patient, mentally ill, mental, insane	Person who has a mental illness... or schizophrenia
Learning disabled, learning difficulty	Person with a learning disability
Visually impaired (as a collective noun), blind	People who have a visual impairment
Disabled sport	Sport for athletes with disabilities
Disabled community	Disability community

Source: Active Living Alliance for Canadians with a Disability.

Photo: Secretary of State Canada.

needs, social needs, and leisure and recreation needs may vary considerably. This has become clearly evident today.

In a recent study, Thomas (2002) outlines how senior volunteers have adapted to the use of computers and technology to implement the services of the Evergreen Seniors Centre of Guelph, Ontario. Moreover, a study by Romsa and Blenman (1989), through the use of an activity diary, reported that the leisure and recreation needs of the aged are many and that leisure and recreation researchers need to be cognizant and appreciative of these needs. Romsa and Blenman concluded by stating that research surveys on "elderly need to be rethought and procedures modified to ensure accuracy of findings" (p. 47). Indeed, the need for better research methods to understand leisure and recreation for the aged in Canada has never been greater.

LEISURE FOR A COLD CLIMATE

Canadians adapt their leisure and recreation activities to Canada's environment, meaning its cold climate (Horna, 1995).

SPECIAL POPULATIONS

The past thirty years has witnessed a significant increase in research in the area of special populations. This research has expanded beyond mere inquiry into what persons with disabilities do for leisure and recreation to a broader understanding as to how they participate, issues of terminology and concern for their self-betterment through leisure and recreation involvement.

The designation of 1981 as the International Year of Disabled Persons, combined with a mid-1980s national survey on Health and Disability that reported that 2.8 million Canadians had a disability, prompted greater emphasis on inclusion, accessibility, integration and adaptability by leisure and non-leisure professionals. Heightened awareness of persons with disabilities brought increased concern as to how language could be detrimental to their full integration into society (MacCauley and Gilbert, 1993), including its leisure and recreation opportunities. As a result, the Active Living Alliance for Canadians with a Disability put together a document entitled "Words With Dignity" to describe persons with disabilities in words and expressions that portray them in an appropriate, positive and sensitive manner. This document suggests that, instead of "disabled," we should use "person with a disability," and rather than use the word "lame," we should use "person who has a mobility impairment." Table 10.3 presents the most recent version of "Words With Dignity," dated October 19, 2001.

In addition to "identity labels" and stereotypes, the over 4 million persons with disabilities in Canada face many other barriers to their full integration into society. These barriers, as presented by the Canadian Centre for Justice (2001b), include yet are not limited to transportation, employment and income. Roughly 20 percent of persons with disabilities have difficulty getting around their local community without transportation assistance. A little less than half of the persons with disabilities in Canada are unemployed while the average income of persons with disabilities is well below that of persons without disabilities.

LEISURE NEEDS OF SPECIAL POPULATIONS

Perhaps the most difficult part of providing leisure and recreational services for the homeless is that this group of individuals is not homogeneous. To be able to best serve the recreation needs of this group, leisure and recreation service providers must first be able to recognize the demographic makeup of this population and, second, explore the leisure and recreation needs and preferences of these individuals as well as the specific benefits to be gained.

The 1970s and early 1980s was a period in which the leisure and recreation field pulled away from the ideology of direct service provision to a focus on facilitation of leisure and recreation services (Gold, 1990). It was in the 1980s that increased focus took place on establishing independent living opportunities to enhance full inclusion of persons with disabilities in all services of society, including leisure and recreation (Marlett, Gall and Wight-Felske, 1984). Today, independent living opportunities for special populations, including the well-being of the client, has come to the forefront of priorities for leisure and recreation service providers. This point was made clear by Mahon (1995) when he stated that "self-determination in leisure for persons with a disability will ultimately be one important measure of societies ability to enhance the quality of life of its citizens" (p. 24).

Since 1987, the **Active Living Alliance for Canadians with a Disability** has attempted to enhance and incorporate a more physically active lifestyle for persons with disabilities. This alliance is composed of national organizations, community partners and various individuals concerned with implementing an active lifestyle for persons with disabilities (Lawrence and Legg, 1998).

Another recent trend to enhance inclusion of people with disabilities into leisure and recreation experiences is the focus on "integration" (Schibberas and Hutchison, 2002). Hutchison (1990) describes this trend by stating that "recreationists are beginning to realize the importance of extending integration to include the provision of supports and structures which facilitate friendships" (p. 44). An example of a recently established organization that focuses on increasing involvement of persons with disabilities in leisure and recreation is the West Island Committee for Integration and Recreation, established in 1990. The intent of this organization is to work closely with municipal leisure and recreation departments in the Montreal area to help persons with disabilities integrate into existing mainstream programs. "Integration" is a good means for activity choice selection as it allows persons with disabilities the ability to choose and participate in leisure and recreational activities (Luken, 1993). Nonetheless, "integration" of persons with disabilities into existing programs may be beneficial for some persons with disabilities yet not all. As Pelot (1998) posits, "integrating persons with special needs into mainstream programming is the ultimate goal but not the only one. By learning more about the needs of these individuals, you may need to offer segregated or tailored programs in some instances" (p. 34).

In 1994, the Active Living Alliance for Canadians with a Disability reported that a number of organizations and services concerned with leisure and recreation in Canada had moved towards a model of inclusion. The Canadian Special Olympics and the Canadian Cerebral Palsy Sports Association were presented as two examples of organizations with an inclusion mandate.

In addition, a number of integration services are currently provided by municipalities. One example is the City of Ottawa and the efforts it has made for Special Needs Recreation Programming. The City of Ottawa has initiated an Inter-Action and Buddy Program that helps identify an appropriate leisure and recreation program for children and adults with disabilities. Through this program, children, youth and adults with disabilities are matched with community volunteers to facilitate attendance in programs or city summer camps (Stewart, 2002b).

Another example is the Persons with Disabilities Partnership Association of Industrial Cape Breton. Since 1993, this association has taken action to ensure equality in the workforce through education and awareness issues. Indeed, the philosophical approach behind this organization is that integration can enhance quality of life (www.nsnet.org/ pdpaicb/mail.html). That is, though integration in the workforce, one's potential to experience leisure and recreation opportunities is also enhanced.

In a study of selected older persons with mental disabilities in Western Canada, Mactavish, Mahon and Rodrigue (1996) found leisure and recreation to be a means of establishing independent living. It was found to be an avenue that helped members of this sample group to make decisions and set personal goals. Leisure and recreation may thus be a useful activity in assisting persons with mental disabilities to perform daily tasks. Indeed, leisure and recreation is an important component of life for persons with mental disabilities (Stanley and Applebaum, 1996).

Of primary concern for leisure and recreation researchers in Canada is the understanding that many of the barriers and factors related to participation are people-oriented. A study by Levinson and Reid (1991) used a questionnaire fashioned after the Canada Fitness Survey. This study revealed that, for groups such as youngsters with developmental disabilities, a dependency on parents exists for leisure and recreation participation. It was suggested by the authors that participants and their families need more information about community facilities and accessibility in order to be able to overcome barriers to involvement.

Research in Canada in the area of leisure and disability has focused on making suggestions for enhancing the quality of life of persons with disabilities. A study by Lyons (1993) makes a strong argument for the development of a network system of outreach recreation services for persons with disabilities in Canada. According to Lyons, these services help alleviate many of the problems experienced by persons with disabilities such as social isolation and inactivity. Leisure and recreation, as shown by Pedlar (1990), can play a key role in the social integration of persons with disabilities into the community.

On December 1, 2001, an article appeared in the *Ottawa Citizen* entitled "Recreational Therapy A Growing Field." The writer of this article, Patricia Rivera, concluded after conducting a series of interviews that the need for leisure and recreation to serve persons with disabilities has grown tremendously. She went on to state that the demand for therapeutic recreationists is greater than the supply and that this trend will continue.

In 1992, a textbook entitled *Leisure, Integration and Community* was published as the first Canadian book on leisure and persons with disabilities. This book, authored by Peggy Hutchison and Judith McGill, overviews the type of change needed so that people with disabilities can experience full leisure and recreation lifestyles. The focus of this text is on providing a philosophical framework for the role that people need to undertake to bring about necessary change. This text is a needed resource in Canada not only to enhance our body of knowledge of leisure, recreation and people with disabilities, but also to help shape the future direction of research in this area.

CONCLUSION

Statistics in Canada present walking as the highest reported physical activity, while watching television and reading are popular sedentary activities. In this chapter, a number of statistical findings were presented, yet it should be noted that limitations exist with these data. The main problem with leisure and recreation participation surveys stems from the process used to define the "activity universe." More specifically, the problem is that there has not been consistency in defining the "activity universe" (i.e., the classification giving to various activities such as leisure, recreation, sport, or even work).

This lack of consistency stems from the fact that some activities may be defined differently by different people. For example, for some, "playing hockey" may be "leisure," for others it may be "recreation," whereas for still others, it may be "sport" or even "work." The exact nature of the "activity universe" is not taken into account in a number of leisure and recreation participation studies such as the 1967-1972 Canadian Outdoor Recreation Demand Study, the 1976 Survey of Fitness, Physical Recreation and Sport (Statistics Canada), or the 1988 Well-Being of Canadians survey (Zuzanek, 1996).

In examining Canadian research on leisure and recreation for leisure studies students, the homeless, youth, women, the aged and special populations, the intent was not only to present the state of each group but also to reveal that the provision of leisure and recreation opportunities in Canadian society cannot be viewed as homogeneous. The leisure and recreation activity patterns experienced by selected populations depend on a number of factors including socio-demographic, lifestyle and societal conditions (Singleton and Harvey, 1995).

CHAPTER 10: CANADIANS, LEISURE AND RECREATION

Study Questions

1. List, in rank order of highest reported popularity, the five most popular physical activities of Canadians.

2. What do the results of Hall and Rhyme's study on Ontario's ethno-cultural population reveal?

3. What impact does the cold climate have on the leisure and recreation pursuits of Canadians?

4. What are the favourite leisure and recreation activities for undergraduate leisure studies students?

5. What makes the provision of leisure and recreation services for Canada's homeless difficult?

Selected Websites

- **Active Living Alliance for Canadians with a Disability**
  http://www.als.ca

- **Saskatchewan Recreation Facility Association**
  http://www.spra.sk.ca/

- **Sport North Federation**
  http://http://www.sportnorth.com

- **Sport P.E.I.**
  http://www.sportpei.pe.ca/

- **Recreation Facilities Association of British Columbia**
  http://www.rfabc.com

Key Concepts

- **Canadian Fitness and Lifestyle Research Institute**

- **National Policy on Youth**

- **Gender equity policies**

- **Active Living Alliance for Canadians with a Disability**

Lunenburg, Nova Scotia. Photo: Canadian Tourism Commission.

11

TOURISM

LEARNING OBJECTIVES

- To define tourism.
- To describe tourism in Canada through the use of recent travel and tourism statistics.
- To explore tourism in Canada.
- To profile the Canadian Tourism Commission.
- To examine the special interest areas of heritage tourism, sport tourism, cultural tourism, educational tourism and ecotourism.

ourism has traditionally been regarded as being the largest industry within the leisure and recreation field. Tourism is not only about the tourist and his or her travel experiences, it is also about the people who make a living serving tourists. This chapter examines tourism in Canada. It begins by presenting definitions of tourism, followed by an exploration of tourism in Canada. It examines tourism trends in Canada, describes the role played the Canadian Tourism Commission, and ends with a discussion of special interest tourism.

"Increased means and increased leisure are the two civilizers of man."

— Benjamin Disraeli (1804-1881), speech to the Conservatives of Manchester, 3 April 1872.

DEFINITIONS OF TOURISM

Unlike the concepts of leisure and recreation, tourism is much easier to define. According to the *New Shorter Oxford English Dictionary*, **tourism** is defined as "travelling for pleasure" and the "business of attracting tourists." It is defined as travel from one place to another for business and/or pleasure purposes. A number of Canadian researchers have defined or analyzed the meaning of tourism, including Brayley, D'Amore and Mieczowski.

According to Brayley (1991) tourism is travel away from the home experience for business purposes, religious pilgrimage, military service, satisfaction, obligation, health and rejuvenation, or education. It can be argued, however, that each of these reasons for travel away from home includes leisure and recreation as the mere experience of a new environment may be, in itself, a leisure and recreation experience.

Tourism is also defined according to the roles it plays within society. For D'Amore (1990), if properly designed and developed, tourism "can bridge the psychological and cultural distances that separate people of

Table 11.1: Top Ten States of Origin for U.S. Tourists to Canada, 2001

	Trips '000	Nights '000	Spending $'000,000
New York	1,967	6,751	720
Michigan	1,857	5,024	577
Washington	1,655	5,494	541
California	1,051	5,530	833
Ohio	828	3,013	353
Massachusetts	738	2,757	379
Pennsylvania	705	3,017	393
Illinois	541	2,355	342
Minnesota	531	2,079	251
Texas	378	1,905	318

Source: Canadian Tourism Facts and Figures, Canadian Tourism Commission, 2001.

Table 11.2: Canada's Top Ten Major Overseas Tourist Markets, 2001

	Trips '000	Nights '000	Spending $'000,000
United Kingdom	826	10,092	1,026
Japan	410	5,314	633
France	357	5,254	436
Germany	330	5,281	454
Australia	158	2,464	244
Mexico	148	1,693	187
South Korea	139	4,063	264
Hong Kong	125	2,075	175
Taiwan	118	1,774	183
Netherlands	114	1,737	132

Source: Canadian Tourism Facts and Figures, Canadian Tourism Commission, 2001.

diverse races, colours, religions and stages of economic and social development" (p. 27). Tourism provides an opportunity for cultural exchange and interchange between and among locals.

Mieczowski (1991) argues that recreation is the motivating force behind tourism. Tourism is about seeking pleasure and enjoyment through the activities of leisure and recreation and therefore it is the anticipated pursuit of pleasure that drives one to become a tourist or to seek the tourism experience. Thus, tourism is defined by the pleasure-seeking appeal it holds for the potential traveller.

Finally, tourism in Canada can be defined through a composition of key terms used by the Canadian Tourism Commission to measure tourism patterns in Canada. These key terms include travel for business, travel for pleasure, and travel to visit friends and family. These key terms provide a good general classification of reasons why "tourists" travel. For the Canadian Tourism Commission, a tourist is someone who takes a trip for one or more nights.

ANTICIPATED PLEASURES

Tourism is about seeking pleasure and enjoyment through the activities of leisure and recreation. It is the anticipated pleasure that drives one to become a tourist or to seek the tourism experience.

TOURISM IN CANADA

Tourism is a major player in the leisure and recreation industry of Canada. It is a major income generator with a total Gross Domestic Product (GDP) of $22 billion reported in 2001. This translates into 2.3 percent of Canada's GDP (Canadian Tourism Commission, 2001). In 2001, tourism spending in Canada was $54.6 billion of which 70 percent or $38.4 billion was spent by Canadians. Foreigners accounted for $16.2 billion or 30 percent (Canadian Tourism Commission, 2001).

Tourism has economic benefits for Canada, for the provinces, for the regions within the provinces, and for the people of Canada. For instance, communities such as Nanaimo in British Columbia have in recent years realized that tourism is an important dimension of the local economy. The local industry of Nanaimo has been developed around various tourism services such as marinas, golf, sport fishing and skiing (Rollins and Delamere, 1996) to attract business. Each of these services offers a unique experience of Nanaimo and its culture to capture a part of the domestic and international tourism market.

It is no surprise that most international tourists in Canada come from the United States. In fact, geography plays a huge role in determining who visits Canada. This is evident in Table 11.1, which indicates that New York, Michigan and Washington, the states bordering Canada, are the top states of origin for U.S. tourists to Canada (Canadian Tourism Commission, 2001).

Internationally, the top three overseas tourist markets for Canada are, in rank order, the United Kingdom, Japan and France (see Table 11.2). It is no surprise that the United Kingdom and France are in the top three, based on the political, social and historical ties between these nations. The strong Yen and the availability of discretionary income for travel may be the reasons that Japan ranks second.

Table 11.3: Top Ten Overseas Countries Visited by Canadians, 2001

	Overnight Visits '000s	Nights '000s	Spending $'000,000
Mexico	689	7,003	691
United Kingdom	673	8,881	807
France	481	5,938	585
Cuba	348	3,026	312
Dominican Republic	251	2,371	229
Germany	251	2,579	215
Italy	231	2,983	379
Spain	162	2,213	179
Netherlands	146	1,403	103
Switzerland	142	930	113

Source: Canadian Tourism Facts and Figures, Canadian Tourism Commission, 2001.

Table I1.4: Top Ten States Visited by Canadians, 2001

	Overnight Visits '000s	Nights '000s	Spending $'000,000
New York	2,200	6,337	605
Florida	1,887	37,370	2,300
Washington	1,538	4,728	281
Michigan	1,133	2,729	215
California	910	8,015	862
Nevada	658	3,360	542
Maine	644	2,241	155
Vermont	577	1,620	96
Pennsylvania	573	1,371	107
Minnesota	496	1,491	142

Source: Canadian Tourism Facts and Figures, Canadian Tourism Commission, 2001.

Most U.S. and international tourists visiting Canada come during the third quarter of the year, that is, during the months of July, August and September (Canadian Tourism Commission, 2001). The months of April, May and June comprise the second most popular quarter for international tourism to Canada (Canadian Tourism Commission, 2001). According to the Canadian Tourism Commission (2001), the main reason why U.S. and international tourists visit Canada is for a holiday and/or vacation. Visiting friends or relatives is the second most frequently reported reason for visiting Canada, whereas business trips rank as the third most frequently stated reason for visiting Canada.

Most Canadian tourists who travel domestically within Canada do so during the months of July, August and September. Surprisingly, the fourth quarter, October, November, and December, is the second most frequent time period of the year for domestic tourism as reported by the Canadian Tourism Commission (2001).

Geography influences the travel destinations selected by Canadians. Table 11.3 presents Mexico, a country geographically close to Canada, as being the top country visited by Canadians. Similarly, as indicated in Table 11.4, the states of New York, Washington and Michigan rank at the top of the list for visits by Canadians. Moreover, Canada's most populated provinces, Ontario and Quebec, have continued to be popular in attracting domestic travellers (see Table 11.5).

It is interesting to note that the top three urban tourist destinations for both U.S. and international visitors to Canada are Toronto, Vancouver and Montreal (see Table 11.6). St. Catherines-Niagara (Niagara Falls), a destination offering one of the greatest natural attractions of the world, surpasses Quebec, Ottawa-Hull and Halifax, cities rich in Canadian history, in number of visitors per year.

When travelling, tourists engage in various leisure and recreation activities. Table 11.7 depicts the top activities participated in by tourists in Canada in 2001. For domestic tourists, visiting friends or relatives was the top reported activity. For international tourists, U.S. residents report shopping as the most popular activity, which may be due to the strength of the U.S. dollar. Similarly, overseas residents report shopping as the number one activity. This may also be the result of the favourable exchange rates of the Euro, Yen and other foreign currencies.

It should be mentioned that the degree of accuracy of some of the aforementioned statistics may be subject to question. This becomes the case when information sought focuses on "purpose of trip." The three main classifications used for "purpose of trip" – pleasure, business, or to visit friends/family – tend to, in reality, sometimes overlap. In some cases, for instance, the purpose of trip may be both pleasure and business, yet the respondent may only indicate "business" as the purpose of trip. As a result, the reported statistical result may lack in accuracy and therefore not be a true representation of the actual nature of the trip for that individual.

Cathedral Grove Provincial Park in B.C. is a popular tourist destination.

Table 11.5: Trips by Canadians in Canada

	1996[3]	1998	1999	2000	2001
	Trips (000s of destination)				
Canada	**150,844**	**159,219**	**164,097**	**162,106**	**144,202**
Newfoundland and Labrador	3,421	3,488	3,356	3,218	3,170
Prince Edward Island	678	902	889	1,019	908
Nova Scotia	5,626	6,191	6,806	7,019	6,960
New Brunswick	4,476	4,915	5,208	4,652	5,383
Quebec	35,408	35,835	37,541	37,592	29,943
Ontario	53,877	56,076	57,930	58,177	51,910
Manitoba	6,601	7,207	6,875	6,700	6,366
Saskatchewan	7,945	8,211	8,434	7,919	7,108
Alberta	17,486	20,193	20,296	19,338	17,332
British Columbia	15,235	16,019	16,676	16,332	15,055
Yukon/Northwest Territories/ Nunavut	93	183	88	41	68

1. Estimates are based on the 1996 Census population counts.

2. 80 km or more.

3. The 1997 data are protected because they were not adjusted and are not comparable with the estimates for the other years.

Source: Statistics Canada, CANSIM II, Table 426-0001. Last modified: 2002-10-25.

TOURISM TRENDS IN CANADA

Prior to the attacks of September 11, 2001, tourism was booming, not only in Canada, but globally as well. Not only did the events of September 11, 2001, shock the world, they have also had a significant impact on the travel industry.

Although it may still be too early to determine the long-term impacts of September 11, 2001, on travel and tourism, tourism data released since that date indicate that it has decreased dramatically, not only in Canada, but also in Canada's key overseas markets. In a report prepared by the Canadian Tourism Commission on September 5, 2002, with reference to the International Travel Survey of Statistics Canada (2001c), it was noted that U.S. overnight trips to Canada increased by 2.5 percent in 2001, while international travel to Canada decreased by 8.1 percent.

Reports from the first part of 2002 indicate trends similar to those of 2001. According to the report prepared by the Canadian Tourism Commission on September 5, 2002, U.S. entries to Canada decreased by 0.2 percent whereas international travel to Canada decreased by 13.0 percent. It is important to note that travel to Canada by all modes, other than automobile, decreased by 10.2 percent during the first six months of 2002. There is no doubt that the travel and tourism industry is going through a difficult time period. As a result, some major airline companies are going bankrupt and others are downsizing in search of means to become more economically efficient for long-term survival. How long will this trend continue? Will the travel and tourism industry ever recover from September 11, 2001?

According to Jim Watson, former president and CEO of the Canadian Tourism Commission, the "Canadian Tourism Commission's ongoing marketing efforts, along with initiatives to provide timely in-depth information and analysis, are helping the industry weather difficult times, even though a full recovery is not expected until 2003" (Corporate Author, 2002b: 5). The Canadian Tourism Commission is allocating a significant amount of its budget on marketing and marketing efforts in the hopes that this will assist in increasing travel and tourism to and from Canada.

In addition to the attacks of September 11, 2001, tourism has also been affected by SARS. The spread of SARS, particularly in the Toronto area, had a devastating impact on the tourism industry of this city. In fact, in 2003, the city of Toronto offered a number of attractive package-deals to attract tourists who had stopped coming due to fear of SARS. The package-deals offered included travel to and from Toronto, hotel, and theatre tickets at prices well below regular cost.

According to *Euromonitor International*, the early years of the new millennium can best be described as years of "constant pressure." Despite this, however, the above events are not expected to influence significantly the decisions of Canadians to travel. Many Canadians will continue to travel to other parts of the wold for business and pleasure (http://www.euromonitor.com/Travel_and_Tourism_in_Canada).

Table 11.6: Top Ten Urban Areas* Visited by International Tourists, 2001

	Total	U.S. Residents '000s overnight visits	Overseas Residents
Toronto	3,733	2,444	1,289
Vancouver	3,033	1,797	1,236
Montreal	2,243	1,418	825
St. Catharines-Niagara	2,080	1,678	401
Quebec	1,009	551	458
Victoria	905	558	347
Ottawa-Hull	803	413	390
Calgary	659	280	380
Edmonton	445	300	145
Halifax	333	230	103

*Data refers to Census Metropolitan Areas

Source: Canadian Tourism Facts and Figures, Canadian Tourism Commission, 2001.

Table 11.7: Top Activities Participated in* by Tourists in Canada, 2001

	Canadian Residents %	U.S. Residents %	Overseas Residents %
Visiting friends or relatives	66	31	55
Participating in sports/outdoor activities	37	31	29
Shopping	36	63	85
Sightseeing	27	54	78
Going to a bar or night club	15	22	30
Visiting a national or provincial nature park	12	23	51
Visiting an historic site	8	29	43
Boating (motor, sail, kayak, canoe, other)	8	9	10
Attending a sport event	7	6	10
Visiting a museum or art gallery	6	21	40

*More than one activity may be participated in while on a trip.

Source: Canadian Tourism Facts and Figures, Canadian Tourism Commission, 2001.

CANADIAN TOURISM COMMISSION

The **Canadian Tourism Commission (CTC)** is a corporation established by the federal government with the primary responsibility for tourism and travel. Although the Canadian Tourism Commission has existed since January 31, 1995, it was not until 2000 that the *Canadian Tourism Commission Act* was passed. The Act (c. 28) commences by stating the following:

> WHEREAS the Canadian tourism industry is vital to the social and cultural integrity of Canada;
>
> WHEREAS the Canadian tourism industry makes an essential contribution to the economic well-being of Canadians and to the economic objectives of the Government of Canada;
>
> WHEREAS the Canadian tourism industry consists of mainly small and medium sized businesses that are essential to Canada's goals for entrepreneurial development and job creation;
>
> AND WHEREAS it is desirable to strengthen Canada's commitment to Canadian tourism by establishing a Tourism Commission that would work with the governments of the provinces and the territories and the Canadian tourism industry to promote the interests of the industry and to market Canada as a desirable tourists destination.

The Canadian Tourism Commission is a part of Industry Canada, a federal government department. It is managed by a board of directors consisting of not more than twenty-six persons, which includes the chairperson and president. In addition, up to sixteen private sector directors of the tourism industry are appointed by the Minister to serve on the executive of this commission.

The objectives of the Canadian Tourism Commission as stated in the *Canadian Tourism Commission Act* (c. 28) are to: (1) sustain a vibrant and profitable Canadian tourism industry; (2) market Canada as a desirable tourist destination, (3) support a co-operative relationship between the private sector and the governments of Canada, the provinces and territories with respect to Canadian tourism; and (4) provide information about Canadian tourism to the private sector and to the governments of Canada, the provinces and the territories.

It is relevant to note that the Canadian Tourism Commission is viewed primarily as a marketing agency. In fact, roughly 4.5 percent of its budget goes to research. Recently, Marc Rosenberg, the Chair of the Research Committee for the Canadian Tourism Commission, affirmed the CTC's commitment to research by stating that, "research plays such a vital role in any of the other committees and any of the work that is being done relative to tourism. It really is the foundation for making business decisions and testing concepts; I think it will always be assessed whether it is satisfying the needs of the industry, however they are defined" (Corporate Author, October 2002c: 5).

WINTERLUDE AND THE QUEBEC WINTER CARNIVAL

A Brief Comparison of Two of Canada's Main Winter Leisure Events

In Canada, two main winter leisure events are provided each year, one in the nation's capital, called Winterlude, and the other in Quebec City, the Quebec Winter Carnival.

Each of these winter events employs a variety of marketing techniques and slogans to attract visitors. The National Capital Commission identifies Winterlude as "North America's greatest festival," whereas the Quebec Winter Carnival identifies itself as the "largest winter carnival in the world."

Both Canada's Capital Region and Quebec City offer ideal winter conditions to host Canada's main winter leisure events. The National Capital Commission makes full use of the longest skating rink in the world, the Rideau Canal Skateway (a 7.8 kilometre pathway of ice) as the central point for its Winterlude activities. Quebec City, on the other hands, makes excellent use of the Plains of Abraham and other historic sites to add to the aesthetics of its carnival's events.

Both Winterlude and the Quebec Winter Carnival attract tourists to Canada and entice domestic travel. Traditionally, the first quarter (January to March) is one of the slowest time periods for travel to and within Canada. Since the advent of these events, tourism in Canada's Capital Region and Quebec City has increased as hundreds of thousands of visitors have come to experience these winter leisure events. For example, in 2003, it is estimated that 656,000 people partook of the activities of Winterlude.

A description of these two main winter leisure events is offered on their respective websites.

Source:
Extracted from: <http://www.canadascaptial.gc.ca> and <http://www.caarnival.qc.ca>.

Ottawa Winterlude	Quebec Winter Carnival
February (3 weekends)	End of January to mid-February (17 days)
26 years (2004)	50 years (2004)
Artists, athletes, visitors (Canada and abroad)	Artists, athletes, visitors (Canada and abroad)
Over 800	Over 1,400
$70 million for region (estimate)	$28 million (average)

Photo: Courtesy of Ted Temertzoglou.

SPECIAL INTEREST TOURISM

A number of special interest areas in tourism have recently been developed and expanded, such as heritage tourism, sport tourism, cultural tourism, educational tourism and ecotourism. Each of these areas has become increasingly popular for Canadians travelling within Canada and abroad. The following review of literature identifies how these areas of special interest tourism relate to Canadian society.

Heritage tourism is a special area of tourism concerned with the visitation of natural, cultural and historical places for educational and nostalgic purposes (Hall and Zeppel, 1990). In Canada, heritage tourism is a form of travel that has been used to explore cultural heritage and/or enhance our sense of cultural identity (MacKay, 1999). Both Canadian Heritage (1995) and the Canadian Tourism Commission (1996) have taken a position in support of heritage tourism as an important means to enhance tourism revenues in Canada and to strengthen Canadian identity.

The experience of heritage tourism can take place in public, private and non-profit facilities and services. These include Canada's museums, galleries, historic sites, Aboriginal heritage sites, cultural festivals, and parks and wilderness areas (MacKay, 1999; Hinch and Delamere, 1993). Heritage tourists tend to be motivated by educational experiences linked to local culture and history (MacKay, 1999).

In Canada, increasing efforts have been placed on expanding heritage tourism opportunities. The Ontario government, for example, has launched a Heritage Property Tax Relief program that will allow owners of designated heritage buildings in municipalities a property tax relief of up to 40 percent. This action highlights the value placed by the Ontario government not only on the preservation and protection of heritage buildings but also on the maintenance and promotion of heritage tourism areas within the province.

Sport tourism is defined as "the use of sports for touristic endeavors" (Kurtzman, 2001: 16). Sports tourism consists of six supply-side tourism categories: sports events, sports resorts, sports cruises, sports attraction, sports adventures and sports tours. Individuals who partake of these supply-side tourism categories are "sports tourists." A sports tourist is defined as someone who is "motivated by sport" to travel outside of her or his home region (Kurtzman, 2001).

Canada's climate is one that entices sports tourism pursuits all kinds. During the winter, a popular sports tourism pursuit is skiing, particularly during "March break." Another popular sports tourism activity is the Grey Cup. Every November, many Canadians football fans travel from all parts of Canada to experience the Grey Cup game, which is played in a different Canadian Football League city each year.

Cultural tourism involves participation in a novel cultural experience. It consists of the pursuit of the touristic experience as a means to explore the lifestyle and/or history of a given society or group of people.

"SPECIAL INTEREST" TOURISM

To aid in better understanding the magnitude of tourism, research in leisure studies concentrates on specific areas within this broad industry. The term "special interest tourism" is thus used to refer to the range of classifications of tourism experiences.

Photo: CN Images of Canada.

The Cabot Trail in Cape Breton (shown above as it was in 1941) honours the historic Canadian explorer John Cabot.

Thus, cultural tourism focuses on learning, observing and experiencing a culture that is foreign (Hinch and Li, 1996). Stebbins (1996) postulates that various cultural forms attract tourists, such as museums, galleries, festivals, architecture, historic ruins, artistic performances and heritage sites.

For Stebbins (1996) cultural tourism can be understood through an exploration of the cultural tourist. In his research on serious leisure, Stebbins identifies two types of cultural tourists: the general cultural tourist and the specialized cultural tourist. The general cultural tourist is someone who makes a hobby out of travelling to different places (e.g., countries, cities, regions). The specialized cultural tourist focuses on one or a small number of geographical sites with repeated visits to find a deeper meaning of the culture of the place or site.

In Canada, cultural tourism is said to be "coming of age." Kingsmill (2002), in a recent article, argues that Canada has a rich cultural history; in fact, a history of well over four thousand years. With reference to survey research, Kingsmill claims that "potential tourism clients want to meet and learn about Canadians. They want to enjoy our music and our spectacles, and gain a sense of our history" (p. 3). For Kingsmill, cultural tourism in Canada is about "conversations with local people in neighbourhood pubs, visiting ecomuseums, or taking in community pageants" (ibid.).

In the same article, Kingsmill (2002) eloquently makes the point that the Canadian Tourism Commission has been successful in selling the ski holiday, the whale-watching excursion and the fishing trip, yet it has overlooked marketing the rich cultural history of Canada to prospective tourists. For Kingsmill, cultural tourism is coming of age in Canada and it is now the time for the Canadian Tourism Commission to "package and present it properly" (p. 3).

Educational tourism is a special area that focuses on learning, and in some cases, the earning of university credits. The Canadian Tourism Commission recently developed a selection of learning travel experiences with the purpose of promoting travel and tourism within Canada for educational reasons.

Since the early 1990s, the University of Ottawa's Department of Leisure Studies has offered international study tour courses for credit. The intent of these international study tour courses is to provide a comparative learning experience of the recreation, sport and tourism industries of Canada with the selected international country. This course is unique in that it provides "students with an opportunity not made possible through the Internet, that is, to feel, to touch, to smell and experience foreign recreation services" (Karlis, 1997b: 33).

The University of Ottawa's international study tour courses are a great way to learn while travelling. In Greece, for example, students study and learn first-hand from administrators at sites such as the Acropolis, the Ancient Theatre of Epidavros, Sparta-Mystra, Ancient Olympia, Delphi, the Monastery of Osios Loukas and the island of Crete.

This unique way of learning has caught the attention of the media. In an article appearing in *The University of Ottawa Gazette,* Lougheed (2002) depicts how this study tour course can be an excellent means to learn about a culture first-hand. Hickman (1998: 3) in another article appearing in *The University of Ottawa Gazette* discusses how this course "challenges students to compare what they have learned about Canada and the country they visit." In an article in the *Ottawa Sun,* Anderson (2002) describes the learning appeal experienced through the University of Ottawa international study tour course.

Similarly, students at University College of the Cariboo in Kamloops, British Columbia, indicated that study tours are an excellent way to learn. Through their study tour experience to Chile, students of tourism management experienced hands-on international development through the exchange and interchange of knowledge (http://www. cariboo.bc.ca /pubref/mediareleases/jan.html).

A definition of **ecotourism**, another special interest form of tourism, has been developed by the Canadian Environmental Advisory Council. This definition states that "ecotourism is an enlightened nature travel experience that contributes to the conservation of the ecosystem, while respecting the integrity of host societies" (Scace, Grifone and Usher, 1992: 14). Ecotourism is focused on the enhancement or maintenance of natural systems through tourism (Farrell, 1991). Moreover, the term ecotourism refers to an environmentally and/or culturally friendly tourism experience (Cukier, 2001) that includes activities such as trekking/hiking, bird watching, nature photography, wildlife safaris, camping, mountain climbing, river rafting/canoeing/kayaking and botanical study.

Research by MacKay, Lamon and Partridge (1996) on ecotourism in Churchill, Manitoba, reveals that this site, as do many others in Canada, presents a wide array of wildlife opportunities for the ecotourist. Moreover, ecotourists tend to have other interests in the tourism experience beyond wildlife exploration, such as visiting museums and outdoor opportunities. Marketing approaches to attract ecotourists to Canadian destinations should thus include cultural and educational touristic opportunities.

The concept of ecotourism has evolved out of the conservation trend (Boo, 1990). Research in Canada suggests that small-scale, community-based tourism is best for conserving the natural and/or cultural characteristics of the touristic site. However, as noted by Cukier (2001), ecotourism does not always include sustainability. The concept "ecotourism is used broadly to describe tourism in natural areas but does not necessarily adhere to the criteria of true ecotourism, which provides some level of sustainability" (Cukier, 2001: 7).

CONCLUSION

The Canadian Tourism Commission holds the primary mandate for tourism in Canada. It also disseminates the bulk of statistical research and trend analysis studies for tourism. Canada relies greatly on tourism. It helps create jobs, keeps people employed and helps stimulate economic growth in Canada.

The tourism industry is currently feeling the effects of September 11, 2001, as international travel to Canada, particularly by air, has drastically decreased. The Canadian Tourism Commission is currently implementing research and marketing approaches to increase the number of visitors to Canada. However, it will likely take some time before the tourism industry experiences a full recovery.

Special interest tourism may help in resurrecting tourism. Heritage tourism, sport tourism, cultural tourism, educational tourism and ecotourism have all grown in popularity in recent years. The field of leisure studies has a role to play in helping stimulate tourism and travel to Canada by further researching these areas of tourism.

CHAPTER 11: TOURISM

Study Questions

1. Define tourism.

2. What do recent statistics indicate for travel to Canada?

3. What is the main reason that American and international tourists visit Canada?

4. What impact has September 11, 2001, had on tourism to Canada? Explain using recent travel indicators.

5. What are the objectives of the Canadian Tourism Commission?

Selected Websites

- **Discover Canada**
  http://www.discovercanada.com

- **Atlantic Travel Net**
  http://english.aliant.net/home.jsp

- **Canada Travel Information and Travelogues**
  http://www.travel-library.com/north_america/canada

- **Imperial Hotel Management School**
  http://www.ihmc.ca

- **Canada's Virtual North**
  http://www.virtualnorth.com

Key Concepts

- **Tourism**
- **Canadian Tourism Commission (CTC)**
- **Heritage tourism**
- **Sport tourism**
- **Cultural tourism**
- **Educational tourism**
- **Ecotourism**

Dalhousie University. Photo: Nova Scotia Information Service.

12

EDUCATION, RESEARCH JOURNALS AND CONFERENCES IN LEISURE STUDIES

LEARNING OBJECTIVES

- To describe university programs in leisure studies.
- To describe community college leisure studies programs.
- To overview the main national Canadian-based leisure studies journals.
- To overview Canada's main national research conference in leisure studies, the Canadian Congress on Leisure Research.
- To profile the Canadian Parks and Recreation Association National Annual Conference and Trade Show.

ince the 1960s university and community college programs in leisure studies or related areas have been offered in Canada. The number of higher education leisure studies or related programs has witnessed a steady, yet not rapid, increase in the past forty years. Currently, more than seventy-five community college and university programs in leisure studies or related areas exist in Canada. Once the first academic programs of leisure studies were in place, it was time to enhance the means for the dissemination of research. The 1970s was the decade when most Canadian-based research journals in leisure studies were created. Although the Canadian Parks and Recreation Association had held annual conferences since the 1940s, it was not until the 1960s that research-focused leisure studies conferences were introduced in Canada.

This chapter commences by describing university study, the intent of university programs in leisure studies, curricula in university leisure studies programs, and employment preparation for students in university leisure studies programs. This is followed by a description of all of the above for community college education in leisure studies. Canadian-based research journals in leisure studies are introduced, and the chapter ends with an overview of Canadian-based research conferences in leisure studies.

"Light, joy, and leisure; but shall they persevere?"

— *Echo Ever.* George Herbert (1593-1633), British poet. "Heaven" (l. 19-20). *The Complete English Poems* [George Herbert]. John Tobin, ed. Penguin Books (1991).

UNIVERSITY STUDY

Although the first attempt to offer a leisure studies-related degree program took place in the late 1940s at the University of Western Ontario, it was not until the 1960s that leisure studies degree programs found success in universities in Canada. Programs established at the University of Ottawa and the University of Waterloo (McFarland, 1970) led the way to the creation of similar programs.

A recent listing of university programs provided by the Canadian Parks and Recreation Association (1998) identified thirty universities in Canada that offer leisure studies or related degree programs: (1) Acadia University, (2) Augustana University, (3) Brandon University, (4) Brock University, (5) Concordia University, (6) Dalhousie University, (7) Lakehead University, (8) Laurentian University, (9) McGill University, (10) Memorial University, (11) Trinity Western University, (12) University of Alberta, (13) University of British Columbia, (14) University of Calgary, (15) University of Guelph, (16) University of Manitoba, (17) Université de Moncton, (18) Université de Montreal, (19) University of New Brunswick, (20) University of Northern British Columbia, (21) University of Ottawa, (22) Université de Quebec à Trois Rivières, (23) University of Regina, (24) University of Saskatchewan, (25) University of Toronto, (26) University of Victoria, (27) University of Waterloo, (28) University of Winnipeg, (29) York University, and (30) University of Windsor.

Most university degree programs in leisure studies at the bachelor degree level are four years in length. To successfully complete a four-year degree in leisure studies students are usually required to complete a work-term semester (internship), and in some cases, an independent research project (honours thesis). Three-year programs in leisure studies do exist, but they are few. For example, the University of Ottawa offers a general concentration degree. This three-year degree program has been designed at the university as an entry-level preparation program, and students completing this degree are not as well prepared for higher administrative careers in leisure or for graduate school.

Leisure studies programs offered in Canadian universities focus on educating students about the importance of leisure in society, including the benefits and merits of activities that may be defined as "leisure," "recreation" and "play" (Karlis, 1996). The intent of these programs is to prepare students to be administrators, leaders and decision-makers in the leisure and recreation industry. It is through the passing on of knowledge pertaining to administrative techniques and principles and practices of leisure service delivery that the goals of formal university education in leisure studies are achieved (ibid.).

It should be noted that no formal accreditation process exists in Canada for leisure studies degree programs. Canadian leisure studies programs rely on internal and external reviews by experts in the field to ascertain required standards. Canadian departments of leisure studies that wish to be accredited in the field need to pursue the accreditation process outside of Canada. For instance, the University of Ottawa's Department of Leisure Studies is accredited by the U.S.-based National Recreation and Parks Association, a global leader for the educational accreditation of higher learning leisure studies programs.

• Intent of University Programs

In Canada, early leisure studies-related degree programs in leisure studies were designed to address the needs of a post-war society. Students who registered in early degree-granting programs at the University of Toronto and the University of Western Ontario studied curricula that focused largely on professional preparation (McFarland, 1970). Degree-granting curricula had two major thrusts: (1) to prepare individuals to direct recreation, park and leisure service programs in governmental, voluntary, commercial, therapeutic and other types of agencies; and (2) to conduct scholarly investigations of leisure as a human experience and social institution (Kraus, 1994: 14).

All university degree programs differ. Cordes and Ibrahim (1999), however, posit that university degree programs in leisure studies in Canada take a philosophical approach. The objective of university degree programs in leisure studies is to prepare students for administrative careers in leisure and recreation.

The intent of university education in leisure studies is to: (1) provide students with a thorough understanding of the concepts and philosophies of leisure and recreation, (2) professionally prepare students for careers in leisure and recreation, (3) provide students with a comprehensive knowledge of leisure behaviour, (4) identify applied techniques of leisure and recreation programming, (5) pass on to students a general knowledge of the arts, humanities and social sciences so that links can be drawn to leisure studies, (6) provide students with professional education for planning leisure and recreation services, (7) present to students theories and processes of administration and management for application in the service sectors of leisure and recreation, and (8) prepare students for graduate and professional studies (Karlis, 2002c).

The Department of Recreation and Leisure Studies at the University of Waterloo, for example, is ranked as one of the top three recreation departments from a pool of almost three hundred in North America. The leisure studies program at this university has existed for more than thirty years. The goal of the undergraduate leisure studies program is to combine knowledge of people, environments and management to prepare students for careers in public and private agencies. The four-year honours program at the University of Waterloo is also designed to act as a solid foundation for graduate school preparation. The structure of the program is designed to allow students to choose an area of specialization in the field, either "recreation and leisure studies," "therapeutic recreation," or "recreation and business" or to take courses from a broad range of disciplines. Moreover, the opportunity to obtain a joint honours degree in Drama, English, Environment and Resource Studies,

CREDENTIALS COUNT

Someone with a degree or diploma in leisure studies is more likely to find employment in the leisure sector than someone who has no higher education in this field.

Geography, History, Music, Political Science, Psychology, Social Development Studies, and Sociology helps prepare students to enter the workforce in an administrative capacity.

Graduate degree programs in leisure studies are offered at select universities in Canada. For instance, Dalhousie University offers an M.A. (Leisure Studies), Simon Fraser University has an M.S. (Parks and Recreation Management) and a Ph.D. (Parks and Recreation Management). The University of Waterloo offers an M.A. (Recreation and Leisure Studies) and a Ph.D. (Recreation and Leisure Studies), and the University of New Brunswick (Fredericton) offers a M.S. (Parks and Recreation Management) and a Ph.D. (Parks and Recreation Management).

The objective of graduate programs in leisure studies is to prepare students for professional careers. In general, there are five main goals: (1) to prepare students for higher administrative careers (middle and upper management positions), (2) to pass on to students a knowledge of research methods, (3) to pass on to students the knowledge of how to conduct research in leisure, recreation and related areas, (4) to prepare students for doctoral programs, and (5) to train students to be leaders in the field of leisure and recreation (Karlis, 2002c).

• University Curricula

Leisure studies programs in Canada are found in a variety of faculties. For instance, the University of Ottawa's program had been housed since 1969 in the Faculty of Social Sciences and recently moved to Health Sciences. The University of Waterloo's program is in the Faculty of Applied Health Sciences. Acadia University's program is in the faculty of Professional Studies. At the University of Guelph, you can complete a Bachelor of Commerce (Tourism Management) degree in the Faculty of Management.

The reason why leisure studies programs are found in various faculties across Canada is that the orientation of the discipline is interpreted differently by various universities. The field of leisure studies has often been described as a multidiscipline area of inquiry. Students take a wide variety of courses that overlap with other fields, such as psychology, sociology, philosophy, political science, economics, history, geography, environmental studies and law. Students registered in university leisure studies degree programs are required to take courses in the socio-psychology of leisure, recreation and political process, leisure concepts and values, and socio-economic aspects of leisure.

In most leisure studies degree programs, curricula emphasis is placed primarily on Western philosophies and the Western notion of leisure. Courses tend to focus mostly on the economic, social, psychological and political issues of leisure and recreation while overlooking the examination of cultural differences. It is for this reason "that leisure studies curricula, including faculty and student enrolment have not, for the most part, reflected the cultural diversity of Canada" (Karlis, 1997c: 29). A number of strategies could be implemented to enhance diversity and pluralism in the field of leisure studies, such as the following:

- Expanding the horizons of curricula.

- Hiring more minority/ethnic faculty.

- Recruiting specialists in ethnic and/or racial relations.

- Recruiting minority/ethnic students.

- Expanding extension, outreach programs to serve community needs.

- Increasing faculty/student awareness of diversity.

- Organizing international conferences focusing on diversity and recreation (ibid., pp. 29-30).

Most university leisure studies programs in Canada include courses in tourism, parks and parks management, therapeutic recreation and selected populations. Some programs focus primarily on tourism or therapeutic recreation and offer a large number of courses in this area. One study found that eight university programs in Canada offered at least one course on leisure and disability, with some courses focusing on therapeutic recreation, while others explored programming implications for special populations (Karlis, 1998a).

A large number of courses in leisure studies curricula focus on youth and recreation. In fact, of all population groups, youth may indeed be the group that is focused on the most, not only in curricula but also in research. For Levy, Losito and Levy (1996), studies of other populations such as the aged need to be expanded in the curricula.

A further concern of leisure studies curricula is that focus has been placed primarily on theory with little emphasis on practice. Research by Burton (1991) indicates that the curricula needs to concentrate on a perspective grounded in an understanding of the nature and characteristics of leisure in social development. The ultimate objective of curricula development in leisure studies is to prepare the recreation professional to enhance the experience of leisure for individuals and groups in the community (ibid.).

In a paper published in 1993, McDonald made reference to work conducted by the British Columbia Recreation and Parks Association and the provincial ministries responsible for post-secondary education and community recreation development. The intent of this joint effort was to encourage educational institutions to put more emphasis on the future development of leisure studies curricula. McDonald discusses how educators in British Columbia view additions to leisure studies curricula, the incorporation of active living and well-being into existing programs, and a focus on special populations, the environment, management and tourism. The results revealed the following desirable changes (top ten in rank order according to the most desirable) to meet the challenges of the future: (1) the establishment of a co-op or fieldwork as a part of each

Many courses and programs focus on the needs of youth in specific communities.

FIRST, VOLUNTEER

To best be prepared for employment in the leisure studies industry, it is recommended that university and college leisure studies students gain work experience while pursuing their degrees or diplomas. This work experience, which may be in the form of volunteer work, will help students realize whether education in leisure studies, and ultimately, a career in this field is the right choice for them.

program, (2) increase networking with tourism, social services and health, (3) more degrees at universities/colleges, (4) stronger formalized links between educators and practitioners, (5) increased student demand for quality and accountability, (6) more mature students, (7) more numbers and diversity of students, (8) central data bank used to advise potential students, (9) increased computer use taught and in teaching, and (10) programs that deliver more packaged workshops to the field (p. 97).

• Employment Preparation

Graduates of leisure studies degree programs have a number of employment avenues open to them. By virtue of their education, they are trained for employment in areas such as administration, research, facilities and programming.

Administration positions in leisure and recreation consist of Administrative Officers, Managers/Directors, Assistant Directors and Recreation Supervisors. The duties of administrative positions may consist of budget preparation, coordination of decision making, hiring of staff members, supervising staff, preparation of strategic plans and coordinating of supervisory tasks. Usually, administrative positions, particularly those in middle and higher management, are among the highest paid in the leisure and recreation profession.

Research positions are numerous. All service sectors of leisure and recreation hire researchers and planners. The government, for example, hires researchers or consultants on a permanent basis. The commercial sector hires external consultants to do marketing and feasibility studies. And the voluntary sector hires researchers or consultants to do feasibility studies.

Recreation facilities positions exist in the public, commercial and voluntary sectors. Facility supervisors may perform the following tasks: scheduling facility bookings, scheduling staff, supervising programs, coordinating activities, maintaining financial records and ensuring the safety of facility users.

Similar to recreation facilities, programming positions are found in all service sectors. Persons in these positions may be designated as Leisure Programmers, Recreation Program Assistant, Program Coordinators, Programmers, and Recreation Techniques. Typical programming job descriptions involve the planning, organizing and supervising of a wide variety of leisure and recreation programs.

In 1989, Claude Cousineau and Patricia Bolla, two professors at the University of Ottawa, conducted a study to understand better the careers of leisure studies graduates. The purpose of this study was to create an up-to-date description of the career profile of leisure studies graduates of the University of Ottawa; specifically, its intent was to examine the types of jobs and careers experienced by leisure studies graduates. This study concluded that:

- The majority of leisure studies graduates are finding work in the leisure field although there has been a decline since 1979.

- The most frequent employer continues to be quasi-government agencies with most being in community recreation, therapeutic recreation and tourism.

- Approximately one-half of the positions held by graduates are at the middle or senior management level.

- There continues to be substantial job mobility. However, most graduates are satisfied that their current job meets or exceeds their expectations.

- Those graduates working in the leisure field do not differ from those working in leisure with respect to type of employer, job level, satisfaction, or salary.

- A minority of graduates were not in the work force, mostly women who were raising a family.

- When compared to national data, leisure studies graduates appear slightly advantaged in finding full-time employment. Furthermore, they seem more able to find work in their field of study than other social sciences graduates (Cousineau and Bolla, 1989: 37-39).

In addition to these main findings, Cousineau and Bolla (1989) state that leisure studies graduates gain access to management positions while earning salaries greater than $30,000 per year. A subsequent study by Smale and Frisby (1990) examined the availability of job outcomes of recreation graduates from the University of Waterloo. The results of this study indicated that many recreation graduates have moved to employment positions outside of their field for a number of reasons, such as: (1) greater opportunities, (2) the development of new skills, (3) for challenge and work stimulation, and (4) for bonuses and pay increases.

COMMUNITY COLLEGE CURRICULA

Just as the focus of leisure studies programs differs from college to college, so does the curricula. Some of the most common courses offered are: leisure management, field placement/practicum, therapeutic recreation, recreation programming, sports and recreation in Canada, leadership, community development and recreation facilities.

Programs that focus on tourism and travel tend to have a curricula that is more commercially oriented. Popular courses include tourism industry studies, marketing and selling destinations, travel law and insurance, travel management and leadership, tourism trends, travel accounting and business practices.

COMMUNITY COLLEGES

Community college programs in leisure studies or related areas have existed since the 1960s. Research by McFarland (1970) finds that Mount Royal College, Centennial College and Lethbridge College were among the first community college programs to offer leisure or leisure-related diplomas.

The Canadian Parks and Recreation Association (Corporate Author, 1998) reported forty leisure studies and leisure studies related programs in Canadian community colleges in 1998. These include college programs at: (1) Malaspina University-College, (2) Medicine Hat College, (3) Mohawk C.A.A.T., (4) Mount Royal College, (5) Newfoundland and Labrador College of Trades and Technology, (6) Niagara College, (7) Northern Alberta Institute of Technology, (8) Nova Scotia Agriculture College, (9) Deer College, (10) Saskatchewan Institute of Applied

THE INTENT OF COMMUNITY COLLEGE PROGRAMS

The program at Mohawk College in Hamilton, Ontario, provides a good example of the intent of community college programs in leisure studies across the country. Its stated intention is

- to promote an appreciation and knowledge of the scope of the recreation profession;
- to facilitate the development of competencies necessary to provide leisure services to all individuals;
- to provide an opportunity for the student to develop and demonstrate skills through identified competencies at a recreation agency;
- to develop and improve the students' interpersonal skills;
- to encourage the development of personal leisure attitudes and philosophies consistent with a changing society and profession.; and
- to maintain a link with agencies and professional bodies to incorporate current trends and resources in the field of recreation and into the program of studies.

Arts and Sciences, (11) Sault C.A.A.T., (12) Selkirk College, (13) Seneca C.A.A.T., (14) Sir Sanford Fleming C.A.A.T. (Applied Arts and Hospitality), (15) Sir Sanford Fleming C.A.A.T., (School of Natural Resources), (16) Southern Alberta Institute of Technology and Arts, (17) Algonquin C.A.A.T., (18) Arctic College, (19) Brescia College, (20) British Columbia Institute of Technology, (21) Camrose Lutheran College, (22) Canadian Union College, (23) Canadore C.A.A.T., (24) Capilano College, (25) Cariboo College, (26) CEGEP Dawson College, (27) CEGEP de Rivière-du-Loup, (28) CEGEP Saint-Laurent, (29) CEGEP du Vieux-Montreal, (30) Centennial C.A.A.T., (31) College of the Rockies, (32) Conestoga C.A.A.T., (33) Confederation C.A.A.T., (34) Dawson College, (35) Douglas College, (36) Fairview College, (37) Fanshawe C.A.A.T., (38) Georgian C.A.A.T., (39) George Brown College, (40) Grande Prairie Regional College, (41) Grant MacEwan Community College, (42) Holland College, (43) Humber C.A.A.T., (44) Huron College, the University of Western Ontario, (45) Lakeland College, (46) Lambton C.A.A.T., (47) Lethbridge Community College, and (48) Vancouver Community College (Langara).

• Intent of Community College Programs

The intent of "complete" community college programs in leisure studies is to prepare individuals for entry-level positions in the service-oriented field of leisure. These programs teach practical skills for the technician (Cordes and Ibrahim, 1999). "Complete" college diplomas refer to programs that are terminal, such as the two-year diploma program in recreation and leisure services at Algonquin College in Ottawa. Those who pursue this program tend to not transfer into a university programs, but rather enter the work force directly.

The second type of community college program offered in leisure studies are university transfer programs. In this case, students begin their studies in community colleges that offer them an opportunity to transfer directly into a university degree program, normally after two years. One example is the collaborative program between Red Deer College and the University of Alberta.

In general, however, most students who pursue community college programs tend to enter the "complete" stream rather than the "university transfer program." One reason for this is that very few "university transfer programs" are offered in Canada. A subsequent reason may be that students entering community college are primarily interested in working at the grassroots level in people-oriented positions and have no desire to pursue administrative careers in leisure.

In general, the intent of community college programs in leisure studies is to: (1) stimulate personal growth, (2) provide necessary skills for practical training, (3) assist in the development of leadership skills, (4) pass on knowledge on the concepts and philosophy of leisure and education, and (5) disseminate information on leisure and recreation behaviour patterns.

Table 12.1: The University versus Community College Leisure Studies Programs Spectrum

	University	College
INTENT	Career Preparation	Career Preparation/Job Training
LENGTH	4 years	2 years
FOCUS	Theory/Administration	Leadership Skills/Programming/Planning
SKILLS	Research	People-Oriented
EDUCATONC	Ph.D.	Masters/Bachelors
FURTHER STUDY	Graduate School	University Transfer Programs

• Employment Preparation

Graduates of community college diploma programs in leisure studies are well prepared to enter entry-level positions in community and therapeutic recreation. Graduates are qualified to find employment in the public, commercial and volunteer sectors, and in the areas of activity leadership and recreation programming in municipal recreation centres. Moreover, graduates are qualified to work in outdoor and sport camps, in commercial fitness facilities such as fitness, squash and tennis clubs, and in leisure entertainment complexes and theme parks.

The most frequent employers for college graduates in leisure studies include: (1) hospitals, (2) municipal recreation departments, (3) homes for the aged, (4) non-profit organizations, (5) correctional services, (6) YMCA/YWCAs, (7) Boys' and Girls' Clubs, (8) rehabilitation centres, (9) community schools, (10) industrial recreation, (11) older adult centres, (12) retail outlets, (13) government agencies, (14) theme and amusement parks, and (15) fitness centres.

Those who graduate from community college diploma programs in tourism and related areas are qualified for a number of positions in the travel industry. Some of the most popular positions include tourist attraction operator, tour wholesalers, visitor/convention bureau information officers, government tourist centres, service-oriented positions at Walt Disney World, cruise lines service positions, sales and service positions in hospitality organizations, tour escort, travel counsellor, tourism marketing manager, meetings/special events coordinator, resort activities director, tour operator/reservationist, and hotel front desk associate.

CANADIAN-BASED RESEARCH JOURNALS IN LEISURE STUDIES

Two classifications of leisure studies journals exist in Canada: national-based and local-based journals. National-based journals cover a market that includes Canada as a whole and the international community. *Leisure/Loisir, Society and Leisure, Journal of Leisurability, Parks and Recreation Canada* and *Tourism* are all national-based leisure studies journals. Most of these focus solely on the dissemination of research in leisure studies.

Local-based journals are usually in the form of newsprint. These tend to be published by provincial or municipal recreation associations as local news releases and focus minimally on research. For example, the Recreation Facility Association of Nova Scotia publishes *Facility Focus On-Line,* whereas the Alberta Recreation and Parks Association publishes *Newsletter.* This *Newsletter* will periodically present research findings. However, its focus is mostly on the state of local services.

• Leisure/Loisir

In November 1970 the first issue of the first volume was published under the name *Recreation Review.* It was prepared by the Ontario Recreation Research Committee. During September 1971, the preparation of this publication became the responsibility of the Ontario Research Council on Leisure. Despite name changes, the Ontario Research Council on Leisure continued to have major responsibility for the preparation of this journal for almost thirty years until 1999-2000.

In November 1976, *Recreation Review* changed its name to *Recreation Research Review* with the publication of Volume 5, Number 2. In 1989, with the introduction of Volume 15, Number 1, this journal changed its name yet again to the *Journal of Applied Recreation Research.* In 1999-2000 (Volume 24, Numbers 1 and 2), it changed to its current name, *Leisure/Loisir.*

Not only did the name of this journal change to **Leisure/Loisir** in 1999-2000, but its major affiliation also shifted. This journal is now recognized as a publication of the Canadian Association for Leisure Studies, prepared in co-operation with the Ontario Research Council on Leisure. Recent research by Heywood (2000/2001) suggests that this journal does not focus as much on applied research as it did in the past. Heywood points out that, in the 1980s and 1990s, the objective of the *Journal of Applied Recreation Research* was to attract "applied research papers on a wide variety of topics concerning recreation and leisure. Of interest to both academic researchers and practitioners, the *Journal of Applied Recreation Research* emphasizes the practical implications of empirical research in recreation and leisure" (p. 10).

Today, *Leisure/Loisir* is not so much committed to the applied dimension of research, but rather focuses on the dissemination of all types of research in leisure, recreation and tourism. *Leisure/Loisir* encompasses an interdisciplinary nature of use to academics, practitioners,

A predecessor of *Leisure/Loisir,* one of the premier journals for applied leisure and recreation.

administrators and students. It publishes text in English and French with abstracts in both languages.

Wilfred Laurier University Press prints *Leisure/Loisir* four times per year. *Leisure/Loisir* publishes peer-reviewed articles and accepts contributions from Canada and abroad. A wide array of articles are considered and accepted for publication. These include quantitative and qualitative research, conceptual articles, comprehensive reviews, policy and economic impact analyses studies, and innovative practice descriptions and evaluations. Submitted articles are reviewed by an associate editor and two anonymous reviewers. Each journal includes, on average, three to six articles.

On occasion, this journal has designated theme issues. Theme issues of the past include: two Special Retrospective Issues, Volume 25, Numbers 1 and 2 and Numbers 3 and 4, 2000/2001; two Community Development and Recreation Practice issues, Volume 21 and Volume 22, 1996; and Applied Ethics and Recreation Practice, Volume 20, Number 2, 1995.

Recent articles include: "Identification of key influences on heritage tourism activity participation," authored by Kelly J. Mackay, Volume 26, Number 1-2, 2001/2002; "A forest recreation decision support system: The woodlot outdoor recreation opportunity spectrum," authored by Glynn Bissix in Volume 24, Number 3-4, 1999-2000; and "A call for the increased use of longitudinal methods in research on adult leisure," authored by Gaylene Carpenter and Brenda Robertson, Volume 24, Number 1-2, 1999-2000.

• Society and Leisure

In the late 1970s, the UNESCO journal, **Society and Leisure**, became the responsibility of the Research Group on Leisure from the International Sociological Association with editorial responsibilities falling in the hands of Université B Quebec de Trois Rivières (Burton, 1979). The first issue of *Society and Leisure* was published in 1978, and it contained an editorial note entitled "From the President." Here, Max Kaplan (1978) described how the first issue of *Society and Leisure* was a continuation of a publication that existed for a few years under the leadership of the European Center for Leisure and Education in Prague. In this editorial, Kaplan also embraced the executive secretary, Gilles Pronovost, from the Université de Quebec à Trois Rivières for undertaking the responsibility as editor of this new journal.

The international scope of this journal was made clear in the selection of the editorial committee for its first issue. The committee consisted of Phillip Bosserman from Salisbury State College, U.S.; Gyorgy Fukasz from Budapest, Hungary; Max Kaplan from the University of South Florida, U.S.; and, Michael A. Smith from the University of Salford, Great Britain. The international nature of this journal was also evident in the diverse group of contributors to the first issue, who were from the U.S., Great Britain, Hungary and Canada.

This journal focuses on the social analysis of leisure and recreation.

In the first volume of *Society and Leisure,* Max Kaplan made an eloquent argument supporting the need to broaden the term "sociology" in studies of leisure, making it clear that the emphasis of this journal would be on the social sciences and a social analysis of leisure. More specifically, Kaplan intended to lay the foundation for a journal that expanded beyond quantitative research:

> Some of us, therefore, while respectful to the need to work with primary and secondary data, have felt impelled to emphasize the holistic or comprehensive approach; in it, the data falls into constructs or systems of analysis that enrich the difficult middle-range of theory that links the micro- and the macrosmic. If our journal is to provide a maximum source of exchange and stimulation, its pages must reflect this range: tables of data will have their rightful place, but so will discussions of values, methods, and ideologies (Kaplan, 1978:4).

Today, *Society and Leisure* continues to operate out of Quebec, Canada, and the emphasis continues to be on the social aspects of leisure. This journal is published two times and year (spring and fall) by the Université de Quebec press in Ste-Foy, Quebec. Articles appear in English or French with abstracts in English, French, German and Spanish.

Society and Leisure tends to devote its issues towards specific theme topics. Recent theme issues include: Culture and Lifestyle, Volume 24, Number 2, 2001; Leisure and Social Agenda, Volume 23, Number 1, 2000; and Working Time and Non-Work Time, Volume 20, Number 1, 1997.

Contributors to this journal continue to come from the international community. Articles are not restricted to Canadian content, yet on occasion, papers focusing on Canada do appear. Some of the most recent papers focusing on Canada or Canadian-based research include: "Leisure and spirituality: A theoretical model," authored by George Karlis, Sotiria Grafanaki, and Jihan Abbas, Volume 25, Number 1, 2002; "Testing an optimal matching hypothesis of stress, coping and health: Leisure and general coping," authored by Yoshi Iwasaki, Volume 24, Number 1, 2001; and "Leisure and spiritual well-being relationships: A qualitative study," authored by Paul Heintzman, Volume 23, Number 1, 2000.

• Journal of Leisurability

The **Journal of Leisurability** first appeared in January 1974 (Volume 1, Number 1) as a publication of the Leisure and Disability Publications Steering Committee. This committee, acting from a grant approved in the 1973-74 budget of the Sport and Recreation Branch of the Ontario Ministry of Community and Social Services, set out to establish "the best possible information services to the practitioner in the field of Therapeutic Recreation" (Pullman, 1974:1).

Unlike other journals, the establishment of the *Journal of Leisurability* did not come from a professional society or association. Rather, it was the result of the efforts of the Leisure and Disability Publications

Steering Committee, made up of an independent functioning group of practitioners. The members of this committee included Lorna Evans, Vince Gilles, Fred Martin, Jim Mountings, Lee Pullman, Jody Witt and Peter Witt.

The original goal of this journal was "to continue to function as practitioners while hopefully answering the needs of other practitioners" (Rullman, 1974: 2). It set out to cater to an interdisciplinary audience from various academic fields and professions, such as recreation, psychology, social work, physical education, rehabilitation, nursing and occupational therapy. Thus, the *Journal of Leisurability* encouraged practitioners of therapeutic recreation and professionals in the field of leisure and disability to share experiences and research with the ultimate intent of improving their practice. The initial targeted readership of this journal were professionals, lay board members, volunteers, students, municipalities, agencies, institutions, government and educational settings.

Originally this journal focused on disseminating information on traditional and innovative programs and practice on leisure and disability. Its underlying objective was to bridge the gap between theory and practice through the publication of articles, reviews and editorial notes. Moreover, the *Journal of Leisurability* intended to present research on "what works" and "what doesn't work" in programs and practices in leisure and disability. It was found that much research was needed to better comprehend this area of inquiry.

Today, more that twenty-five years later, the *Journal of Leisurability* continues to address the area of leisure and disability yet has expanded its focus to a greater emphasis on selected populations in general. Its intent is to publish articles on leisure and disability, community, advocacy and integration. This quarterly consists of a "Current Research" section that presents research on leisure and disability or devalued persons. Also included is a section on "Sharing Program Ideas," which allows those practising in the area of leisure and disability with an opportunity to describe innovative and interesting approaches to programming and development. This journal states in its "Information for Contributors" that it is "committed to maintaining a high Canadian content."

The *Journal of Leisurability* is published by Leisurability Publications Inc., in Toronto, Ontario. It regularly publishes theme issues on selected topics. Recent theme issues include: Youth in Volume 27, Number 2, Spring 2000; Privatization in Volume 26, Number 4, Fall 1999; and Access in Volume 26, Number 1, 1999.

Today, as throughout its history, the *Journal of Leisurability* publishes articles with an interdisciplinary audience in mind. Although this journal is Ontario-based and focuses mainly on Canadian content, from time to time it publishes articles from authors in other countries, such as the U.S., Belgium and Australia. This has not always been the case, as most articles that appeared in the early issues of this journal came mostly from local communities. The local presence of this journal continues to be

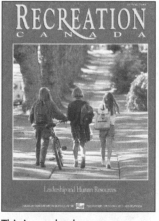

This journal enhances our knowledge of the parks and recreation industry in Canada.

emphasized as article submissions tend to come from the Ontario region.

Recent articles that have appeared in the *Journal of Leisurability* include: "Leisure education as a rehabilitative tool for youth in incarcerated settings," by Brenda Robertson, Volume 27, Number 2, Spring 2000; "Institutionalization of seniors: A necessary practice?" by Elaine Wiersma, Volume 27, Number 1, Winter 2000; and "Personal relationship, illness, and disability," by Renee Lyons, Volume 2, Number 3, Summer 1999.

• Parks and Recreation Canada

The oldest of all national journals in the field of leisure studies in Canada is a publication by the Canadian Parks and Recreation Association, currently entitled *Parks and Recreation Canada.* However, as is the case with *Leisure/Loisir,* this journal has gone through a number of name changes throughout its history.

The first volume appeared in late 1940s bearing the name *Parks and Recreation in Canada.* In September 1969, the name of the journal was changed to *Recreation Canada* in Volume 27, Number 5. Its current name, *Parks and Recreation Canada,* was introduced in Volume 54, Number 1 of the March/April 1996 issue.

Although **Parks and Recreation Canada** is now published six times a year, this was not always the case. From 1981 to 1995, it was published five times a year, and prior to 1980, the frequency of publication varied. For instance, in 1954 it was published monthly, whereas in 1960, it was published quarterly.

The focus of *Parks and Recreation Canada* is on offering information about the parks and recreation field in Canada. Its primary concern is to address the needs of parks and recreation practitioners so as to enhance the body of knowledge and the provision of services in the park and recreation industries and practices of Canada.

The current editorial committee of *Parks and Recreation Canada,* as in the past, consists of park and recreation professionals and practitioners. Unlike, *Leisure/Loisir, Society and Leisure* and the *Journal of Leisurability,* it is uncommon to find academics on its editorial committee. Nonetheless, university professors from various universities in Canada and the United States do contribute articles to this journal.

Currently, *Parks and Recreation Canada* is published bi-monthly by the Canadian Parks and Recreation Association in Ottawa, Ontario. Almost all of its issues address specific themes. Some of the most recent themes are: Levelling the Playing Field, Volume 60, Number 2, May/June 2002; Focus on Extreme Recreation, Volume 59, Number 5, November/December 2001; and Children and Youth, Volume 58, Number 1, March/April 2000.

Recent articles include: "Allocation of Ice Time," authored by Roland Cote, Volume 60, Number 2, May/June 2002; "Discover Northeastern

Table 12.2: Comparison of Canadian-Based Peer-Reviewed Leisure Studies Journals

Journal	Year Started	Focus	Issues/ Year	Contributors	Location/ Publisher
Leisure/Loisir	1970	Applied/Empirical Research	4	Highly Canadian	Waterloo, Ont.
Journal of Leisurability	1974	Leisure and Disability	4	Canadian/ International	Toronto, Ont.
Society and Leisure	1978	Social Analysis of Leisure	2	Highly International	Ste-Foy, Que.

Ontario in a technological way," authored by Cathy Deline, Volume 60, Number 1, March/April 2002; and "Reclaiming play in the serious work of our lives," authored by Lanie Melamed, Volume 59, Number 4, September/October 2001.

• Tourism

In the late 1990s, the Canadian Tourism Commission released its first issue of **Tourism**. Although this journal does not publish peer-reviewed articles, it acts as a leader for the distribution of research on tourism to subscribers. *Tourism* is published ten times per year and is printed by St. Joseph in Ottawa. With the exception of January/February and July/August, issues are published monthly.

The first page of each issue of *Tourism* features a statement by the Canadian Tourism Industry, followed by a "vision" and "mission" statement. The vision statement reads: "Canada will be the premier four-season destination to connect with nature and to experience diverse cultures and communities." The mission statements is as follows: "Canada's tourism industry will deliver world-class cultural and leisure experiences year round, while preserving and sharing Canada's clean, safe and natural environments. The industry will be guided by the values of respect, integrity and empathy."

Appearing regularly in *Tourism* is an editorial, and sections on news, markets, industry, research, tourism roundup and people. On occasion, a section of the journal is dedicated to articles on markets and industry. Recent articles include: "New realities in the German Market" by Roger Laplante, Volume 6, Number 9, November 2002; "Developing a travel and tourism Website" by Greg Klassen, Volume 6, Number 8, October 2002; and, "Small airports feel the pinch" by Raymon J. Kaduck, Volume 6, Number 8, October 2002.

CANADIAN-BASED RESEARCH CONFERENCES IN LEISURE STUDIES

Two national conferences exist in leisure studies. These are the Canadian Congress on Leisure Research, and the Canadian Parks and Recreation Association's Annual Conference.

• Canadian Congress on Leisure Research

The **Canadian Congress on Leisure Research** takes place in a different Canadian location every three years. The responsibility for the selection of a location for this congress falls within the hands of the Canadian Association for Leisure Research, the same association primarily responsible for the journal *Leisure/Loisir*.

The first Canadian Congress on Leisure Research took place in 1975 in Quebec City. To date, there have been a total of ten Canadian Congresses on Leisure Research, with the most recent being held at the University of Alberta in Edmonton in 2002. The next Canadian Congress on Leisure Research will take place at Malaspina University in Nanaimo, British Columbia, in 2005.

It was at the Second Canadian Congress on Leisure Research in Toronto that the idea was put forth to hold these conferences triennially. At that time, Jack Ellis from the University of Toronto and Bill Knott from the Ontario government led a group of conference delegates in the preparation of a formal organization and constitution for the establishment of, not only a congress, but also a permanent organization made up of individuals attending the conference. This organization of conference delegates, that is, those who have attended the Canadian Congress on Leisure Research, make up the membership of the Canadian Association for Leisure Studies.

Although the Canadian Congress on Leisure Research is held in a Canadian location, it has become an international conference and is attended by delegates from various parts of the world including the United States, Australia, Great Britain and Turkey. Research presented at this conference is not only Canadian in nature, but extends towards a global understanding of leisure and leisure theory.

During the 1990s, registration at this triennial conference showed a steady increase. Markham-Starr (2000/2001) reports that, in 1990, one hundred and fifty delegates attended the conference in Waterloo. In 1993, one hundred and twenty-five delegates attended the conferences in Winnipeg. In 1996, one hundred and fifty-nine delegates attended the conference in Ottawa.

Despite the fact that the Canadian Congress on Leisure Research is heavily attended by Canadian academics and researchers (Jackson, 2000/2001), the research that is presented does not focus specifically on Canada. Presentations at the 10th Canadian Congress on Leisure Research on leisure in Canadian society include: "Understanding commonalities and differences: A case study of a provincial sport organization's attempt to recreate their understanding of recreation," by Ted

Alexander; "The meaning of community on a cognitive support unit," by Anne-Marie Cantwell and Alison Pedlar; and "Developing agri-tourism in Nova Scotia: Issues and challenges," by John Colton and Glyn Bissix.

Partnerships have been established with *Society and Leisure, Journal of Leisurability* and *Leisure/Loisir* for the publication of papers presented at these conferences (Markham-Starr, 2000/2001). This conference has become an excellent vehicle for the sharing of Canadian-based research, both orally and in print.

• **Canadian Parks and Recreation Association National Conference and Trade Show**

Unlike the Canadian Congress on Leisure Research, the **Canadian Parks and Recreation Association National Conference and Trade Show** focuses primarily on bringing together parks and recreation practitioners to learn about research trends and innovations in the industry. Minimal focus is placed on theory and research, while heavy focus is placed on the practice, techniques and process of the provision, distribution and implementation of parks and recreation services in Canada.

Each year, the Canadian Parks and Recreation Association's National Conference and Trade Show has a designated theme. The theme of the 2002 conference held in Winnipeg, Manitoba, was "Inside-Out: The Value of People." This conference offered educational program sessions, a trade-show, keynote speakers and presentations, and a social program for delegates.

This conference features keynote presentations and educational sessions. Some of the presentations conducted at the Winnipeg conference in 2002 included: "Personal Power/Personal Success," by Kit Grant; "Improving the life quality and life chances of Canadian children and youth: The contribution of recreation," by Dr. Dan Offord; and Demystifying the nexus generation and understanding and working with the nexus generation," by Karen Ward.

The delegates of the Canadian Parks and Recreation Association National Conference and Trade Show are, for the most part, practitioners from the leisure and recreation industry who come from all service sectors: public, commercial and voluntary. One of the main reasons for attending this conference is to find out the latest trends and fads in leisure and recreation. Trade show displays exhibit the most recent developments in equipment, supplies, services and technology for use in the industry. At the Winnipeg conference in 2002, there were forty-two companies occupying fifty-six display booths.

As this conference is primarily practitioner-oriented, the outstanding work of those in the leisure and recreation field is recognized. A number of awards are presented each year to those who have made a significant contribution to the profession. Some of the awards presented include the Award of Excellence for Innovation, the National Benefits Award, and the Award of Merit.

"Parks for people" – a popular theme at the 2002 conference in Winnipeg.

Photo: Courtesy of George Karlis.

CONCLUSION

Although the shared intent of university and community college programs in leisure studies is to prepare students for employment, a number of differences exist. The length, focus, skills passed on, and the education level of instructors differ considerably in the two types of institutions. Table 12.1 provides a comparison between university and community college programs in leisure studies.

A study of forty-four Canadian leisure studies programs and related areas concluded that ten general areas of concentration exist in both universities and community college. These are: (1) recreation leadership, (2) tourism, (3) recreation management, (4) recreation facilities management, (5) therapeutic recreation, (6) older adult recreation, (7) parks and recreation, (8) resort management, (9) recreation for special populations, and (10) recreation technology (Gagnon, Ostiguy and Swedburg, 1993).

University and college programs in Canada have evolved significantly in the past forty years. Changes are inevitable as the study of leisure in Canada heads towards maturity. One of the biggest challenges for the development of leisure studies programs and curricula in universities and colleges will be to keep pace with societal changes, in particular those that effect leisure and recreation services. Indeed, "academic programs need to keep pace with these changes and more collaborative efforts between academics and professionals for applied research will continue to be encouraged" (Mitsui, 1999: 7).

The 1970s was an important decade for leisure research as it witnessed the creation of most Canadian research journals. The creation of higher education programs in leisure studies in Canadian universities and colleges in the 1960s and 1970s helped not only to launch the establishment of Canadian research journals, but also the inauguration of the Canadian Congress of Leisure Research. Today, both of these avenues are highly relied upon for the dissemination of leisure research in Canadian society.

The number of university and college leisure studies programs in Canada has increased rapidly since the 1970s. The fact that only three Canadian-based peer-reviewed journals exist is of concern, as the number of research endeavours conducted by Canadians has increased tremendously over the past three decades (see Table 12.2). Not only are more Canadian-based leisure studies research journals needed, but also more avenues for sharing academic research. The creation of an annual Canadian leisure studies conference would enhance the spreading of Canadian leisure-based research of the increasing number of Canadian academics, researchers and students in leisure studies.

CHAPTER 12: EDUCATION, RESEARCH JOURNALS AND CONFERENCES

Study Questions

1. What is the intent of undergraduate university programs in leisure studies?

2. What is the objective of graduate programs in leisure studies?

3. In what broad areas are graduates of university leisure studies programs trained for employment?

4. What is the difference between "complete" and "university transfer programs" in community college?

5. What is the intent of community college programs in leisure studies?

Selected Websites

*   **Academy of Leisure Sciences**
    http://www.academyofleisuresciences.org

*   **World Leisure and Recreation Association**
    http://www.worldleisure.org

*   **Leisure on the Net**
    http://www.leisurestudies.uiuc.edu/resources/
    degrees/world/CA/NS.html

*   **Canadian Universities**
    http://www.uwaterloo.ca/canu/univ3.html

*   **Study in Canada**
    http://www.studyincanada.com

Key Concepts

*   **Leisure/Loisir**

*   **Society and Leisure**

*   **Journal of Leisurability**

*   **Parks and Recreation Canada**

*   **Tourism**

*   **Canadian Congress on Leisure Research**

*   **Canadian Parks and Recreation Association National Conference and Trade Show**

13

THE FUTURE OF LEISURE AND RECREATION IN CANADA

LEARNING OBJECTIVES

- To examine the evolution of social trends that may have an impact on leisure and recreation in Canadian society.
- To overview the changing face of the Canadian population.
- To look at future predictions for leisure and recreation activity participation.
- To overview provincial and territorial perspectives for the future of leisure and recreation.
- To examine what may unfold for the future of leisure and recreation for the year 2020.

The evolution of various social trends can provide us with hints in understanding the people of society and the people of the leisure and recreation industry. These social trends may be directly linked to our comprehension of both the current and future leisure and recreation patterns for the people of Canada. Although it is difficult to conceptualize leisure and recreation in the future, nothing stops us from making educated guesses based on current social trends. By putting together more than one future scenario for leisure and recreation we view what may happen from multiple perspectives.

This final chapter presents an overview of current social trends in Canada and also depicts future scenarios for the future of leisure and recreation. In addition, the chapter offers four scenarios for the future of leisure and recreation in Canada for the year 2020.

CANADA'S POPULATION

In 1996, Tina Chui reported that Canada's demographic future probably consists of a slow population growth and an ageing population, largely due to low fertility and the ageing of the baby boomers. There is a third factor that also influences size of population, that of immigration. From Census Canada 2002, we know that immigration in Canada has increased and that a great number of Canadians were born outside of Canada. As immigration increases, projected figures for population growth in Canada also increase.

"The most remarkable aspect of the transition we are living through is not so much the passage from want to affluence as the passage from labor to leisure.... Leisure contains the future, it is the new horizon.... The prospect then is one of unremitting labor to bequeath to future generations a chance of founding a society of leisure that will overcome the demands and compulsions of productive labor so that time may be devoted to creative activities or simply to pleasure and happiness."

— Henri Lefebvre (b. 1901), French philosopher. "What Should the New Society Be Called?" in *Everyday Life in the Modern World*, ch .1 (1962).

Table 13.1: Components of Population Growth, July 1, 2001 – June 30, 2002

	Canada	Newfound-land and Labrador	Prince Edward Island	Nova Scotia	New Brunswick
Births	327,187	4,689	1,428	8,918	7,719
Deaths	231,232	4,420	1,188	8,104	6,427
Immigrants	255,888	417	146	1,591	762
Total emigrants[1]	71,042	402	46	751	356
Net interprovincial migrants	x	-2,510	683	-1266	-871
Non-permanent residents	22,624	5	-14	1493	412

"X" data unavailable, not applicable or confidential.

[1] Total emigration is comprised of emigrants, returning emigrants and net variation in the number of persons temporarily abroad.

Source: Statistics Canada, CANSIM, Table 051-0004.

Statistics Canada has put together three population growth scenarios for Canada up to 2016. The first of these is a high-growth scenario with an increase in fertility to 1.9 children; life expectancies of 81 years for men and 86 for women; and annual immigration of 330,000 people by 2005. The second scenario is medium-growth. Here, fertility remains at 1.7 births per woman, life expectancy for males is 78.5 years and 84 years for women, while annual immigration remains at 250,000. The third scenario is one of low-growth. In this case, fertility declines to 1.5 births per women, men live to 77 years while women live to 83 years, and annual immigration decreases to 150,000 people annually (Statistics Canada, 1993).

In general, however, recent trends reveal the following: (1) Canada is an ageing society as baby boomers, the largest age cohort born between 1946 and 1966, approach their senior years; (2) Canadians are living longer as mortality rates have declined due to improved quality of life and health care; (3) immigration has grown in the early part of the new millennium as there are now more new Canadians and more Canadians who were born outside of Canada (Statistics Canada, 2003a); (4) low fertility rates have continued; (5) a slow, but continuous growth of the young adult population exists; (6) Canada has an older work force that is rapidly ageing; and (7) a smaller proportion of the future Canadian population will be of working age (Chui, 1996).

Table 13.1 clearly illustrates that the Canadian population is growing. From July 1, 2001, to June 30, 2002, there were more births than deaths and more immigrants than migrants. Moreover, the fifth round of the 2001 Census of Population data released on January 21, 2003, reveals that the population of foreign-born people in Canada was the highest in seventy years. Indeed, as of May 15, 2001, 5.4 million people or 18.4 percent of the Canadian population had been born in countries other than Canada. During the 1990s, most immigrants who arrived in Canada had been born in Asia and the Middle East while most now reside in Toronto, Montreal or Vancouver (Statistics Canada, 2003a).

A further growth trend in Canada's population is occurring for Aboriginal Peoples. Since 1996, the population of Aboriginal Peoples of Canada has grown by 22 percent. As of 2001, 3.3 percent of Canada's population identified themselves as Aboriginal persons, an increase of .5 percent from 1996 (Statistics Canada, 2003a).

AGEING BOOMERS

Canada is an ageing society. The main contributor to this is the baby boomers, the large age cohort born between 1946 and 1966. This group is rapidly approaching their senior years.

EDUCATION

In 1996, Statistics Canada reported that the education level of Canadians continues to rise. During the past few years, a shift has occurred as the number of Canadians having completed university now surpasses the number of Canadians with less than a Grade 9 education. In fact, during the past fifty years, the level of schooling in Canada has risen steadily and rapidly.

A little more than 10 percent of the Canadian population have university degrees (Statistics Canada, 1996d). Indeed, this number is reflective of the high value placed by Canadian society on higher education. In 1997, among G7 countries, Canada was ranked second in spending on education as a proportion of GDP. Only the United States surpassed Canada in this category (Clark, 2000a). Higher education entails a number of benefits. First and foremost is a higher median income. The 1996 Census indicated that Canadians with university degrees were more likely than high-school graduates to earn more money and be employed full time and full year. During that year, the median income for university graduates was $43,600, whereas for high-school graduates it was $27,900 (Clark, 2000a).

Women now outnumber men at Canadian universities. It used to be that men outnumbered women. However, during the onset of 1990s it became evident that a shift had taken place (Clark, 2000a; Normand, 2000). This is only the case in undergraduate studies as men continue to outnumber women in graduate studies (Normand, 2000).

In addition, recent findings reveal that parents in Canada are strongly committed to post-secondary education for their children. Indeed, most parents (74 percent) with children up to the age of five have expectations that their child will complete a university degree (Statistics Canada, 2003b).

INCOME AND EXPENDITURES

The early 1990s was a turbulent time for the Canadian economy as this decade commenced with a recession. Canada witnessed an economic downturn leading to cutbacks in government social programs. Unemployment rates remained over at 10 percent whereas annual inflation was less than 3 percent. In addition, from 1990 to 1995, the average individual income of Canadians decreased by more than 2 percent from $26,991 to $26,327. The result was that consumers were left with little discretionary income and less spending power (Williams, 2000).

Despite having less discretionary income and spending power, Canadians spent more on consumer goods and services. In fact, from 1990 to 1999, the spending of Canadians on these goods and services increased by almost 12 percent from $14,801 to $16,533. However, some of this spending was financed by credit as the volume of consumer debt continued to increase in the 1990s while personal savings dropped from 9.5 percent to 1.4 percent (Williams, 2000).

The 1990s ended with a strong economic recovery as unemployment started to decrease, income tax rates started to drop and disposable income started to rise at rates faster than inflation. Indeed, the close of the 1990s brought a sense of hope into the new millennium for the income and expenditures of Canadians.

In 2001, households in Canada spent an average of 3.4 percent more on everything from food and shelter to recreation than they did in 2000. This means that total household spending was slightly higher than the rate of inflation, measured at 2.6 percent in 2001 by the Consumer Price Index. In 2001, households spent $57,730 as compared to $55,830 in 2000. Moreover, during the three most recent reported years, the average expenditures on recreation also increased (Statistics Canada, 2002b). In 1999, Canadians spent $2,960 on recreation, whereas in 2000 and 2001, average household expenditures on recreation were $3,170 and $3,450 respectively. In 2001, Canadians spent 6 percent of their household expenditures budget on recreation as compared to 5.7 percent in 2000 and 5.5 percent in 1999 (ibid.).

Preliminary indicators for November 2002 show average weekly earnings at $684.76, an increase of 2.0 percent from November 2001. In November 2002, the average weekly earnings for employees in the arts, entertainment and recreation industries was well below the national average at $480.92 (Statistics Canada, 2003c). The average weekly earnings for employees in these industries were higher in November 2001 at $493 than in November 2002 (Statistics Canada, 2002b).

The year 2000 marked the lowest number of reported low-income families since 1989. In 2000, a family of four dwelling in a city of over 500,000 people earning below $29,163 as after-tax income was classified as "low-income." Similarly, a family living in a rural area would be classified as low-income if its after-tax income was less than $19,120. It was estimated that 666,000 families fell under the low-income category in 2000 (Statistics Canada. 2002c).

HEALTH

During the past one hundred years, the leading causes of death in Canada have changed dramatically. In the early 1920s, the three main causes were reported as cardiovascular and renal disease; influenza, bronchitis and pneumonia; and diseases of early infancy. In the later part of the 1990s, the three leading causes of death were: cardiovascular diseases (heart disease and stroke); cancer; and chronic obstructive pulmonary diseases (see Table 13.2).

In general, Canadians today are healthier than they were in the 1970s and early 1980s. In fact, it appears as though the general overall level of health of Canadians is increasing with each generation (Crompton, 2000). "Advances in public health measures and sanitary control, pharmaceuticals and medical technology in the 20th century have had a dramatic effect on the overall level of health in Canada" (p. 17). It is not surprising that the World Health Organization identifies Canada as a society with a trend towards longevity while predicting that the average lifetime of Canadians will be 81 years of age in 2025.

The fact that Canadians are becoming better educated helps enhance the health of society. Risk behaviour, health status and education are closely linked. "People with more education are less likely to smoke, drink heavily or be overweight; they tend to be more physically active and to have a positive outlook on life and good mental health" (Crompton, 2000: 17). As reported by the *Statistical Report on the Health of Canadians 1999*, Canadians with university degrees are more likely to have health-care coverage through work, including dental care, vision care and prescription drugs (Statistics Canada, 1999a). Thus, a higher educated population is more likely to take preventative measures to health care and healthy living.

LIVING PATTERNS

In Canada, smaller urban and rural communities are losing residents as urbanization has continued to increase. Nonetheless, since the 1950s and 1960s the rapid growth of car ownership has enticed suburban development. Canadians have moved to suburban homes while continuing to work in the urban city. Today, more than 80 percent of Canadian husband-wife families own their own homes (Kremarik, 2000).

A recent trend was reported by Foot and Stoffman (1998), who claim that some Canadians are now living in smaller cities and towns outside big urban cities. These individuals desire country living while being close enough to commute to the city. Another trend reported by Statistics Canada, based on the 2001 General Survey, is that one in twelve Canadians live in separate homes from their partners. Most are young adults in their twenties (56 percent), yet 19 percent of people were in their thirties, 14 percent were in their forties, and 11 percent were aged fifty or over. Some of the reasons cited for couples living apart are: family responsibilities or to save money (Statistics Canada, 2003d).

Photo: Health Canada.

Canadians are living longer and are more physically active than ever before.

Table 13.2: Leading Causes of Death in the Twentieth Century

	Rate per 100,000
1921-25	
All causes	**1,030.0**
Cardiovascular and renal disease	221.9
Influenza, bronchitis and pneumonia	141.1
Diseases of early infancy	111.0
Tuberculosis	85.1
Cancer	75.9
Gastritis, duodenitis, enteritis and colitis	72.2
Accidents	51.5
Communicable diseases	47.1
1996-97	
All causes	**654.4**
Cardiovascular diseases (heart disease and stroke)	240.2
Cancer	184.8
Chronic obstructive pulmonary diseases	28.4
Unintentional injuries	27.7
Pneumonia and influenza	22.1
Diabetes mellitus	16.7
Hereditary and degenerative diseases of the central nervous system	14.7
Diseases of arteries, arterioles and capillaries	14.3

Note: Disease categories not identical over time. Rates in 1996-97 are age-standardized.
Source: Statistics Canada, Catalogue nos. 11-516 and 84-214.

FAMILY STRUCTURES

In the recent past, Canada has undergone a steady decline of the traditional two-parent family in which the father was employed and the mother was the homemaker and had child-care responsibilities. Following World War II, there has been a greater involvement of women in the workforce. More married women are now employed and more Canadians are valuing two-income families (Zukewich Ghalan, 1997).

From 1986 to 1996 the number of "three generations living together" has increased in Canada. This is a trend that is likely to continue in the future as Canadian society ages, Canadians start to live longer, and immigration continues to grow (Che-Alford and Hamm, 1999). The number of young adults living at home has also increased since 1981 as more and more young women and men between the ages of twenty to thirty-four live at home (Boyd and Norris, 1999).

Canadians choosing to get married are doing so later in life. More than ever before, Canadians are choosing common-law unions, at least as a start, while in some cases these lead to marriage (Oderkirk, 2000). Statistics Canada (1992) reported that the average age of first marriage for men is twenty-nine whereas for women it is twenty-seven. However, with the liberalization of divorce laws in 1968, the number of divorces in Canada has increased while the number of remarriages has also increased (Oderkirk, 2000). The number of Canadians living alone has also increased in the past fifty years (Clark, 2002).

Clark (1998) posits that weekly attenders of religious services tend to place more importance on home life. Findings by Statistics Canada (1995) indicate that religious people are more likely to want to keep the family together. These same findings reveal that religious people tend to place greater emphasis on marriage, family and children. Studies by Myers and Diener (1995), Bradley (1995), and Larsen and Larsen (1994) indicate that religious people feel better while Clark (1998) claims that weekly attenders of religious services have happier, healthier marriages. Nonetheless, trends in Canada indicate that "attendance at religious services" continues to decrease (ibid.).

Moreover, a further trend in Canada indicates a decline in the size of the family. For example, from 1970 to 1995 the average size of the Canadian family decreased from 3.72 persons in 1970 to 3.05 persons in 1995 (Statistics Canada, 1999c). A number of factors may have contributed to this decrease such as cost of living and birth control. Yet it should be noted that, during the aforementioned period, average income per family member increased 60.9% (Statistics Canada, 1999c).

A study by Crompton and Kemeny (2000) reports that, healthy or not, most seniors that were married were doing well psychologically. Furthermore, Statistics Canada's National Population Health Survey (1996/1997b) indicates that senior men in good health living with a healthy partner were more likely to feel happy as the majority of seniors living in two-person households tend to receive high levels of emotional support.

Today, children tend to belong to smaller and less traditional families.

Photo: Health Canada.

WORK

According to Fast and Da Pont (1997) work is important for our sense of identity as employment discontinuity can affect our emotional and psychological well-being. It may thus be that, similar to leisure, work and the employment experience is critical for the enhancement of quality of life.

A National Graduates Survey conducted by Statistics Canada (1997) reveals that graduates from the class of 1995 were least successful in finding full-time work in comparison to graduates from the classes of 1990, 1986 and 1982. In addition, this same survey revealed that high pay, job location and "liking the kind of work" were reported as the most important job selection criteria for 1995 graduates (see Table 13.3).

Clark (2000b) reports a number of trends that are important in the pursuit of finding work. These include networking, particularly for a first job, volunteering and previous work experience. Making contacts and having volunteer and paid work experience prior to graduating from university or college enhance the likelihood of finding work after graduation (Karlis, 2002c).

Further trends on work in Canadian society indicate that: (1) one in five well-educated Canadians feels overqualified for his or her job, (2) women are more likely than men to feel overqualified, (3) young adults feel overqualified for their jobs, and (4) low employment income has a strong effect on the workers' opinion of the job (Kelly, Howatson-Leo, and Clark, 2000). As Canadians become more highly educated, they seem to expect more from their job and work experiences. Despite this, Statistics Canada (1994) reveals that a high proportion of post-secondary graduates work in clerical, sales, service or blue collar jobs (see Table 13.4). In fact, a high proportion of recreation graduates feel overqualified for their jobs (see Table 13.5).

Since the 1980s the number of self-employed Canadians has increased. Self-employed Canadians are from diverse backgrounds and work in a different range of occupations. These include well-educated professionals, such as dentists and consultants, with high average annual salaries. The self-employed also include those with little education in lower paid positions such as tradespeople, barbers and hairdressers (Gardner, 2000).

Technology has also changed the work force. Today, computers have the processing capability to take the place of some highly paid, well-educated positions. This means that highly educated professionals have become subject to "deskilling" positions and now feel overqualified for their jobs (Kelly, Howatson-Leo and Clark, 2000). Moreover, technology has become an important part of the work force as more and more people are plugging into the Internet (Dickenson and Ellison, 1999).

All-in-all, Canadians report that there are not enough hours in the day. In 1999 "the most time-stressed men reported spending 9.7 hours on paid or unpaid work, while women in that group said they spend 9.4

Table 13.3: Importance of Job Selection Criteria for 1995 Graduates

Criteria considered when selecting a job (Importance score 0 to 3)	College			Bachelor's		
	Total	Men	Women	Total	Men	Women
Highly salary/pay	1.53	1.61	1.47	1.34	1.43	1.28
Job location	0.80	0.76	0.84	0.73	0.69	0.75
Like the kind of work	0.57	0.56	0.59	0.67	0.63	0.70
Job is in my field of study	0.45	0.47	0.44	0.52	0.45	0.56
Uses and develops my skills and abilities	0.32	0.30	0.34	0.44	0.39	0.48
Job security	0.28	0.33	0.24	0.17	0.20	0.14
Career advancement	0.27	0.36	0.21	0.37	0.45	0.32
Able to work with people	0.24	0.19	0.28	0.20	0.18	0.22
Feeling of accomplishment	0.17	0.17	0.17	0.32	0.34	0.31
Job allows flexibility	0.16	0.13	0.18	0.13	0.12	0.14
Well-respected or prestigious occupation	0.10	0.11	0.09	0.07	0.08	0.07

Note: Graduates identified the three most important criteria they would consider when selecting a job. A value of 3 was assigned to criterion selected as the most important, a 2 for the second most important, a 1 for the third most important and a value of 0 for those criteria that were not in the top three. An importance score was calculated by averaging the values assigned across all graduates for each job selection criterion.

Source: Statistics Canada, National Graduates Survey, 1997.

PROTECTING LAND

The proportion of protected land in Canada has increased significantly from 29 million hectares in 1989 to 82 million hectares in 2003. In addition, industries in Canada spent more than 3 billion dollars on environment protection in 2000 (Statistics Canada, 2003f).

hours working" (Stonehouse, 1999: 1). This tends to be more common for twenty-five to forty-four year olds in which one in three claims to be a workaholic. In fact, men working long hours averaged fifty-five hours a week on the job whereas the average for women in this category was fifty-one hours (Statistics Canada, 1999b).

More Canadians appear to be working more hours to make ends meet and/or to afford a specific leisure lifestyle. Canadians are spending more time at work and less time on leisure and recreation (DeMont, 1999). Switching from a standard work week of thirty-five to forty hours to a longer workweek in excess of fifty hours may increase the risk of certain negative impacts on health, such as high blood pressure and cardiovascular disease (Statistics Canada, 1999b). Nonetheless, preliminary Statistics Canada reports from November 2002 indicate that the average weekly hours for hourly employees is thirty-two hours per week (Statistics Canada, 2003e).

In 2002, employment in Canada increased by 3.7 percent. This rate of growth was the highest since 1987. Yet, despite this growth in employment, a large number of Canadians continued to be unemployed as the unemployment rate continues to remain consistent at 7.5 percent for December of 2002 (Statistics Canada, 2003e).

ENVIRONMENT

The 1990s witnessed a trend towards a greater appreciation of the environment and our natural resources. A number of initiatives were undertaken by government at all levels not only to enhance our appreciation of the natural environment and its resources, but to encourage us to "do our part" in protecting and conserving the environment and our natural resources for future generations. The concepts of "recycling" and "re-using" became household terms. Neighbourhood communities, shopping centres and office buildings began to encourage people to not dispose of but rather recycle goods that could be recycled. Advertisements and promotional campaigns relayed the message that the earth's resources are not finite and that we all have to do our part not only to eliminate waste, but to assist with conservation.

A number of efforts and public subsidies have been put into curbing pollution. Despite these efforts, water quality remains of concern to Canadians (Statistics Canada, 2000), as does our use of energy. Society has become more intent on measuring, preventing, limiting and correcting environmental damage to water, air and soil as well as problems related to waste, noise and ecosystems (Statistics Canada, 2002d). Moreover, the protection, conservation and maintenance of our national parks and green spaces have become a primary concern for public decision-makers as well as concerned citizens. Society as a whole has come to realize that the environment needs to be protected and conserved for the benefits of not only the present generation but of future generations as well.

Table 13.4: Employment of Post-Secondary Graduates

	Type of job held when interviewed			
	Felt Over-Qualified	Management, Professional	Clerical, Sales, Service	Blue Collar
Educational attainment	% distribution by occupation			
Post-Secondary graduates	22	64	23	13
Community college certificate or diploma	21	46	30	24
Undergraduate diploma or certificate	23	58	32	10
Bachelor's or first professional degree	22	78	17	5
Master's degree, earned doctorate[1]	27	83	12	5

1. Includes university diplomas or certificates above a bachelor's degree.
Source: Statistics Canada, General Social Survey, 1994.

Table 13.5: Feelings of Overqualification by Field of Study (%)

Field of Study	College	Bachelor's and First Professional Degree
Total	21	22
Education, recreation, counselling	30	18
Fine and applied arts, humanities, social sciences	24	27
Commerce, management and business administration	33	26
Engineering and applied science[1]	-	24
Engineering and applied science technologies and trades[2]	10	-
Health professions, sciences and technologies	14	-
Mathematics and physical sciences	-	20

"-" Sample too small to be released.
1. University-level engineering and applied science programs.
2. Technology and trades programs in engineering and applied science field.
Source: Statistics Canada, General Social Survey,1994.

CUTBACKS, DOWNSIZING AND CONTRACTING OUT

The leisure and recreation service sector has gone through changes as government cutbacks, downsizing and contracting out initiatives have led to greater involvement of and opportunities for the commercial and voluntary sectors.

THE SERVICE SECTOR

A growing trend in Canada is for two or more organizations of society to join forces and operate partnerships for the provision of services. This merger has occurred in the commercial sector, such as the merger of the Toronto Dominion Bank and Canada Trust, and in the public sector, such as in the amalgamation of municipalities. In 2000 the City of Ottawa became a mega-city as it amalgamated with its neighbouring municipalities. A few years earlier, the City of Toronto did the same.

Similarly, a recent trend has emerged for two or more sectors to work together for the provision of leisure and recreation services. This has been a popular alternative for the leisure and recreation field as the public sector has encouraged and enticed collaboration with the commercial and voluntary sectors.

Kraus (1997) discusses how in Ontario, municipalities have started to complete joint construction of school-community centres. Kraus (1997) uses the district of Etobicoke as an example in which a multi-service centre includes an elementary school, a recreation and day care centre, and a library and natural interpretive area. The staff and authorities of this facility consist of school members, the municipality and other authorities.

Another trend prevalent in the recreation industry has been that of "**contracting out**." A number of public sector organizations have been contracted out to the commercial sector as a popular "money-saving" alternative as operational responsibilities are passed over to the agency in the commercial sector, including staffing and management.

The leisure and recreation service sector has gone through changes as government cutbacks, downsizing and contracting-out initiatives have led to greater involvement of and opportunities for the commercial and voluntary sectors. Indeed, this trend is one that continues to exist as labour force indicators released in 2002 show a significant increase in commercial sector employment (Statistics Canada, 2003e).

PREDICTING THE FUTURE

To predict the future, one needs to recognize what may happen, what needs to be done, how it may be done, and who will be doing it. Predicting the future is complex. Long-term predictions are even more complex and prone to unexpected events. It may be that the best way to predict the future is to examine past trends. The more recent the trend, the more likely it is to continue to happen in the short-term future. Predicting the distant future is much more complicated as recent trends are more likely to change through time.

According to David Foot (2000), demography is not only the most powerful, but also the most underutilized tool we have to understand the past and predict the future. Foot posits that demographics explain almost two-thirds of everything. Demographics tell us what recreation products will be in demand in the future while also helping us to predict participation patterns in recreation activities. In fact, the use of demography as a means to predict the future is not often used. As Foot argues, "if our decision-makers understood demographics, Canada would be a better place to live because it would run more smoothly and efficiently." (p. 8).

To predict the future of leisure and recreation in Canada, leisure professionals, practitioners, academics and students would be wise to consider both trends (predictors of change) and demographics.

PREDICTORS OF CHANGE

Social trends can be regarded as being predictors of change as they lead us towards an understanding of the direction of future social happenings. **Predictors of change** are thus shaped from today's social trends with an understanding as to how these social trends might evolve in the future.

In 1998, the work of a number of resource persons from the field of leisure studies was used to compile a list of predictors of change for the future of leisure and recreation in Canada. Below is an overview of these predictors of change and their implications as presented by three of these resource persons. In addition, predictors for change put together by David R. Mitsui, President of the Canadian Parks and Recreation Association, are also presented.

Dr. Geoffrey Godbey, a professor of leisure studies in the College of Health and Human Development at Pennsylvania State University, has written extensively on the future of leisure and recreation. Godbey (1999) presented the nine best predictors of changes in leisure patterns in Canada. These are: (1) the ageing of the population, (2) the huge amount of immigration into urban areas, (3) higher levels of formal education, (4) more diverse roles for women, (5) the emergence of a have and have-not culture, (6) the unpredictability of Generation X in terms of recreation, (7) the loss of agricultural jobs resulting in increased urbanization, (8) more people living alone and smaller household sizes, and (9) the economic erosion and the concomitant concern for the value of money (p. 37).

For leisure and recreation, it may be that these predictors of change lead to: (1) declines in most forms of sport participation; (2) greater interest in nature, plant life, animal life and the environment, but only on terms in which the participant is comfortable; (3) greater concern for a sense of place, what is real, quality experiences and the environmental impact of the experience; (4) more diversity of leisure expression; (5) recreation and parks not functioning as stand-alone professions with employees not functioning as stand-alone professionals; (6) a need to re-think leisure and the organization of work; and (7) local governments becoming more important and senior levels of government less important (Godbey, 1999: 37).

Photo: Health Canada.

Ethnicity, age and the evolving role of women all affect leisure choices.

CLIMATE CHANGE ON THE PRAIRIES: WHAT DOES IT MEAN TO RECREATION?

By: Jim Nick, Saskatchewan Environment

Recreation and its support industries on the prairies are largely based on outdoor activities. Clearly, these will be greatly affected by climate change. Prairie provinces have typically had a short season for summer recreation. Now, with general warming trends, outdoor recreation demands will increase in the shoulder seasons of late spring and early fall. This will put added demand on recreation programming, park maintenance and general operations.

Water We Going to Do?

Lower water availability will cause stress to vegetation and higher costs for maintaining outdoor recreation areas. There will also be a lowering of lake levels, heating of water bodies, an increase in algae blooms and a general deterioration of water quality.

As a result, beach experiences will suffer, which will drive recreational users to find alternative locations. Fishing quality may drop with the loss of cold-water species, resulting in less angling and boating. Communities and local businesses will suffer unless alternative recreation options are developed.

Longer periods of warm weather will encourage more outdoor recreational events, which could be an economic benefit to communities and agencies that hold them.

Snow No More

Winter recreation on the Prairies will be the area that is most dramatically affected, especially in the southern regions. The winter recreation season will be greatly shortened. Ice fishing will decline as the number of ice-free days increases.

The ski and snowmobile industries will be affected as increased use of snowmaking machines will be required. Winter recreationists may also seek alternative locations where snow cover is better.

I Think That I Shall Never See...

The northern areas will not experience the same dramatic shifts in temperature, but the environ-

mental consequences could still be quite extreme. Longer, warmer and drier summers will result in an increased risk of forest fires. As in the south, cold-water fish may die off due to warmer water temperatures. This will keep anglers away and therefore damage one of the major economic generators in the northern Prairie provinces.

The Prairies will see a loss of forest cover over time. Current tree species will have a less favourable climate for regeneration and will face extreme events such as fire more frequently. This will result in the grasslands of the southern Prairies pushing further north.

Where forest recreation is important, decisions need to be made about how to deal with this in the long term. Forest recreationists will go somewhere else. New recreation opportunities will have to be developed by communities.

Local agencies may also actively seek to manage the effects of climate change by restructuring programs such as mosquito control spray programs (with biological agents only of course), watering programs or water rationing, or introducing non-indigenous species in recreation areas where the current species are at risk.

Conclusion

Short-term climate change effects on Prairie recreation will be felt most severely in water-based activities. Businesses such as marinas, boat rentals and beach cabin rentals will need to adapt to lower water levels. Winter recreation enthusiasts and businesses will need to consider how they will adapt to shorter, warmer winters. In the long term, we will see dramatic change in the prairie and boreal ecosystems, with some estimating grasslands pushing northwards as much as 500 kilometres. In some areas, some species will die off while non-indigenous species move in. All of this will add up to shifts in traditional recreation patterns.

Jim Nick is a Park Management Specialist for Saskatchewan Environment. This article is reproduced from Canadian Parks and Recreation *(Winter 2003) with permission.*

John McIntyre, the acting commissioner of Parks and Recreation for the Etobicoke district of Toronto, lists the four best predictors of change in the service sector of leisure. These are: (1) tax pressures from the federal, provincial and municipal governments bringing on continued restraint in the public sector of leisure; (2) government restructuring leading to amalgamation and fewer municipal recreation departments; (3) the changing role of the government from provider to facilitator; and (4) an increase in private sector interest and private/public partnerships (McIntyre, 1999: 37).

William R. Neale, the manager of service development for BC Tel Advanced Communications, focuses extensively on technology and how innovations are good predictors for change. Neale (1999) presents four major shifts in technology: (1) increasing band width for all communication means larger volumes of information is transferred faster, (2) wireless communication technology (i.e., low orbit satellites) allows people to communicate from anywhere to anywhere without being tied to land-based lines, (3) processing speeds and power will continue to increase dramatically so that multi-media interfaces and large scale modelling will become easier, and (4) voice activated computers will make keyboards obsolete (p. 38).

For Neale (1999) these technological predictors of change will have the following implications for parks and recreation: (1) there will be little freedom as people will always be reachable, (2) easy access to information will be a great "leveller" with maximum equity of access to services, (3) increased use of virtual office and teleworking options, (4) virtual classroom opportunities will bring recreation and community information into homes, (5) registration and community information will be increasingly available via the Internet and there will be increased use of virtual work groups and teams, and (6) instantaneous communication will continue to increase pressure on decision-makers (p. 38).

Finally, David R. Mitsui, the president of the Canadian Parks and Recreation Association, states that during the onset on the new millennium, "one has to look at trends evident in today's society as these will continue to affect us all in the next century" (1999: 6). Mitsui identifies six trends that are predictors of change. These are: (1) globalization, (2) the ageing of society and health care, (3) immigration, (4) youth and violence in our communities, (5) gender issues of equality and discrimination, and (6) the gap between the haves and have-nots including barriers to participation and poverty.

For the future, Mitsui (1999) suggests that (1) we need to be proactive to ensure that the benefits of recreation and parks are part of the solution, (2) we need to be at the table to address these issues as part of any multi-sectoral initiative, (3) we must be able to adapt to imposed changes and be a catalyst for change as the need arises, and (4) we need to do more field research and benchmarking to demonstrate the value of recreation in our communities (p. 6).

"BOOM, BUST AND ECHO" EFFECTS

The most powerful demographic variable for predicting the future is the variable of age (Foot, 2000).

DEMOGRAPHICS

The age cohort that we most often hear about is the baby boomers. This group refers to those born between 1947 and 1966. In 1998, baby boomers constituted 9.9 million people or 32.4 percent of the Canadian population. In each of the years of the baby boom, no less than 400,000 births occurred each year. In fact, the baby boom group of Canada was the "loudest boom" in the industrialized world.

The baby bust age cohort encompasses those born between 1967 and 1979. Only 5.6 million Canadians were reported to belong to this age cohort in 1998. The third major age cohort necessary for understanding the demographic makeup of Canada in the future is the baby-boom echo generation. Statistics from 1998 reveal that 6.5 million Canadians belong to this age cohort, which consists of individuals born between 1980 and 1995. The final generation, the millennium busters, are those who were born and will be born between 1996 and 2010. As of 1998, one million had gained membership in this group, but it is not expected to be as large as the baby-boom echo group (Foot, 2000).

The study of **demographics** utilizes a broad spectrum of data such as the size of a given population, birth and death rates, immigration and migration patterns, and the ethnic composition of society. However, the most powerful demographic variable for predicting the future is the variable of age (Foot, 2000). Age tells us who and how many will be what age at any given time in the future. It tells us the number of each group, and the probability that each person will engage in a particular behaviour (ibid.). For example, youth are more likely than seniors to experience active physical recreation activities.

Through the use of demographics we can predict which age groups will be populous in the future. We can use this information, and past and current activity trends, to predict what leisure and recreation activities and experiences will most likely be experienced in the future. David Foot has derived four leisure and recreation activities that he feels will continue to grow in the future in Canada, based primarily on age demographics.

The first of these activities, gambling, is identified as one of the fastest-growing leisure and recreation pursuits in North America. Serious and recreational gamblers tend to be in their fifties and sixties, with discretionary income. As society ages, this age cohort will increase and the number of potential gamblers will also increase.

Gardening is identified by Foot as another leisure and recreation activity that will continue to grow in the future. His rationale for this continued growth is that gardening is an activity that is mostly experienced by the fifty-plus plus age group. As baby boomers age, this age cohort will increase and a large number will turn to gardening as a pastime activity.

The third leisure and recreation activity that will grow in the future in Canada is what Foot calls "up-market travel." Up-market travel refers to rare, exclusive experiences that few can afford, such as a cruise for twenty people down the coast of Antarctica with naturalists on board explaining the sights.

The last activity is "home fitness." Foot argues that the day of the fitness club is over and Canadians, particularly ageing baby boomers, will save time by buying their own home equipment. People will prefer to work out at home as they will be able to afford the necessary equipment needed to build a home fitness centre. Foot claims that this trend, which began in the 1990s, will continue into the future.

Foot also mentions tourism as an activity that will continue to grow and be a popular pursuit for the baby boomer and ageing population. The reasons given were time, money and an inclination to travel. It is predicted that tourism activities in the future will include ecotourism and educational travel.

The Canadian population is ageing. The Ministry of Goods and Services reported in 1990 that, by the year 2031, 22 percent of the total Canadian population will be sixty-five years of age and older. The ageing of the population in Canada means that past activity growth rates will, more than likely, provide an inadequate picture as to what recreation activities Canadians will undertake in the future (Foot, 1990).

Other research by Gravelle, Wood and Karlis (1995) describes the future of recreation for Canada's aged. Based on this growing number of seniors, there is the possibility that not all seniors will be recreationally fulfilled. This research suggests that "future recreation practitioners play a lead role in making sure that the merits of an active living philosophy is instilled in all seniors" (p. 11). To assist practitioners in passing on this philosophy, Gravelle at al. present the following recommendations:

- Recreation practitioners should become aware of active living and its applicability to the aged;

- Recreation practitioners should become aware of the fact that Canada is an aging society, and that Canadians are retiring to recreation and active living rather than from it;

- Recreation practitioners should act as leaders in educating and instilling an active living philosophy in all seniors and aging Canadians;

- Recreation practitioners should encourage the development of programs and services oriented towards active living; and

- Recreation practitioners at the public, private and non-profit sectors should work closely with Fitness Canada's Active Living Department to assure that the needs of seniors are met (ibid.)

In addition, recreation practitioners can aid in passing on an active living philosophy to seniors by having them acting as role models. As society ages, it would be wise to hire seniors as recreation practitioners. By doing so, senior recreation practitioners can lead by example to promote a philosophy of active living to others in the same age cohort.

Photo: Health Canada.

Active seniors can serve as role models for other Canadian seniors.

ILLUMINATING OUR FUTURE

In February 1998, with the intent of charting a course for parks and recreation in Canada for the new millennium, fifty-five parks and recreation practitioners from all over Canada met in British Columbia. This group of individuals held a three-day "think-tank" called **Illuminating Our Future**. This event, organized by the Canadian Parks and Recreation Association, was the first comprehensive look at the future of parks and recreation since *The Elora Prescription* of 1978 (Webster, 1999a).

The primary purpose of Illuminating Our Future was to "draft a strategy to respond to the future challenges and opportunities in the field of parks and recreation" (Johnstone, 1999: 34). The intent was to focus on trends occurring in demographics, leisure behaviour, the role of government, the economy and technology up to the year 2010. To come up with a draft strategy, the efforts of government officials, educators, private consultants and members of the non-profit sector were pooled.

Johnstone (1999: 35-36) presents a detailed overview of the scenario put forth for parks and recreation in 2010 from Illuminating Our Future:

- Public resources will be constrained yet demand for services will increase faster than the rate of growth in the community. Increase in demand for services by seniors and unemployed or underemployed youth who have learned to understand each other and share services and facilities.

- The best use of public resources will be made by targeting priority areas to achieve the greatest benefits at the least possible cost. Focus will be on most important community needs, customer-centered approaches, alternative delivery systems, economies of scale through round the clock use of facilities, and much improved measurement of outcomes.

- There will be interest in experiences of spiritual quest that give meaning to life and escape from the complexities of life (safe, high-risk, stimulating experiences).

- Traditional 9-to-5 jobs will have declined and recreational services will be demanded around the clock with very high quality services packaged in short duration "hits."

- There will be a decline in participation in many organized sports.

- There will be a focus on celebrating diversity thus bringing together and better addressing the needs of diverse groups (i.e., visible minorities, people with special needs). The target is to address individual needs rather than use traditional homogeneous approaches.

- There will be reduced barriers to participation for the "have nots" by redesigning financial support systems.

- There will be integration of environmental management systems into all services and programs offered as the environment and nature are given utmost priority by the people of the community.

- There will be a greater reliance on part-time staff and volunteers to operate programs and services. Most paid employees will work under contract and will be assigned a wide number of tasks. Focus will be on "outcomes" not "work activity."

- Success will be found in contracting out services and public/private partnerships.

- Technology will be used to make better decisions, free up staff to serve customers better and increase access to services. Customer data bases will help to better address individual needs.

- Although there will never be enough financial resources, there will be an increased relationship with individuals and groups in the community.

ILLUMINATING OUR FUTURE

In February 1998, the Canadian Parks and Recreation Association organized the first comprehensive look at the future of parks and recreation since *The Elora Prescription* of 1978. This was a three-day "think-tank" event called Illuminating Our Future.

THE FUTURE OF PARKS AND RECREATION IN CANADA

In a theme issue of *Parks and Recreation Canada* published in November/December 1999, authors representing the provinces and territories of Canada were asked to comment on the future of parks and recreation in Canada up to the year 2010. The comments were based on the social trends of demographics, financial constraints, partnerships of the service sector and the positive benefits of recreation. Below is an overview of some of the key points addressed.

• Nova Scotia

Linda Atkinson, Wendy Bedingfield, Carol Davis-Jamison, Janet Landry, Carol Pickings-Anthony, Debbie Pyne, Brenda Robertson and Debby Smith, all with many years of experience in the recreation field, joined together to brainstorm the current and future state of recreation in Nova Scotia. They commenced by pointing out how we like to predict the future but live our lives for today by polluting our environment and expending our natural resources. The authors claim that "the economic, social, and environmental conditions we presently endure" are a result of how we have been unsuccessful and ineffective in predicting or preparing for the future (1999: 23). The authors conclude by stating that "caring and service based on caring need to re-emerge in our efforts. Caring about each other, our communities, our environment, our resources, our country, our world, our universe – caring enough that we will make a difference" (ibid.).

• New Brunswick

For Shanks (1999), the future of recreation is one of promise as the ageing population is becoming more actively involved in the provision

Photo: Health Canada.

Meeting leisure and recreation needs of special communities will be key.

MULTI-PURPOSING

"The trend to multi-purpose, multi-generational (recreation) facilities will continue. Their design will shift to allow for more individualized use, but they will also continue to be the main gathering places in the community."

– Don Hunter, retired General Manager of Parks, Recreation and Culture in Surrey, British Columbia (Hunter in Webster, 2003: 33).

of recreation services. The author argues that trends for more volunteers will be met by a greater involvement of the ageing population in the volunteer sector. This fact, coupled with the current trend of recreation directors broadening their mandates and becoming more innovative in service provision, indicates the direction the service industry of recreation will take in the future.

• Prince Edward Island

Focus is placed on two specific trends: active living and outdoor recreation. Canada's smallest province is active in promoting active living and outdoor recreation through trail development, more specifically its leg of the Trans Canada trail. By referring to the recreation experience offered by the trail, the Government of Prince Edward Island uses the slogan "Canada's New Outdoor Adventure." Emphasis on the development of this trail hints that addressing outdoor recreational needs will be paramount in the future (Corporate Author, 1999a).

• Newfoundland and Labrador

In Newfoundland and Labrador leisure and recreation has developed out of traditional values and emerging program and policy development in Canada. In this province, many leisure experiences take place within the family as social and family recreation pursuits are highly valued. It is thus no surprise that the future of parks and recreation for this province is one that focuses on addressing the individual and social needs of its population. The philosophy behind the provision of the leisure service industry is one in which municipalities, either as direct services agents or catalysts, work towards addressing the total needs of their citizens. To this end, the Newfoundland and Labrador Parks and Recreation Association has provided a vision for the future that places focus on a clean environment, an active lifestyle for all people of all ages and a commitment to provide recreation for all (Corporate Author, 1999b).

• Quebec

In Quebec, Fournier (1999) implies that a dialogue between individuals responsible for the provision of leisure and recreation services and participants must take place in order to successfully implement leisure and recreation services in the province. More specifically, Fournier calls on the provincial government of Quebec to prioritize a number of necessary conditions in its action plan. These necessary conditions include: (1) accessibility, (2) the recognition of the benefits of leisure and recreation, (3) collaborative research between universities and organizations interested in the development of leisure and recreation services, and (4) opportunities for innovation through partnerships between municipalities and citizens (pp. 21-22).

• Ontario

In this article, six factors are identified that will affect recreation for individuals and recreation service providers in the future: technology, funding, leadership, values, environment and change. It is argued that technology is currently, and will continue to be, an integral part of recreation. Affordable funding is needed to ascertain equitable service delivery. Sound leadership is needed for the future. Future values for quality of life, humanitarianism, and community and ecological ethics will probably evolve. A need to better address the relation between recreation and the environment will become paramount. Becoming comfortable with change will also be of prime concern (Corporate Author, 1999c).

The author concludes that "organizationally the parks and recreation field must work together, build together and find solutions together. If parks and recreation is to be an essential service in the next century, we will need strong leaders to advocate, go against the tide, and to challenge. We will also need a participative, not a parochial and/or passive public" (Corporate Author, 1999c: 19).

• Manitoba

In Manitoba, the focus of the future of parks and recreation lies in the recognition of the many benefits of leisure. The Manitoba Parks and Recreation Association is playing a key role in addressing the current and future needs of the residents of this province. It is perceived by this association that the goal of the twenty-first century is to continue with what it has set out to do, that is, create strong partnerships with the service sector of recreation. Through these partnerships, the benefits of leisure can be promoted and endorsed (Corporate Author, 1999d).

• Saskatchewan

According to Bakes and Schaad (1999) the future of recreation will be a continuation of current demographic shifts. There will be changing volunteer patterns, new forms of communication bringing together the recreation community, and quality education for recreation and parks professionals. The future of recreation will also be based on a recognition of the many benefits of recreation.

The authors conclude by stating that "the Saskatchewan population will have more recreation and parks opportunities, be more active, and more healthy. We will all live longer. As we embrace the excitement of change and continue our wonderful pioneer spirit, recreation and parks volunteers and professionals alike will continue to hold to our belief that the benefits of recreation make Saskatchewan the best place in the world to live" (Bakes and Schaad, 1999: 15).

WELCOMING DIVERSITY

"The continued influx of immigrants will require us to take cultural diversity and needs into consideration even more than we do at the present time."

– Neil Semenchuk, Director of Culture, Sports, Recreation, and Social Development for the City of Montreal, Kirkland Borough (Semenchuck in Webster, 2003: 33).

• Alberta

In Alberta, the future of parks and recreation has evolved out of an understanding of the many benefits of leisure, and a strategy as to how the societal needs of leisure can be addressed so that all can benefit. Emphasis is placed on the importance of community recreation providers and government to work together to address leisure needs and concerns. Agencies of leisure such as the Alberta Parks and Recreation Association and the provincial government have take action to recognize the many benefits of leisure. The future is focused on placing recreation within the community as it contributes to individual, family and community well-being (Corporate Author, 1999e).

• British Columbia

Fifteen professionals from the leisure industry of British Columbia provided input. Suggestions for the future focused on addressing current social, economic and demographic trends. The future was pictured as one in which the leisure industry will rely more on partnerships between all service sectors in order to address the plethora of leisure and recreation needs of society. Mention is made of the need for leisure and recreation professionals to broaden their scope and to recognize the need for change. Issues of accessibility, equal opportunity and financial accountability appear to be at the forefront of concerns (Corporate Author, 1999f).

• Northwest Territories

Theresa Ross, the president of the Northwest Territories Parks and Recreation Association, argues that the future of parks and recreation is one of great reliance on the working relationship between partnerships. Through successful partnership relationships between all sectors of the leisure industry, healthy individual and healthy communities will be developed. For Ross (1999), leadership development, the appropriate training of recreation professionals and active living are all areas of focus for the future of the leisure industry.

• Yukon

In the Yukon, recreation is viewed as a means to an end: "In the Yukon, the end is the development and growth of Yukon people and communities, and the means to this end is the promotion, development and delivery of meaningful, relevant and affordable programs, services and facilities" (Corporate Author 1999g: 32). The future of parks and recreation is depicted as one with greater strategic alliances, new approaches to funding, a greater emphasis on the needs of the marginalized sectors, greater accountability, and an awareness of the benefits of leisure and recreation and the economic impacts of leisure and recreation (Corporate Author, 1999g).

SCENARIOS FOR THE FUTURE AND FINAL THOUGHTS

According to Searle and Brayley (2000), the "future of recreation and leisure in Canada depends on many things, not the least of which are: (1) the evolving role and nature of family, (2) economic prosperity, (3) cultural diversification, (4) government policy, (5) technological advancement, and (6) our ageing population" (p. 28). Thus, social trends, and the projection of the evolution of these trends, will help shape the picture of leisure and recreation in the future. In addition, demographics will give us an understanding as to the nature and composition of each age cohort (Foot, 2000). This will assist us in predicting needs, demands and participation patterns based on information that we currently have on each demographic group (i.e., seniors, young adults, children, and forth).

According to Bregha (1978), those concerned with the future forecasting of leisure and recreation should present a range of scenarios, not just one. By presenting more than one scenario, it is more likely that a more holistic perspective of what may happen in the future will be presented.

More than fifteen years ago, Seymour Gold put together four scenarios for the future of recreation up to the year 2000. At that time, Gold (1985) posited that the construction of various scenarios for the future depicts innovation and change that may unfold. What made Gold's analysis interesting is that he provided four different viewpoints for the future of leisure and recreation as follows: (1) the traditional view, (2) the humanistic view, (3) the pessimistic view, and (4) the optimistic view. Gold provided a more holistic analysis of different scenarios that may or may not happen. As the establishment of future scenarios is based on putting forth educated guesses, Gold's four viewpoints were effective in that he attempted to cover as much ground as possible in their establishment.

The traditional view relied on social and demographic trends and the extent to which these may evolve. The humanistic view emphasized human services and a people-oriented focus. The pessimistic view presented the world as one of complexity, scarcity and turmoil. The optimistic viewpoint depicted positive changes towards work and leisure lifestyles.

Although Gold's work was put together in the United States and focuses primarily on the American situation, it is possible to adapt the general orientation of the four scenarios and apply these to current social trends in Canadian society.

Photo: CN Images of Canada.

Technology spurred on activities such as the snowmobile craze of the seventies.

• Traditional View

Despite low fertility rates, the Canadian population will continue to increase in size as Canadians will live longer. Other factors will also contribute to this growth, such as more immigration than migration, and a high birth rate in Aboriginal communities. The personal income of Canadians will continue to rise slightly above the rate of inflation. The average workweek will consist of from 35 to 40 hours yet some members

GREY POWER: THE FUTURE IS NOW

By: Jill Johnson, Recreation Supervisor, West Vancouver

What do Tina Turner, Paul McCartney, Sophia Loren and Anne Murray have in common? They are seniors, aged fifty-five and over.

As futurists have predicted, the baby boomers are knocking on the door of pensions and fixed incomes. They will be joining an already large population of elderly seniors aged eighty and over.

We are facing a time of massive change in the provision of seniors' services. Over the next twenty-five years, we will have the largest growth in senior population that we have ever seen. What will seniors' services look like in the future?

Demographics

According to the Statistics Canada (StatsCan) 2001 Census, the oldest population group, eighty and over, is the fastest growing. It has risen by 41 percent between 1991 and 2001. During the next decade, this group is expected to increase by 43 percent.

These seniors have been active in creating buildings to house programs for learning. This group has set the stage for today's service provision model, where centres are service providers.

Statscan reports that the second largest percentage increase in population over the past decade has occurred in the forty-five to sixty-four age group, which has grown by 35 percent. During the next decade, it is expected to increase an additional 30 percent. The boomers are ready to take the plunge into retirement. This will create the largest group of seniors that we have experienced to date.

A Look at Today

As providers of services to seniors, we have become very good at providing a cornucopia of diverse programs that offer the basics on how to do just about anything. We offer good value programs that are cost effective and have low overhead.

Aiding this endeavour are the volunteers that continue to participate in providing services from peeling potatoes to teaching computer skills. These seniors have learned to do more with less. They have learned to pitch in to survive through the Depression and World Wars. This mentality leads their strong community volunteer efforts.

Boomer Traits

The boomers have grown up with the Beatles, Donovan, Elvis, George Car in the Cheese Whiz. This group is not so willing to accept their retirement as being a time to slow down and learn. Most of this age group is well educated and have geared their lives around acquiring wealth at a fast pace for fear that it will not be there as they age. They have not lived in an environment where they have had to go without, as their parents and grandparents did. They are obsessed with staying healthy, but do not like the confines of a structured pursuit. The boomers seek solace in programs designed to reduce stress and balance their obsession with youthfulness, financial success and family.

According to David Baxter of the Urban Futures Institute, while boomers believe in community involvement, they are more willing to donate money than time when it comes to providing for the common good. They will volunteer but often only in areas that may help them attain status or improve the opportunities in their business world. This group wants to be heard and will be involved in community consultation in a greater way than we have seen to date.

A Look at Tomorrow

In the future, there will be less need to provide "How To" programs at a basic level. People will look for more complex and more specialized services. Self-directed groups may spur an increase in inexpensive yet healthy and mind stimulating alternatives, such as investment groups, community gardening, biking and tai chi clubs.

Photo: Health Canada.

and specialized services tailored to complex needs.

Preparing for the Future

As we prepare for the future, the transition from service provider to service facilitator will be a slow, but sure, change. Expectations will increase as a seniors-driven decision-making process makes staff and politicians more accountable.

With shrinking tax dollars, the look of public service delivery will change. It will become more common to see facilities provide for general socialization and encourage rental groups and self-group leadership. Special interest groups will begin to organize themselves using the community senior centres as gathering places. The seniors centres will always provide some programming, but where the tax dollars go will be thoroughly scrutinized.

Further efforts to encourage this community involvement model will help us to prepare for this transition. Continued efforts to make our facilities more accessible to those with physical limitations should be a focus from now on. The importance of social interaction will become more and more evident as people speak through face-to-face dialogue. The coffee house mentality will encourage happy-feeling spaces with places to play.

All services must be high quality and created with consideration for meeting the needs of this new thinking senior. Our centres will become a more important hub of social interaction and involvement. It is our readiness to accept this challenge that will allow for a smooth transition into the future.

As the Beatle's sang, "Let It Be."

Fitness and health will continue to be important. The centres will likely become gathering places. This will create an ambience where the centres are oriented to facilitation.

Facility and Program Response

Facility development will have to encourage multi-use spaces along with cozy food establishments that encourage chats and discussions. All facilities will have to be focused on providing accessible, user-friendly options with special attention given to people with physical limitations.

There will also need to be smaller spaces for more specialized activities. We will need to provide space for one-to-one or small group services such as counselling, tax preparation, legal assistance and even health-care services. As people start to cope with smaller living spaces, they will want community spaces to express creativity. Drop-in specialized spaces such as garage shops and woodworking rooms will be popular. In essence seniors' centres will become facilitators of services, providing unique spaces

Jill Johnson has been a Recreation Supervisor for the District of West Vancouver for eleven years. Over the past five years, she has overseen the West Vancouver Seniors Activity Centre. This article is reproduced from Canadian Parks and Recreation *(Winter 2003) with permission.*

GATHERING PLACES

"Tomorrow's community centre will have a large, comfortable foyer, serving as a community gathering place. The facility will be big enough to provide a variety of activities for individuals and families. Each centre will be linked to others, utilizing the latest in technology."

– Clem Pelot, President of Clem Pelot Consulting (Pelot in Webster, 2003: 35).

of society will work more than fifty hours not only to enhance personal income, but also because a work ethic will prevail. The number of Canadians with university degrees will continue to increase as will the number of Canadians with graduate degrees.

An energy crisis and economic depression will not occur as we will have an unlimited consumption of resources. Sub-urbanization will be valued as more people would prefer to own homes outside of bigger cities. As Canada's population will be more diverse, leisure and recreation services will become more "cultural specific" to address the multi-ethnic needs of society. The percentage of household expenditures on recreation will remain at 6 percent as Canadians will continue to participate in specialized activities. The public sector will not have the major responsibility for the provision of leisure and recreation services. However, it will continue to work in partnership with the commercial and voluntary sectors for service provision.

• Humanistic View

The emphasis of society will be on human services instead of material things. Society will place equal value on work and leisure as both will be deemed equally important to the enhancement of quality of life. The public sector will be more active in the leisure and workforce, aiding in making both of these "people-oriented."

Education systems will prepare people for a life of leisure as well as a life of work. However, a leisure ethic will replace the work ethic and humanism will replace materialism. The orientation of society will be on social welfare as the production of wealth will not be as important as the fair distribution of wealth. Although unemployment will continue to be high, those out of work will find meaning in the humanistic side of leisure.

The percentage of household expenditures on recreation would account for 20 percent of household budgets. Households will invest more in leisure and recreation to assist individual and community development and enhance social functioning. A plethora of leisure and recreation opportunities will exist in all sectors of society as leisure and recreation will not only be valued as a necessary experience, but also as a basic right for all in society.

• Pessimistic View

The future will be one of complexity, scarcity and turmoil as the industrialized world will be faced with diminishing resources. Our relationship with things will be more temporary as products produced will be of lower quality, that of a "use-and-throw-away" nature. Technology will change rapidly and the accelerated pace of change will be negative rather than positive as it will cause increased stress on educators and consumers.

Inflation rates will hover at all-time highs. Most Canadians will credit a high percentage of their purchases as household expenditures will exceed household earnings. The cost of being entertained will also increase. The average household expenditures on recreation will be 2 percent as Canadians will have a difficult time paying for high priced leisure goods and services. An energy crisis and recession will also make leisure experiences, in particular travel, an activity for the affluent few.

The public sector will only be minimally involved in the provision of leisure and recreation services with most of its focus on the aged, the growing number of low-income families, the high number of unemployed individuals, and the low-income immigrant population. The commercial sector will witness its first decline in years as high costs will deter people from participation. The voluntary sector will be in huge demand. However, few services will exist as many organizations will not be economically sustainable. Limited partnerships will exist between the public and voluntary sectors for the provision of services as public financial resources will be scarce.

• Optimistic View

Leisure and recreation will become the focus of society. Work will be considered as part of leisure as few jobs will be boring and monotonous. This highly educated society will find the mostly technological-oriented work challenging. These challenges will enhance the work experience and make it pleasurable. Canadians will have new work attitudes, lifestyles and a leisure ethic will shape our leisure patterns at work and outside of the work environment.

Three-day workweeks and flex-time schedules will be popular as work-sharing, extended vacations, sabbaticals and early retirement will allow for more vacation and leisure time for travel and participation in local recreation programs. The home office and the home classroom will come of age as most Canadians will prefer to live in suburban and rural communities. The focus on society will be on active living and all recreation service sectors will experience growth while targeting programs around this need.

Inflation and declining discretionary income will force people to discover simple active activities, yet the percentage of household expenditures on recreation will be quite high as leisure will be viewed as necessary for physical, social and emotional well-being. Energy costs will be moderately priced and members of society will value the preservation, conservation and maintenance of the environment. Tourism will increase as Canadians will seek cultural tourism, ecotourism and sport tourism pursuits more than ever before. Canadian society will be a consumer society with a growing preference for active, appreciative activities such as cross-country skiing and hiking. A decline of mechanized activities (e.g., snowmobiling, trail biking) will also take place as society will become environmentally friendly.

Towards a future where quality leisure and recreation are a main focus.

Photo: Health Canada.

The aforementioned scenarios provide us with differing viewpoints of the future of leisure and recreation in Canada. The traditional scenario calls, for the most part, for a continuation of current trends. This may or may not happen, but as my predictions are for the year 2020, the likelihood of current trends continuing for more than fifteen years is slim. The world is constantly changing and the nature of our society is constantly evolving.

The humanistic scenario places emphasis on the social welfare dimension of leisure with a prevailing leisure ethic. Throughout the history of Canada, leisure has never been the central focus of life. We have been busy building this young nation, and work and production remain the central focus. This will more than likely continue to be the case in 2020 and beyond.

The pessimistic scenario illustrates a viewpoint of complexity, turmoil and scarcity of resources as the industrialized world experiences diminishing resources. High costs will make leisure and recreation involvement an expensive experience and few will be able to afford such activities. High inflation, minimal discretionary income and a recession will limit our involvement in leisure while work will continue to be the central focus. The pessimistic scenario of an economically driven perspective of leisure and recreation may unfold by 2020.

Finally, the optimistic scenario depicts a positive future for leisure and recreation with society being driven by leisure, particularly "active pursuits." Citizens will be better educated, value the simple things in life, and live in suburban and rural communities. Activity pursuits will be conserver-oriented as discretionary income will not be plentiful but Canadians will make the most of leisure opportunities. As society is ageing with a value for leisure, the likelihood of this scenario taking place in 2020 is quite probable.

One thing is certain: change is inevitable. We must be prepared to face the future no matter how it unfolds. To do so, we must first value and appreciate our past. The following quote is from Bill Webster, principle of Professional Environmental Recreation Consultants. This quote assures us that we have come a long way in this profession and the future can be a positive one if we continue to work towards it.

> As we look back on our brief history we have many reasons to feel good about the work we do. We have excellent park, trail and open space systems. We have superb recreation facilities. We have well qualified professionals, who work closely with diverse groups in every community to ensure the delivery of a wealth of recreation opportunities. Despite this, we can't sit back and rest. The challenges facing the field – especially related to financial resources – will require all of our imagination, creativity, enthusiasm and patience as we step into the future (Webster, 1999b: 5).

CHAPTER 13: THE FUTURE OF LEISURE AND RECREATION IN CANADA

Study Questions

1. Describe Statistics Canada's three scenarios for population growth for 2016.

2. Summarize the findings of the 2001 Census of Population.

3. What was the spending of Canadians on consumer goods and services from 1990-99?

4. How do the average weekly earnings of national data compare to the average weekly earnings for those employed in arts, entertainment and recreation (based on November 2002 data)?

5. Which viewpoint for the future of leisure and recreation do you feel is more likely to take place in 2020? Why?

Selected Websites

- **Statistics Canada**
  http://www.statcan.ca

- **About Canada**
  http://canada.gc.ca/canadiana/cdaind_e.html

- **Pan Canadian Community Futures Network**
  http://www.communityfutures.ca

- **Ontario Sport**
  http://www.ontariosport.com

- **Health Canada – Commission on the Future of Health Care in Canada**
  http://www.hc-sc.gc.ca/english/care/romanow

Key Concepts

- **Contracting out**
- **Predictors of change**
- **Demographics**
- **Illuminating Our Future**

References

• Abrams, J. (1969). Cybernetic and automation. *Leisure in Canada: The Proceedings of the Montmorency Conference on Leisure*. Ottawa: Fitness and Amateur Sport Directorate, Department of National Health and Welfare Canada. (pp. 63-75).

• Active Living Alliance for Canadians with a Disability. (1994). *Proceedings Report: Annual Stakeholders Forum 1993, February 10-13*. Ottawa, Ontario.

• Active Living Alliance for Canadians with a Disability. (2001). *Words With Dignity*. Ottawa, Ontario.

• Active Living Canada. (1993). Active Living Communities – Collective Action: The Community-Driven Approach. Ottawa: Active Living Canada.

• Alberta Recreation Survey. (1992). Alberta Tourism, Parks and Recreation: Edmonton.

• Allen, L.R. (1991). Benefits of leisure services to community satisfaction. In B.L. Driver, P.J. Brown, and G.L. Peterson (Eds.). *Benefits of Leisure*. State College, PA: Venture Publishing.

• Anderes, S., and Fortier, A. (1987). A case study of an altered lifestyle. *Journal of Leisurability*, 14(3): 13-14.

• Anderson, L. (2002). In step with the ancient Greeks. *The Ottawa Sun*, Saturday, June 15.

• Annual Report of the Public School of the Province. (1934-1935). Victoria: King's Printer.

• Arai, S.M. (1996). Benefits of citizen participation in a healthy communities initiative: Linking community development and empowerment. *Journal of Applied Recreation Research*, 21(1): 25-44.

• Arai, S.M. (2001). Typology of volunteers for a changing sociopolitical context: The impact on social capital, citizenship and civil society. *Leisure and Society*, 23(2): 327-352.

• Arnstein, S.R. (1969). *Ladder of citizen participation*. American Institute of Planners, July: 216-217.

• Atkinson, L., Bedingfield, W., Davis-Jamison, C., Landry, J., Pickings-Anthony, C., Pyne, D., Robertson, B., and Smith, D. (1999). Nova Scotia: Thoughts on the millennium. *Parks and Recreation Canada*, November/December: 23.

• Auger, D., and Karlis, G. (2000) Culture, tourism and northern aboriginal peoples in Canada: The impacts of technology. Paper accepted for presentation at the Technology Impact on Cultural Tourism Conference, Instanbul, Turkey, June 27.

• Auger, D., Dawson, D., Gravelle, F., Karlis, G., Pageot, J-C., and Zalatan, A. (1999). The interests for and participation in cultural leisure activities: A study of students enrolled in undergraduate leisure studies courses. *Book of Abstracts: 9th Canadian Congress on Leisure Research*, Acadia University, Wolfville, Nova Scotia: 204-205.

• Backman, K.F., and Backman, S.J. (1997). Retiree's choice of community: The importance of recreation and parks. *Journal of Applied Recreation Research*, 22(3): 211-231.

• Baker, W. (1982). *Sports in the Western World*. Totowa, NJ: Rowan and Littlefield.

• Bakes, R., and Schaad, C. (1999). Saskatchewan: One hundred years of recreation and parks in Saskatchewan. *Parks and Recreation Canada*, November/December: 14-15.

• Bakopanos, E. (2004). As an MP, our health is at great risk: Liberal MP Bakopanos. *The Hill Times*, Monday, March 22-28: 19.

• Ballantyne, B. 1988. *Leisure Lifestyles*. Toronto: Ministry of Tourism and Recreation and the Kitchener Parks and Recreation Department.

• Beaman, J. (1978). Leisure research and its lack of relevance to planning management and policy formulation: A problem of major proportions. *Recreation Research Review*, 6(3): 18-25.

* Bella, L., and Lanthier, L. (1984). *Direct and Indirect Recreation Programming: Final Report.* Edmonton, AB: University of Alberta.

* Bennett, A. (1973). Professional staff members' contribution to community development. *Journal of the Community Development Society,* 4(1): 58-68.

* Berlin, S. (1989). Defining the Canadian Healthy Communities Project. *Recreation Canada,* 47(2): 10-13.

* Betke, C. (1990). Winter sports in the early urban environment of prairie Canada. In E. Corbet and A. Rasporich (Eds.). *Winter Sports in the West.* Calgary: Historical Society of Alberta. (pp. 52-67).

* Bishop, D., and Jeanrenaud, C. 1985. Creative growth through play and its implications for recreation practice. In T.L. Goodale and P.W. Witt. *Recreation and Leisure: Issues In An Era of Change.* (Revised Edition). State College, PA: Venture. (pp. 87-104).

* Bolla, P., and Dawson, D. (1989). *Recreation Programs and Multiculturalism in Ontario.* Toronto: Ministry of Tourism and Recreation.

* Bolla, P., and Dawson, D. (1990). Meeting the recreation needs of ethnic communities. *Recreation Canada,* October: 10-15.

* Bolla, P., Dawson, D., and Karlis, G. (1991). Serving the multicultural community: Directions for leisure service providers. *Journal of Applied Recreation Research,* 16(2): 116-132.

* Boo, E. (1990). *Ecotourism: The Potentials and Pitfalls.* (Vol. 1). Washington, DC: World Wildlife Fund.

* Bowen, R. (1970). *Cricket: A History of its Growth and Development Throughout the World.* London.

* Bowler, V., and Wanchuk, M. (1986). *Volunteers.* Edmonton, AB: Lone Pine.

* Boyd, M., and Norris, D. (1999). The crowded nest: Young adults at home. *Canadian Social Trends.* Spring, 2-5, Statistics Canada-Catalogue No. 11-008.

* Bradley, D.E. (1995). Religious involvement and social resources: Evidence from the data set Americans. *Journal for the Scientific Study of Religion,* 34(2): 259-267.

* Brayley, R.E. (1991). Recreation and tourism: Partners in the community. *Recreation Canada,* October: 19-22.

* Bregha, F. (1978). Future directions of leisure research. *Recreation Research Review,* 6(3): 57-62.

* Bregha, F. (1985). Leisure and freedom re-examined. In T.L. Goodale and P.W. Witt. *Recreation and Leisure: Issues In An Era of Change.* (Revised Edition). State College, PA: Venture. (pp. 35-43).

* Breton, R., Reitz, J.G., and Valentine, V. (1980). *Cultural Boundaries and the Cohesion of Canada .* Montreal: The Institute for Research on Public Policy.

* Brightbill, C. (1960). *The Challenge of Leisure.* Englewood Cliff, NJ: Prentice-Hall.

* Bullaro, J., and Edginton, C. (1986). *Commercial Leisure Services.* New York: Macmillan.

* Burnet, J.R., and Palmer, H. (1988). *Coming Canadians: An Introduction to a History of Canada's People.* Toronto: McClelland and Stewart.

* Burton, P. (1987). *Why We Act Like Canadians: A Personal Exploration.* Markham, ON: McClelland and Stewart.

* Burton, T.L. (1979). The development of leisure research in Canada: An analogy tale. *Society and Leisure,* 2(1): 13-32.

* Burton, T.L. (1991). A model curriculum for a baccalaureate degree in recreation and leisure studies. *Schole,* Fall, 6: 80-93.

* Butler, D. (1990). The role of ethnic clubs in providing leisure opportunities. *Proceedings: 6th Canadian Congress on Leisure Research,* University of Waterloo, Waterloo, ON: 279-282.

* Caldwell, L.L., and Smith, E.A. (1996). Adolescent problem behavior and leisure participation. *Proceedings: 8th Canadian Congress on Leisure Research,* University of Ottawa, Ottawa, Ontario: 29-31.

* Canadian Centre for Justice. (2001a). Statistics Profile Series-Seniors in Canada. Statistics Canada-Catalogue no. 85F0033MIE.

* Canadian Centre for Justice. (2001b). Statistics Profile Series-Canadians with Disabilities. Statistics Canada-Catalogue no. 85F0033MIE.

* Canadian Encyclopedia. (1985). Edmonton: Hurtig Publishers, 1144.

* Canadian Heritage (1995). *Discovering the Opportunity.* Alberta Region: Department of Canadian Heritage.

* Canadian Tourism Commission. (1996). *Domestic Tourism Market Research Study: Main Report.* Ottawa, ON: Coopers and Lybrand, March.

* Canadian Tourism Commission. (2001). *Pamphlet of Canadian Tourism Facts and Figures 2001.* Ottawa, ON.

* Che-Alford, J., and Hamm, B. (1999). *Canadian Social Trends.* Summer, 6-9, Statistics Canada-Catalogue No. 11-008.

* Christenson, J.A. (1980). Three items of community development. In J.A. Christenson and J.W. Robinson (Eds.). *Community Development in America.* Ames, IA: The Iowa State University Press.

* Christenson, J.A., Fendley, K., and Robinson, J.W. (1989). In J.A. Christenson and J.R. Robinson (Eds.). *Community Development in Perspective.* Ames, IA: Iowa State University Press, 3-25.

* Chui, T. (1996). Canada's population: Charting into the 21ˢᵗ century. *Canadian Social Trends.* Autumn, 1-5, Statistics Canada-Catalogue No. 11-008-XPE.

* City of Gloucester (1991). *Proposal for Cadboro Shelter Recreation and Culture Program.* Gloucester, Ontario: Department of Recreation, Parks and Culture.

* City of Ottawa (1989). *Provision of Recreation Programs for the Homeless.* Ottawa: Department of Recreation and Culture.

* Clark, W. (2000a). Education. *Canadian Social Trends.* Winter, 3-7, Statistics Canada-Catalogue No. 11-008.

* Clark, W. (2000b). Search for success: Finding work after graduation. *Canada Social Trends (Volume 3).* Toronto: Thompson Educational Publishers. (pp. 175-179).

* Clark, W. (2002c). Time alone. *Canadian Social Trends.* Autumn, 2-6, Statistics Canada-Catalogue No. 11-008.

* Colbert, F., and Mitchell, C. (1991). *Proceedings: First International Conference on Arts Management.* Montreal: Ecole des Hautes Etudes Commerciales de Montreal.

* Cole, D. (1993). Recreation practices of the Stoney of Alberta and the Mohawks of the Six Nation Confederacy. *Journal of Applied Recreation Research,* 18(2): 103-114.

* Colley, L. (1985). Work occupation and leisure patterns of self-supporting women in pre- and post-retirement. *Society and Leisure,* 8(2): 631-658.

* Colton, J.W. (1999). Motivations for indigenous tourism development in northern Canada. *Book of Abstracts: 9ᵗʰ Canadian Congress on Leisure Research,* Acadia University, Wolfville, Nova Scotia: 256-258.

* Colton, J.W. (2002). Building community capacity for indigenous sustainable tourism development. *Abstract: 10ᵗʰ Canadian Congress on Leisure Research,* Edmonton, Alberta, 68-70.

* Community Constitution. (1984). Ottawa, ON: Hellenic Community of Ottawa and District.

* Community Services Administration. (1978, January 7). *Citizen Participation.* Washington, DC: Community Services Administration.

* Condon, R.G. (1995). The rise of the leisure class: Adolescence and recreational acculturation in the Canadian Arctic. *Ethos,* 23(1): 47-68.

* Connolly, C. (1992). *City of Cambridge Municipal Policy Support Services to Neighbourhood Associations.* Cambridge, ON: City of Cambridge Community Services Department.

* Connelly, K., and Smale, B.J.A. (1999). Changes in the financing of local recreation and cultural services: An examination of trends in Ontario from 1988-1996. *Book of Abstracts:*

9th *Canadian Congress on Leisure Research*, Acadia University, Wolfville, Nova Scotia: 190-193.

* Cordes, K.A., and Ibrahim, H.M. (1999). *Applications in Recreation and Leisure For Today and the Future.* (2nd Edition). Dubuque, IO: McGraw-Hill.

* Clark, W. (1998). Religious observance: Marriage and family. *Canadian Social Trends.* Autumn, 3-7, Statistics Canada-Catalogue No. 11-008-XPE.

* Corporate Author. (1998). Professional development: College and university listings. *Parks and Recreation Canada*, 56(3): 18-19.

* Corporate Author. (1999a). Prince Edward Island: On the beaten track…The Island's millennium legacy. *Parks and Recreation Canada*, November/December: 26-27.

* Corporate Author. (1999b). Newfoundland: Prosperous past-Promising future. *Parks and Recreation Canada*, November/December: 28-29.

* Corporate Author. (1999c). Ontario: The roots of parks and recreation in Canada. *Parks and Recreation Canada*, November/December: 18-19.

* Corporate Author. (1999d). Manitoba: Where we have been and where we are going. *Parks and Recreation Canada*, November/December: 16-17.

* Corporate Author. (1999e). Alberta: Past, present and future. *Parks and Recreation Canada*, November/December: 12-13.

* Corporate Author. (1999f). British Columbia: A view from the west coast. *Parks and Recreation Canada*, November/December: 10-11.

* Corporate Author. (1999g). Yukon: Canada's Yukon-The magic and the mystery. *Parks and Recreation Canada*, November/December: 32-33.

* Corporate Author. (2000). The National Recreation Roundtable on Aboriginal/Indigenous Peoples. *Parks and Recreation Canada*, May/June: 32-33.

* Corporate Author. (2002a). The voluntary sector and the government of Canada: A historic past and a new beginning. *Parks and Recreation Canada*, 59(6): 34.

* Corporate Author. (2002b). PM joins World Tourism Day celebration. *Tourism*, November, 6(9): 5.

* Corporate Author. (2002c). Marc Rosenberg to head CTC's research committee. *Tourism*, October, 6(8): 5.

* Cousineau, C., and Bolla, P. (1989). Leisure studies graduates and their careers: A follow-up study at the University of Ottawa. *Journal of Applied Recreation Research*, 15(1): 25-40.

* Craig, J. (1977). *The Years of Agony 1910/1920.* Toronto: Jack McClelland.

* Crompton, J.L., and McGregor, B.P. (1994). Trends in the financing and staffing of local government park and recreation services 1964/65-1990/91. *Journal of Park and Recreation Administration*, 12(3): 19-37.

* Crompton, S. (2000). Health. *Canadian Social Trends.* Winter, 12-17, Statistics Canada-Catalogue No. 11-008.

* Crompton, S. and Kemeny, A. (2000). In sickness and in health: The well-being of married seniors. *Canada Social Trends (Volume 3).* Toronto: Thompson Educational Publishers. (pp. 45-50).

* Cross, G. (1990). *A Social History of Leisure Since 1600.* State College, PA: Venture.

* Crossley, J.C., and Jamieson, L.M. (1993). *Introduction to Commercial and Entrepreneurial Recreation.* (2nd Edition). Champaign, IL: Sagamore.

* Cukier, J. (2001). Tourism sustainability: An elusive concept or tangible goal. *Proceedings of the 9th Annual Graduate Leisure Research Symposium*, University of Waterloo, Waterloo, ON: 7.

* D'Amore, L. (1977-1978). *Community Development and Public Leisure Services Seminars.* Ottawa, ON: Canadian Parks and Recreation Association.

* D'Amore, L. (1990). Tourism: The world's peace industry. *Recreation Canada*, March, 48(1): 25-30.

* Dail, P.W. (1990). The quality of life context of the homeless. Paper presented at Symposium for Selected Populations: Homeless, Migrant Workers, New Immigrants, and Urban Elderly, September 17.

* Darby, J.P., and Morris, G. (1975). Community groups and research in Northern Ireland. *Community Development Journal*, 10(2). 110-119.

* Dauphinas, P.R. (1990). A class act: French-Canadians in organized sport, 1840-1910. *History of Sport*, 7(3): 432-442.

* Davis, A., and McKenzie, M. (1981). Disaffection with government. *Recreation Research Review*, March, 8(3): 51-57.

* Davis-Jamieson, C. (1990). The politics of creating a recreation service. *Recreation Canada*, July: 22-25.

* Dawson, D., Andrew, C., and Harvey, J. (1991). Leisure, the local state and the welfare society: A theoretical overview. *Society and Leisure*, 14(1): 191-217.

* Dawson, D., Karlis, G., and Georgescu, D. (1998). Contemporary issues in recreation and leisure for Aboriginal Peoples in Canada. *Journal of Leisurability*, 25(1): 3-9.

* Decarie, G. (2000). Lacrosse: Culture and sociological drive. *Parks and Recreation Canada*, May/June: 28-29.

* Decker, J.M. (1991). Seven steps to sponsorship. *Parks and Recreation*, 26(12): 45-49.

* Delisle, M-A. (1993). Changes in the leisure activities of older Quebecers from 1979 to 1989. (In French). *Canadian Journal of Aging*. 12(3): 338-359.

* Delorme, G. (2000). Recreational development in Nunavik: A holistic approach. *Parks and Recreation Canada*, May/June: 16-17.

* Dembrowski, K. (1988). *Survey on Recreation for Ethnic Older Adults*. Toronto: Ontario Ministry for Tourism and Recreation.

* DeMont, P. (1999). Too much stress, too little time. *The Ottawa Citizen*, Wednesday, November 10, pages A1-2.

* Dickenson, P., and Ellison, J. (1999). Plugged into the internet. *Canadian Social Trends*. Winter, 7-10, Statistics Canada-Catalogue No. 11-008.

* Douse, L. (1974). Older people: Recreology's greatest challenge. *Journal of Leisurability*, 1(4): 18-24.

* Drysdale, A.C. (1970). Twenty-five years of unity: Canadian Parks/Recreation Association. *Recreation Canada*, August, 28: 18-37.

* Dunbar, J.O. (1972). The bedrock of community development. *Journal of the Community Development Society*, 3(2): 42-53.

* Duncombe, L.D. (1998). Traditions of the past partner with energy of the future. *Parks and Recreation Canada*, July/August, 56(3): 36-37.

* Eagles, P.F.J., and Martens, J. (1997). Wilderness tourism and forestry: The possible dream in Algonquin Provincial Park. *Journal of Applied Recreation Research*, 22(1): 79-97.

* Edgington, C., Compton, D., and Hanson, C. (1980). *Recreation and leisure programming: A guide for the professional*. Philadelphia, PA: Saunders College Publishing.

* Edwards, A.D., and Jones, D. (1976). *Community and Community Development*. Mouton: New Babylon.

* Eisenhardt, I. (1945). Canada's National Fitness Act. *Journal of Health, Physical Education and Recreation*, April, 186.

* Ellis, R., and Nixon, E. (1986). *Saskatchewan's Recreation Legacy*. Saskatoon, SK: Modern Press.

* Ellis, T., and Norton, R.L. (1988). *Commercial Recreation*. St. Louis, MI: Times/Mirror Mosby College Publishing.

* England, E.F. (1975). *Historic Newfoundland*. St. John's, Newfoundland: The Newfoundland Department of Tourism.

* Epitropoulos, M. (2002). Tourism and culture. Presentation made to University of Ottawa Study Tour Course in Greece. Ancient Olympia, Greece, May 14.

- Epperson, A. (1977). *Private and Commercial Recreation: A Text and Reference.* New York, NY: John Wiley and Sons.

- Farina, J. (1969a). Comments by Dr. John Farina. *Leisure in Canada: The Proceedings of the Montmorency Conference on Leisure.* Ottawa: Fitness and Amateur Sport Directorate, Department of National Health and Welfare Canada. (pp. 3-4).

- Farina, J. (1969b). Towards a philosophy of leisure. *Leisure in Canada: The Proceedings of the Montmorency Conference on Leisure.* Ottawa: Fitness and Amateur Sport Directorate, Department of National Health and Welfare Canada. (pp. 5-15).

- Farina, J. (1985). Perceptions of time. In T.L. Goodale and P.W. Witt. *Recreation and Leisure: Issues In An Era of Change.* (Revised Edition). State College, PA: Venture. (pp. 23-34).

- Farrell, B. (1991). Ecology and tourism. *Annals of Tourism Research,* 18: 26-40.

- Fast, J., and Da Pont, M. (1997). Changes in women's work continuity. *Canadian Social Trends.* Autumn, 2-7, Statistics Canada-Catalogue No. 11-008-XPE.

- Federal, Provincial/Territorial Ministers Responsible for Sport, Fitness and Recreation. (2002). Canada Sport Policy. Ottawa: Federal, Provincial/Territorial Ministers Responsible for Sport, Fitness and Recreation.

- Ferris, B.F., Kisby, R., Craig, C.L., and Landry, F. (1987). Fitness promotion and research in Canada. *Journal of Physical Education, Recreation and Dance,* 58(7): 26-30.

- Foot, D. (1990). The age of outdoor recreation in Canada. *Journal of Applied Recreation Research,* 15(3): 159-178.

- Foot, D. (2000). *Boom, Bust and Echo.* Toronto: Macfarlane, Walter and Ross.

- Foot, D.K., and Stoffman, D. (1998). *Boom, Bust and Echo: Profiting From the Demographic Shift in the New Millennium* Toronto: Macfarlane, Walter and Ross.

- Forsey, E.A. (1982). *How Canadians Govern Themselves.* Ottawa: Ministry of Supply and Services, Government of Canada.

- Fournier, J-Y. (1999). Loisir: vers un renouveau. *Parks and Recreation Canada,* November/December: 21-22.

- Fowler, I., and Cohoon, J. (2002/2003). Partnering in community services. *Parks and Recreation Canada,* Winter, 60(4): 18-19.

- Fox, K.M. (1993). Strengthening the web of life: Women, community and "leisure." *Proceedings: The 7th Canadian Congress on Leisure Research,* The University of Manitoba, Winnipeg, Manitoba: 274-278.

- Fox, K.M. (1994). The power and promise of leisure based on diversity. *Recreation Canada,* 52(1): 23-25.

- Fox, K.M., Ryan, S., van Dyck, J., Chivers, B., Chuchmach, L., and Quesnal, S. (1998). Cultural perspectives, resilient aboriginal communities, and recreation. *Journal of Applied Recreation Research,* 23(2): 147-191.

- Frederick, C.J., and Shaw, S.M. (1995). Body image as a leisure constraint: Examining the experience of aerobics classes for young women. *Leisure Sciences,* 17: 57-73.

- Frederickson, G.H. (1975). Strategy for development administration. *Journal of the Community Development Society,* 6(1): 88-101.

- Friars, K. (1994). Toward a gender equity policy for parks and recreation: A discussion paper. *Recreation Canada,* 52(4): 25-28.

- Gagnon, N., Ostiguy, L., and Swedburg, R. (1993). The ivory tower syndrome. *Recreation Canada,* 51(2): 27-29.

- Gardner, A. (2000). Their own boss: The self-employed in Canada. *Canada Social Trends (Volume 3).* Toronto: Thompson Educational Publishers. (pp. 188-192).

- Glover, T.D. (1999). Reinventing local government in Canada: Contemporary challenges facing leisure practitioners. *Book of Abstracts: 9th Canadian Congress on Leisure Research,* Acadia University, Wolfville, Nova Scotia: 97-100.

- Glover, T.D., and Burton, T.L. (1998). A model of alternative forms of public leisure services delivery. In M.F. Collins, and I.S. Cooper (Eds.). *Leisure Management: Issues and Applications.* Wallingford, OX: CAB International.

* Godbey, G. (1999). Illuminating our future: Parks and recreation in Canada-What did the resource people have to say? *Parks and Recreation Canada*, November/December: 37.

* Godin, C. (1996). Community cultural development: The Calgary parks and recreation department. *Journal of Applied Recreation Research*, 21(1): 67-73.

* Gold, D. (1990). The other side of the "forgotten client" concept. *Recreation Canada*, October: 18-23.

* Gold, S.M. (1985). Future leisure environments in cities. In T.L. Goodale and P.W. Witt. *Recreation and Leisure: Issues In An Era of Change*. (Revised Edition). State College, PA: Venture. (pp. 135-151).

* Goodale, T. (1985). If leisure is to matter. In T.L. Goodale and P.W. Witt. *Recreation and Leisure: Issues In An Era of Change*. (Revised Edition). State College, PA: Venture. (pp. 44-55).

* Government of Canada. (2000). *Constitution Act*. Ottawa, ON: Queens Printer.

* Government of Ontario. (1998). *Ontario Government Business Plans: 1998-1999* . Toronto, ON. Ministry of Citizenship, Culture and Recreation.

* Grace, S. (2001). *Canada and the Idea of the North*. Montreal and Kingston: McGill-Queen's University Press.

* Gravelle, F., Wood, J., and Karlis, G. (1995). The future of recreation for Canada's aged: Focus on active living. *Recreation Canada*, 53(1): 9-12.

* Grey, T., and Johnston, D. (2000). City of Winnipeg-Aboriginal Services: A new paradigm preparing for growth. *Parks and Recreation Canada*, May/June: 10-11.

* Gruneau, R., and Whitson, D. (1993). *Hockey Night in Canada*. Toronto: Garamond Press.

* Gurney, H. (1983). *The CAPHER Story 1933-1983* . Ottawa, ON: Canadian Association for Health, Physical Education and Recreation.

* Guy, S. (1993). Youth 2000. *Recreation Canada*, 54(4): 33-35.

* Haasen, B., Hornibrook, T., and Pedlar, A. (1998). Researcher and practitioner perspectives on a research partnership. *Journal of Leisurability*, 25(3): 25-32.

* Haensel, R., Bliss, J., Brownridge, J., and Twardochleb, T. (1991). Encouraging grassroots cultural development: The burning issues forums. *Recreation Canada*, October: 34-35.

* Hall, M., and Banting, K.G. (2000). The nonprofit sector in Canada: An introduction. In K.G. Banting (Ed.) *The Nonprofit Sector in Canada*. Kingston: School of Policy Studies, Queens University. (pp. 1-28).

* Hall, M., and Zeppel, H. (1990). Culture and heritage tourism: The new grand tour. *Historic Environment*, 7(3,4): 86-98.

* Hall, M., Knighton, T., Reed, P., Bussiere, P., McRae, D., and Bowen, P. (1998). *Caring Canadians, Involved Canadians: Highlights from the 1997 National Survey of Giving, Volunteering and Participating*. Ottawa, ON: Ministry of Industry. Cat. No: 71-542-XIE.

* Hall, M.H. (1988). Survey on Recreational Services for Ontario's Ethnocultural Populations. Toronto, ON: Ontario Ministry for Tourism and Recreation.

* Hall, M.H., and Macpherson, L.G. (1997). A provincial portrait of Canada's charities. *Research Bulletin*, 4(2&3). Toronto: Canadian Center for Philanthropy.

* Hall, M.H., and Rhyme, D. (1989). Leisure Behaviors and Recreation Needs of Ontario's Ethnocultural Populations. Toronto: Ontario Ministry of Tourism and Recreation.

* Hammock, J.C. (1973). Community development: Organization-building and political modernization. *Journal of the Community Development Society*, 4(2): 12-19.

* Harper, J., Mahon, M.J., Foreman, S., and Godbey, G. (1999). The use and benefits of local government parks and recreation services in Canada and the United States: A Perspective of People with Disabilities. *Book of Abstracts: 9ᵗʰ Canadian Congress on Leisure Research*, Acadia University, Wolfville, Nova Scotia: 113-116.

* Harper, J., Neider, D., and Godbey, G. (1997). Use and benefits of public parks and recreation services in Canada. *Parks and Recreation Canada*, November/December: 22-24.

* Harper, J.A., and Balmer, K.R. (1989). The perceived benefits of public leisure services: An exploratory investigation. *Leisure and Society*, 12: 171-188.

* Harper, J.A., and Johnston, B.L. (1992). Balancing the scales in public parks and recreation departments. *Recreation Canada*, October: 18-20.

* Harrington, M., and Dawson, D. (1993). No rest for mom: The effects of motherhood on women's leisure. *Proceedings: The 7ᵗʰ Canadian Congress on Leisure Research*, The University of Manitoba, Winnipeg, Manitoba: 130-133.

* Harrington, M., and Dawson, D. (1996). Recreation and homelessness. *Proceedings: 8ᵗʰ Canadian Congress on Leisure Research*, University of Ottawa, Ottawa, Ontario: 99-102.

* Harrington, M., Dawson, D., and Bolla, P. (1992). Objective and subjective constraints on women's enjoyment of leisure. *Society and Leisure*, 15:203-222.

* Henderson, K.A. (1993). "The changer and the changed:" Leisure research in the 1990s. *Proceedings: The 7ᵗʰ Canadian Congress on Leisure Research*, The University of Manitoba, Winnipeg, Manitoba: 1-4.

* Henhawk, C. (1993). Recreation development in first nation communities: A six nations perspective. *Journal of Applied Recreation Research*, 18(2): 82-86.

* Herchmer, B. (1996). Benefits in action: First things first. *Parks and Recreation Canada,* 54(4): 26-27, 37,42.

* Heron, P. (1990). The institutionalization of leisure: Cultural interpretation. *Proceedings: 6ᵗʰ Canadian Congress on Leisure Research*, University of Waterloo, Waterloo, ON: 82-88.

* Heywood, L.A. (2000/2001). A retrospective commentary on "need assessment in selected municipal recreation departments. *Leisure/Loisir*, 25(1-2): 9-12.

* Hickman, S. (1998). Digging behind the scenes. *The University of Ottawa Gazette.* 10(7): 3, February 19.

* Hillier, H.H. (2000). *Canadian Society: A Macro Analysis* (4ᵗʰ Edition). Toronto: Prentice-Hall.

* Hills, S. (1989). What wellness really means. *Recreation Canada,* 47(2): 8-9.

* Hinch, T.D., and Delamere, T.A. (1993). Native festivals as tourism attractions: A community challenge. *Journal of Applied Recreation Research*, 18(2): 131-142.

* Hinch, T.D., and Li, Y. (1996). Cultural tourist attractions: A comparative study of ethnic interpretive centers in China and Canada. *Proceedings: 8ᵗʰ Canadian Congress on Leisure Research*, University of Ottawa, Ottawa, Ontario: 120-122.

* Hoffman, D. (2002). National cultures in transnational worlds: The future of culture in comparative. Paper presented at the 4ᵗʰ Annual Athens Institute for Education and Research Conference, Athens, Greece, May 25.

* Hollands, R. (1988). Leisure, work and working-class cultures: The case of leisure on the shop floor. In H. Cantelon and R. Hollands (Eds.). *Leisure, Sport and Working-Class Cultures: Theory and History.* Toronto: Garamond Press.

* Horna, J.L.A. (1980). Leisure re-socialization among immigrants in Canada. *Society and Leisure*, 3(1): 97-110.

* Horna, J.L.A. (1987a). Leisure and ethnic minorities. In Graefe, A., and Parker, S. (Eds.). *Recreation and Leisure: An Introductory Handbook.* State College, PA: Venture.

* Horna, J.L.A. (1987b). The process of choosing leisure activities and preferences: A stream model. *Society and Leisure*, 10(2): 219-234.

* Horna, J.L.A. (1987c). The arts in Canada. In L. Hantrais, and T. Kamphorst (Eds.). *Trends in the Arts: A Multinational Perspective.* Amersfoort, The Netherlands: Giordano Bruno. (pp. 33-65).

* Horna, J.L.A. (1995). The impact of the cold climate on leisure in Canada. *World Leisure and Recreation*, 37(2): 10-14.

* Horton, H.D. (1992). A sociological approach to black community development: Presentation of the black organizational autonomy model. *Journal of the Community Development Society*, 23(1): 1-19.

* House of Commons Debates: Official Report, May 12, 1994. Ottawa: Government of Canada.

* House of Commons Debates: Official Report, Volume VIII, October 8, 1971. Ottawa: Government of Canada.

* Howard, D.R., and Crompton, J.L. (1980). *Financing, Managing and Marketing Recreation and Park Resources.* Dubuque, IA: Wm. C. Brown.

* Howell, M.L., and Howell, R.A. (1985). *History of Sports in Canada.* Champaign, IL: Stripes.

* Hubbard, R.H. (no date). *Rideau Hall: An Illustrated History of Government House.* Ottawa.

* Hunt, P. (1994, November 1). Leisure, Recreation and Community Development. Presentation made in LSR 2126 (Recreation and Community Development) class, University of Ottawa, Ottawa, Ontario.

* Hunt, P. (1995, October 30). "Leisure, Recreation and Community Development." Presentation made to LSR 2136 (Recreation and Community Development Class, University of Ottawa, Ottawa, Ontario).

* Hunter, D. (1986). The municipal role in community development. *Recreation Canada,* 44(5): 18-21.

* Hunter, D. (2003). Back to the Future. *Parks and Recreation Canada,* Winter: 14-15.

* Hunter, P.L., and Whitson, D.J. (1991). Women, leisure and familism: Relationship and isolation in small town Canada. *Leisure Studies,* 10(3): 219-233.

* Hutchison, P. (1990a). A qualitative study of the friendships of people with disabilities. *Proceedings: Sixth Canadian Congress on Leisure Research,* University of Waterloo, Waterloo, ON: 44-51.

* Hutchison, P. (1990b). *Making Friends: Developing Relationships Between People With A Disability and Other Members of the Community.* Downsview, ON: G. Allen Roeher Institute.

* Hutchison, P. (1996). Community development and recreation practice: An introduction to Part 1. *Journal of Applied Recreation Research,* 21(1): 3-4.

* Hutchison, P., and Campbell, J. (1996). Innovative community development approaches in recreation and leisure in Canada. Eighth Canadian on Leisure Research, University of Ottawa, Ottawa, Ontario, 137-140.

* Hutchison, P., and McGill, J. (1992). *Leisure, Integration and Community.* Concord, ON: Leisurability Publications.

* Hutchison, P., and Nogradi, G. (1993). Community development in recreation and leisure: A study to clarify concepts, process and strategies. Proceedings: 7th Canadian Congress on Leisure Research, University of Manitoba, Winnipeg, Manitoba.

* Hutchison, P., and Nogradi, G. (1996). The concept and nature of community development in recreation and leisure services. *Journal of Applied Recreation Research,* 21(2): 93-130.

* Ibrahim, H. (1991). *Leisure and Society: A Comparative Approach.* Dubuque, IA: Wm. C. Brown.

* Inglis, S. (1994). Exploring volunteer board member and executive director needs: Importance and fulfillment. *Journal of Applied Recreation Research,* 19(3): 171-189.

* Ipson, N.M. (1993). The market segmentation of campus recreation programs: The mature student market. *Proceedings: The 7th Canadian Congress on Leisure Research,* The University of Manitoba, Winnipeg, Manitoba: 52-56.

* Jackson, E. (2000/2001). The North American leisure research community in the 1990s: An exploratory quantitative analysis of participation in the Leisure Research Symposium and the Canadian Congress on Leisure Research. *Leisure/Loisir,* 25(1-2): 79-107.

* Jackson, E.L., and Henderson, K.A. (1995). Gender-based analysis of leisure constraints. *Leisure Sciences,* 17(1): 31-51.

* Jackson, R.L., and Jackson, D. (1990). *Politics in Canada.* (2nd Edition). Scarborough, ON: Prentice-Hall.

* Jenson, J., and Phillips, S.D. (2000). Distinctive trajectories: Homecare and the voluntary sector in Ontario and Quebec. In K.G. Banting (Ed.) *The Nonprofit Sector in Canada.* Kingston: School of Policy Studies, Queens University. (pp. 29-68).

* Johnson, R., and Johnson-Tew, P. (1999a). A longitudinal study of leisure opportunities in three Ontario communities. . *Book of Abstracts: 9ᵗʰ Canadian Congress on Leisure Research,* Acadia University, Wolfville, Nova Scotia: 187-189.

* Johnson, R., and Johnson-Tew, P. (1999b). "Moving in harmony with nature's laws" – Sport, leisure, and health in Victorian North America. *Book of Abstracts: 8ᵗʰ Canadian Congress on Leisure Research,* University of Ottawa, Ottawa, Ontario: 267-268.

* Johnson, R., and McLean, D. (1996a). Rationing recreation: A reality of the 1990s. *Proceedings: 8ᵗʰ Canadian Congress on Leisure Research,* University of Ottawa, Ottawa, Ontario: 150-151.

* Johnson, R., and McLean, D. (1996b). Public sector marketing: Improving services or compromising values? *Parks and Recreation Canada,* May/June: 21-24.

* Johnson-Tew, P., Havitz, M., and McCarville, R. (1999). Current trends in the pricing and marketing of public leisure services. *Parks and Recreation Canada,* 57(2): 10-11.

* Johnstone, B. (1999). Illuminating our future: Parks and recreation in Canada. *Parks and Recreation Canada,* November/December: 34-36.

* Kaminski-Morris, P. (1987). Service brokerage and recreation: One model. *Journal of Leisurability,* 14(3): 15-18.

* Kaplan, M. (1978). From the president. *Society and Leisure,* 1(1): 3-4.

* Karlis, G. (1987). Perceptions of Greek immigrants and descendants toward Greek culture and participation in the Hellenic Community of Ottawa. Unpublished Masters Thesis, Department of Recreation and Physical Education, Acadia University, Wolfville, Nova Scotia.

* Karlis, G. (1989a). MBO: A sustainable process of operation for the future management of volunteer organizations. *Recreation Canada,* July: 40-42.

* Karlis, G. (1989b). Cultural perceptions, ethnicity and recreation: The case of the Greek community of Halifax. *Tidings,* Summer: 3, 11, 16.

* Karlis, G. (1990a). Aged immigrants: Forgotten clients in the provision of recreation services. *Recreation Canada,* October: 36-41.

* Karlis, G. (1990b). *Ethnicity and Leisure: A Bibliographic Review of Current Theory and Research.* Ottawa: The Department of Leisure Studies, University of Ottawa.

* Karlis, G. (1991a). Research, technology transfer and programming for recreation. *Tidings,* Winter: 11-14.

* Karlis, G. (1991b). Recreation preferences, participation and cultural assimilation: A comparison of Greek immigrants and their descendants in Toronto. Paper presented at the Canadian Parks and Recreation Association Conference, Regina, Saskatchewan, August 12.

* Karlis, G. (1991-1992). Recommendations for ethno-culturally sensitive leisure counselling. *Leisure Information Quarterly,* 18(3): 1-3.

* Karlis, G. (1993a). The relationship between cultural recreation and cultural identity among Greek immigrants of Toronto. Unpublished Doctoral Dissertation, Department of Park and Recreation Resources, Michigan State University, East Lansing, Michigan.

* Karlis, G. (1993b). Ethnicity and recreation in Canada: The constraints of Canada's ethnic population. *Proceedings: The 7ᵗʰ Canadian Congress on Leisure Research,* The University of Manitoba, Winnipeg, Manitoba: 284-285.

* Karlis, G. (1994a). Community development and community recreation. *Tidings,* Summer: 10-11.

* Karlis, G. (1994b). Managing recreation services for immigrants: Recommendations for leaders, programmers and administrators. *Visions in Leisure and Business,* 12(4): 39-43.

* Karlis, G. (1995a). Strategic planning for recreation administrators in private sector recreation organizations. *Visions in Leisure and Business,* 14(2): 4-12.

* Karlis, G. (1995b). Aboriginal cultural recreation in Quebec: On-reserve recreation, off-reserve recreation and cultural maintenance. Technical Report, Faculty of Social Sciences (Research), University of Ottawa: Ottawa.

* Karlis, G. (1996). Leisure studies: A means to understand, practice and implement active living. *Active: The Active Living Community Action Update,* January: 7.

* Karlis, G. (1997a). The evolution of ethnic community organizations in multicultural societies: The role of recreation. *World Leisure and Recreation Journal,* 39(3): 41-45.

* Karlis, G. (1997b). International comparative study tours: A trend in recreation and parks education in Canada. *Parks and Recreation Canada,* September-October, 55(4): 33.

* Karlis, G. (1997c). Cultural diversity in recreation and leisure studies: Curricula, faculty and students. *Parks and Recreation Canada,* September-October, 55(4): 29-30.

* Karlis, G. (1998a). Identifying and serving the disenfranchised: University programs of leisure studies and disability. *Parks and Recreation Canada,* November/December: 10-11.

* Karlis, G. (1998b). Privatizing recreation experiences: The Canadian experience. Paper presented at the 1st International Conference of the Athens Institute for Education and Research on Entrepreneur and Entrepreneurship at the Dawn of the 21st Century. Athens, Greece, May 29.

* Karlis, G. (1998c). Citizen participation : Managing public and non-profit recreation services. *World Leisure and Recreation Journal,* 12(1): 37-40.

* Karlis, G. (1998d). Social cohesion, social closure, and recreation: The ethnic experience in multicultural societies. *Journal of Applied Recreation Research,* 23(1): 3-21.

* Karlis, G. (1999). Cultural recreation and cultural identity: Greek immigrants and descendants in a Canadian city. *Journal of Business and Society,* 12(1): 95-108.

* Karlis, G. (2000). Leisure, recreation and sports: Concepts and management. (In Greek). In G.T. Papanikos (Ed.). *Athletics, Economics, Management and Marketing.* Athens: Athens Institute for Education and Research. (pp. 105-115).

* Karlis, G. (2002a). The concepts of leisure and recreation in Canada. Presentation made to MBA course on Athletic Management and Marketing, Economic University of Athens, June 3.

* Karlis, G. (2002b). Higher education and research in leisure studies: Current state of condition. Paper presented at the 4th Athens Institute for Education and Research Conference, Athens, Greece, May 25.

* Karlis, G. (2002c). Career development. Presentation given at University of Ottawa Study Tour Course, Gouves Beach, Crete, Greece, May 15.

* Karlis, G. (2003). Culture and identity: Bringing back Greeks from the diaspora to volunteer for Athens 2004. (In Greek). *Economics and Athletics,* forthcoming.

* Karlis, G., and Bolla, P. (1989). The state of research into ethnicity and leisure. Paper presented at the Canadian Ethnic Studies Association Conference, Calgary, Alberta, October 19.

* Karlis, G., and Dawson, D. (1990). Ethnic maintenance and recreation: A case study. *Journal of Applied Recreation Research,* 15(2): 85-99.

* Karlis, G., and Dawson, D. (1994). Mental health promotion through recreation: A look at qualitative program evaluation. *Journal of Applied Recreation Research,* 19(4): 267-280.

* Karlis, G., and Dawson, D. (1995a). Ethnicity and recreation: Concepts, approaches and programming. *Canadian Ethnic Studies,* 37(2): 166-179.

* Karlis, G., and Dawson, D. (1995b). On-reserve recreation, off-reserve recreation and cultural maintenance: A study of the Kitigan Zibi reserve of Quebec. Paper presented at the Ontario Research Council on Leisure Research Symposium, Waterloo, April 7.

* Karlis, G., and Dawson, D. (1996). Native culture and recreation in Canada: A preliminary enquiry. *Native Studies Review,* 11(2): 157-166.

* Karlis, G., and Gravelle, F. (1997). Displacement and the administration of recreation services. *Supplementary Proceedings: Association of Management and the International Association of Management 15th Annual International Conference (Ed. S. LeMah).* Montreal. August. (pp. 1-16).

* Karlis, G., and Kartakoullis, N. (1992). Leisure in multicultural societies: Learning from the Canadian experience. *Journal of Business and Society,* 5(1,2): 94-102.

• Karlis, G., and Kartakoullis, N. (1996). Recreation and the preservation of ethnic cultural identity in multicultural Canada. *Journal of Business and Society,* 5(1,2): 153-161.

• Karlis, G., and Lithopoulos, S. (1991). The management of volunteers in ethnic community organizations. *Proceedings: First International Conference on Arts Management.* Ecoles des Hautes Commerciales de Montreal: Montreal, Quebec. (pp. 351-363.

• Karlis, G., Auger, D., and Gravelle, F. (1996). Three approaches to community development in recreation organizations: The development of a theoretical model. *Journal of Applied Recreation Research,* 21(2): 131-141.

• Karlis, G., Bolla, P., and Dawson, D. (1992). Leisure studies and ethnicity: A review and resource for educators. *New Education,* 14(1): 21-30.

• Karlis, G., Gravelle, F., and Pawlick, M.T. (1997). L'Importance de la récréation pour les immigrants au Canada: Les Grecs de Toronto. *Journal of Applied Recreation Research,* 22(3): 245-257.

• Kelly, K., Howatson-Leo, L., and Clark, W. (2000). "I feel overqualified for my job...". *Canada Social Trends (Volume 3).* Toronto: Thompson Educational Publishers. (pp. 182-187).

• Kent, S. (1993). Vandalism: A youth's perspective on how to stop the destruction. *Recreation Canada,* 54(4): 41-42.

• Kerr, M. (1990). Recreation: A collaborator in healthy communities. *Recreation Canada,* 48: 32-34.

• Khinduka, S.K. (1975). Community development: Potentials and limitations. In R.M. Kraner and H. Specht (Eds.). *Readings in Community Organization Practice.* Englewood Cliffs, NJ: Prentice-Hall. (220-228).

• Kingsmill, P. (2002). Cultural tourism coming of age. *Tourism,* November, 6(9): 3.

• Kraus, R. (1984). *Recreation and Leisure in Modern Society.* Glenview, IL: Scott and Foresman.

• Kraus, R. (1994). *Leisure in a Changing America: Multicultural Perspectives.* New York: Macmillan College Publishing Company.

• Kraus, R. (1997). *Recreation Programming: A Benefits-Driven Approach.* Boston: Allyn and Bacon.

• Kremarik, F. (2000). Urban development. *Canadian Social Trends.* Winter, 18-22, Statistics Canada-Catalogue No. 11-008.

• Kurtzman, J. (2001). Economic impact: Sport tourism and the city. *Journal of Sport Tourism,* 6(3): 14-42.

• Labonte, R. (1993). *Health promotion and Empowerment: Practice Frameworks.* Montreal, QU: Black Rose Books.

• Labossiere, S., and Gemmell, B. (1989). Volunteerism in Canada. *Recreation Canada,* December, 47(5): 30-33.

• Lakey, J. (1998). Lastman finds New York tough on homeless but he likes crackdown on squeegee kids. *Toronto Star,* Thursday, November 19.

• Lamirande, T. (2000). Manitoba recreation council helps aboriginals participate in sport. *Parks and Recreation Canada,* May/June: 22-23.

• Laplante, M. (1967). Pour une politique du temps libre. Paper presented at the Conference canadienne du bien-etre social. Inn of the Park, Toronto.

• Lappage, R. (1985). The Canadian scene and sports, 1921-1976. In M.L. Howell and R.A. Howell (Eds.). *History of Sport in Canada.* Champaign, IL: Stripes.

• Larabee, E., and Meyersohn, E. (1958). *Mass Leisure.* Glencoe, IL: Free Press.

• Larocque, L., Gravelle, F., and Karlis, G. (2002). Volunteerism and serious leisure: The case of the Francophone Games. *Abstracts: 10ᵗʰ Canadian Congress on Leisure Research,* Edmonton, Alberta: 85-87.

• Larsen, D.B., and Larson, S. (1994). *The Forgotten Factors in Physical and Mental Health: What Does the Research Show.* Washington, DC: National Institute for Health Care Research.

* Larsen, J.K., and Montelpare, W.J. (1990). The status of volunteerism in recreational and cultural services. *Proceedings: 6th Canadian Congress on Leisure Research*. University of Waterloo, Waterloo, Ontario: 285-287.

* Larsen, J.K., Montelpare, W., and Donovan-Neale, W. (1992). The development of municipal policy for volunteers in recreation and cultural services. *Journal of Applied Recreation Research*, 17(2): 130-143.

* Larsen, R., and Kleiber, D.A. (1993). Free time activities as factors in adolescent adjustment. In P. Tolan and B. Cohler (Eds.). *Handbook of Clinical Research and Practice with Adolescents*. New York: Wiley.

* Lawrence, L., and Legg, D. (1998). A linkage initiative: A cross Canada approach to creating active living opportunities for persons with a disability. *Parks and Recreation Canada*, November/December: 8-9.

* LeClair, J. (1992). *Sport and Physical Activity in the 90s*. Toronto: Thompson Educational Publishing.

* Legaree, I., Schofield, D., and Hayden, L. (1994). Developing recreation leaders in Canada's Arctic. *Recreation Canada*, 52(5): 4-7.

* Leith, D.A., and Shaw, S.M. (1997). Physical inactivity in leisure: Why some women adopt inactive lifestyles. *Journal of Applied Recreation Research*, 22(4): 339-364.

* Levinson, L.J., and Reid, G. (1991). Patterns of physical activity among youngsters with developmental disabilities. *CAHPER Journal*, 57(3): 24-28.

* Levy, J. (1983). *Leisure Today*. Guelph, ON: The Backdoor Press.

* Levy, J., Losito, V., and Levy, R. (1996). Ontario senior games: Determinants, constraints and benefits. *Proceedings: 8th Canadian Congress on Leisure Research*, University of Ottawa, Ottawa, Ontario: 164-166.

* Lohmann, R.A. (1992). *The Commons: New Perspectives on Nonprofit Organizations and Voluntary Action*. San Francisco: Jossey-Bass.

* Lothian, W.F. (1976). *A History of Canada's National Parks*. Ottawa: Parks Canada.

* Lougheed, T. (2002). Exploring leisure makes for an academic marathon. *The University of Ottawa Gazette*. 15(1): 6, September 27.

* Lower, A.R.M. (1958). *Canadians in the Making: A Social History of Canada*. Toronto: Longmans, Green and Company.

* Luken, K. (1993). Reintegration through recreation. *Parks and Recreation*, April: 52-57.

* Lyons, R.F. (1981). Profile of municipal leisure services for special populations in Canada. *Journal of Leisurability*, Fall, 8(4): 14-24.

* Lyons, R.F. (1993). Meaningful activity and disability: Capitalizing upon the potential of outreach recreation networks in Canada. *Canadian Journal of Rehabilitation*, 6(4): 256-265.

* MacCauley, M., and Gilbert, A.A. (1993). Newspaper portrayal of persons with a disability. *Proceedings: The 7th Canadian Congress on Leisure Research*, The University of Manitoba, Winnipeg, Manitoba: 181-183.

* Macdonald, C. (1998). City at leisure: An illustrated history of parks and recreation services in Winnipeg, 1893-1993. *Manitoba History*, Spring-Summer, 35: 32-33.

* MacKay, K.J. (1996). A first nation interpretation of a national park's image. *Proceedings: 8th Canadian Congress on Leisure Research*, University of Ottawa, Ottawa, Ontario: 171-174.

* MacKay, K.J. (1999). Heritage tourists: Profiling an important segment of provincial travelers. *Book of Abstracts: 9th Canadian Congress on Leisure Research*, Acadia University, Wolfville, Nova Scotia: 153-156.

* MacKay, K.J., Lamont, D.E., and Partridge, C. (1996). Northern ecotourists and general tourists: An intra-provincial comparison. *Journal of Applied Recreation Research*, 21(4): 335-337.

* MacLean, J., Peterson, J., and Martin, D. (1985). *Recreation and Leisure: The Changing Scene*. (4th Edition). New York: John Wiley and Sons.

• Mactavish, J., Mahon, M., and Rodrique, M. (1996). Older adults with a mental disability: Exploring the meaning of independence. *Proceedings: 8ᵗʰ Canadian Congress on Leisure Research*, University of Ottawa, Ottawa, Ontario: 175-179.

• Mahon, M.J. (1995). Leisure education: Promoting self-determination in persons with a disability. *Recreation* Canada, 53:(1): 22-24.

• Malloy, D. C. (1991). Cross-cultural awareness in administration: An interview with Harold Cardinal. *Recreation Canada*, July: 40-44.

• Malloy, D.C., Nilson, R.N., and Yoshioka, C. (1993). The impact of culture upon the administrative process in sport and recreation: A Canadian Indian perspective. *Journal of Applied Recreation Research*, 18(2): 115-130.

• Malpass, D. (1993). The total community includes the ethnic groups. *Recreation Canada*, 31(3): 46-47.

• Mannell, R.C., Zuzanek, J., and Schneider, M. (2002). Adolescents' experience of busyness, time pressure and well-being: Positive and negative effects of school, work, volunteer and extracurricular involvement. *Abstracts: 10ᵗʰ Canadian Congress on Leisure Research*, 12-15.

• Markham, S. (1992). Our leaders speak up. *Recreation Canada,* May: 15-19.

• Markham, S.E. (1980). *The Halifax Common 1749 to 1979.* Unpublished M.A. Thesis, Dalhousie University, Halifax, Nova Scotia.

• Markham, S.E. (1995). The early years: 1944 to 1951. *Recreation Canada,* July, 53: 6-16.

• Markham, S.E. (1996). Early efforts to professionalize leisure services in Canada. *Proceedings: 8ᵗʰ Canadian Congress on Leisure Research*, University of Ottawa, Ottawa, Ontario: 181-185.

• Markham-Starr, S. (2000/2001). Reflections from the garden: A commentary on "worlds apart: Thoughts on a Canadian Association of Leisure Studies." *Leisure/Loisir*, 25(1-2): 27-29.

• Marlett, N.J., Gall, R., and Wight-Felske, A. (1994). *Dialogue on Disability: A Canadian Perspective (Volume 1): The Service System.* Calgary: The University of Calgary Press.

• Matheson, J.R. (1997). Ideology in culture: "Canadian Flag." In E. Cameron (Ed.). *Canadian Culture: An Introduction .* Toronto: Canadian Scholars Press (pp. 353-395).

• McCarville, R.E., and Smale, B.J. (1992). The use of pricing by municipal recreation agencies in the delivery of leisure services. *Journal of Applied Recreation Research*, 16(3): 200-219.

• McCarville, R.E., Flood, C.M., and Froats, T.A. (1996). The effectiveness of selected promotions on spectators' assessments of a non-profit sporting event sponsor. *Proceedings: 8ᵗʰ Canadian Congress on Leisure Research.* University of Ottawa, Ottawa, Ontario: 285-287.

• McClaughlin, M. (1897). *Homelessness in Canada: The Report of the National Inquiry.* Ottawa: Canadian Council on Social Development.

• McCormick, S. (1991). Parks and recreation + social change = future. *Parks and Recreation,* 2: 30-35, 142.

• McCue, W. (1986). Involving ethnic older adults in community recreation programs. *Recreation Canada,* July: 15-16.

• McDonald, D.J. (1993). The future of recreation education. *Proceedings: The 7ᵗʰ Canadian Congress on Leisure Research*, The University of Manitoba, Winnipeg, Manitoba: 95-99.

• McFarland, E.M. (1970). *The Development of Public Recreation in Canada.* Ottawa, ON: Canadian Parks and Recreation Association.

• McFarland, E.M. (1982). The development of supervised playgrounds. In G. Wall and J.S. Marsh (Eds.). *Recreation Land Use .* Ottawa: Carleton University Press.

• McGill, J. (1996). *Developing Leisure Identities: A Pilot Project.* Brampton: Brampton Caledon Community Living.

• McInnis, E. (1969). *Canada: A Political and Social History.* Toronto, ON: Holt, Rinehart and Winston.

* McIntosh, R., and Goeldner, C. (1984). *Tourism: Principles, Practices, Philosophy*. (4th Edition). New York, NY: John Wiley and Sons.

* McIntyre, J. (1999). Illuminating our future: Parks and recreation in Canada-What did the resource people have to say? *Parks and Recreation Canada*, November/December: 37.

* McLeod, W., and Wright, A. (1992). Older adults: The role of physical activity in aging. *Recreation Canada*, March, 50(1): 8-15.

* McNamee, K. (2002). From wild places to endangered spaces. In P. Deardon and R. Rollins (Eds.). *Parks and Protected Areas in Canada*. (2nd Edition). Don Mills, ON: Oxford.

* Metcalfe, A. (1987). *Canadians Learn to Play: The Emergence of Organized Sport 1807-1914* . Toronto, ON: McClelland and Stewart.

* Mieczowski, Z.T. (1991). Some notes on the geography of tourism: A comment. *Canadian Geographer*, 25: 186-191.

* Ministry of Culture and Recreation. (1978). *The Elora Prescription: A Future for Recreation*. Ontario: Ministry of Culture and Recreation.

* Ministry of Natural Resources. (1974). *Algonquin Provincial Park Master Plan*. Toronto, ON.

* Ministry of State for Urban Affairs. (1973). Local Leisure Activity Studies. Ottawa, ON: Urban Affairs, Canada.

* Ministry of Supply and Services Canada (1982). *The Charter of Rights and Freedoms: A Guide for Canadians*. Ottawa, ON: Publications Canada.

* Minshall, L. (1984a). Shifting demographics. *The Recreationist*, 4(2): 49-60.

* Minshall, L. (1984b). Volunteerism. *The Recreationist*, 4(2): 13-24.

* Minutes of the Corporation of the City of Ottawa. (1899). Ottawa: Ottawa Printing Company.

* Mirecki, G. (1992). Shaping Canada's future… The essential benefits of recreation. *Recreation Canada*, October, 50(4): 8-9.

* Mitsui, D.R. (1999). The Millennium Issue. *Parks and Recreation Canada*, November/December: 6-7.

* Mitsui, D.R. (2000). National Recreation Roundtable on Aboriginal Peoples. *Parks and Recreation Canada*, May/June: 6, 43.

* Mobily, K., Nilson, R., Ostiguy, L.J., and McNeil, R.D. (1993). Seasonal variation in physical activity in elderly adults. *Proceedings: The 7th Canadian Congress on Leisure Research*, The University of Manitoba, Winnipeg, Manitoba: 174-180.

* Morinis, E. (1982). Getting straight: Behavioral patterns in a skid row community. *Urban Anthropology*, 11(2): 193-212.

* Morris, M. (1969). *Voluntary Work in the Welfare State*. London: Routledge.

* Morrow, D. (1981). Little men of iron: The 1902 Montreal Hockey Club. *Canadian Journal of History of Sport*, 12 ADD: 51-60.

* Multiculturalism and Citizenship Canada. (1990). *The Canadian Multiculturalism Act: A Guide for Canadians*. Ottawa.

* Munson, W.W. (1996). Leisure and adolescent career development. *Proceedings: 8th Canadian Congress on Leisure Research*, University of Ottawa, Ottawa, Ontario: 197-201.

* Murray, N., and McGrath, D. (1990). Politics: The art of the possible. *Recreation Canada*, May: 39-42.

* Myers, D.G., and Diener, E. (1995). Who is happy? *Psychological Science*, January, 6(1): 10-19.

* Nash, J.B. (1953). *The Philosophy of Recreation and Leisure*. Dubuque, IO: Wm. C. Brown.

* *National Recreation Statement*. (1987). Ottawa, ON: Fitness and Amateur Sport.

* Neale, W.R. (1999). Illuminating our future: Parks and recreation in Canada-What did the resource people have to say? *Parks and Recreation Canada*, November/December: 38.

* Neulinger, J. (1974). *The Psychology of Leisure*. Springfield, IL: Charles C. Thomas Publisher.

* Neumeyer, M., and Neumeyer, E. (1949). *Leisure and Recreation.* New York: Roland Press.

* Nielson, R. (1993). Brief to the Royal Commission on Aboriginal Peoples. *Recreation Canada.* 51(5): 34.

* Nogradi, G. (1992). The potential for co-operation between academics and recreation practitioners: More a reality than a myth. *Journal of Applied Recreation Research,* 17(1): 87-108.

* Normand, J. (2000). Education of women in Canada. *Canada Social Trends (Volume 3).* Toronto: Thompson Educational Publishers. (pp. 73-77).

* Oderkirk, J. (2000). Marriage in Canada: Changing beliefs and behaviours 1600-1990. *Canada Social Trends (Volume 3).* Toronto: Thompson Educational Publishers. (pp. 93-98).

* Ofori, G., and Hammer, K. (2002). Community-based sustainable aboriginal tourism product development: A proposed model. *Abstract: 10th Canadian Congress on Leisure Research,* Edmonton, Alberta, 38-41.

* Ontario Ministry of Attorney General. (2000). Draft standard objects clauses for non-profit non-charitable corporations under Part III of the Corporations Act. Queen's Printer for Ontario.

* Ontario Ministry of Tourism and Recreation. (1987). *A Community Recreation Policy Statement.* Toronto: Government of Ontario.

* Osawabine, C. (2000). Manitoulin/Sagamok tourism opportunity. *Parks and Recreation Canada,* May/June: 30-31.

* Ottawa Charter for Health Promotion. (1986). Ottawa, ON: Ottawa Charter for Health Promotion (Adapted at the First International Conference on Health Promotion, November 17-21).

* Parker, S. (1992). Volunteering as serious leisure. *Journal of Applied Recreation Research,* 17(1): 1-11.

* Parks and Recreation Federation of Ontario and the Ontario Ministry of Tourism and Recreation. (1992). *The Benefits of Parks and Recreation: A Catalogue.* Toronto, ON: Parks and Recreation Federation of Ontario and the Ontario Ministry of Tourism and Recreation.

* Parsons, L. (2001). Community portals: The sustainability factor. *Parks and Recreation Canada,* March/April, 60(1): 32-33.

* Pavelka, J., and Godin, C. (1994). *Canadian Parks/Recreation Association: National Policy on Youth,* 52(2): 24-27.

* Pawlick, M.T., and Karlis, G. (1998). The state of condition of recreation services for immigrant women. *Parks and Recreation Canada,* 56(5):14-15.

* Pearson, N. (1969). Planning for a leisure society. *Leisure in Canada: The Proceedings of the Montmorency Conference on Leisure.* Ottawa: Fitness and Amateur Sport Directorate, Department of National Health and Welfare Canada. (pp. 81-98).

* Pedlar, A. (1990). Deinstitutionalization and the role of therapeutic recreationists in social integration. *Journal of Applied Recreation Research,* 15(2): 101-112.

* Pedlar, A. (1996). Community development: What does it mean for recreation and leisure. *Journal of Applied Recreation Research,* 21(1): 5-23.

* Pedlar, A., and Hutchison, P. (1999). Maximizing participatory processes in leisure research: Moving the social agenda forward. *Proceedings: The 9th Canadian Congress on Leisure Research,* Acadia University, Wolfville, Nova Scotia: 21-23.

* Pedlar, A., Gilbert, A., and Gove, L. (1993). The role of action research in facilitating participation in integrated recreation for older adults. *Therapeutic Recreation Journal,* 28(2): 99-106.

* Peepre, J., and Dearden, P. (2002). The role of aboriginal peoples. In P. Dearden and R. Rollins (Eds.). *Parks and Protected Areas in Canada.* (2nd Edition). Don Mills, ON: Oxford. (pp. 323-353).

* Pelot, C. (1998). Serving those with special needs. *Parks and Recreation Canada,* November/December: 34.

* Physical Activity Monitor. (2001). Canadian Fitness and Lifestyle Research Institute.

* Ploch, L. (1976). Community development in action: A case study. *Journal of the Community Development Society,* 7(1): 5-16.

* Poplin, D.E. (1972). *Communities: A Survey of Theories and Methods of Research.* New York, NY: Macmillan.

* Provincial Ministers Responsible for Recreation and Sport. (1983). *An Interprovincial Recreation Statement.* Fredericton, New Brunswick.

* Public Works and Government Services Canada. (1996). *For Seven Generations: An Information Legacy of the Royal Commission on Aboriginal Peoples.* CD-ROM, Ottawa.

* Redmond, G. (1989). Imperial viceregal patronage: The Governors-Generals of Canada and sport in the dominion. *The International Journal of the History of Sport,* September, 6(2): 193-217.

* Rehman, L.A. (1999). Sport, fitness, and recreation entrepreneurship: "The double-edged sword." *Proceedings: 9ᵗʰ Canadian Congress on Leisure Research.* Acadia University, Wolfville, Nova Scotia: 24-27.

* Reid, D. (1989). Implementing senior government policy at the local level: The case of the Province of Ontario's Community Recreation Policy. *Journal of Applied Recreation Research,* 15(1):3-13.

* Reid, D. (1993a). The role of future analysis in planning for leisure and recreation development. *Journal of Leisurability,* 20(4): 3-11.

* Reid, D. (1993b). Recreation and social development in Ontario First Nation communities. *Journal of Applied Recreation Research,* 18(2): 87-102.

* Reid, D. (1993c). Community recreation service delivery in First Nation communities: A preliminary report. *Proceedings: The 7ᵗʰ Canadian Congress on Leisure Research,* The University of Manitoba, Winnipeg, Manitoba: 278-281.

* Reid, D., and van Dreunen, E. (1996). Leisure as a social transformation mechanism in community development practice. *Journal of Applied Recreation Research,* 21(1): 45-65.

* Report of the Minister. (1945). Ontario: Department of Education.

* Report of the Study Committee on Environmental Resources. (1969). *Leisure in Canada: The Proceedings of the Montmorency Conference on Leisure.* Ottawa: Fitness and Amateur Sport Directorate, Department of National Health and Welfare Canada. (pp. 81-98).

* Reville, R.H. (1920). *Golf in Canada.* Montreal, QU: Canadian Pacific Railways.

* Rivera, P. (2001). Recreational therapy a growing field. *Ottawa City,* Saturday, December 1.

* Roberts, H. (1979). *Community Development: Learning and Action.* Toronto, ON: University of Toronto Press.

* Robertson, B. (1993). The roots of at-risk behaviour. *Recreation Canada,* 54(4): 19, 21-23, 25, 27.

* Robertson, B., and Singleton, J.F. (1996). Leisure patterns and behaviors of Nova Scotians. *Proceedings: 8ᵗʰ Canadian Congress on Leisure Research,* University of Ottawa, Ottawa, Ontario: 221-227.

* Rollins, R., and Delamere, T. (1996). The good, the bad, and the ugly: Measurement of tourism impacts. *Proceedings: 8ᵗʰ Canadian Congress on Leisure Research,* University of Ottawa, Ottawa, Ontario: 228-231.

* Romsa, G.H., and Blenman, M. (1989). Recording activity patterns: Some comments from a southwestern Ontario study on retirees. *Journal of Applied Recreation Research,* 15(1): 41-50.

* Rosener, J.B. (1975). A cafeteria of techniques and critiques. *Public Management,* 57(2): 11-20.

* Ross, T. (1999). Northwest Territories: Northwest Territories Recreation and Parks Association-A community development approach to sport and recreation. *Parks and Recreation Canada,* November/December: 24.

* Rothman, J., Erlich, J.L., and Theresa, J.G. (1981). *Changing Organizations and Community Programs.* Beverly Hills, CA: Sage.

* Royal Commission on Aboriginal Peoples. (1993). Canada: Ministry of Supply and Services.

* Rublee, C.B., and Shaw, S.M. (1991). Constraints on the leisure and community participation of immigrant women: Implications for social integration. *Society and Leisure*, 14(1): 133-150.

* Rullman, L. (1974). Welcome to the Journal of Leisurability. *Journal of Leisurability*, 1(1): 1-2.

* Sandys, J., and Leaker, D. (1987). The impact of integrated employment on leisure lifestyles. *Journal of Leisurability,* 14(3): 19-23.

* Saskatchewan Senior Citizens' Provincial Council. (1998). A study of the unmet needs of off-reserve Indian and Métis elderly in Saskatchewan. Regina, Saskatchewan.

* Scace, R., Grifone, E., and Usher, R. (1992). *Ecotourism in Canada*. Canadian Environmental Advisory Council. Ottawa, ON: Ministry of Supply and Services Canada.

* Schauerte, G. (2000). Evolution of recreation administration in the Northwest Territories. *Parks and Recreation Canada*, May/June: 24-25.

* Schmidt, L. (1996). The cultural challenge: Bridging the gap. *Parks and Recreation Canada*, March/April: 8-9.

* Schrodt, B. (1984). Federal programmes of physical recreation and fitness: The contributions of Ian Eisenhardt and B.C.'s PRO-REC. *Canadian Journal of Sport History*, December, 15(2): 45-61.

* Scibberas, J., and Hutchison, P. (2002). Close friendships of integrated youth: Parents as partners. *Abstracts: 10th Canadian Congress on Leisure Research*, University of Alberta, Edmonton, AB: 3-6.

* Scott, J. (1998). *Fundamental of Leisure Business Success: A Manager's Guide to Achieving Success in the Leisure and Recreation Industry*. New York: The Haworth Press.

* Searle, M.S., and Brayley, R.E. (2000). *Leisure Services in Canada*. (2nd Edition). State College, PA: Venture.

* Secretary of State of Canada. (1987). *Multiculturalism*. Ottawa: Ministry of Supply and Services Canada.

* Selbee, L.K., and Reed, P.B. (2001). Patterns of volunteering over the life cycle. *Canadian Social Trends*. Summer, Statistics Canada-Catalogue No. 11-008.

* Shanks, J. (1999). Recreation in New Brunswick: Looking back and to the future.

* Shaw, S. (1985). Gender and leisure: Inequality in the distribution of leisure time. *Journal of Leisure Research*, 17(4): 266-282.

* Shaw, S. (1992). Dereifying family leisure: An examination of women's and men's everyday experiences and perceptions of family time. *Leisure Sciences*, 14(4): 171-286.

* Shaw, S.M., Bonen, A., and McCabe, J. (1991). Do more constraints mean less leisure? Examining the relationship between constraints and participation. *Journal of Leisure Research*, 23(4): 286-300.

* Shaw, S.M., Kleiber, A.K., and Caldwell, L.L. (1993). The role of leisure activities in the identity formation process of male and female adolescents. *Proceedings: 7th Canadian Congress on Leisure Research*. University of Manitoba, Winnipeg, MA: 166-169.

* Sheard, J. (1986). *The Politics of Volunteering*. London: Advice and Development for Volunteering and Neighbourhood Care.

* Siegal, D. (1997). Local government in Ontario. In G. White (Ed.). *The Government and Politics of Ontario* (pp. 126-157). Toronto: The University of Toronto Press.

* Skerrett, A. (1992). *History of Provincial Government Services in Sport and Recreation: 1975-1982*. Waterloo, ON: The Ontario Research Council on Leisure.

* Smale, B.J.A., and Frisby, W. (1990a). Managerial competencies of municipal recreationists in Ontario. *Proceedings: 6th Canadian Congress on Leisure Research*, University of Waterloo, Waterloo, Ontario: 104-109.

* Smale, B.J.A., and Frisby, W. (1990b). The availability of job outcomes for recreation graduates: A comparison of those who have stayed in the field with those who have not. *Journal of Applied Recreation Research*, 15(2): 113-124.

* Smith, S.J. (1981). Worlds apart: Thoughts on the Canadian Association of Leisure Studies. *Recreation Research Review,* 8(4): 10-11.

* Sport Canada Policy on Women in Sport. (1986). Ottawa, ON: Canadian Heritage.

* St. Jean, J. (2002). Report on Ottawa's Community Action Plan to Prevent and End Homelessness (2002-2005). City of Ottawa: People Services Department. Ref. No. ACS2002-PEO-HOU-0009.

* Standup, M. (2000). Kahnawake reviews its sport and recreation structure. *Parks and Recreation Canada*, May/June: 27.

* Stanley, D.A., and Applebaum, R.A. (1996). Long-term care and leisure: The leisure of disabled, low-income older adults. *Proceedings: 8th Canadian Congress on Leisure Research*, University of Ottawa, Ottawa, Ontario: 274-277.

* Statistics Canada. (1992). Marriage and conjugal life in Canada. Catalogue number 91-534E.

* Statistics Canada. (1993). Population projections for Canada, provinces and territories, 1993-2016. Catalogue number 91-520-XPB.

* Statistics Canada. (1994). General social survey. Ottawa: Statistics Canada.

* Statistics Canada. (1995). General social survey. Ottawa: Statistics Canada.

* Statistics Canada. (1996-1997a). Leading causes of death. Catalogue numbers 11-516 and 84-214.

* Statistics Canada. (1996-1997b). National population health survey. Ottawa: Statistics Canada.

* Statistics Canada. (1996a). 1996 Census: Population by Ethnic Origin.

* Statistics Canada. (1996b). 1996 Census: Population by Aboriginal Group.

* Statistics Canada. (1996c). 1996 Census: Persons Registered Under the Indian Act, Living On and Off Reserve.

* Statistics Canada. (1996d). Census of Canada. Catalogue number 93-328 and special tabulations.

* Statistics Canada. (1997). National graduates survey. Ottawa: Statistics Canada.

* Statistics Canada. (1998a). Average Time Spent on Activities, Total Population and Participants, by Sex. Statistics Canada General Social Survey 1998.

* Statistics Canada. (1998b). Average Hours Per Week of Television Viewing. Statistics Canada, Catalogue no. 87F0006XPB.

* Statistics Canada. (1998c). Most Popular Sports. Statistics Canada General Social Survey.

* Statistics Canada. (1998d). Participation in Cultural Activities By Sex. Statistics Canada General Social Survey.

* Statistics Canada. (1998e). Most popular sports among children aged 5-14. Statistics Canada General Social Survey.

* Statistics Canada. (1999a). Statistical report on the health care of Canadians. Catalogue number 82-570-XIE.

* Statistics Canada. (1999b). Longer working hours and health. Statistics Canada: Ottawa, *The Daily,* Tuesday, November 16.

* Statistics Canada. (1999c). Family Income. Statistics Canada: Ottawa, *The Daily*, Wednesday, March 3.

* Statistics Canada. (2000). Human activity and the environment. Statistics Canada: Ottawa, *The Daily,* Thursday, June 29.

* Statistics Canada. (2001a). 2001 Census. 96F0030XIE2001007.

* Statistics Canada. (2001b). Population in Shelters by Age and Sex. 2001 Census Analysis Series. Catalogue no. 96F0030XIE2001004.

* Statistics Canada. (2001c). International Travel Survey. Ottawa, Ontario.

* Statistics Canada. (2002a). Trips by Canadians in Canada. Ottawa, Ontario, CANSIM II, Table 426-0001.

* Statistics Canada. (2002b). Household spending. Statistics Canada: Ottawa, *The Daily,* Wednesday, December 11.

* Statistics Canada. (2002c). Family income. Statistics Canada: Ottawa, *The Daily,* Wednesday, October 30.

* Statistics Canada. (2002d). Environment industry: business sector. Statistics Canada: Ottawa, *The Daily,* Thursday, April 25.

* Statistics Canada. (2003a). Census of population: Immigration, birthplace and birthplace of parents, citizenship, ethnic origin, visible minorities and Aboriginal peoples. Statistics Canada: Ottawa, *The Daily,* Tuesday, January 21.

* Statistics Canada. (2003b). Survey of approaches to educational planning. Statistics Canada: Ottawa, *The Daily,* Thursday, November 20.

* Statistics Canada. (2003c). Employment, earnings and hours. Statistics Canada: Ottawa, *The Daily,* Tuesday, January 28.

* Statistics Canada. (2003d). Couples living apart. Statistics Canada: Ottawa, *The Daily,* Tuesday, June 10.

* Statistics Canada. (2003e). Labour force survey. Statistics Canada: Ottawa, *The Daily,* Friday, January 10.

* Statistics Canada. (2003f). Human activity and the environment: Annual statistics. Statistics Canada: Ottawa, *The Daily,* Wednesday, December 3.

* Statistics Canada. (July 1, 2001-June 30, 2002). Components of population growth. CANSIM II, table 051-0004.

* Statutes of Canada. (1942). Vocational Training Co-ordination Act, Chapter 34, 6 George vi, August 1st.

* Stebbins, R.A. (1982). Serious leisure: A conceptual framework. *Pacific Sociological Review,* 25(2): 251-272.

* Stebbins, R.A. (1996). Cultural tourism as serious leisure: A conceptual elaboration. *Proceedings: 8th Canadian Congress on Leisure Research,* University of Ottawa, Ottawa, Ontario: 282-284.

* Stebbins, R.A. (2000/2001). Introduction: Antinomies in Volunteering-Choice/Obligation, Leisure/Work. *Leisure and Society,* 23(2): 313-324.

* Stewart, D. (2002a). Report on the Community Services Branch Facility Allocation Policy. City of Ottawa: People Services Department. Ref. No. ACS2002-PEO-COM-0009.

* Stewart, D. (2002b). Report on the City of Ottawa Special Needs Recreation Programming. City of Ottawa: People Services Department. Ref. No. ACS2002-PEO-COM-0010.

* Stonehouse, D. (1999). There are not enough hours in the day. *The Ottawa Citizen,* Sunday, November 14, pages A1-2.

* Storey, E.H. (Ted). (1990). The quest for a national policy on recreation: A brief history. *Recreation Canada,* May: 7-9.

* Stroick, S. (1996). The development of community associations and federations. *Journal of Applied Recreation Research,* 21(1): 165-183.

* Sutherland, H. (1990). Taking volunteerism into the 21st century. *American Red Cross,* March.

* Swedburg, R. (2002). The grammatical use of leisure: An analysis of the research of the 9th Canadian Congress on Leisure Research. *Abstracts: 10th Canadian Congress on Leisure Research,* University of Alberta, Edmonton, Alberta: 32-34.

* Tessier, Y. (1984). *Histoire du Hockey et des Sports.* Sillery, QU: Editions Tessier.

* Thayer Scott, J. (1997). Defining the nonprofit sector. In R. Hishorn (Ed.). *The Emerging Sector in Search of a Framework.* Ottawa: Renouf.

* Thomas, J. (2002). Seniors leading the way: The Evergreen Seniors Centre of Guelph, Ontario takes on technology. *Parks and Recreation Canada*, 60(1): 28-29.

* Thornton, M. (2001). Aspects of the history of aboriginal peoples and their relationships with colonial, national and provincial governments in Canada. In M. Thornton and R. Todd (Eds.). *Aboriginal Peoples and Other Canadians: Shaping New Relationships*. Ottawa: University of Ottawa Press (pp. 7-24).

* Tirone, S. (1995). Cultural variation in leisure: The experiences of immigrant women from India. *Proceedings: 3rd Graduate Leisure Research Symposium*. Department of Recreation and Leisure Studies, University of Waterloo, Waterloo, ON: 1-3.

* Tirone, S.C. (1999). Racism and intolerance in recreation and leisure: A Canadian experience. *Book of Abstracts: 9th Canadian Congress on Leisure Research*, Acadia University, Wolfville, Nova Scotia: 200-203.

* Tirone, S.C. (1999/2000). Racism, indifference, and the leisure experiences of South Asian Canadian teens. *Leisure/Loisir*, 24(1-2): 89-114.

* Tirone, S.C., and Shaw, S.M. (1997). At the center of their lives: Indo-Canadian women, their families, and leisure. *Journal of Leisure Research*, 29:225-244.

* Toward a National Policy on Recreation. (1977). Ottawa: Fitness and Amateur Sport.

* Trottier, A. (1990). Children and youth living actively. *Recreation Canada*, October, 48(4): 30-35.

* Trudeau, P.E. (1978). A letter from the Prime Minister of Canada to the President of the Canadian Parks and Recreation Association. Ottawa, July 12.

* Tryphonas, L., Karakasis, D., and Sophianopoulos, A. (1985). *The Hellenes of Ottawa: The First Hundred Years*. Ottawa: The Hellenic Community of Ottawa and the Yearbook Committee.

* United Nations. (1955). *Social Progress Through Community Development*. New York: United Nations.

* Vail, S. (1994). Better together: Partnerships building between recreation and sport leaders. *Recreation Canada*, 52(5): 11-14.

* Vail, S., and Carmichael, J. (1993). More than just facilities: The role of municipal recreation in community sport development. *Recreation Canada*, 51(1): 24, 26-27, 43-44.

* Vandermay, S. (1990). A provincial perspective: An interview with The Honourable Colin Maxwell, Minister Responsible for Saskatchewan Culture, Multiculturalism and Recreation. *Recreation Canada, May: 11-14*.

* Vaughan, G. (1996). *The Puck Starts Here*. Fredericton, NB: Goose Lane Editions.

* Voluntary Sector Initiative. (2001). Ottawa, ON: Government of Canada.

* Volunteer Centre of Ottawa-Carleton. (1992). Why People Volunteer: A Report to the Voluntary Action Directorate. Ottawa: Multiculturalism and Citizenship Branch.

* Walsh, K. (1995). *Public Services and Market Mechanisms: Competition, Contracting and the New Public Management*. London: Macmillan Press Limited.

* Ward, J. (1986). Community development and municipal recreation. *Recreation Canada*, 44(5): 6-14.

* Ward, J. (1991). Empowering street youth. *Journal of Leisurability*, 18: 19-22.

* Watson, W.G. (1988). *National Pastimes: The Economics of Canadian Leisure*. Vancouver, B.C.: The Fraser Institute.

* Webster, B. (1999a). The future of parks and recreation. *Parks and Recreation Canada*, November/December: 5.

* Webster, B. (1999b). The Leading Edge – The Future of Parks and Recreation. *Parks and Recreation Canada*, November/December: 5.

* Webster, B. (----).A Look at Tomorrow's Recreation Facilities. *Parks and Recreation Canada*, Winter: 32-36.

* Wellman, B. (1987). The community question re-evaluated. (Research Paper No. 165). Toronto: University of Toronto, Center for Urban and Community Studies.

* Westland, C. (1977). Recreation leadership in Canada. *Proceedings and Papers: The First World Conference of Experts on Leadership for Leisure,* Michigan State University, East Lansing, Michigan, September. (pp. 192-204).

* Westland, C. (1979). *Fitness and Amateur Sport in Canada-The Federal Government's Programme: An Historical Perspective.* Ottawa, ON: Canadian Parks and Recreation Association.

* Westland, C. (1985). The development of national recreation policies. In T.L. Goodale and P.W. Witt. *Recreation and Leisure: Issues in an Era of Change.* (Revised Edition). State College, PA: Venture. (pp. 391-406).

* Westland, C. (1991). Leisure and mental health. *Recreation Canada,* 49(4): 24-29.

* Wetherell, D.G., and Kmet, I. (1990). *Useful Pleasures: The Shaping of Leisure in Alberta 1896-1945.* Regina, SK: Canadian Plains Research Centre.

* Wharf Higgins, J. (1995). Leisure and recreation: Achieving health for all. *Journal of Applied Recreation Research,* 20(1): 17-36.

* Whelan, L. (1987). Working with refugee newcomers in Saskatchewan. *Recreation Canada,* October: 30-33.

* Whyte, D.N.B. (1992). Key trends impacting local government recreation and park administration in the 1990's: A focus for strategic management and research. *Journal of Park and Recreation Administration,* 10(3): 89-100.

* Wilkinson, P.F., and Murray, A.L. (1991). Centre and periphery: The impacts of the leisure industry on a small town (Collingwood, Ontario). *Society and Leisure,* 14(1): 235-260.

* Williams, C. (2000). Income and expenditure. *Canadian Social Trends.* Winter, 7-12, Statistics Canada-Catalogue No. 11-008.

* Witt, P.A., and Ellis, G.D. (1985). Conceptualizing leisure: Making the abstract complete. In T.L. Goodale and Witt, P.A. (Eds.). *Recreation and Leisure: Issues In An Era of Change.* (Revised Edition). State College, PA: Venture. (pp. 105-117).

* Wright, J.R. (1983). *Urban Parks in Ontario, Part I: Origins to 1860.* Ottawa, ON: Ontario Ministry of Tourism and Recreation.

* Wright, J.R. (1984). *Urban Parks in Ontario, Part II: 1860-1914.* Ottawa, ON: Ministry of Tourism and Recreation.

* Wright, J.R. (2000). *Urban Parks in Ontario: The Modern Period.* Ottawa, ON: The Ontario Ministry of Citizenship, Culture and Recreation.

* Zentner, H. (1964). The state and the community. *Sociology and Social Research,* 48: 415-430.

* Zukewich Ghalam, N. (1997). Attitudes toward women, work and family. *Canadian Social Trends.* Autumn, 13-17, Statistics Canada-Catalogue No. 11-008-XPE.

* Zuzanek, J. (1996). Studies of leisure participation and the use of time in Canada, 1967-1992: Conceptual and methodological considerations. *Proceedings: 8th Canadian Congress on Leisure Research,* University of Ottawa, Ottawa, Ontario: 322-326.

* Zuzanek, J., and Mannell, R. (1993). Gender and life-cycle variations in the daily and leisure life: Participation and experience. *Proceedings: The 7th Canadian Congress on Leisure Research,* University of Manitoba, Winnipeg, Manitoba, 133-135.

Index

AGMV Marquis

MEMBER OF SCABRINI MEDIA

Quebec, Canada
2004